Chalmers' Marine Insurance

Editors of Previous Editions

First Edition 1901:	M D Chalmers, CSI, and Douglas Owen
Second Edition 1913:	Sir M D Chalmers, KCB, CSI, and Douglas Owen
Third Edition 1922:	Sir M D Chalmers, KCB, CSI, and J G Archibald, MA
Fourth Edition 1932:	J G Archibald, MA, assisted by Charles Stevenson, BA
Fifth Edition 1956:	J Milnes Holden, LLB, PhD, AIB, and C B Drover, ACIS, AIB
Sixth Edition 1966:	E R Hardy Ivamy, LLB, PhD
Seventh Edition 1971:	E R Hardy Ivamy, LLB, PhD, LLD
Eighth Edition 1976:	E R Hardy Ivamy, LLB, PhD, LLD
Ninth Edition 1983:	E R Hardy Ivamy, LLB, PhD, LLD

Chalmers'
Marine Insurance Act 1906

by the late Sir Mackenzie D Chalmers, KCB, CSI,
Draftsman of the Act

Tenth edition

E R Hardy Ivamy, LLB, PhD, LLD
of the Middle Temple, Barrister,
Emeritus Professor of Law in the University of London

London, Dublin and Edinburgh
Butterworths
1993

United Kingdom	Butterworth & Co (Publishers) Ltd, 88 Kingsway, LONDON WC2B 6AB and 4 Hill Street, EDINBURGH EH2 3JZ
Australia	Butterworths, SYDNEY, MELBOURNE, BRISBANE, ADELAIDE, PERTH, CANBERRA and HOBART
Belgium	Butterworth & Co (Publishers) Ltd, BRUSSELS
Canada	Butterworths Canada Ltd, TORONTO and VANCOUVER
Ireland	Butterworth (Ireland) Ltd, DUBLIN
Malaysia	Malayan Law Journal Sdn Bhd, KUALA LUMPUR
New Zealand	Butterworths of New Zealand Ltd, WELLINGTON and AUCKLAND
Puerto Rico	Butterworth of Puerto Rico, Inc, SAN JUAN
Singapore	Butterworths, Asia, SINGAPORE
USA	Butterworth Legal Publishers, CARLSBAD, California; and SALEM, New Hampshire

All rights reserved. No part of this publication may be reproduced in any material form (including photocopying or storing it in any medium by electronic means and whether or not transiently or incidentally to some other use of this publication) without the written permission of the copyright owner except in accordance with the provisions of the Copyright, Designs and Patents Act 1988 or under the terms of a licence issued by the Copyright Licensing Agency Ltd, 90 Tottenham Court Road, London, England W1P 9HE. Applications for the copyright owner's written permission to reproduce any part of this publication should be addressed to the publisher.

Warning: The doing of an unauthorised act in relation to a copyright work may result in both a civil claim for damages and criminal prosecution.

© Butterworth & Co (Publishers) Ltd 1993

A CIP Catalogue record for this book is available from the British Library.

ISBN 0 406 02229 1

Typeset by Phoenix Photosetting, Chatham, Kent
Printed and bound in Great Britain by
Mackays of Chatham PLC, Chatham, Kent

Preface to Tenth Edition

The aim of this edition is the same as that of previous ones: 'To support the [sections of the Marine Insurance Act 1906], where possible, by references to leading cases or to cases containing good expositions of principle by eminent commercial Judges. . . . Where rules of law seem difficult to apply, illustrations drawn from decided cases are inserted . . . to show the application of the abstract [rule] to concrete states of fact.' (Chalmers, Preface to First Edition).

In this edition two important changes have been made—(1) the notes on each section of the Act are now set out immediately after the text of the section, and these are followed by illustrations; and (2) the notes on the Institute Clauses have been considerably expanded.

With regard to the first change, it is hoped that this will help to explain the meaning of the sections of the Act more readily.

In respect of the second change the following Institute Clauses are considered: Institute Time Clauses (Hulls), Institute Voyage Clauses (Hulls), Institute War and Strikes Clauses (Hulls-Time), Institute War and Strikes Clauses (Hulls-Voyage), Institute Time Clauses (Freight), Institute Voyage Clauses (Freight), Institute War and Strikes Clauses (Freight-Time), Institute War and Strikes Clauses (Freight-Voyage), Institute Cargo Clauses (A), Institute Cargo Clauses (B), Institute Cargo Clauses (C), Institute War Clauses (Cargo) and Institute Strike Clauses (Cargo). Permission to reproduce them has been given by Lloyd's and the Institute of London Underwriters, to both of whom I tender my thanks.

The principal cases included in the new edition are: *Stone Vickers Ltd v Appledore Ferguson Shipbuilders Ltd* [1992] 2 Lloyd's Rep 578, CA (mixed sea and land risks); *Hong Kong Borneo Services Ltd v Pilcher* [1992] 2 Lloyd's Rep 593 (mixed sea and land risks); *Smit Tak Offshore Services v Youell and General Accident Fire and Life Assurance Corpn* [1992] 1 Lloyd's Rep 154, CA (marine adventure); *Sharp and Roarer Investments Ltd v Sphere Drake Insurance plc, The Moonacre* [1992] 2 Lloyd's Rep 501 (insurable interest); *Black King Shipping Corpn v Massie, The Litsion Pride* [1985] 1 Lloyd's Rep 437 (duty of good faith); *Banque Financière de la Cité v Westgate Insurance Co Ltd* [1990] 2 All ER 947, CA (duty of good faith); *Allden v Raven, The Kylie* [1983] 2 Lloyd's Rep 444 (non-disclosure); *Inversiones Manria SA v Sphere Drake Insurance plc, The Dora* [1989] 1 Lloyd's Rep 69 (non-disclosure); *Bank* of *Nova Scotia v Hellenic Mutual War Risks Association (Bermuda) Ltd, The Good Luck* [1991] 3 All ER 1, HL (warranty); *Seaview Investment SA v Evennett and Clarkson Puckle Ltd, The Tiburon* [1990] 2 Lloyd's Rep 418 (warranty); *Outhwaite v Commercial Bank of Greece SA, The Sea Breeze* [1987] 1 Lloyd's Rep 372 (warranty); *Pindos Shipping Corpn v Raven, The Mata Hari* [1983] 2 Lloyd's Rep 449 (warranty); *JJ Lloyd Instruments Ltd v Northern Star Insurance Co Ltd, The Miss Jay Jay* [1987] 1 Lloyd's Rep 32, CA (latent defect); *T M Noten BV v Harding* [1990] 2 Lloyd's Rep 283 (inherent vice); *CCR Fishing Ltd v Tomenson, The La Pointe* [1991] 1 Lloyd's Rep 89, Supreme Court of Canada (proximate cause rule); *Bank of America National Trust and Savings Association v Chrismas, The Kyriaki* [1993] 1 Lloyd's Rep 137 (constructive total loss); *Castle Insurance Co Ltd v Hong Kong Islands Shipping Co Ltd, The Potoi Chau* [1983] 2 Lloyd's Rep 376, PC (general average); and *Ventouris v Mountain, The Italia Express (No 2)* [1992] 2 Lloyd's Rep 281 (measure of indemnity).

The Association of Average Adjusters has kindly allowed me to set out in Appendix V the latest version of their Rules of Practice and for this I am indeed grateful.

My thanks go to the staff of Butterworths for preparing the Index, the Table of Statutes and the List of Cases and for seeing the book through the press.

November 1993   E R Hardy Ivamy

Introduction to First Edition of Digest (1901)

The large-type propositions of this Digest are taken, with a few slight corrections, and with the necessary verbal alterations (such as the substitution of the indicative for the imperative), from the clauses of the Marine Insurance Bill, which was introduced in the House of Lords in 1894, 1895, 1896 and 1899.

The object of that Bill was to reproduce as exactly as possible the existing law, without making any attempt to amend it. Lord Herschell, who originally took charge of the Bill, was strongly of opinion that a codifying Bill, in its inception, ought to be a mere reproduction of existing law. If amendments in the law are made in the initial stage, the whole Bill becomes controversial. Any amendment which seems desirable should be deliberately inserted by the Legislature when the Bill is under consideration. In some instances, of course, the Bill has to deal with questions where the law is unsettled, and the framers of the Bill must decide what they believe the law to be. In the Digest, propositions which appear to be unsettled law are included in square brackets, and the doubt is dealt with in the notes. Again, in one or two instances the Lords Select Committee, which partially examined the Bill, introduced some small amendment in the law. In those cases the Digest reverts to the original draft, and the point is mentioned in the notes.

The law of marine insurance rests almost entirely upon common law. Only a few isolated points are dealt with by statute. The reported cases are very numerous, being over 2,000 in number. On some points there is a plethora of authority. On other points of apparently equal importance the decisions are meagre, and not always satisfactory. Some important questions are still untouched by authority, and the rule depends on recognised commercial usage. Again, many of the older cases turn upon commercial conditions which are now obsolete. The subject, therefore, is not an easy one to deal with in a brief Digest. It would be altogether beyond the scope of this Digest to attempt even to refer to the great bulk of decided cases, much more so to endeavour to criticise them in detail. The objects of the Digest are twofold: first, to state the main principles of marine insurance law in brief consecutive propositions; and secondly, to support those propositions, where possible, by references to leading cases, or cases containing good expositions of principle by eminent commercial judges. Each case is dated, and if a later case reviews previous cases, only a reference to the later case is given. Where rules of law seem difficult to apply, illustrations drawn from decided cases are inserted after the section to show the application of the abstract proposition to concrete states of fact.

After the list of cases referred to, there is added a list of important cases, which have been overruled, doubted, and explained. This list has no pretensions to completeness, but may be useful as far as it goes.

Occasional reference is made to foreign codes by way of illustration, but no attempt has been made to compare the English rules systematically with any foreign code.

The Marine Insurance Bill was first introduced by Lord Herschell in 1894. Its history up to the present time (1901) sufficiently appears from the following extract from the Memorandum attached to it, viz:—

'The Bill is founded on the Bill which was introduced in 1894. Its provisions and suggestions received from various sources have been carefully considered by a Committee appointed by the late Lord Chancellor (Lord Herschell). The Committee met at first under the presidency of the late Attorney-General (Sir R T Reid QC), and afterwards under the presidency of Lord Herschell. It consisted of Mr John Glover and Mr Milburn, representing the shipowners, Mr Charles McArthur (Chairman of the Liverpool Chamber of Commerce), and Mr Hogg representing the average adjusters, and Mr J E Street, Deputy-Chairman of Lloyd's, Mr Douglas Owen, of the Alliance Marine and General Assurance Company, Mr William Walton (legal adviser to Lloyd's), representing the underwriters and insurance companies, Mr C B Vallence, Chairman of the Liverpool Underwriters' Association, and the draftsman, Mr Chalmers.*

'In dealing with rules of law, which may be modified by the stipulations of the parties, it is to be borne in mind that the certainty of the rule laid down is of more importance than its theoretical perfection. As Willes J said in 1786, "In all commercial transactions the great object is certainty; it will therefore be necessary for the Court to lay down some rule, and it is of more consequence that the rule should be certain than

---

* After Lord Herschell's death, Lord Chancellor Halsbury again took up the Bill, and introduced it in the House of Lords in 1899, but did not proceed with it.

Further criticisms on the Bill were obtained from Lord Justice Mathew, the Right Hon Arthur Cohen KC, and other friends, and the Bill was again introduced in 1900. Lord Halsbury then appointed another committee, on which the underwriters, shipowners and average adjusters were represented, and, presiding himself, went through the Bill with them clause by clause.

After this conference the Bill was passed through the Lords, but it was always blocked in the House of Commons until, in 1906, it was taken up by Lord Chancellor Loreburn in conjunction with Lord Halsbury. In the Commons the Bill was sent to Grand Committee, and was in the charge of the Solicitor-General (Lord Robson). A good many amendments were made in committee and on the report stage, and most of them were agreed to, with occasional modification, when the Bill returned to the Lords.

whether it is established one way or the other." (*Lockyer v Offley* 1 T R at 259. See, too, *Sailing Ship Blairmore v Macredie* [1898] AC at 597, per Lord Halsbury.) What mercantile men require is a clear rule to provide for cases where the parties have either formed no intention or have failed to express it clearly. Where the rule of law is certain, the parties know when to stipulate and what to stipulate for.'

The future which awaits the Bill is uncertain, Mercantile opinion is in favour of codification, but probably the balance of legal opinion is against it. As along as freedom of contract is preserved, it suits the man of business to have the law stated in black and white. The certainty of the rule laid down is of more importance than its nicety. It is cheaper to legislate than to litigate; moreover, while a moot point is being litigated and appealed, pending business is embarrassed. The lawyer, on the other hand, feels cramped by codification. Discussions on the wording of the Act in question have to take the place of discussions of principles. No code can provide for every case that may arise, or always use language which is absolutely accurate. The cases which come before lawyers are the cases in which the code is defective. In so far as it works well it does not come before them. Every man's view of a question is naturally coloured by his own experience, and a lawyer's view of commerce is perhaps affected by the fact that he sees mainly the pathology of business. He does not often see its healthy physiological action.

If the Bill passes, this Digest may be useful as showing the foundations on which it was built up. If it does not pass, it is hoped that the Digest may be useful as a brief and succinct exposition of the existing law.

I may add that I am mainly responsible for the purely legal part of this Digest, though I have had throughout the benefit of the criticisms of my colleague, Mr Douglas Owen.

M D C

January 1901

Contents

Preface to Tenth Edition   v
Introduction to First Edition of Digest (1901)   vii
Table of Statutes Cited   xv
List of Cases Cited   xix
Table of Books Cited or Used   xxxix

MARINE INSURANCE ACT 1906

Marine Insurance
1. Marine insurance defined   1
2. Mixed sea and land risks   3
3. Marine adventure and maritime perils defined   5

Insurable Interest
4. Avoidance of wagering or gaming contracts   8
5. Insurable interest defined   10
6. When interest must attach   13
7. Defeasible or contingent interest   14
8. Partial interest   15
9. Reinsurance   16
10. Bottomry   17
11. Master's and seamen's wages   18
12. Advance freight   18
13. Charges of insurance   19
14. Quantum of interest   20
15. Assignment of interest   20

Insurable Value
16. Measure of insurable value   21

Disclosure and Representations
17. Insurance is uberrimæ fidei   24
18. Disclosure by assured   26
19. Disclosure by agent effecting insurance   32
20. Representations pending negotiation of contract   33
21. When contract is deemed to be concluded   36

The Policy
22. Contract must be embodied in policy   37
23. What policy must specify   38
24. Signature of insurer   39
25. Voyage and time policies   40
26. Designation of subject-matter   40
27. Valued policy   42
28. Unvalued policy   45
29. Floating policy by ship or ships   45
30. Construction of terms in policy   47
31. Premium to be arranged   47

Double Insurance
32. Double insurance 48

Warranties etc
33. Nature of warranty 50
34. When breach of warranty excused 53
35. Express warranties 54
36. Warranty of neutrality 56
37. No implied warranty of nationality 57
38. Warranty of good safety 57
39. Warranty of seaworthiness of ship 58
40. No implied warranty that goods are seaworthy 62
41. Warranty of legality 63

The Voyage
42. Implied condition as to commencement of risk 65
43. Alteration of port of departure 66
44. Sailing for different destination 66
45. Change of voyage 67
46. Deviation 68
47. Several ports of discharge 70
48. Delay in voyage 70
49. Excuses for deviation or delay 72

Assignment of Policy
50. When and how policy is assignable 73
51. Assured who has no interest cannot assign 75

The Premium
52. When premium payable 76
53. Policy effected through broker 76
54. Effect of receipt on policy 77

Loss and Abandonment
55. Included and excluded losses 78
56. Partial and total loss 86
57. Actual total loss 87
58. Missing ship 89
59. Effect of transhipment etc 90
60. Constructive total loss defined 90
61. Effect of constructive total loss 98
62. Notice of abandonment 99
63. Effect of abandonment 104

Partial Losses (including Salvage and General Average and Particular Charges)
64. Particular average loss 106
65. Salvage charges 107
66. General average loss 109

Measure of Indemnity
67. Extent of liability of insurer for loss 114
68. Total loss 115
69. Partial loss of ship 116
70. Partial loss of freight 118
71. Partial loss of goods, merchandise etc 119
72. Apportionment of valuation 121

73. General average contribution and salvage charges   122
74. Liabilities to third parties   123
75. General provisions as to measure of indemnity   124
76. Particular average warranties   124
77. Successive losses   126
78. Suing and labouring clause   127

Rights of Insurer on Payment
79. Right of subrogation   131
80. Right of contribution   135
81. Effect of under-insurance   136

Return of Premium
82. Enforcement of return   136
83. Return by agreement   137
84. Return for failure of consideration   137

Mutual Insurance
85. Modification of Act in case of mutual insurance   140

Supplemental
86. Ratification by assured   142
87. Implied obligations varied by agreement or usage   142
88. Reasonable time etc, a question of fact   143
89. Slip as evidence   144
90. Interpretation of terms   144
91. Savings   145
94. Short title   149

Schedule I
Form of policy   151
Rules for construction of policy   152

Schedule II
Repealed   155

APPENDIX I – STATUTES
The Marine Insurance (Gambling Policies) Act 1909   157
The Sale of Goods Act 1979   158

APPENDIX II – MARINE POLICY FORMS
(1) Lloyd's Form   160
(2) Insurance Companies' Form   163

APPENDIX III – THE INSTITUTE CLAUSES
(1) Hull Clauses
    Time   167
    Voyage   196

xiv *Contents*

        War and Strikes (Time)   208
        War and Strikes (Voyage) 212
(2) Freight Clauses
        Time   215
        Voyage   225
        War and Strikes (Time)   232
        War and Strikes (Voyage) 236
(3) Cargo Clauses
        (A)   239
        (B)   249
        (C)   256
        War   264
        Strikes   271

APPENDIX IV – THE YORK-ANTWERP RULES 1974   277

APPENDIX V – RULES OF PRACTICE OF THE ASSOCIATION OF AVERAGE ADJUSTERS 1986 (amended 1992)   285

APPENDIX VI – SHIP'S PAPERS – RULES OF THE SUPREME COURT   304

Index   307

Table of statutes

References in this Table to *Statutes* are to Halsbury's Statutes of England (Fourth Edition) showing the volume and page at which the annotated text of an Act may be found. Page references printed in **bold** type indicate where the Act is set out in part or in full.

	PAGE
Admiralty Court Act 1840	
s 6	12, 13
Atomic Energy Act 1946 (47 *Statutes* 712)	195
s 18(1)	195
Bills of Exchange Act 1882 (5 *Statutes* 334)	
s 91	39
Companies Act 1862	145
Companies Act 1985 (8 *Statutes* 104):	140, 148
s 716(1)	141
County Courts Act 1984 (11 *Statutes* 603)	
s 69	38
Customs Consolidation Act 1853	64
Explosives Act 1875 (17 *Statutes* 455)	195
s 3	195
Finance Act 1959 (41 *Statutes* 248) Sch 8	
Pt II	37, 39, 40
Forgery and Counterfeiting Act 1981 (12 *Statutes* 753)	
s 1	2
6(1), (2)	3
Gaming Act 1845 (5 *Statutes* 12)	
s 18	9
Insolvency Act 1986 (4 *Statutes* 717)	
s 323	75
Interpretation Act 1978 (41 *Statutes* 899)	149
s 9	148
23(3)	148
Judicial Committee Act 1833 (11 *Statutes* 752)	
s 4	175
Law of Property Act 1925 (37 *Statutes* 72)	
s 136	74
Law Reform (Frustrated Contracts) Act 1943 (11 *Statutes* 215)	
s 1	140

	PAGE
Law Reform (Frustrated Contracts) Act 1943—*contd*	
s 2(5)	140
Limitation Act 1980 (24 *Statutes* 648)	98, 110
Lloyd's Act 1871 Schedule	
Rule 4	39
Magistrates' Courts Act 1980 (27 *Statutes* 143)	
s 6(5)	3
32, 143	3
Marine and Aviation Insurance (War Risks) Act 1952 (22 *Statutes* 73)	
s 7	38
Marine Insurance Act 1745	8
s 4	16
Marine Insurance Act 1788	38
Marine Insurance Act 1906 (22 *Statutes* 15)	7, 8, 9, 16, 24, 104, 171
s 1	**1**, 16, 145
2	**3**, 145
3	5, 12, **63**, 145
4	8, 63, **106**, 140, 158
(2)	89, 139
5	9, **10**
6	9, 12, **13**
7	9, 12, **14**, 18
8	9, 12, **15**
9	9, 12, **16**
10	9, 12, **17**
11	9, 12, **18**
12	9, 12, **18**, 23, 145
13	12, **19**, 22
14	12, **20**
(2)	15
15	12, 13, **20**, 75, 142
16	19, **21**, 45, 50, 114, 115, 121, 122, 136
(2)	3, 119, 145
(3)	3, 120, 121, 122

xvi *Table of statutes*

Marine Insurance Act 1906—*contd*
Section	Page
s 17	**24**, 27
18	7, 24, 25, **26**, 43, 44, 57, 64
(3)	24
19	27, **32**
20	**33**
(4)	52
(7)	34
21	2, 30, **36**, 38, 144
22	2, **37**, 145
23	37, **38**
(1)	142
24	**39**, 76
25	**40**
26	16, 17, **40**, 48
27	**42**, 49, 115, 119
(2)	3
(4)	96, 187
28	3, **45**, 115, 119
29	44, **45**
(4)	44
30	**47**, 151
31	**47**, 69, 73, 144
(2)	52
32	16, 20, **48**, 124, 132, 139, 140
33	10, 34, 36, 48, **50**
(2)	35
(3)	51
34	10, 34, 48, 51, 52, **53**
(3)	52
35	10, 34, 48, 52, **54**
36	10, 34, 48, 52, **56**
37, 38	10, 34, 48, 52, **57**
39	10, 34, 48, 52, 55, **58**
40	10, 34, 48, 52, **62**, 145
(2)	61
41	6, 7, 10, 12, 34, 48, 52, 53, 54, 56, **63**
42	40, **65**
43, 44	40, **66**
45	40, 48, **67**
46	40, 48, 67, **68**
47	40, **70**
48	40, 65, 66, **70**, 73
49	40, 69, **72**
50	13, 21, **73**
(1)	14
(2)	145

Marine Insurance Act 1906—*contd*
Section	Page
s 51	13, 21, **75**
52, 53	2, **76**, 136
54	2, **77**
55	2, **78**
(2)	8, 128, 130
56	2, **86**
(3)	98
(4)	145
57	2, **87**
(1)	97
58	2, **89**
59	2, **90**
60	2, 7, 22, 65, 66, 87, **90**, 104, 118, 145
61	2, **98**, 100, 104
62	2, 87, 96, 98, **99**, 134
(7)	10
(9)	16
63	2, 98, 99, 100, **104**, 131, 132
64	2, **106**, 125
(2)	108, 125
65	2, **107**, 122, 125, 130
(2)	130
66	2, 82, **109**, 113, 119, 122, 125, 130
(1)	108
67	22, **114**, 136
68	22, 45, 114, **115**, 136
69	45, 107, **116**, 136
70	45, **118**, 136
71	45, 87, 107, **119**, 122, 124, 136
(1), (2), (4)	145
72	87, **121**, 125, 136
73	111, **122**
(2)	108
74	7, 114, **123**, 136
75	120, 121, **124**
(2)	43, 44
76	87, 107, 122, **124**
(1)	87
(2)	107
77	115, 117, 118, **126**
(2)	45
78	82, 107, 109, 114, 115, 125, 126, **127**
(4)	83, 106
79	10, 20, 21, 45, 50, 99, 100, 104, 105, **131**, 136

Table of statutes

	PAGE
Marine Insurance Act 1906—*contd*	
s 80	45, 49, 50, **135**
(2)	145
81	45, 49, 100, 104, 114, 122, 132, 134, **136**
82	74, **136**
83	74, **137**
84	10, 49, 74, **137**
(3)	136
85	2, **140**
86	13, 21, 31, 37, 39, **142**
87	**142**, 167
(1)	76
88	47, 65, 71, 89, 102, **143**
89	2, 37, 38, **144**
90	7, 23, 62, **144**
91	40, 54, 111, **145**
(2)	7, 63, 64, 124
94	**149**, 173
Sch 1	47
r 1	14, 23–57, **152**
2	65, **152**
3	65, 145, **153**
4	**153**
5	40, **153**
6	69, **153**
7	61, 83, **153**
8, 9	**154**
10	96, 97, 103, **154**, 192
11, 12	**154**
13	107, **154**
14	**154**
15	7, 22, **154**
16	22, **155**
17	7, 18, 41, 145, **155**
Marine Insurance Act 1963 (India):	134
Marine Insurance (Gambling Policies) Act 1909 (22 *Statutes* 66):	9, 158
s 1	**157**
2	**158**
Maritime Conventions Act 1911 (39 *Statutes* 637)	
s 1–5	123
6	73
7	148
Merchant Shipping Act 1854	
s 183	18
Merchant Shipping Act 1894 (39 *Statutes* 424)	
s 5	15

	PAGE
Merchant Shipping Act 1894—*contd*	
21	95
544, 557–564	109
Merchant Shipping Act 1970 (39 *Statutes* 761)	
s 15	18
Merchant Shipping Act 1979 (39 *Statutes* 904)	
s 17	178
Merchant Shipping (Salvage) Act 1916	109
Nuclear Installations Act 1965 (47 *Statutes* 785)	195
s 26	195
Policies of Marine Assurance Act 1868	
s 1, 2	74
Public Order Act 1986 (12 *Statutes* 1030)	
s 1(1)–(5)	194
Reinsurance (Acts of Terrorism) Act 1993	
s 2(2), (3)	194
Revenue (No 2) Act 1864	
s 1	16
Sale of Goods Act 1979 (39 *Statutes* 106)	14
s 20	14, 75, **158**
32	14, 75, **159**
56	144
61(2)	145
Stamp Act 1891	145
Summer Time Act 1972 (45 *Statutes* 641)	146
s 1(2)	148
2(1)	148
Supreme Court Act 1981 (11 *Statutes* 966)	
s 35A	38
69(5)	148
151(1)	145
Supreme Court of Judicature (Consolidation) Act 1925	
s 226	13
Sch 6	13
Third Parties (Rights against Insurers) Act 1930 (4 *Statutes* 688)	
s 1(1)	123
(5)	16
Trading with the Enemy Act 1939 (48 *Statutes* 808)	
s 2	147

List of cases

	PAGE
Adam SS Co Ltd v London Assurance Corpn (1914)	26
Admiralty Comrs v Ropner & Co Ltd (1917)	2
African Merchants Co v British and Foreign Marine Insurance Co (1873)	71, 72
Agenoria SS Co Ltd v Merchants Marine Insurance Co Ltd (1903)	118
Aifanourios, The. See West of Scotland Ship Owners Mutual Protection and Indemnity Association (Luxembourg) v Aifanourios Shipping SA, The Aifanourios	
Aitchison v Lohre. See Lohre v Aitchison	
Ajum Goolam Hossen & Co v Union Marine Insurance Co (1901)	61
Al-Jubail IV, The. See Almojil (M) Establishment v Malayan Motor and General Underwriters (Private) Ltd, The Al-Jubail IV	
Alexion Hope, The. See Schiffshypothekenbank Zu Luebeck AG v Compton, The Alexion Hope	
Allden v Raven, The Kylie (1983)	32
Allgemeine Versicherungs-Gesellschaft Helvetia v German Property Administrator (1931)	106
Allison v Bristol Marine Insurance Co (1876)	13, 19, 42
Allkins v Jupe (1877)	10, 140
Almojil (M) Establishment v Malayan Motor and General Underwriters (Private) Ltd, The Al-Jubail IV (1982)	40, 56, 61, 72
Alps, The (1893)	84

	PAGE
Amalgamated General Finance Co Ltd v C E Golding & Co Ltd (1964)	75
American Surety Co of New York v Wrightson (1910)	50, 136
Andersen v Marten (1908)	64, 85
Anderson v Morice (1875); affd (1876)	3, 10, 14, 15, 42, 61
Anderson v Ocean SS Co. See Ocean SS Co v Anderson	
Anderson v Pacific Fire and Marine Insurance Co (1872)	35, 36
Anderson v Thornton (1853)	36, 140
Andreas Lemos, The. See Athens Maritime Enterprises Corpn v Hellenic Mutual War Risks Association (Bermuda) Ltd, The Andreas Lemos	
Angel v Merchants Marine Insurance Co (1903)	96, 187
Anglo-Californian Bank Ltd v London and Provincial Marine and General Insurance Co Ltd (1904)	39, 114, 136
Anglo-International Bank Ltd, Re (1943)	148
Anglo-Mexican (Part Cargo ex), The (1918)	149
Annen v Woodman (1810)	140
Anstey v Ocean Marine Insurance Co (1913)	18
Apollinaris Co v Nord Deutsche Insurance Co (1904)	4
Arab Bank Ltd v Barclays Bank (Dominion, Colonial and Overseas) (1954)	148
Argonaut Marine Insurance Co Ltd, Re (1932)	4
Aron (J) & Co v Miall (1928)	74, 75
Aronsen (Oscar L) Inc v Compton, The Megara (1974)	17

List of cases

Arrow Shipping Co v Tyne Improvement Comrs, The Crystal (1894) 106, 134
Asfar & Co v Blundell (1896) . 89
Assicurazioni Generali De Trieste v Empress Assurance Corpn Ltd (1907) 17, 134, 135
Associated Oil Carriers Ltd v Union Insurance Society of Canton Ltd (1917) . 30, 31, 32, 57, 89, 103
Astrovlanis Compania Naviera SA v Linard, The Gold Sky (1972); on appeal (1972) . 83, 84, 130
Athel Line Ltd v Liverpool and London War Risks Insurance Association Ltd (1944) . . . 113
Athel Line Ltd v Liverpool and London War Risks Insurance Association Ltd (1945) . . . 86
Athens Maritime Enterprises Corpn v Hellenic Mutual War Risks Association (Bermuda) Ltd, The Andreas Lemos (1982) 175
Atlantic Maritime Carriers SA v Hellenic Mutual War Risks Association Ltd, The Mitera (1969) 142
Atlantic Maritime Co Inc v Gibbon (1953) 222, 265
Atlas, The (1876) 241
A-G v Ard Coasters Ltd, Liverpool and London War Risks Insurance Association Ltd v SS Richard de Larrinaga Marine Underwriters. See Richard de Larrinaga, SS (Owners) v Admiralty Comrs
Atwood v Sellar (1880) . 90, 112, 143
Aubert v Gray (1862) 193
Austin v Drewe (1816) . . . 175
Austin Friars SS Co Ltd v Spillers & Bakers Ltd (1915); affd (1915) 113
Australia and New Zealand Bank Ltd v Colonial and Eagle Wharves Ltd (1960) . . 23, 25
Australian Coastal Shipping Commission v Green (1971) . 109, 113, 130

Bah Lias Tobacco and Rubber Estates Ltd v Volga Insurance Co Ltd (1920) 66
Bainbridge v Neilson (1808) . . 103
Baines v Holland (1855) . . . 52
Baker v Adam (1910) . . 17, 38, 75
Baker-Whiteley Coal Co v Marten (1910) 221
Ballantyne v Mackinnon (1896) . 85, 109
Balmoral SS Co v Marten (1900); on appeal (1901); affd (1902) 45, 108, 123
Bamburi, The (1982) . . 96, 97, 103
Bank Line Ltd v Arthur Capel & Co (1919) 97
Bank of America National Trust and Savings Association v Chrismas, The Kyriaki (1993) 96, 99
Bank of England v Vagliano Bros (1891) 149
Bank of Nova Scotia v Hellenic Mutual War Risks Association (Bermuda) Ltd, The Good Luck (1991) 52
Banque Financière de la Cité SA (formerly Banque Keyser Ullmann SA) v Westgate Insurance Co Ltd (formerly Hodge General and Mercantile Co Ltd) (1991) 25
Barber v Fleming (1869) . . 12, 13, 15
Baring Bros & Co v Marine Insurance Co (1894) . . 124, 145
Barker v Janson (1868) . . 44, 45
Barraclough v Brown (1897) . . 134
Bates v Hewitt (1867) 31
Baxendale v Fane, The Lapwing (1940) 83, 174, 176
Beaconsfield, The (1894) . . . 241
Becker, Gray & Co v London Assurance Corpn (1916); affd (1918) 85, 97
Bedouin, The (1894) . . 31, 36, 84
Behn v Burness (1863) . . 36, 55
Bell v Bromfield (1812) . . . 57
Bell v Humphries (1818) . . . 15
Belle of Portugal, The. See Rosa v Insurance Co of the State of Pennsylvania, The Belle of Portugal

List of cases

Bennett SS Co v Hull Mutual SS Protecting Society (1913); affd (1914) 124, 179
Bensaude v Thames and Mersey Marine Insurance Co (1897) . 84, 222
Benson v Chapman (1849) . 87, 97, 130
Bentsen v Taylor, Sons & Co (1893) 55
Bergens Dampskibs Assurance Forening v Sun Insurance Office Ltd (1930) 17
Berger and Light Diffusers Pty Ltd v Pollock (1973) . 23, 30, 31, 32, 37, 45, 89
Berk (F W) & Co Ltd v Style (1955) 8, 83, 130, 242
Berridge v Man on Insurance Co (1887) 10
Besnard (Robert S) Co Ltd, Barque v Murton (1909) . . 97
Bhugwandass v Netherlands India Sea and Fire Insurance Co of Batavia (1888) . . . 38
Biccard v Shepherd (1861) . 60, 61, 62
Biddle, Sawyer & Co Ltd v Peters (1957) 83
Birkley v Presgrave (1801) . . 113
Birrell v Dryer (1884) . . . 55, 143
Black King Shipping Corpn and Wayang (Panama) SA v Massie, The Litsion Pride (1985) 25, 74, 77, 102
Blackburn v Liverpool, Brazil and River Plate Steam Navigation Co (1902) . . . 174
Blackburn, Low & Co v Haslam (1888) 31, 33
Blackburn, Low & Co v Vigors (1887) 30, 33
Blackett v Royal Exchange Assurance (1832) 143
Blackett, Magalhaes and Colombie v National Benefit Assurance Corpn (1921) . . 63
Blackhurst v Cockell (1789) . 52, 57
Blairmore Co Ltd (Sailing Ship) v Macredie (1898) . 87, 96, 103, 115
Blane Steamships Ltd v Minister of Transport (1951) 106
Boag v Standard Marine Insurance Co Ltd (1937) . 134, 135

Boehm v Bell (1799) . 7, 12, 15, 139
Bold v Rotheram (1846) . . . 90
Bolivia Republic v Indemnity Mutual Marine Assurance Co Ltd (1908); affd (1909) . 4, 7, 30, 33, 36, 173, 175, 194
Boon and Cheah Steel Pipes Sdn Bhd v Asia Insurance Co Ltd (1975) 89, 97, 121, 247
Booth v Gair (1863) 90
Boston Corpn v Fenwick & Co Ltd (1923) 106, 134
Boston Fruit Co v British and Foreign Marine Insurance Co (1905); affd (1906) . . . 39, 142
Bosworth (No 3), The. See Grand Union (Shipping) Ltd v London SS Owners' Mutual Insurance Association Ltd, The Bosworth (No 3)
Bottomley v Bovill (1826) . . 68
Bouillon v Lupton (1863) . 61, 73
Boulton v Houlder Bros & Co (1904) 26
Boyd v Dubois (1811) . . . 63
Braconbush, The. See United Scottish Insurance Co Ltd v British Fishing Vessels Mutual War Risks Association Ltd, The Braconbush
Bradford v Symondson (1881) . 2, 16, 139, 140
Brandeis Goldschmidt & Co v Economic Insurance Co Ltd (1922) 113
Brandon v Curling (1803) . . 148
Brankelow SS Co v Canton Insurance Office (1899); affd sub nom Williams & Co v Canton Insurance Office Ltd (1901) 83, 85, 89
Brentwood, The. See Coast Ferries Ltd v Century Insurance Co of Canada, The Brentwood
Brigella, The (1893) 113
Briggs v Merchant Traders' Ship Loan and Insurance Association (1849) 7, 12
Bristol Steam Navigation Co Ltd v Indemnity Mutual Marine Insurance Co (1887) . . . 118
Britain SS Co Ltd v R (1921) . 85

	PAGE
British American Tobacco Co v Poland (1921)	72
British and Foreign Insurance Co Ltd v Wilson Shipping Co Ltd (1921)	3, 114, 118, 127, 136, 148
British and Foreign Marine Insurance Co v Gaunt (1921)	8, 30, 47, 83, 130
British and Foreign Marine Insurance Co v Sturge (1897)	144
British and Foreign Marine Insurance Co Ltd v Samuel Sanday & Co. See Sanday & Co v British and Foreign Marine Insurance Co	
British Columbia and Vancouver's Island Spar, Lumber and Sawmill Co Ltd v Nettleship (1868)	121
British Dominions General Insurance Co Ltd v Duder (1915)	3, 16, 17, 103
British Marine Mutual Insurance Co v Jenkins (1900)	141
Brooking v Maudslay, Son and Field (1888)	25
Brooks v MacDonnell (1835)	127, 135
Brough v Whitmore (1791)	23, 143
Brown v Tayleur (1835)	70
Brown Bros v Fleming (1902)	121
Browning v Provincial Insurance Co of Canada (1873)	74, 99
Brownlie v Campbell (1880)	25
Bruce v Jones (1863)	45, 50, 136
Buchanan & Co v Faber (1899)	42
Buchanan Co v London & Provincial Marine Insurance Co Ltd (1895)	89, 109
Burger v Indemnity Mutual Marine Assurance Co (1900)	124, 180
Burges v Wickham (1863)	61, 76
Burnand v Rodocanachi, Sons & Co (1882)	45, 134, 135
Byas v Miller (1897)	142
Byrne v Schiller (1871)	19
CCR Fishing Ltd v Tomenson Inc, The La Pointe (1991)	84, 175
Cahill v Dawson (1857)	77

	PAGE
Caine v Palace Steam Shipping Co (1906); affd sub nom Palace Shipping Co Ltd v Caine (1907)	7, 64
Cammell v Sewell (1860)	90
Canada Rice Mills Ltd v Union Marine and General Insurance Co Ltd (1940)	83
Canadian General Electric Co Ltd v Liverpool and London and Globe Insurance Co Ltd (1980)	175
Cantiere Meccanico Brindisino v Janson (1912)	25, 31, 32, 61
Cap Tarifa, The. See Simons (trading as Acme Credit Services) v Gale, The Cap Tarifa	
Cape Borer, The. See Rudolph (M J) Corpn v Lumber Mutual Fire Insurance Co (Luria International, Third Parties), The Cape Borer	
Capital Coastal Shipping Corpn and Bulk Towing Corpn v Hartford Fire Insurance Co (United States of America, Third Party), The Cristle (1975)	54, 56, 61
Captain Panagos DP, The. See Continental Illinois National Bank and Trust Co of Chicago and Xenofon Maritime SA v Alliance Assurance Co Ltd, The Captain Panagos DP	
Caribbean Sea, The. See Prudent Tankers Ltd SA v Dominion Insurance Co Ltd, The Caribbean Sea	
Carlton SS Co Ltd v Castle Mail Packets Co Ltd (1898)	144
Carras v London and Scottish Assurance Corpn Ltd (1936)	89, 97, 222
Carter v Boehm (1766)	25, 30
Caruthers v Graham (1811)	77
Castellain v Preston (1883)	3, 20, 134, 135
Castle Insurance Co ltd v Hong Kong Islands Shipping Co Ltd, The Potoi Chau (1983)	113
Cates (Captain J A) Tug and Wharfage Co Ltd v Franklin Insurance Co (1927)	89, 102, 103

List of cases

	PAGE
Cator v Great Western Insurance Co of New York (1873)	121, 126
Chandler v Blogg (1898)	123, 179
Chandris v Argo Insurance Co Ltd (1963)	113
Chapman v James Fisher & Sons (1904)	180
Chapman v Royal Netherlands Steam Navigation Co (1879)	179
Charlesworth v Faber (1900)	16, 31
Charlotte, The (1908)	134
Chattahoochee, The (1899)	241
Cheshire (T) & Co v Thompson (1919)	31
Cheshire (Thomas) & Co v Vaughan Bros & Co (1920)	10
China (Republic of), China Merchants Steam Navigation Co and United States of America v National Union Fire Insurance Co of Pittsburgh, Pennsylvania, The Hai Hsuan (1958)	176
China (Republic of), China Merchants Steam Navigation Co Ltd and United States of America v National Union Fire Insurance Co of Pittsburgh, Pennsylvania, The Hai Hsuan (No 2) (1958)	10
China Traders' Insurance Co Ltd v Royal Exchange Assurance Corpn (1898)	16, 26
Chippendale v Holt (1895)	16
Christie v Secretan (1799)	60
City Equitable Fire Insurance Co Ltd (No 2), Re (1930)	38
Clan Line Steamers Ltd v Liverpool and London War Risks Insurance Association Ltd (1942)	86
Clapham v Cologan (1813)	57
Clapham v Langton (1864)	61
Coast Ferries Ltd v Century Insurance Co of Canada, The Brentwood (1973); on appeal (1974)	176
Cobequid Marine Insurance Co v Barteaux (1875)	85
Cockrane v Fisher (1835)	55
Cohen (G) Sons & Co v Standard Marine Insurance Co Ltd (1925)	30, 61, 89, 103
Coker v Bolton (1912)	106
Colonial Insurance Co of New Zealand v Adelaide Marine Insurance Co (1886)	14, 15
Commercial Union Assurance Co v Lister (1874)	134
Commonwealth Smelting Ltd v Guardian Royal Exchange Assurance Ltd (1984); affd (1986)	175
Commonwealth, The. See Welsh Girl, The	
Compania Colombiana de Seguros v Pacific Steam Navigation Co (1964)	74, 134
Compania Maritima San Basilio SA v Oceanus Mutual Underwriting Association (Bermuda) Ltd, The Eurysthenes (1976)	40, 61
Compania Naviera Bachi v Henry Hosegood & Co Ltd (1938)	176
Compania Naviera Santi SA v Indemnity Marine Assurance Co Ltd, The Tropaioforos (1960)	175
Constantine (Joseph) SS Line Ltd v Imperial Smelting Corpn Ltd, The Kingswood (1941)	97
Container Transport International Inc and Reliance Group Inc v Oceanus Mutual Underwriting Association (Bermuda) Ltd (1982); revsd (1984)	25, 30, 31, 32, 33, 36
Continental Grain Co Inc v Twitchell (1945); affd (1945)	98
Continental Illinois National Bank and Trust Co of Chicago and Xenofon Maritime SA v Alliance Assurance Co Ltd, The Captain Panagos DP (1986); affd (1989)	86, 175
Corfield (W R) & Co v Buchanan (1913)	141
Cory v Patton (1872)	33, 144
Cory v Patton (1874)	36, 37
Cory (John) & Sons v Burr (1883)	64, 82, 85
Cossman v West (1887)	88, 89
Court Line Ltd v R, The Lavington Court (1945)	95, 96, 97
Cousins v Nantes (1811)	9

List of cases

	PAGE
Cousins (H) & Co Ltd v D and C Carriers Ltd (1971)	5, 134, 135
Coxwold, The. See Yorkshire Dale SS Co Ltd v Minister of War Transport, The Coxwold	
Cristie, The. See Capital Coastal Shipping Corpn and Bulk Towing Corpn v Hartford Fire Insurance Co (United States of America, Third Party), The Cristie	
Crocker v Sturge (1897)	16
Crooks v Allan (1879)	113
Crouan v Stanier (1904)	130
Crowley v Cohen (1832)	12, 23, 124
Crystal, The. See Arrow Shipping Co v Tyne Improvement Comrs, The Crystal	
Cunard v Hyde (1859)	64
Cunard SS Co v Marten (1902); affd (1903)	7, 12, 123, 124, 130
Currie & Co v Bombay Native Insurance Co (1869)	102, 130, 144
Czarnikow (C) Ltd v Java Sea and Fire Insurance Co Ltd (1941)	96, 97
Dalglish v Davidson (1824)	182
Daneau v Laurent Gendron Ltée, Union Insurance Society of Canton Ltd (Third Party) (1964)	54, 56
Daniels v Harris (1874)	61, 62
Darrell v Tibbitts (1880)	134
Davidson v Burnand (1868)	85, 123
Davies v National Fire and Marine Insurance Co of New Zealand (1891)	4, 46
Davis v Garrett (1830)	69
Dean v Hornby (1854)	103
De Cuadra v Swann (1864)	62
De Hahn v Hartley (1786); affd (1787)	52, 54, 55
De Hart v Compañia Anonima de Seguros Aurora (1903)	113, 182
Delany v Stoddart (1785)	73
De Mattos v North (1868)	10
De Mattos v Saunders (1872)	97, 126, 174, 221
Dennistoun v Lillie (1821)	36

	PAGE
Denoon v Home and Colonial Assurance Co (1872)	42, 45, 119, 124, 145
Dent v Smith (1869)	57, 85, 182
Deutsch-Australische Dampschiffs-gesellschaft v Sturge (1913)	244
De Vaux v Salvador (1836)	82, 84
Devaux v Steele (1840)	12
De Wolf v Archangel Insurance Co (1874)	65
Dias, The. See Palamisto General Enterprises SA v Ocean Marine Insurance Co Ltd, The Dias	
Dickenson v Jardine (1868)	113, 135, 143
Difiori v Adams (1884)	70
Dixon v Sadler (1839); affd sub nom Sadler v Dixon (1841)	61, 62, 83
Dixon v Sea Insurance Co (1880)	109
Dixon v Stansfield (or Stansfeld) (1850)	77
Dixon v Whitworth (1879); revsd (1879)	130
Dodwell & Co Ltd v British Dominions General Insurance Co Ltd (1955)	83
Dominion Coal Co Ltd v Mackinonge SS Co Ltd (1918)	137
Dora Forster, The (1900)	127
Dora, The. See Inversiones Manria SA v Sphere Drake Insurance Co plc, Malvern Insurance Co Ltd and Niagara Fire Insurance Co Inc, The Dora	
Driefontein Consolidated Gold Mines v Janson (1901); affd sub nom Janson v Driefontein Consolidated Mines Ltd (1902)	4, 148
Dudgeon v Pembroke (1874); on appeal (1875); on appeal (1877)	61, 62, 64, 167
Duff v Mackenzie (1857)	18, 126
Dufourcet v Bishop (1886)	19, 20, 135
Dunlop Bros & Co v Townend (1919)	42, 46

List of cases

	PAGE
Duus, Brown & Co v Binning (1906)	129, 134
Ebsworth v Alliance Marine Insurance Co (1873); revsd (1874)	15, 20
Eddystone Marine Insurance Co, Re, ex p Western Insurance Co (1892)	16
Eden v Parkison (1781)	57
Edwards v Aberayron Mutual Ship Insurance Society Ltd (1876)	141
Edwards v Footner (1808)	35
Edwards (John) & Co v Motor Union Insurance Co Ltd (1922)	3, 10, 134, 135
Eglinton v Norman (1877)	134
Elcock v Thomson (1949)	118
Elgood v Harris (1896)	77
Elton v Brogden (1747)	73
Emanuel & Co v Andrew Weir & Co (1914)	17
Emperor Goldmining Co Ltd v Switzerland General Insurance Co Ltd (1964)	130
Empress Assurance Corpn Ltd v C T Bowring & Co Ltd (1905)	144
Engineer, The. See Tatham, Bromage & Co v Burr, The Engineer	
Ertel Bieber & Co v Rio Tinto Co (1918)	148
Esposito v Bowden (1857)	54, 148
Eurysthenes, The. See Compania Maritima San Basilio SA v Oceanus Mutual Underwriting Association (Bermuda) Ltd, The Eurysthenes	
Evans, Sons & Co v Cunard SS Co Ltd (1902)	70
Evelpidis Era, The. See First National Bank of Chicago v West of England Shipowners Mutual Protection and Indemnity Association (Luxembourg), The Evelpidis Era	
Everett v London Assurance (1865)	175

	PAGE
Fabrique de Produits Chimiques SA, La v Large (1923)	126
Fairfield Shipbuilding and Engineering Co Ltd v Gardner, Mountain & Co Ltd (1911)	77
Falcke v Scottish Imperial Insurance Co (1886)	109
Farnworth v Hyde (1865); on appeal (1866)	89, 96, 97, 103
Fawcus v Sarsfield (1856)	61
Federation Insurance Co of Canada v Coret Accessories Inc and Hirsh (trading as S A Hirsh & Co) (1968)	84
Field SS Co v Burr (1899)	85
Firemen's Fund Insurance Co v Western Australian Insurance Co Ltd and Atlantic Insurance Co Ltd (1927)	16, 17
First National Bank of Chicago v West of England Shipowners Mutual Protection and Indemnity Association (Luxembourg), The Evelpidis Era (1981)	141
Fisher v Liverpool Marine Insurance Co (1874)	38
Fisher v Smith (1878)	77
Fisk v Masterman (1841)	140
Fleming v Smith (1848)	88, 99
Fletcher v Alexander (1868)	113, 121
Flint v Flemyng (1830)	145
Forbes v Aspinall (1811)	119, 124
Forwood v North Wales Mutual Marine Insurance Co (1880)	87
Foster v Driscoll (1929)	7
Fowler v English and Scottish Marine Insurance Co Ltd (1865)	95
France (William), Fenwick & Co Ltd v Merchants' Marine Insurance Co Ltd (1914); affd (1915)	124, 180
France (William), Fenwick & Co Ltd v North of England Protection and Indemnity Association (1917)	85
Francis v Boulton (1895)	89, 121
Fraser & Co v Burrows (1877)	26
Frenkel v MacAndrews & Co Ltd (1929)	70
Fuerst Day Lawson Ltd v Orion Insurance Co Ltd (1980)	5, 8

	PAGE
Furness Withy & Co Ltd v Duder (1936)	124, 179
Gamba v Le Mesurier (1803)	64
Gambles v Ocean Marine Insurance Co of Bombay (1876)	40
Gardner v Salvador (1831)	97
Garrels v Kensington (1799)	57
Garthwaite (Sir William) (Insurance) Ltd v Port of Manchester Insurance Co Ltd (1930)	16, 26
Gaunt v British and Foreign Insurance Co Ltd and Standard Marine Insurance Co Ltd (1920); affd sub nom British and Foreign Marine Insurance Co v Gaunt (1921)	5
Gedge v Royal Exchange Assurance Corpn (1900)	7, 10, 54
Gee and Garnham Ltd v Whittall (1955)	242
Geipel v Smith (1872)	68
General Insurance Co of Trieste (Assicurazioni Generali) v Cory (1897)	55
Genforsikrings Aktieselskabet (Skandinavia Reinsurance Co of Copenhagen) v Da Costa (1911)	37, 38
Gernon v Royal Exchange Assurance (1815)	102
Gibson v Small (1853)	62
Glasgow Assurance Corpn Ltd v William Symondson & Co (1911)	17, 19
Gledstanes v Royal Exchange Assurance (1864)	46
Glover v Black (1763)	42
Gold Sky, The. See Astrovlanis Compania Naviera SA v Linard, The Gold Sky	
Gooding v White (1913)	31
Goodwin v Robarts (1875); affd (1876)	143
Goole and Hull Steam Towing Co Ltd v Ocean Marine Insurance Co Ltd (1928)	3, 45, 118, 134, 135
Gorsedd SS Co Ltd v Forbes (1900)	137, 191

	PAGE
Goulart v Trans-Atlantic Marine Inc and Enos (1970)	141
Graham Joint Stock Shipping Co v Motor Union Insurance Co (1922)	26
Graham Joint Stock Shipping Co Ltd v Merchants Marine Insurance Co Ltd (No 2) (1923); affd (1924)	39
Grainger v Martin (1862); affd (1863)	97
Grand Union (Shipping) Ltd v London SS Owners' Mutual Insurance Association Ltd, The Bosworth (No 3) (1962)	109
Grant v King (1802)	66
Grant, Smith & Co and McDonnell Ltd v Seattle Construction and Dry Dock Co (1920)	83
Gratitudine, The (1801)	175
Grazebrook, Re, ex p Chavasse (1865)	7
Great Indian Peninsula Rly Co v Saunders (1861); on appeal (1862)	90, 126
Great Western Rly Co v Mostyn (Owners), The Mostyn (1928)	106
Green v Brown (1743)	89
Green Lion, The. See Sipowicz v Wimble, The Green Lion	
Green Star Shipping Co Ltd v London Assurance (1933)	112
Greenhill v Federal Insurance Co (1927)	30, 31
Greenock SS Co v Maritime Insurance Co (1903); affd (1903)	48, 61, 84
Greenshields, Cowie & Co v Stephens & Sons Ltd (1908)	83, 112
Greer v Poole (1880)	85, 123, 148
Grover and Grover Ltd v Mathews (1910)	142
Gulfstream Cargo Ltd v Reliance Insurance Co, The Papoose (1971)	30, 32
Gurney v Grimmer (1932)	17
Guthrie v North China Insurance Co Ltd (1902)	97
Haabet, The (1899)	18

List of cases

	PAGE
Hadkinson v Robinson (1803)	68
Hagedorn v Whitmore (1816)	126
Hahn v Corbett (1824)	85
Hai Hsuan, The. See China (Republic of), China Merchants Steam Navigation Co and United States of America v National Union Fire Insurance Co of Pittsburgh, Pennsylvania, The Hai Hsuan	
Hai Hsuan (No 2), The. See China (Republic of), China Merchants Steam Navigation Co Ltd and United States of America v National Union Fire Insurance Co of Pittsburgh, Pennsylvania, The Hai Hsuan (No 2)	
Hall v Hayman (1912)	96, 97, 102, 118, 149, 187
Hall v Janson (1855)	19
Hall Bros SS Co Ltd v Young, The Trident (1939)	124, 179
Hamilton, Fraser & Co v Pandorf & Co (1887)	84, 85, 175
Hammond v Reid (1820)	69
Hansen v Dunn (1906)	90
Harding v Bussell (1905)	26
Harris v Scaramanga (1872)	113, 182
Harrower v Hutchinson (1870)	30
Hart v Standard Marine Insurance Co (1889)	55, 143, 167
Hartley v Buggin (1781)	69
Haughton v Empire Marine Insurance Co (1866)	60
Havelock v Hancill (1789)	176
Haywood v Rodgers (1804)	31
Helen, The (1865)	7
Helmville Ltd v Yorkshire Insurance Co Ltd, The Medina Princess (1965)	44, 96, 118, 187
Henderson Bros v Shankland & Co (1896)	113, 118, 123
Hendricks v Australasian Insurance Co (1874)	182
Herring v Janson (1895)	45
Hewitt v London General Insurance Co Ltd (1925)	48, 69
Hewitt Bros v Wilson (1914); affd (1915)	2, 7, 30, 48
Hibbert v Carter (1787)	21, 75
Hickie and Borman v Rodocanachi (1859)	106

	PAGE
Hill v Wilson (1879)	182
Hine Bros v SS Insurance Syndicate Ltd, The Netherholme, Glen Holme and Rydal Holme (1895)	77
Hobbs v Hannam (1811)	20
Hogarth v Walker (1900)	23
Holman & Sons Ltd v Merchants' Marine Insurance Co Ltd (1919)	123
Home Insurance Co of New York v Victoria-Montreal Fire Insurance Co (1907)	17
Hong Kong Borneo Services Co Ltd v Pilcher (1992)	4
Hood v West End Motor Car Packing Co (1917)	48
Hore v Whitmore (1778)	54
Horlock v Beal (1916)	54
Hoskins v Pickersgill (1783)	23
Houghton and Mancon Ltd v Sunderland Marine Mutual Insurance Co Ltd, The Ny-Eeasteyr (1988)	175
Houstman v Thornton (1816)	89, 103, 135
Hudson v British and Foreign Marine Insurance Co. See Leitrim, The	
Hunter v Leathley (1830); affd sub nom Leathly v Hunter (1831)	77
Hunter v Northern Marine Insurance Co Ltd (1888)	70
Hunter v Potts (1815)	83, 84
Hunter v Wright (1830)	137, 191
Hutchins Bros v Royal Exchange Assurance Corpn (1911)	176
Hydarnes SS Co v Indemnity Mutual Marine Assurance Co (1895)	167
Hyderabad (Deccan) Co v Willoughby (1899)	5, 48, 73
Ide and Christie v Chalmers and White (1900)	4, 245
Ikerigi Cia Naviera SA v Palmer, The Wondrous (1992)	131, 167, 208, 211
Imperial Marine Insurance Co v Fire Insurance Corpn Ltd (1879)	46

	PAGE
Indian City, The. See Reardon Smith Lines Ltd v Black Sea and Baltic General Insurance Co Ltd, The Indian City	
Industrial Waxes Inc v Brown (1958)	245
Inglis v Robertson and Baxter (1898)	149
Inglis v Stock. See Stock v Inglis	
Inman SS Co v Bischoff (1882)	84
Integrated Container Service Inc v British Traders Insurance Co Ltd (1981)	130
Inversiones Manria SA v Sphere Drake Insurance Co plc, Malvern Insurance Co Ltd and Niagara Fire Insurance Co Inc, The Dora (1989)	32, 36
Ionides v Harford (1859)	139
Ionides v Pender (1872)	176
Ionides v Pender (1874)	30, 31, 45
Ionides v Universal Marine Insurance Co (1863)	85
Ionides and Chapeaurouge v Pacific Fire and Marine Insurance Co (1871); affd (1872)	35, 36, 39, 144
Iredale v China Traders Insurance Co (1900)	85, 112
Irvin v Hine (1949)	44, 95, 118, 130
Irving v Manning (1847)	44, 45, 96, 115, 121, 187
Irving v Richardson (1831)	20, 45
Irwin v Eagle Star Insurance Co Ltd, The Jomie (1973)	176
Italia Express (No 2), The. See Ventouris v Mountain, The Italia Express (No 2)	
Jackson v Mumford (1902); affd (1904)	4, 176
Jackson v Union Marine Insurance Co Ltd (1873); affd (1874)	82, 84, 96
Jacob v Gaviller (1902)	5
James W Elwell, The (1921)	18
James Yachts Ltd v Thames and Mersey Marine Insurance Co Ltd (1977)	4, 32, 64
Jamieson and Newcastle SS Freight Insurance Association, Re (1895)	84, 96, 97

	PAGE
Janson v Driefontein Consolidated Mines Ltd. See Driefontein Consolidated Gold Mines v Janson	
Janson v Poole (1915)	42, 144
Janson v Property Insurance Co Ltd (1913)	39
Jardine v Leathley (1863)	103
Johnson v Sheddon (1802)	121
Johnston v Hogg (1883)	175, 193
Jomie, The. See Irwin v Eagle Star Insurance Co Ltd, The Jomie	
Joyce v Kennard (1871)	4, 123
Kacianoff v China Traders Insurance Co Ltd (1914)	85
Kaltenbach v Mackenzie (1878)	89, 95, 99, 102, 103
Karberg (Arnold) & Co v Blythe Green Jourdain & Co (1916)	148
Keevil and Keevil Ltd v Boag (1940)	26
Keighley, Maxsted & Co v Durant (1901)	142
Kellner v Le Mesurier (1803)	64, 137, 140
Kemp v Halliday (1866)	96
Kent v Bird (1777)	3
Kettlewell v Refuge Assurance Co (1908); affd sub nom Refuge Assurance Co Ltd v Kettlewell (1909)	139
Kewley v Ryan (1794)	46
Khedive, The. See Stoomvart Maatschappy Nederland v Peninsular and Oriental Steam Navigation Co, The Khedive	
Kidston v Empire Marine Insurance Co (1866); on appeal (1867)	90, 107, 126, 129, 130
King v Victoria Insurance Co Ltd (1896)	5, 134, 135
King v Walker (1863); on appeal (1864)	87
Kingswood, The. See Constantine (Joseph) SS Ltd v Imperial Smelting Corpn Ltd, The Kingswood	
Kleinwort v Shepard (1859)	175

List of cases

	PAGE
Knight of St Michael, The (1898)	85
Knill v Hooper (1857)	61
Koebel v Saunders (1864)	63, 83
Krüger & Co Ltd v Moel Tryvan Ship Co Ltd (1907)	134
Kuehne and Nagel Inc v Baiden (1975); on appeal (1977)	12, 83
Kulukundis v Norwich Union Fire Insurance Society (1936)	97, 98, 222, 223
Kylie, The. See Allden v Raven, The Kylie	
Kynance Sailing Ship Co v Young (1911)	42, 62, 70
Kyriaki, The. See Bank of America National Trust and Savings Association v Chrismas, The Kyriaki	
Laga, The. See Vermaas' (J) Scheepvaartbedrijf NV v Association Technique de l'Importation Charbonnière, The Laga	
Laing v Union Marine Insurance Co Ltd (1895)	30, 48
Lamb Head Shipping Co Ltd v Jennings, The Marel (1992)	175
Lane v Nixon (1866)	61
Langdale v Mason (1780)	194
La Pointe, The. See CCR Fishing Ltd v Tomenson Inc, The La Pointe	
Lapwing, The. See Baxendale v Fane, The Lapwing	
Larrinaga SS Co Ltd v R (1945)	86
Laurie v West Hartlepool SS Thirds Indemnity Association and David (1899)	74
Laveroni v Drury (1852)	84
Lavington Court, The. See Court Line Ltd v R, The Lavington Court	
Law v Hollingsworth (1797)	61
Lawrence v Aberdein (1821)	85
Lawther v Black (1901)	42, 126
Le Cheminant v Pearson (1812)	127
Lee v Southern Insurance Co (1870)	130

	PAGE
Leitrim, The (1902), sub nom Hudson v British and Foreign Marine Insurance Co	83, 85, 113
Leon v Casey (1932)	4, 26
Letchford v Oldham (1880)	221
Levy v Assicurazioni Generali (1940)	194
Levy & Co v Merchants Marine Insurance Co (1885)	103
Lewis v Rucker (1761)	12, 44, 121, 124
Leyland Shipping Co v Norwich Union Fire Insurance Society Ltd (1918)	84, 85
Liberian Insurance Agency Inc v Mosse (1977)	31, 32, 36, 48
Lidgett v Secretan (1870)	40
Lidgett v Secretan (1871)	44, 45, 127
Lind v Mitchell (1928); on appeal (1928)	83, 95, 176
Lindsay v Klein, The Tatjana (1911)	61
Lindsay and Pirie v General Accident Fire and Life Assurance Corpn Ltd (1914)	193, 194
Lion Mutual Marine Insurance Association Ltd v Tucker (1883)	141
Lishman v Northern Maritime Insurance Co (1875)	144
Litsion Pride, The. See Black King Shipping Corpn v Massie, The Litsion Pride	
Liverpool and London War Risks Association Ltd v Ocean SS Co Ltd (1947)	86
Livie v Janson (1810)	127
Lloyd v Fleming (1872)	2, 3, 12, 74, 76
Lloyd (J J) Instruments Ltd v Northern Star Insurance Co Ltd, The Miss Jay Jay (1987)	84
Loders and Nucoline Ltd v Bank of New Zealand (1929)	3
Lohre v Aitchison (1878); varied sub nom Aitchison v Lohre (1879)	3, 88, 96, 107, 108, 109, 114, 118, 127, 129, 130
London and Manchester Plate Glass Co Ltd v Heath (1913)	195

List of cases

	PAGE
London Assurance Corpn v Williams (1892); affd (1893)	106
London County Commercial Reinsurance Office Ltd, Re (1922)	10, 140
London General Insurance Co v General Marine Underwriters' Association (1921)	17, 32
London SS Owners' Insurance Co v Grampian SS Co (1890)	178, 179
Lower Rhine and Würtemberg Insurance Association v Sedgwick (1899)	16
Lubrafol, M/V (Owners) v SS Pamia (Owners), The Pamia (1943)	148
Lucena v Craufurd (1806)	10, 12, 15, 18
Lysaght (J) Ltd v Coleman (1895)	121
Macbeth & Co Ltd v Maritime Insurance Co Ltd (1908)	96
M'Carthy v Abel (1804)	85
M'Cowan v Baine and Johnston, The Niobe (1891)	123, 179
Macdowall v Fraser (1779)	35
Mackenzie v Whitworth (1875)	7, 42
Maignen & Co v National Benefit Assurance Co Ltd (1922)	2
Main, The (1894)	45, 119, 124
Manchester Liners Ltd v British and Foreign Marine Insurance Co Ltd (1901)	84
Manchester Ship Canal Co v Horlock (1914)	95
Manfield v Maitland (1821)	12, 13
Mann Macneal and Steeves Ltd v General Marine Underwriters Ltd (1921)	30, 32
Maori King, The (Cargo Owners) v Hughes (1895)	63
Marel, The. See Lamb Head Shipping Co Ltd v Jennings, The Marel	
Margetts and Ocean Accident and Guarantee Corpn, Re (1901)	124, 179
Marine Insurance Co v China Transpacific SS Co (1886)	118
Marine Insurance Co Ltd v Grimmer (1944)	17
Marine Mutual Insurance Association Ltd v Young (1880)	141
Marine Sulphur Queen, The (1970)	134
Maritime Insurance Co v Stearns (1901)	16, 66
Maritime Insurance Co Ltd v Alianza Insurance Co of Santander (1907)	40
Marsden v Reid (1803)	70
Marstrand Fishing Co Ltd v Beer (1937)	89, 96, 97, 176
Marten v Nippon Sea and Land Insurance Co Ltd (1898)	4, 245
Marten v SS Owners' Underwriting Association (1902)	16, 187
Marten v Vestey Bros Ltd (1920)	70
Martin (John) of London Ltd v Russell (1960)	245
Mary Thomas, The (1894)	113, 123, 182
Mata Hari, The. See Pindos Shipping Corpn v Raven, The Mata Hari	
Matveieff & Co v Crossfield (1903)	77, 143
Mavro v Ocean Marine Insurance Co (1874); affd (1875)	113, 182
Mead v Davison (1835)	38
Medina Princess, The. See Helmville Ltd v Yorkshire Insurance Co Ltd, The Medina Princess	
Megara, The. See Aronsen (Oscar L) Inc v Compton, The Megara	
Mentz, Decker & Co v Maritime Insurance Co (1909)	7, 48, 176
Mercantile SS Co Ltd v Tyser (1881)	31
Merchants' Marine Insurance Co Ltd v North of England Protecting and Indemnity Association (1926)	179
Metcalfe v Parry (1814)	70
Meyer v Ralli (1876)	97, 130

List of cases

	PAGE
Michalos (N) & Sons Maritime SA v Prudential Assurance Co Ltd, The Zinovia (1984)	175
Middlewood v Blakes (1797)	69, 70
Midland Insurance Co v Smith (1881)	135
Mildred, Goyeneche & Co v Maspons Y Hermano (1883)	76, 77
Miller v Law Accident Insurance Co (1903)	68, 193
Miller v Woodfall (1857)	106
Miss Jay Jay, The. See Lloyd (J J) Instruments Ltd v Northern Star Insurance Co Ltd, The Miss Jay Jay	
Mitera, The. See Atlantic Maritime Carriers SA v Hellenic Mutual War Risks Association Ltd, The Mitera	
Montgomery & Co v Indemnity Mutual Marine Insurance Co (1901); affd (1902)	109, 113
Montoya v London Assurance Co (1851)	85
Montreal Light, Heat and Power Co v Sedgwick (1910)	87
Moore v Evans (1917); affd (1918)	2, 4, 23, 97
Moran, Galloway & Co v Uzielli (1905)	3, 7, 12, 13, 23
Morgan v Oswald (1812)	148
Morgan v Price (1849)	50
Morrison v Universal Marine Insurance Co (1873)	25, 31, 37
Morrison (James) & Co Ltd v Shaw, Savill and Albion Co Ltd (1916)	69
Moss v Smith (1850)	2, 95, 96
Mostyn, The. See Great Western Rly Co v Mostyn (Owners), The Mostyn	
Motor Union Insurance Co Ltd v Boggan (1923)	194
Motor Union Insurance Co Ltd v Mannheimer Versicherungs Gesellschaft (1933)	38
Mount v Larkins (1831)	66
Mountain v Whittle (1921)	61
Mouse's Case (1608)	175
Muirhead v Forth and North Sea Steamboat Mutual Insurance Association (1894)	45

	PAGE
Munro, Brice & Co v War Risks Association (1918); revsd (1920)	90
Munroe, The (1893)	123
National Benefit Assurance Co Ltd, Re (1931)	38, 139
National Oil Co of Zimbabwe (Pte) Ltd v Sturge (1991)	193
Naviera de Canarias SA v Nacional Hispanica Aseguradora SA (1977)	84, 222
Navone v Haddon (1850)	126
Naylor v Taylor (1829)	73
Near East Relief v King, Chasseur & Co Ltd (1930)	77
Nelson v Empress Assurance Corpn Ltd (1905)	16
Neter (N E) & Co v Licenses and General Insurance Co Ltd (1944)	174
Netherholme, Glen Holme and Rydal Holme, The. See Hine Bros v SS Insurance Syndicate Ltd, The Netherholme, Glen Holme and Rydal Holme	
New Zealand Shipping Co Ltd v Duke (1914)	7
Newby v Reed (1763)	50, 136
Newman v Cazalet (circa 1780)	182
Nickels & Co v London and Provincial Marine and General Insurance Co (1900)	66, 68, 85
Nigel Gold Mining Co Ltd v Hoade (1901)	148
Niger Co Ltd v Guardian Assurance Co Ltd (1922)	37, 72
Niobe, The. See M'Cowan v Baine and Johnston, The Niobe	
Norske Atlas Insurance Co Ltd v London General Insurance Co Ltd (1927)	38
North Atlantic SS Co Ltd v Burr (1904)	96, 187
North Britain, The (1894)	180
North British and Mercantile Insurance Co v London, Liverpool and Globe Insurance Co (1877)	20, 50, 136
North British and Mercantile Insurance Co v Moffatt (1871)	13

List of cases

	PAGE
North British Rubber Co v Cheetham (1938)	26
North-Eastern 100A SS Insurance Association v Red S SS Co Ltd (1905); affd (1906)	141
North of England Iron SS Insurance Association v Armstrong (1870)	45, 135
North of England Oil-Cake Co v Archangel Insurance Co (1875)	21, 75, 76
North Shipping Co Ltd v Union Marine Insurance Co Ltd (1918); affd (1919)	137, 191
Northumbrian Shipping Co Ltd v E Timm & Son Ltd (1939)	61
Northwestern Mutual Life Assurance Co v Linard, The Vainqueur (1974)	175
Norwich Union Fire Insurance Society v Colonial Mutual Fire Insurance Co (1922)	17
Norwich Union Fire Insurance Society Ltd v William H Price Ltd (1934)	102
Notara v Henderson (1872)	130
Noten (T M) BV v Harding (1990)	85
Nourse v Liverpool Sailing Ship Owners' Mutual Protection and Indemnity Association (1896)	109
Ny-Eeasteyr, The. See Houghton and Mancon Ltd v Sunderland Marine Mutual Insurance Co Ltd, The Ny-Eeasteyr	
Ocean Iron SS Insurance Association Ltd v Leslie (1887)	2, 39, 141
Ocean SS Co v Anderson (1883); revsd sub nom Anderson v Ocean SS Co (1884)	109, 112
Oceanic SS Co v Faber (1907)	176
Oceanic Steam Navigation Co Ltd v Evans (1934)	106
Odessa, The (1916)	149
Oppenheim v Fry (1863)	126
O'Reilly v Royal Exchange Assurance (1815)	73

	PAGE
Oriental Fire and General Insurance Co Ltd v American President Lines Ltd and Cotton Trading Corpn of San Francisco (1968)	134
Otago Farmers' Co-op Association of New Zealand v Thompson (1910)	2, 167
Outhwaite v Commercial Bank of Greece SA, The Sea Breeze (1987)	53, 55, 189
Overseas Commodities Ltd v Style (1958)	42, 53, 56, 83, 85, 121, 245
Overseas Marine Insurance Co Ltd, Re (1930)	10
Pacific Queen Fisheries v L Symes, The Pacific Queen (1963)	30, 32, 62, 64, 176
Padstow Total Loss and Collision Assurance Association, Re (1882)	141
Page v Fry (1800)	15
Palamisto General Enterprises SA v Ocean Marine Insurance Co Ltd, The Dias (1972)	84
Palm Branch, The (1916)	135, 148
Palmer v Blackburn (1822)	23, 143
Palmer v Fenning (1833)	66
Palyart v Leckie (1817)	140
Pamia, The. See Lubrafol, M/V (Owners) v SS Pamia (Owners), The Pamia	
Pan American World Airways Inc v Aetna Casualty and Surety Co (1974); affd (1975)	195
Panamanian Oriental SS Corpn v Wright (1970); on appeal (1971)	89, 97, 102, 103, 193
Papadimitriou v Henderson (1939)	12, 45, 114
Parchim, The (1918)	148
Parente (Robert A) v Bayville Marine Inc and General Insurance Co of America (1975)	83
Parker, Re, ex p Turquand (1885)	143
Parkin v Tunno (1809)	66
Parkinson v Collier (1797)	143
Paterson v Harris (1861)	12, 174

List of cases

	PAGE
Pawson v Watson (1778)	35, 52
Pearson v Commercial Union Assurance Co (1876)	72
Pellas v Neptune Marine Insurance Co (1879)	74
Pesquerias y Secaderos de Bacalao de España SA v Beer (1946); revsd (1947); on appeal (1949)	103
Peters v Warren Insurance Co (1838); affd (1840)	182
Petrofina SA of Brussels v Compagnia Italiana Trasporto Olii Minerali of Genoa (1937)	55
Phillips v Headlam (1831)	61
Philpott v Swann (1861)	85, 96
Phyn v Royal Exchange Assurance Co (1798)	69
Pickersgill (William) & Sons Ltd v London and Provincial Marine and General Insurance Co Ltd (1912)	32, 38, 74, 75
Pickup v Thames and Mersey Marine Insurance Co Ltd (1878)	61
Pickwick, The (1852)	130
Pillgrem v Cliff Richardson Boats Ltd and Richardson (Switzerland General Insurance Co, third party) (1977)	13, 123
Pindos Shipping Corpn v Raven, The Mata Hari (1983)	56
Pink v Fleming (1890)	83, 85
Piper v Royal Exchange Assurance (1932)	12, 14, 31
Pipon v Cope (1808)	64
Piracy Jure Gentium, Re (1934)	175
Pitman v Universal Marine Insurance Co (1882)	3, 118
Plata American Trading Inc and Nord-Handel Gesellschaft Ruecker-Giehr & Co v Lancashire (1957)	245
Polpen Shipping Co Ltd v Commercial Union Assurance Co Ltd (1943)	124, 179
Polurrian SS Co Ltd v Young (1913); affd (1915)	96, 97, 103, 118
Pomeranian, The (1895)	130, 145
Popham v St Petersburg Insurance Co (1904)	113
Popi M, The. See Rhesa Shipping Co SA v Edmunds, The Popi M	
Porter v Freudenberg (1915)	148
Potoi Chau, The. See Castle Insurance Co Ltd v Hong Kong Islands Shipping Co Ltd, The Potoi Chau	
Potts v Bell (1800)	148
Powell v Gudgeon (1816)	85
Power v Whitmore (1815)	182
Powles v Innes (1843)	21, 76
Price v Maritime Insurance Co (1900); affd (1901)	7, 18, 126
Price & Co v AI Ships' Small Damage Insurance Association (1889)	107, 126
Price & Co v Union Lighterage Co (1903); affd (1904)	83
Probatina Shipping Co Ltd v Sun Insurance Office Ltd (1974)	26
Property Insurance Co Ltd v National Protector Insurance Co Ltd (1913)	17, 30
Proudfoot v Montefiore (1867)	30, 31
Provincial Insurance Co of Canada v Leduc (1874)	53, 54, 102
Prudent Tankers Ltd SA v Dominion Insurance Co Ltd, The Caribbean Sea (1980)	86, 176
Pyman v Marten (1906)	74, 137
Quebec Marine Insurance Co v Commercial Bank of Canada (1870)	4, 52, 54, 55, 60, 61
Quellec, Le et Fils v Thomson (1916)	85
R v International Trustee for Protection of Bondholders Akt (1937)	148
Ralli v Janson (1856)	126
Ralli Bros v Cia Naviera Sota y Aznar (1920)	7
Rankin v Potter (1873)	7, 44, 85, 88, 89, 96, 99, 102, 103, 105, 106, 119, 134
Rayner v Preston (1881)	7, 21

List of cases

	PAGE
Reardon Smith Lines Ltd v Black Sea and Baltic General Insurance Co Ltd, The Indian City (1939)	70
Red Sea, The (1896)	106
Redmond v Smith (1844)	64
Reinhart Co v Joshua Hoyle & Sons Ltd (1961)	245
Reischer v Borwick (1894)	82
Reliance Marine Insurance Co v Duder (1913)	39, 42, 44, 124
Renton (G H) & Co Ltd v Black Sea and Baltic General Insurance Co Ltd (1941)	5, 245
Rhesa Shipping Co SA v Edmunds, The Popi M (1985)	175
Rhind v Wilkinson (1810)	14
Richard de Larrinaga, SS (Owners) v Admiralty Comrs (1920); affd sub nom A-G v Ard Coasters Ltd, Liverpool and London War Risks Insurance Association Ltd v SS Richard de Larrinaga Marine Underwriters (1921)	85, 86
Richardson v Burrows (1880)	179
Richardsons and M Samuel & Co, Re (1898)	194
Rickards v Forestal Land, Timber and Rlys Co Ltd (1942)	68, 73, 95, 96, 97, 103, 264, 265
Rivaz v Gerussi (1880)	30, 31, 35, 36
River Wear Comrs v Adamson (1877)	106
Roberts v Security Co Ltd (1897)	40, 78
Robertson v Petros M Nomikos Ltd (1939)	95, 98, 222
Robinson v Gleadow (1835)	15
Robinson Gold Mining Co v Alliance Insurance Co (1902); on appeal (1904)	193
Roddick v Indemnity Mutual Marine Insurance Co (1895)	10, 23, 55
Rodocanachi v Elliott (1873); affd (1874)	5, 68, 96, 97
Rosa v Insurance Co of the State of Pennsylvania, The Belle of Portugal (1970)	83, 176
Ross v Hunter (1790)	73

	PAGE
Roura and Forgas v Townend (1919)	97, 103, 222
Roux v Salvador (1835)	87, 89, 96, 99
Rowland and Marwood SS Co Ltd v Maritime Insurance Co Ltd (1901)	95, 97
Royal Exchange Assurance Corpn v Sjoforsakrings Akt Vega (1901); affd (1902)	38
Ruabon SS Co v London Assurance (1900)	118
Rudolph (M J) Corpn v Lumber Mutual Fire Insurance Co (Luria International, Third Parties), The Cape Borer (1975)	141
Russell v Provincial Insurance Co Ltd (1959)	47
Russell v Thornton (1859); on appeal (1860)	31, 33
Russian Bank for Foreign Trade v Excess Insurance Co (1918); affd (1919)	68, 84, 102, 103, 222
Ruys v Royal Exchange Assurance Corpn (1897)	103
Sadler v Dixon. See Dixon v Sadler	
Sadlers' Co v Badcock (1743)	10
Safadi v Western Assurance Co (1933)	244
St Margaret's Trust Ltd v Navigators and General Insurance Co Ltd (1949)	86, 89
St Paul Fire and Marine Insurance Co v Morice (1906)	85, 193
Salacia, The (1862)	19
Salem, The. See Shell International Petroleum Co Ltd v Gibbs, The Salem	
Samuel v Royal Exchange Assurance Co (1828)	71
Samuel (P) & Co Ltd v Dumas (1924)	10, 39, 84, 86, 174
Sanday & Co v British and Foreign Marine Insurance Co (1915); affd sub nom British and Foreign Marine Insurance Co Ltd v Samuel Sanday & Co (1916)	23, 68, 87, 95, 97, 148, 149

	PAGE
Sassoon (E D) & Co v Western Assurance Co (1912)	83
Sassoon (E D) & Co Ltd v Yorkshire Insurance Co Ltd (1923); affd (1923)	83
Scaramanga v Stamp (1880)	73
Schiffshypothekenbank Zu Luebeck AG v Compton, The Alexion Hope (1988)	175
Schloss Bros v Stevens (1906)	5, 8, 85
Schroder v Thompson (1817)	71
Scindia Steamships (London) Ltd v London Assurance (1937)	174, 176
Scott v Globe Marine Insurance Co Ltd (1896)	46
Scottish Marine Insurance Co v Turner (1853)	97, 106
Scottish Metropolitan Assurance Co Ltd v Groom (1923); affd (1924)	17
Scottish National Insurance Co Ltd v Poole (1912)	17, 144
Scottish Shire Line Ltd v London and Provincial Marine and General Insurance Co Ltd (1912)	10, 12, 31
Sea Breeze, The. See Outhwaite v Commercial Bank of Greece SA, The Sea Breeze	
Sea Insurance Co v Blogg (1898); on appeal (1898)	55
Sea Insurance Co v Hadden (1884)	106, 135
Seagrave v Union Marine Insurance Co (1866)	12, 20, 124
Seaton v Heath (1899); revsd sub nom Seaton v Burnand (1900)	25
Seavision Investment SA v Norman Thomas Evenett and Clarkson Puckle Ltd, The Tiburon (1990); affd sub nom Seavision Investment SA v Evennett and Clarkson Puckle Ltd, The Tiburon (1992)	53, 56
Sellar v M'Vicar (1804)	66
Seymour v London and Provincial Marine Insurance Co (1872); affd (1873)	64
Sharp v Gladstone (1805)	106

	PAGE
Sharp and Roarer Investments Ltd v Sphere Drake Insurance plc, Minster Insurance Co Ltd and E C Parker & Co Ltd, The Moonacre (1992)	13
Shee v Clarkson (1810)	137
Shelbourne & Co v Law Investment and Insurance Corpn (1898)	4, 83, 123
Shell International Petroleum Co Ltd v Gibbs, The Salem (1982); affd (1983)	175
Shoolbred v Nutt (1782)	31
Sibbald v Hill (1814)	36
Silcock (R) & Sons Ltd v Maritime Lighterage Co (J R Francis & Co) Ltd (1937)	61
Simon, Israel & Co v Sedgwick (1893)	66, 67, 68
Simonds v White (1824)	182
Simons (trading as Acme Credit Services) v Gale, The Cap Tarifa (1957); affd (1958)	52, 53, 56
Simpson v Thomson (1877)	99, 106, 134, 135
Simpson SS Co Ltd v Premier Underwriting Association Ltd (1905)	52, 55, 67
Sipowicz v Wimble, The Green Lion (1974)	176
Slattery v Mance (1962)	31, 36, 175
Sleigh v Tyser (1900)	55, 61, 145
Small v United Kingdom Marine Mutual Insurance Association (1897)	20, 84
Smit Tak Offshore Services v Youell and General Accident Fire & Life Assurance Corpn plc (1992)	7
Smith v Robertson (1814)	102
Smith Hill & Co v Pyman Bell & Co (1891)	19
Société Nouvelle d'Armement v Spillers and Bakers Ltd (1917)	113
South British Fire and Marine Insurance Co of New Zealand v Da Costa (1906)	17
Sovfracht (V/O) v Van Udens Scheepvaart en Agentuur Maatschapij (NV Gebr) (1943)	148

	PAGE		PAGE
Soya GmbH Mainz Kommanditgesellschaft v White (1982); on appeal (1983)	32, 83, 85	Svendsen v Wallace Bros (1884); affd (1885)	112
Spalding v Crocker (1897)	144	Swan and Cleland's Graving Dock and Slipway Co v Maritime Insurance Co and Croshaw (1907)	74, 109
Sparkes v Marshall (1836)	14, 15, 74	Sweeting v Pearce (1859); affd (1861)	77, 143
Spence v Union Marine Insurance Co Ltd (1868)	87, 121	Symington & Co v Union Insurance Society of Canton (1928)	4, 144, 244, 245
Spinney's (1948) Ltd, Spinney's Centres SAL and Michel Doumet, Joseph Doumet and Distributors and Agencies SAL v Royal Insurance Co Ltd (1980)	193, 194	Tait v Levi (1811)	69
Stainbank v Fenning (1851)	12, 18	Tannenbaum & Co v Heath (1908)	26
Stanton v Richardson (1874); on appeal (1875)	63	Tasker v Cunninghame (1819)	68
		Tate v Hyslop (1885)	30, 31
Stearns v Village Main Reef Gold Mining Co Ltd (1905)	135	Tatham v Hodgson (1796)	83
Stephens v Australasian Insurance Co (1872)	46, 143	Tatham, Bromage & Co v Burr, The Engineer (1898)	7, 124, 167, 180
Stewart v Greenock Marine Insurance Co (1848)	105, 106	Tatjana, The. See Lindsay v Klein, The Tatjana	
Stewart v Steele (1842)	118	Taylor v Dunbar (1869)	83
Stewart v West India and Pacific SS Co (1873); affd (1873)	182	Taylor v Liverpool and Great Western Steam Co (1874)	175
Stock v Inglis (1884); affd sub nom Inglis v Stock (1885)	12, 15, 46	Tenneco Oil Co v Tug Tony Coastal Towing Corpn (1972)	134
Stone Vickers Ltd v Appledore Ferguson Shipbuilders Ltd (1992)	4	Thames and Mersey Marine Insurance Co v British and Chilian SS Co (1915); affd (1916)	45, 135
Stoomvart Maatschappij Sophie H v Merchants' Marine Insurance Co Ltd (1919)	85	Thames and Mersey Marine Insurance Co v Gunford Ship Co (1911)	9, 10, 23, 31, 32
Stoomvart Maatschappy Nederland v Peninsular and Oriental Steam Navigation Co, The Khedive (1882)	179	Thames and Mersey Marine Insurance Co Ltd v Hamilton, Fraser & Co (1887)	7, 84, 174, 176
Stott (Baltic) Steamers Ltd v Marten (1914); affd (1916)	7, 84, 174, 176	Thames and Mersey Marine Insurance Co Ltd v Van Laun & Co (1905), (1917)	48, 68
Strang, Steel & Co v A Scott & Co (1889)	113	Theodorou v Chester (1951)	8
Stranna, The (1938)	83	Thomas v Tyne and Wear SS Freight Insurance Association (1917)	61, 62
Strass v Spillers and Bakers Ltd (1911)	21, 75		
Street v Royal Exchange Assurance (1913); affd (1914)	17	Thomas (M) & Son Shipping Co Ltd v London and Provincial Marine and General Insurance Co Ltd (1914)	62
Stringer v English and Scottish Marine Insurance Co (1869); affd (1870)	103	Thompson v Hopper (1856)	84
		Thompson v Hopper (1858)	83
		Thompson v Reynolds (1857)	45
Sutherland v Pratt (1843)	14	Thorsa, The (1916)	61

	PAGE		PAGE
Tiburon, The. See Seavision Investment SA v Norman Thomas Evenett and Clarkson Puckle Ltd, The Tiburon		United States Shipping Co v Empress Assurance Corpn (1907); affd (1908)	19, 23
Tobin v Harford (1863); affd (1864)	121, 124	Universo Insurance Co of Milan v Merchants Marine Insurance Co (1897)	77, 143
Traders and General Insurance Association Ltd, Re, ex p Continental and Overseas Trading Co (1924)	4, 244	Usher v Noble (1810)	19, 23, 121
		Usparicha v Noble (1811)	148
		Uzielli v Boston Marine Insurance Co (1884)	16, 103, 109, 130
Trident, The. See Hall Bros SS Co Ltd v Young, The Trident			
Trinder, Anderson & Co v Thames and Mersey Marine Insurance Co (1898)	57, 64, 82, 83, 84, 103	Vacuum Oil Co v Union Insurance Society of Canton Ltd (1926)	103
Tropaioforos, The. See Compania Naviera Santi SA v Indemnity Marine Assurance Co Ltd, The Tropaioforos		Vainqueur, The. See Northwestern Mutual Life Assurance Co v Linard, The Vainqueur	
Tunno v Edwards (1810)	135	Vallance v Dewar (1808)	30, 66
Turnbull v Janson (1877)	61	Vandyck v Hewitt (1800)	140
Turnbull, Martin & Co v Hull Underwriters' Association (1900)	84, 222	Ventouris v Mountain, The Italia Express (No 2) (1992)	115, 116
		Vermaas' (J) Scheepvaartbedrijf NV v Association Technique de l'Importation Charbonnière, The Laga (1966)	194
Tyrie v Fletcher (1777) cited in (1777)	140		
Tyser v Shipowners Syndicate (Reassured) (1896)	39	Versicherungs und Transport AG Daugava v Henderson (1934)	17
		Vincentelli & Co v John Rowlett & Co (1910)	2, 8
Uhde v Walters (1811)	143	Visscherij Maatschappij Nieuw Onderneming v Scottish Metropolitan Assurance Co Ltd (1922)	25, 31
Union Castle Mail SS Co Ltd v United Kingdom Mutual War Risks Association Ltd (1958)	142		
Union Insurance Society of Canton Ltd v George Wills & Co (1916)	46, 52, 54	Vita Food Products Inc v Unus Shipping Co Ltd (1939)	148
Union Marine Insurance Co v Borwick (1895)	123	Vlassopoulos v British and Foreign Marine Insurance Co Ltd (1929)	113
Union Marine Insurance Co Ltd v Martin (1866)	50	Vortigern, The (1899)	61
		Vrondissis v Stevens (1940)	98
United Railways of Havana and Regla Warehouses Ltd, Re (1960)	148		
		Wadsworth Lighterage and Coaling Co Ltd v Sea Insurance Co Ltd (1929)	83
United Scottish Insurance Co Ltd v British Fishing Vessels Mutual War Risks Association Ltd, The Braconbush (1944)	90	Walker (F B) & Sons Inc v Valentine (1970)	55, 176
		Walpole v Ewer (1789)	182
United States of America v Atlantic Mutual Insurance Co (1952)	241	Watson (Joseph) & Son Ltd v Firemen's Fund Insurance Co of San Francisco (1922)	85, 113

List of cases

	PAGE
Watts Watts & Co Ltd v Mitsui & Co Ltd (1917)	85
Waugh v Morris (1873)	64
Wavertree Sailing Ship Co v Love (1897)	148
Way v Modigliani (1787)	66
Wells v Hopwood (1832)	221
Welsh Girl, The (1906); affd sub nom The Commonwealth (1907)	135, 136
West of England Fire Insurance Co v Isaacs (1896); affd (1897)	134
West of Scotland Ship Owners Mutual Protection and Indemnity Association (Luxembourg) v Aifanourios Shipping SA, The Aifanourios (1980)	141
Western Assurance Co of Toronto v Poole (1903)	17, 130, 136, 144
Westminster Fire Office v Reliance Marine Insurance Co (1903)	244
Westport Coal Co v McPhail (1898)	84
Westwood v Bell (1815)	77
Wetherall (J H) & Co Ltd v London Assurance (1931)	85
Wetherell v Jones (1832)	7
Wharton (J) (Shipping) Ltd v Mortleman (1941)	86
Whincup v Hughes (1871)	140
Whitworth v Shepherd (1884)	136
Wilkinson v Hyde (1858)	126
Williams v Atlantic Assurance Co Ltd (1933)	23, 25, 35, 74
Williams v North China Insurance Co (1876)	124, 142
Williams & Co v Canton Insurance Office Ltd. See Brankelow SS Co v Canton Insurance Office	
Williams Bros (Hull) Ltd v W H Naamlooze Vennootschap Berghuys Kolenhandel (1915)	194
Willmott v General Accident Fire and Life Assurance Corpn Ltd (1935)	36, 37
Wills & Sons v World Marine Insurance Ltd (1911)	176
Wilson v Boag (1956)	40, 65
Wilson v Jones (1867)	7, 9, 10, 12, 13, 15, 42
Wilson v Martin (1856)	12
Wilson v Rankin (1865)	64
Wilson v Salamandra Assurance Co of St Petersburg (1903)	30
Wilson Bros Bobbin Co Ltd v Green (1917)	126, 130
Wilson (Thomas), Sons & Co v Xantho (Cargo Owners), The Xantho (1887)	83, 174, 175
Wingate v Foster (1878)	70
Wondrous, The. See Ikerigi Cia Naviera SA v Palmer, The Wondrous	
Woodside v Globe Marine Insurance Co Ltd (1896)	3, 45, 115, 127
Wooldridge v Boydell (1778)	66
Wyllie v Povah (1907)	7, 89
Xantho, The. See Wilson (Thomas), Sons & Co v Xantho (Cargo Owners), The Xantho	
Xenos v Fox (1868); on appeal (1869)	45, 130, 180
Xenos v Wickham (1866)	40
Yangtsze Insurance Association v Lukmanjee (1918)	21
Yangtze Insurance Association v Indemnity Mutual Marine Assurance Co (1908)	56, 64
Yasin, The (1979)	12, 134
Yates v Whyte (1838)	20
Yorkshire Dale SS Co Ltd v Minister of War Transport, The Coxwold (1942)	86
Yorkshire Insurance Co Ltd v Campbell (1917)	52, 54
Yorkshire Insurance Co Ltd v Nisbet Shipping Co Ltd (1962)	45, 134, 135
Young v Merchants' Marine Insurance Co Ltd (1932)	17, 179
Zinovia, The. See Michalos (N) & Sons Maritime SA v Prudential Assurance Co Ltd, The Zinovia	

Books Cited or Used

NB – Where in this work a book is cited by the author's name only, a reference is intended to the book and edition mentioned below under that author's name.

ARNOULD, SIR, J, *The Law of Marine Insurance and Average* (16th ed, 1981)

CARVER, T G, *Carriage of Goods by Sea* (13th ed, 1982)

CHALMERS, SIR M D, *Sale of Goods Act 1979* (18th ed, 1981)

DICEY, A C and MORRIS, J H C, *The Conflict of Laws* (11th ed, 1987)

GOW, W, *Marine Insurance: A Handbook* (5th ed, 1931)

HALL, W E, *A Treatise on International Law* (8th ed, 1924)

IVAMY, E R HARDY, *General Principles of Insurance Law* (6th ed, 1993)

IVAMY, E R HARDY, *Marine Insurance* (4th ed, 1985)

KENNEDY, W R, *Law of Salvage* (5th ed, 1985)

LOWNDES, R and RUDOLF, G R, *The Law of General Average and the York-Antwerp Rules* (11th ed, 1990)

MARTIN, F, *The History of Lloyd's and of Marine Insurance in Great Britain* (1876)

McARTHUR, C, *The Contract of Marine Insurance* (2nd ed, 1890)

McNAIR, LORD and WATTS, A D, *Legal Effects of War* (4th ed, 1966)

PHIPSON, S L, *The Law of Evidence* (14th ed, 1990)

SCRUTTON, SIR T E, *Charterparties and Bills of Lading* (19th ed, 1984)

SELMER, K S, *The Survival of General Average* (2nd ed, 1974)

WEBBER, G J, *Effect of War on Contracts* (2nd ed, 1946)

WRIGHT, C and FAYLE, C E, *A History of Lloyd's* (1928)

The Marine Insurance Act 1906

(6 Edw 7 c 41)

An Act to codify[1] the Law relating to Marine Insurance.

[21 December 1906]

MARINE INSURANCE

1. Marine insurance defined

A contract of marine insurance is a contract whereby the insurer undertakes to indemnify the assured, in manner and to the extent thereby agreed, against marine losses, that is to say, the losses incident to marine adventure.[2]

Note

The formal instrument in which the contract is embodied is called the 'policy'.[3] The informal note or memorandum which is drawn up when the contract is entered into is called the 'slip'.[4]

The party who undertakes to indemnify the other, ie the promisor, is called the 'insurer' or 'underwriter' (so called because he subscribes or underwrites the policy). The party to be indemnified is called the 'insured,' or more usually, the 'assured'.[5] When a contract of marine insurance is entered into, the underwriters are said 'to take a line'. The subject-matter insured is usually referred to as 'the interest insured'.[6]

The consideration which the insurer receives for his undertaking is called the 'premium'. But in the case of 'mutual insurance' a guarantee or other arrangement may take the place of the premium.[7]

The term 'loss' includes damage or detriment as well as the actual loss of the property.[8]

The term 'risk' is used in different senses, and must always be construed in the light of its context. Sometimes it is used to denote the perils themselves to which insurable property may be exposed, as when sea risks are contrasted with land risks, or when goods are insured against 'all risks'.[9] Sometimes it is used to denote the risk run by the person whose property is exposed to danger. But, more usually perhaps, it is used to denote the liability undertaken by the insurer in respect of his contract as, for example, when goods are lost, and it is said that 'the risk had not attached,' that is to say, that the goods were not at the time of loss covered by the policy.[10]

Marine insurance, in legal theory, is essentially a contract of indemnity.[11] The legal consequences and incidents of the contract are deductions from this cardinal principle. Hence arise its distinctive characteristics, such as the rules requiring an insurable interest, the rules as to double insurance, the right of subrogation consequent upon settlement of the loss, and the right to a return of premium in certain events.

But it has often been pointed out that, in practice, marine insurance is not a perfect contract of indemnity.[12] For example, under an unvalued policy[13] on goods, in the ordinary form, and without any special clause, the assured would probably receive an amount less than his real loss,[14] while under a valued policy[15] he may receive an amount which either exceeds or falls short of his real loss.[16] But this departure in practice from the principle of indemnity depends rather on the form of policies in actual use than on the nature of the contract itself.

The lawful contract is always, in principle, a contract of indemnity, but the extent and amount of indemnity are matters of agreement between the parties. An 'honour' (or wager) policy is not a contract of indemnity.[17] But a policy of reinsurance is a contract of indemnity.[18]

Forgery of a marine insurance policy is an offence under the Forgery and Counterfeiting Act 1981, s 1.[19]

1 For the short title, and the rule of construction in respect of a codifying statute, see s 94 and notes thereto.
2 Cf definition by Blackburn J in *Lloyd v Fleming* (1872) LR 7 QB 299 at 302: 'A policy of marine insurance is a contract of indemnity against all losses accruing to the subject-matter of the policy from certain perils during the adventure.' See also *Admiralty Comrs v Ropner & Co Ltd* (1917) 86 LJKB 1030, distinguishing the Admiralty charter-party with marine indemnity clauses (which was used in the First World War) from marine insurance; *Moore v Evans* [1918] AC 185, 193, distinguishing marine from non-marine risks.
3 From Latin *pollicitatio*, a promise, through Italian *polizza* or French *police*. Oddly enough, in an English policy the promise to pay in case of loss is implied, not expresssed. Continental policies contain an express promise to pay within so many days after notice of loss.
4 See ss 21, 22, 89, and *Arnould*, paras 163–165. Cf *Maignen & Co v National Benefit Assurance Co* (1922) 38 TLR 257 (as to short slip and closing slip).
5 As to what is included in the term 'assured,' see *Ocean Iron SS Insurance Association Ltd v Leslie* (1887) 22 QBD at 722n, 726n, per Mathew J.
6 Cf *Hewitt Bros v Wilson* (1915) 20 Com Cas 241 at 243, CA distinguishing the 'interest insured' from 'insurable interest'.
7 As to the premium, see ss 52–54, and as to mutual insurance, see s 85.
8 As to loss, see ss 55–66. For a useful discussion of the meaning of 'loss', see *Moss v Smith* (1850) 19 LJCP 225, at 228. As to the clause 'FPA *and loss*,' see *Otago Farmers' Co-op Association of New Zealand v Thompson* [1910] 2 KB 145.
9 Even then the term may have a double meaning, and may refer either to the quantum of loss or the cause of the accident: *Vincentelli & Co v John Rowlett & Co* (1910) 16 Com Cas 310 at 317.
10 Cf *Bradford v Symondson* (1881) 7 QBD at 464, per Lord Bramwell.

11 Per Lord Mansfield, *Kent v Bird* (1777) 2 Cowp at 585 (wager policy); per Blackburn J, *Lloyd v Fleming* (1872) LR 7 QB at 302 (assignment after loss); per Blackburn J, *Anderson v Morice* (1875) LR 10 CP at 615 (insurable interest); per Jessel MR, *Pitman v Universal Marine Insurance Co* (1882) 9 QBD at 204 (partial loss); per Lord Esher and Bowen LJ, *Castellain v Preston* (1883) 11 QBD at 386 and 397 (subrogation); *Moran, Galloway & Co v Uzielli* [1905] 2 KB at 563, CA (insurable interest). See further, Ivamy, *Marine Insurance* (4th ed, 1985), pp 4–7.
12 *Aitchison v Lohre* (1879) 4 App Cas at 761; *British and Foreign Insurance Co v Wilson Shipping Co Ltd* [1921] 1 AC at 214, 26 Com Cas at 35, per Lord Sumner; *Goole and Hull Steam Towing Co Ltd v Ocean Marine Insurance Co Ltd* [1928] 1 KB at 594.
13 As to unvalued policies, see s 28.
14 See s 16(3). In practice, the valuation generally allows for freight and expected profit so that the assured receives more. In the case of freight insurance the indemnity is exceeded. See s 16(2).
15 As to valued policies, see s 27(2).
16 Cf *Woodside v Globe Marine Insurance Co Ltd* [1896] 1 QB at 107; *Loders and Nucoline Ltd v Bank of New Zealand* (1929) 45 TLR 203.
17 See note to s 4, and *Kulen Kemp v Vigne* (1786) 1 Term Rep at 309; *Arnould*, para 385; *John Edwards & Co v Motor Union Insurance Co* [1922] 2 KB 249 (no right of subrogation on payment).
18 *British Dominions General Insurance Co Ltd v Duder* [1915] 2 KB 394, 20 Com Cas 270, CA.
19 Which states: 'A person is guilty of forgery if he makes a false instrument with the intention that he or another shall use it to induce somebody to accept it as genuine, and by reason of so accepting it to do or not to do some act to his own or any other person's prejudice.' A person guilty of an offence under s 1 is liable on summary conviction (a) to a fine not exceeding the statutory maximum; or (b) to imprisonment for a term not exceeding 6 months; or to both: Forgery and Counterfeiting Act 1981, s 6(1). On conviction on indictment he is liable to imprisonment for a term not exceeding 10 years: ibid, s 6(2). 'Statutory maximum' in relation to a fine on summary conviction means the prescribed sum within the meaning of the Magistrates' Courts Act 1980, s 32 (£1,000 or another sum fixed by order under s 143 of the Act to take account of changes in the value of money): ibid, s 6(5).

2. Mixed sea and land risks

(1) A contract of marine insurance may, by its express terms, or by usage of trade, be extended so as to protect the assured against losses on inland waters or on any land risk which may be incidental to any sea voyage.[1]
(2) Where a ship in course of building, or the launch of a ship, or any adventure analogous to a marine adventure, is covered by a policy in the form of a marine policy, the provisions of this Act, in so far as applicable, shall apply thereto; but, except as by this section provided, nothing in this Act shall alter or affect any rule of law applicable to any contract of insurance other than a contract of marine insurance as by this Act defined.[2]

Note

The normal insurance on goods now contains the 'transit' clause,[3] which covers the goods from the time they leave the shipper's or manufacturer's warehouse until they reach the warehouse of the consignee.[4] These mixed sea and land risks may be compared, by the way of analogy, with 'through bills of lading,' which are the invention of modern commerce.

Thus, goods may be insured 'from Japan to London, via Marseilles and/or Southampton';[5] wool may be insured 'at and from Townsville to London, including risk of fire and flood, from sheep's back until waterborne at Townsville';[6] bullion may be insured 'at and from Boodini to London, including all risks of every description, from the mines by escort to railway station at Raichur, thence by rail to Bombay, and thence to London';[7] a fox terrier may be insured 'against all risks from London to Bombay, and thence by rail to Lahore';[8] goods may be insured 'against all risks by land or by water' from Cartagena to any place in the interior of Colombia;[9] timber may be insured 'whilst on board the ocean-going vessel until discharged at port of destination and whilst in transit by land and/or water to final destination there or in the interior';[10] a consignment of clothing may be insured from 'Hong Kong to Scotland via the Port of London';[11] and oil may be insured in steel or iron drums 'on steamer and/or steamers and/or conveyances or any other method of transportation from anywhere to anywhere'.[12]

It is usual to insure a vessel under construction and also while she is being launched.[13]

1 *Ide and Christie v Chalmers and White* (1900) 5 Com Cas 212 (warehouse to warehouse); *Republic of Bolivia v Indemnity Mutual Marine Assurance Co* [1909] 1 KB 785 at 802 (riverine policy up the Amazon). As to trade usage, which hitherto has been of very limited scope, see *Rodocanachi v Elliott* (1873) 43 LJPC at 254, per Lord Esher. For a non-marine policy which incidentally covered a sea transit, see *Moore v Evans* [1918] AC 185, 23 Com Cas 124, HL (no constructive total loss); and for a policy in a marine form which was in substance one of fire insurance and ultra vires the company, see *Re Argonaut Marine Insurance Co Ltd* [1932] 2 Ch 34.

2 *Jackson v Mumford* (1904) 9 Com Cas 114, CA (ships when building insured against 'fire in shops and on board on stocks, trials, and all marine risks to completion and acceptance by Admiralty'); *James Yachts Ltd v Thames and Mersey Marine Insurance Co Ltd* [1977] 1 Lloyd's Rep 206, British Columbia, Supreme Court (policy on 'hull, tackle . . . boats and other furniture and fixtures and all material belonging to and destined for inclusion in all vessels being built at the premises of the assured as specified elsewhere herein'); *Stone Vickers Ltd v Appledore Ferguson Shipbuilders Ltd* [1992] 2 Lloyd's Rep 578, CA, where the question was whether the plaintiffs were entitled to be protected against a subrogated claim; *Hong Kong Borneo Services Co Ltd v Pilcher* [1992] 2 Lloyd's Rep 593, QB (Commercial Court) (reinsurance), where the risk of delay in delivery of two vessels under construction caused by strikes was reinsured. As to the words 'so far as applicable,' see *Quebec Marine Insurance Co v Commorcial Bank of Canada* (1870) LR 3 PC 234 (lake, river, and canal insurance); *Joyce v Kennard* (1871) LR 7 QB 78 (insurance of lighterman's liability); *Shelbourne v Law Investment and Insurance Co* (1898) 8 Asp MLC 445 (river insurance); *Apollinaris Co v Nord Deutsche Insurance Co* [1904] 1 KB 252 (deck cargo on the Rhine canal, usage).

3 See Institute Cargo Clauses (A), Clause 8, p 243, post; Institute Cargo Clauses (B), Clause 8, p 252, post; Institute Cargo Clauses (C), Clause 8, p 259, post; Institute War Clauses (Cargo), Clause 5, p 266, post.

4 *Ide and Christie v Chalmers and White* (1900) 5 Com Cas 212; *Marten v Nippon* (1898) 3 Com Cas 164; *Re Traders and General Insurance Association Ltd* [1924] 2 Ch 187; *Symington & Co v Union Insurance Society of Canton Ltd* (1928) 34 Com Cas 23; *Leon v Casey* [1932] 2 KB 576, CA (transit by land and sea, loss on land, policy substantially one of marine insurance). See further Ivamy, *Marine Insurance* (4th ed, 1985), pp 122–126.

5 *Rodocanachi v Elliott* (1873) LR 8 CP 649; affd (1874) LR 9 CP 518, Ex Ch (goods detained in Paris during siege).
6 *King v Victoria Insurance Co* [1896] AC 250, PC; see, too, *Davies v National Insurance Co of New Zealand* [1891] AC 485.
7 *Hyderabad (Deccan) Co v Willoughby* [1899] 2 QB 530; see, too, *Janson v Driefontein Consolidation Mines* [1902] AC 484 (bullion insured from Transvaal mines to London).
8 *Jacobs v Gaviller* (1902) 7 Com Cas 116.
9 *Schloss Bros v Stevens* [1906] 2 KB 665, approved in *British and Foreign Marine Insurance Co v Gaunt* [1921] 2 AC 41, HL; affg SC [1920] 1 KB 903, CA (all risks from sheep's back by land or water to warehouse).
10 *G H Renton & Co Ltd v Black Sea and Baltic General Insurance Co Ltd* [1941] 1 All ER 149, KB. (*Held*, in this case, that the risk ended when the timber was unloaded on the quay, and not after the subsequent sorting and stacking by the port authority.)
11 *H Cousins & Co Ltd v D and C Carriers Ltd* [1971] 2 QB 230, [1971] 1 All ER 55, CA.
12 *Fuerst Day Lawson Ltd v Orion Insurance Co Ltd* [1980] 1 Lloyd's Rep 656.
13 See the cases cited in footnote 2, supra.

3. Marine adventure and maritime perils defined

(1) Subject to the provisions of this Act, every lawful[1] marine adventure may be the subject of a contract of marine insurance.[2]
(2) In particular there is a marine adventure where—
  (a) Any ship[3], goods,[4] or other moveables[5] are exposed to maritime perils. Such property is in this Act referred to as 'insurable property';
  (b) The earning or acquisition of any freight, passage money,[6] commission, profit, or other pecuniary benefit, or the security for any advances, loan, or disbursements, is endangered by the exposure of insurable property to maritime perils;[7]
  (c) Any liability to a third party may be incurred by the owner of, or other person interested in or responsible for, insurable property, by reason of maritime perils.[8]

'Maritime perils' means the perils consequent on, or incidental to, the navigation of the sea, that is to say, perils of the seas, fire, war perils, pirates, rovers, thieves, captures, seizures, restraints and detainments of princes and peoples, jettisons, barratry, and any other perils, either of the like kind, or which may be designated by the policy.[9]

Note

Lawfulness of adventure. If an insurer, with his eyes open, insures an unlawful adventure, the policy is obviously a mere 'honour' policy, for *ex turpi causa non oritur actio*.[10] Speaking generally, an adventure is illegal if it is prohibited by statute, or contrary to good morals or public policy;[11] and illegality in any integral part of the adventure taints the whole of it.[12]

An adventure will usually be unlawful when its performance involves a breach of the laws of a foreign country. The cases which held that this principle did not apply to infringements of trade and revenue laws are now of doubtful authority.[13] But if two foreign States are at war, there is nothing unlawful in sending an

English ship to run a blockade, though the ship may be liable to confiscation by the blockading belligerent.[14]

But a distinction must be drawn between the lawfulness of the adventure and the implied warranty of legality by the assured (see s 41). If the insurer and the assured like to insure an illegal adventure, the contract is an 'honour' contract; but where the assured does not disclose the illegality of the adventure, the contract is binding neither in law nor honour. Again, if there is anything in foreign law or international relations which increases the particular risk and is not a matter of common knowledge, it must be disclosed to the insurer before the contract is concluded.[15]

Subject of insurance. Strictly speaking, it is the risk or adventure of the assured and not the property exposed to peril, which is the subject of insurance. Ex hypothesi, the ship or goods may be lost. What is really insured is the pecuniary interest of the assured in or in respect of the property exposed to peril, in other words, the risk or adventure.[16] Lord Esher sought to reconcile the underlying facts with popular language, by drawing a distinction between the subject insured and the subject-matter of insurance.[17] In mercantile language the subject insured is referred to as 'the interest insured.'[18]

'The subject-matter', said Lord Blackburn, 'is generally described very concisely as being so much "on ship," "on goods," "on freight," "on profit on goods," "on advances on coolies," "on emigrant money," and so on.'[19]

Maritime perils. The result of maritime perils is to cause 'marine damage,' which, said Lord Herschell, does not mean only damage which has been caused by the seas, 'but damage of a character to which a marine adventure is subject. Such an adventure has its own perils, to which either it is exclusively subject or which possess in relation to it a special or peculiar character. To secure an indemnity against these is the purpose and object of marine insurance.'[20]

The terms of sub-s (2) are inclusive, not exhaustive. As the conditions of maritime commerce change, new dangers and matters require to be covered by insurance. For example, shipments of live cattle, which are insured against mortality and all other risks, and pilferage risks, have to be covered by special provisions, as such risks are not contemplated by the ordinary form of policy.

The insurer, as a rule, is not liable for loss consequent on delay, even though the delay is caused by a peril insured against.[21] But policies may be framed to protect the assured against the cancelling clause in charter-parties, and to protect the owner of perishable goods.

Insurances are often effected against 'all risks,' or even against 'all risks by land or by water.'[22]

As regards 'all risks' policies there are, as Lord Sumner pointed out, certain necessary limits. 'The expression does not cover inherent vice, or mere wear and tear, or British capture. It covers a risk, not a certainty; it is something which happens to the subject-matter from without, not the natural behaviour of the subject-matter, being what it is, in the circumstances under which it is carried. Nor is it a loss which the assured brings about by his own act, for then he has not merely exposed the goods to the chance of injury, he has injured them himself. Finally, the description "all risks" does not alter the general law; only risks are covered which it is lawful to cover, and the onus of proof remains where it would have been on a policy against ordinary sea perils.'[23]

If it is desired to cover goods against all risks, the usual course is to embody in the policy the Institute Cargo Clauses (A).[24]

In order for the subject-matter to be insured against war risks, the appropriate Institute Clauses must be inserted in the policy.[25]

Cover against loss by strikes is covered by the Institute Strike Clauses.[26]

1 As to 'lawfulness,' see note to this section, and s 41 (warranty of legality), and note the saving for Common Law in s 91(2).
2 *Wilson v Jones* (1867) LR 2 Ex Ch 139, Ex Ch.
3 As to 'ship,' see Sch 1, r 15. References in whatever terms in the Marine Insurance Act 1906 to ships, vessels or boats or activities or places connected therewith are extended to include hovercraft or activities or places connected with hovercraft: Hovercraft (Application of Enactments) Order 1972 (SI 1972/971).
4 As to 'moveables', see s 90.
5 As to 'goods,' see Sch 1, r 17.
6 Ie fares payable by passengers.
7 Cf *Rankin v Potter* (1873) LR 6 HL 83 (chartered freight on homeward voyage insured by policy on outward voyage); *Price v Maritime Insurance Co* (1900) 5 Com Cas 332; affd [1901] 2 KB 412, CA (advances); *Moran, Galloway & Co v Uzielli* [1905] 2 KB 555 (disbursements); *Wyllie v Povah* (1907) 12 Com Cas 317 (profits on cargo); *Mentz Decker & Co v Maritime Insurance Co* (1909) 15 Com Cas 17 (commission); *New Zealand Shipping Co v Duke* [1914] 2 KB 682, 19 Com Cas 223 (passage money, disbursements consequent on transhipping passengers after an accident).
8 *Boehm v Bell* (1799) 8 Term Rep at 161 (damages and costs for illegal capture); *Tatham v Burr* [1898] AC at 385 (liability for running down another ship); *Cunard SS Co v Marten* [1902] 2 KB 624 (liability of shipowner under contract of carriage); *Briggs v Merchant Traders' Association* (1849) 13 QB 167 (liability for salvage charges insured as 'average expenses'); *Smit Tax Offshore Services v Youell and General Accident Fire and Life Assurance Corpn plc* [1992] 1 Lloyd's Rep 154, CA where it was held, on the true construction of the policy, that the insurers were under no liability to remove the insured vessel which sank outside Dubai waters for the Dubai authorities had not passed a decree compelling the assured to remove her. (See the judgment of Mustill LJ, ibid, at 158.) See further s 74, as to 'collision' clause.
9 Cf *Thames and Mersey Marine Insurance Co Ltd v Hamilton, Fraser & Co* (1887) 12 App Cas at 498, per Lord Herschell.
10 Cf *Gedge v Royal Exchange Assurance Corpn* [1900] 2 QB at 220.
11 *Wetherell v Jones* (1832) 3 B & Ad at 225, 226.
12 See *Arnould*, para 749 and as to illegality generally, see ibid, paras 743–760.
13 See *Ralli Bros v Compania Naviera Sota y Aznar* [1920] 2 KB 287 at 300, CA; and *Foster v Driscoll* [1929] 1 KB 470 at 518, CA.
14 *The Helen* (1865) LR 1 A & E 1; *Ex p Chavasse* (1865) 34 LJ Bcy 17. Similar considerations apply to carrying contraband of war: *Caine v Palace Shipping Co* (1906) 12 Com Cas at 109, 111, CA and see note to s 41 (implied warranty of legality).
15 *Republic of Bolivia v Indemnity Mutual Marine Assurance Co Ltd* (1908) 14 Com Cas at 166, and see s 18, as to disclosure.
16 A good illustration of this principle is furnished by the rule that there may be a total loss of goods, freight or profits when the adventure is wholly frustrated, though the goods themselves remain in specie (see s 60).
17 *Rayner v Preston* (1881) 18 Ch D at 9, CA. See further, Ivamy, *General Principles of Insurance Law* (6th ed, 1993), pp 11–12.
18 Cf *Hewitt Bros v Wilson* (1915) 20 Com Cas 241 at 243, CA distinguishing the 'interest insured' from 'insurable interest.'
19 *Mackenzie v Whitworth* (1875) 1 Ex D at 40, CA.
20 *Thames and Mersey Marine Insurance Co Ltd v Hamilton, Fraser & Co* (1887) 12 App Cas at 498. Cf *Stott (Baltic) Steamers v Marten* [1916] 1 AC 304, 21 Com Cas 144, HL.

21 See s 55(2)(b).
22 *Schloss Bros v Stevens* [1906] 2 KB 665; *Vincentelli & Co v John Rowlett & Co* (1910) 16 Com Cas 310, and see cases cited, pp 4–5, ante.
23 *British and Foreign Marine Insurance Co v Gaunt* (1921) 26 Com Cas 247 at 259, [1921] 2 AC 41 at 57, HL; applied in *Theodorou v Chester* [1951] 1 Lloyd's Rep 204, KB; *F W Berk & Co Ltd v Style* [1955] 3 All ER 625. It must, of course, be shown that the risk attached: *Fuerst Day Lawson Ltd v Orion Insurance Co Ltd* [1980] 1 Lloyd's Rep 656, where a cargo of oil drums was insured against 'all risks' and on arrival the drums were found to contain water with slight traces of oil, and judgment was given for the insurers because the assured had failed to discharge the burden of proof that the oil in the drums had ever started on its transit. (See the judgment of Mocatta J, ibid, at 664.)
24 See Appendix III, p 239, post.
25 See Institute War Clauses (Cargo), p 264 post; Institute War and Strikes Clauses (Hulls-Time), p 208, post; Institute War and Strikes Clauses (Hulls-Voyage), p 212, post; Institute War and Strikes Clauses (Freight-Time), p 232, post.
26 Institute Strikes Clauses (Cargo), p 271, post; Institute War and Strikes Clauses (Hulls-Time), p 208, post; Institute War and Strikes Clauses (Hulls-Voyage), p 212, post; Institute War and Strikes Clauses (Freight-Time), p 232, post.

INSURABLE INTEREST

4. Avoidance of wagering or gaming contracts

(1) Every contract of marine insurance by way of gaming or wagering is void.
(2) A contract of marine insurance is deemed to be a gaming or wagering contract—
  (a) Where the assured has not an insurable interest as defined by this Act, and the contract is entered into with no expectation of acquiring such an interest;[1] or
  (b) Where the policy is made 'interest or no interest,' or 'without further proof of interest than the policy itself,' or 'without benefit of salvage to the insurer,' or subject to any other like term:[2]

Provided that, where there is no possibility of salvage, a policy may be effected without benefit of salvage to the insurer.[3]

Note

Gaming or wagering policies. This section substantially reproduces the effect of the Marine Insurance Act 1745, which prohibited policies that bore on the face of them the *indicia* of wagering, whether, in fact, they were wager policies or not. The following points may be noted:—
(1) The statute of 1745 was confined in terms to British ships, and goods and effects laden on them. Therefore a ppi policy on a foreign ship was not illegal if, as a fact, the insurer had a lawful interest and could prove it. As, however, such a policy bears the mark of wagering on the face of it, the Lords Select Committee concerned with the passage of the Marine Insurance Act 1906 through Parliament thought that the provision should be generalised.
(2) The statute of 1745 spoke of ships, and goods and effects laden on them. But a wide construction was put on these terms, and the scope of the statute was by judicial decision extended to policies on profits and commission effected 'without benefit of salvage'.[4]

(3) The scope of the statute was not confined to the exact terms prohibited. Any similar terms avoided the policy. Thus, a policy on cash advances, 'full interest admitted,' was void.[5].
(4) The statute of 1745 further contained two more or less obsolete exceptions, viz, policies on privateers, and policies on ships in the Spanish trade.
(5) The statute of 1745 did not extend to Ireland.[6] The present section extends to the whole of the United Kingdom.

A policy 'without interest' is not necessarily a wager policy. For example, when the assured bona fide expects to have an interest, but the expectation is not realised, the policy is not a wager policy.[7] The assured cannot recover on the policy, but he may be entitled to a return of the premium.[8].

The Marine Insurance Act 1906, s 4(1) is supported by the Gaming Act 1845, s 18.[9]

Section 4 of the Act is now supplemented by the Marine Insurance (Gambling Policies) Act 1909.[10] That Act penalises contracts of marine insurance in cases where there is no interest or bona fide expectation of interest either in the safe arrival of a ship or in the safety or preservation of the subject-matter insured, or where an 'honour' policy in relation to a ship is effected by any person in the employment of a shipowner unless that person is a part owner.

'Honour' policies. An 'honour' policy, eg a ppi policy, 'is one in which the parties, by express terms, disclaim, on the face of it, the intention of making a contract of indemnity' (*Arnould*, para 386). Though an 'honour' policy is void in the eye of the law, the issue of such a policy may constitute a breach of a warranty to keep a certain proportion of the value of a ship uninsured.[11] Again, a policy on ship may be avoided for non-disclosure of over-insurance by concurrent policies on disbursements.[12]

A distinction must be drawn between ppi policies and policies 'without benefit of salvage,' that is to say, in modern language, 'without benefit of abandonment'. The nature of an insurance may be such that, in case of loss, there could be nothing to abandon to the insurer, and therefore such a policy may lawfully be effected 'without benefit of salvage'.[13] For example, a man may have an interest, but no property, in the thing imperilled, and then he has nothing which he can abandon.[14]

Illustrations

1. Policy on ship, insurer to pay a total loss if she does not arrive at Yokohama on or before 31 December. The insurance is a speculation, assured having no interest in the ship or adventure. He cannot recover.[15]
2. An agent is instructed by warehousemen to effect a ppi policy on profits dependent on the arrival of a cargo from abroad. He negligently omits to disclose a material fact, and the insurer consequently refuses to pay for the loss which occurred. The principal cannot recover even nominal damages from the agent.[16]

1 *Kulen Kemp v Vigne* (1786) 1 Term Rep 304, 309; *Cousins v Nantes* (1811) 3 Taunt 513 Ex Ch (presumption of interest and averment in pleading); *Wilson v Jones* (1867) LR 2 Ex Ch at 141, per Willes J. See ss 5–15, as to interest. And as to the purpose of this enactment, see *Thames and Mersey Marine Insurance Co Ltd v Gunford Ship Co Ltd* [1911] AC at 543, per Lord Shaw.

2 Cf *Murphy v Bell* (1828) 4 Bing 567, 569. As to an equivalent clause 'freight at risk or not,' see *Scottish Shire Line v London and Provincial Marine Insurance Co* (1912) 17 Com Cas at 261, per Hamilton J. For the history of the introduction of the term 'interest or no interest,' see *The Sadler's Co v Badcock* (1743) 2 Atk 554, per Lord Hardwicke.
3 Cf *Lucena v Craufurd* (1806) 2 Bos & P NR 310. Cf s 62(7), as to notice of abandonment.
4 *De Mattos v North* (1868) LR 3 Ex Ch 185; *Allkins v Jupe* (1877) 2 CPD 375; see at 388 as to possibility of salvage in such a case.
5 *Berridge v Man On Insurance Co* (1887) 18 QBD 346, CA; see, also *Gedge v Royal Exchange* [1900] 2 QB 214.
6 *Keith v Protection Marine Insurance Co* (1882) 10 LR Ir 51.
7 See eg *Anderson v Morice* (1876) 1 App Cas 713.
8 See s 84.
9 Which provides that 'all contracts or agreements, whether by parol or in writing, by way of gaming or wagering shall be null and void.'
10 See Appendix I, p 157, post.
11 *Roddick v Indemnity Mutual Marine Insurance Co* [1895] 2 QB 380, CA; *Samuel (P) & Co Ltd v Dumas* [1924] AC 431, 29 Com Cas 239, HL; cf *Thames and Mersey Marine Insurance Co Ltd v Gunford Ship Co Ltd* [1911] AC at 538, per Lord Alverstone. As to promissory warranties generally, see ss 33–41.
12 *Thames and Mersey Marine Insurance Co Ltd v Gunford Ship Co Ltd* (supra).
13 *Lucena v Craufurd* (1806) 2 Bos & P (NR) at 310, 6 RR at 694, per nine of the Judges.
14 Cf *Wilson v Jones* (1867) LR 2 Ex Ch 139 (policy on successful laying of submarine cable effected by shareholder in company).
15 *Gedge v Royal Exchange Assurance Corpn* [1900] 2 QB 214, 217. The fact that the policy was ppi was not set up as a defence.
16 *Cheshire & Co v Vaughan Bros* (1919) 25 Com Cas 51; affd [1920] 3 KB 240, 25 Com Cas 242, CA. If the policy is ppi, it is none the less void because the insured has an insurable interest in fact: ibid. But the position in the USA is different. See *Aetna Insurance Co v United Fruit Co* 304 US 430 at 432, [1938] AMC 707: 'But in the United States it is held that, while a wager policy on property in which the insured has no interest is void as against public policy, the provision in the policy that that instrument shall be proof of interest does not render the policy void if the insured in fact had an insurable interest, and that such policies are to be deemed policies on interest if the contracting parties so understood and agreed.' See further, *Republic of China, China Merchants Steam Navigation Co Ltd and United States of America v National Union Fire Insurance Co of Pittsburgh, Pennsylvania, The Hai Hsuan (No 2)* [1958] 2 Lloyd's Rep 578, District Council of Maryland. See especially the cases cited in the footnote on p 580. See per Scrutton LJ, as to practice of pinning on and detaching ppi clauses from policy, and cf *Re London County Commercial Reinsurance Office* [1922] 2 Ch 67, 81; *Re Overseas Marine Insurance Co Ltd* (1930) 36 Ll L Rep 183; *John Edwards & Co v Motor Union Insurance Co* [1922] 2 KB 249 (no subrogation on payment under a ppi policy). For subrogation, see s 79.

5. Insurable interest defined

(1) Subject to the provisions of this Act,[1] every person has an insurable interest who is interested in a marine adventure.[2]

(2) In particular a person is interested in a marine adventure where he stands in any legal or equitable relation to the adventure or to any insurable property at risk therein, in consequence of which he may benefit by the safety or due arrival of insurable property, or may be prejudiced by its loss, or by damage thereto, or by the detention thereof, or may incur liability in respect thereof.[3]

Note

Three questions, often confused, must be kept distinct, viz: 1. Has the assured an insurable interest? 2. Is the subject-matter in respect of which his interest arises sufficiently described in the policy? 3. What is the quantum of his interest?

The definition of 'insurable interest' has been continuously expanding, and dicta in some of the older cases, which would tend to narrow it, must be accepted with caution. The essence of 'interest' is (*a*) that there should be a physical object exposed to sea perils, and (*b*) that the assured should stand in some relationship, recognised by law, to that object, in consequence of which he either benefits by its preservation, or is prejudiced by its loss or mishap to it.

It is clear, since *Wilson v Jones* (illustration 2), that 'interest' is not confined to rights in the nature of property or arising out of contract, for the assured had no property in the cable nor any contract respecting it.

Suppose A is offered an appointment abroad on the condition that his acceptance of the offer is received by return of post. Why should he not insure the safe arrival of the letter, although he has no legal rights in respect of it after it is posted? Sub-s (2) is, therefore, framed as being inclusive, not exhaustive, and its language was somewhat broadened in the Commons Committee.

'Interest' can hardly be defined exhaustively, and probably the criterion proposed by Lawrence J, cannot be improved upon: 'Interest,' he said, 'does not necessarily imply a right to the whole or part of a thing, nor necessarily or exclusively that which may be the subject of privation; but the having some relation to or concern in the subject of insurance, which relation or concern, by the happening of the perils insured against, may be so affected as to produce a damage, detriment, or prejudice to the person insuring. . . . To be interested in the preservation of a thing, is to be so circumstanced with respect to it as to have benefit from its existence, prejudice from its destruction.'[4]

Elsewhere, speaking of liability to third persons, he said, 'Did they mean to game, or was there not a loss against which they might indemnify themselves by insurance?'[5]

'The general rule,' said Willes J, 'is clear, that to constitute interest insurable against a peril, there must be an interest such that the peril would, by its proximate effect, cause damage to the assured.'[6]

'Any interest may be insured,' said Walton J, 'which is dependent on the safety of the thing exposed to [the risks insured against], still it must in all cases at the time of the loss be an interest legal or equitable, and not merely an expectation, however probable.'[7]

The 'interest' must be real and not merely a colourable interest.[8]

Illustrations

1. Floating policy for £1,200 'on goods as interest may appear'. The assured, who are canal carriers, have an insurable interest in respect of their liability for the safe carriage of the goods, and this interest is sufficiently described as 'on goods'.[9]
2. Policy effected by shareholder in submarine cable company in respect of the successful laying of the cable. The assured has an insurable interest in the adventure, although he has no property in the cable.[10]
3. A lends money to B, a small shipowner, whose solvency depends on the safe arrival of his ship, but the loan is not secured on the ship or freight. The loan

12 Insurable interest

is not at risk, and A has no insurable interest which can be covered by a marine policy.[11]

4. Policy on freight, 'chartered or otherwise, per *Cambodia* from Bombay to Howlands Island, and thence to a port of discharge in the United Kingdom'. Under charter, the ship is to go to Howlands Island in ballast, and then load a cargo for England. On the way to Howlands Island she is disabled by perils of the sea, so the freight cannot be earned. The assured has an insurable interest, and the risk has attached.[12]

5. The agents of a foreign ship effect a policy on disbursements against the risk of total loss only. The ship becomes a constructive total loss. The agents have an insurable interest in the advances they have made to the ship in so far as they could arrest the ship under s 6 of the Admiralty Court Act 1840, for the purpose of founding an action in rem.[13]

6. A marina operator insures against legal liability for loss of or damage to craft belonging to third parties whilst in his care. He has a valid insurable interest because he will be prejudiced if the craft are lost or damaged.[14]

7. The owner of a yacht conferred on S by a power of attorney a wide authority to enjoy the use of her exclusively for his own purposes and to exercise over her such control as he thought fit. *Held*, he had an insurable interest in her for he stood in a legal relationship to her in consequence of which he would benefit from her preservation and, if she were lost or damaged, he would suffer the loss of a valuable benefit.[15]

1 See ss 6–15 for sub-rules, and s 3 as to lawfulness of adventure, and s 41, warranty of legality.
2 *Wilson v Jones* (1867) LR 2 Ex Ch 139, Ex Ch.
3 See s 3, defining 'marine adventure'; as to equitable assignee of freight, see *Wilson v Martin* (1856) 11 Exch 684.
   Conversely, a prospect or possibility of loss or gain which is not founded on any right or liability in, or in respect of the subject-matter insured, is not insurable: *Lucena v Craufurd* (1806) 2 Bos & P NR 269, 6 RR 623, HL; *Seagrave v Union Marine Insurance Co* (1866) LR 1 CP 305 at 320 (cargo); *Barber v Fleming* (1869) LR 5 QB at 71 (freight); and see eg *Manfield v Maitland* (1821) 4 B & Ald 582 (loan to shipowner); *Devaux v Steele* (1840) 6 Bing NC 358, 54 RR 818 (expected fishing bounty from French Government); *Stainbank v Fenning* (1851) 11 CB 51 (invalid bottomry bond); *Paterson v Harris* (1861) 1 B & S at 354, 355 (shares in a cable company); *Scottish Shire Line v London and Provincial Marine Insurance Co* [1912] 3 KB 51, 17 Com Cas 240 (freight 'chartered or as if chartered'); *Papadimitriou v Henderson* [1939] 3 All ER 908, KB (shipowner has an insurable interest in 'anticipated freight').
4 *Lucena v Craufurd* (1806) 2 Bos & P NR at 302, cited and approved by Blackburn J in *Lloyd v Fleming* (1872) LR 7 QB at 302. Cf *Piper v Royal Exchange Assurance* (1932) 44 Ll L Rep 103 KB at 116–17.
5 *Boehm v Bell* (1799) 8 Term Rep 154 (prize insured by captors).
6 *Seagrave v Union Marine Insurance Co* (1866) LR 1 CP at 326. Cf *Briggs v Merchant Traders' Association* (1849) 13 QB 167 (average expenses per ship T).
7 *Moran, Galloway & Co v Uzielli* [1905] 2 KB at 562.
8 *Lewis v Rucker* (1761) 2 Burr 1167 at 1171. But in case of doubt the court should lean in favour of interest: *Stock v Inglis* (1884) 12 QBD 864 at 871, per Brett J.
9 *Crowley v Cohen* (1832) 3 B & Ad 478, 37 RR 472; *The Yasin* [1979] 2 Lloyd's Rep 45 at 53 (per Lloyd J); see *Cunard SS Co v Marten* [1902] 2 KB 624, for an insurance in express terms against liability of carrier owing to the omission of the negligence clause in a charter party. For an example of a policy issued to a charterer in respect of loss of or damage to cargo owned by third parties, see *Kuehne and Nagel Inc v Baiden* [1977]

1 Lloyd's Rep 90, Court of Appeals of New York, where it was held that the cargo owners' claim had been reasonably settled by the assignees of the assured. (See the judgment of Gabrielli J, ibid, at 92.) As to insurance by a bailee (who is not responsible by virtue of his special property in the goods bailed), see *North British Insurance Co v Moffatt* (1871) LR 7 CP 25 at 31 (fire insurance).
10 *Wilson v Jones* (1867) LR 2 Ex Ch 139.
11 Cf *Manfield v Maitland* (1821) 4 B & Ald 582; *Allison v Bristol Marine Insurance Co* (1876) 1 App Cas at 220. Of course, B's solvency can be insured by an appropriate policy, but that is not a marine policy. See Ivamy, *Personal Accident, Life and Other Insurances* (2nd ed, 1980), pp 314–322.
12 *Barber v Fleming* (1869) LR 5 QB 59.
13 *Moran, Galloway & Co v Uzielli* [1905] 2 KB 555. Section 6 of the Admiralty Court Act 1840 was repealed by the Supreme Court of Judicature (Consolidation) Act 1925, s 226 and Sch 6.
14 *Pillgrem v Cliff Richardson Boats Ltd and Richardson: Switzerland General Insurance Co, Third Party* [1977] 1 Lloyd's Rep 297, Supreme Court of Ontario, where the question was whether the loss had occurred in the 'alteration, repair or maintenance' of a cabin cruiser.
15 *Sharp and Roarer Investments Ltd v Sphere Drake Insurance plc, The Moonacre* [1992] 2 Lloyd's Rep 501, QB (Commercial Court). See the judgment of AD Colman, QC, sitting as a Deputy Judge, ibid, at 512–513.

6. When interest must attach

(1) The assured must be interested in the subject-matter insured at the time of the loss though he need not be interested when the insurance is effected:[1]

Provided that where the subject-matter is insured, 'lost or not lost,' the assured may recover although he may not have acquired his interest until after the loss unless at the time of effecting the contract of insurance the assured was aware of the loss, and the insurer was not.[2]

(2) Where the assured has no interest at the time of the loss, he cannot acquire interest by any act or election after he is aware of the loss.[3]

Note

This section relates only to the existence of interest as a condition of effective insurance. A policy founded on interest may, of course, be assigned after loss.[4] As to assignment of policy, see ss 50 and 51. As to assignment of interest, see s 15, and as to ratification by the assured of insurance effected by another, see s 86.

It has been argued that the rule contained in the proviso to sub-s (1) only applies to the case of a partial loss, but that is not so. Suppose a man buys a cargo while at sea. It turns out that before the purchase was completed the cargo had perished. As a rule the contract is void, and therefore the buyer has no insurable interest, but there is such a thing as an emptio spei, as opposed to the purchase of a thing itself.[5]

It is often a difficult question to determine the exact moment when under a contract of sale, the risk passes from seller to buyer. Prima facie, the risk passes when the property passes, but under the terms of the contract they may pass at different times. When goods are insured by the buyer, the question is whether,

Insurable interest

on the true construction of the contract, the risk has passed to him at the time when the loss occurs.[6]

Illustrations

1. Policy on rice 'as interest may appear, by ship *Sunbeam* from Rangoon to London'. The assured has contracted to buy a 'cargo' of rice to be shipped in that ship. When three-fourths of the cargo are on board, the ship and rice are lost by perils of the sea. The rice is not at the assured's risk until a complete cargo is loaded, and he has therefore no insurable interest.[7]
2. Policy on 'wheat cargo now on board or to be shipped' in the ship *Sutherland* from New Zealand to England. Under the terms of the contract between the sellers and the assured, the property (and risk) pass to him as the wheat is shipped. Before the whole cargo is loaded the ship and wheat are lost by perils of the sea. The assured has an insurable interest which has attached, and can recover for the wheat lost.[8]
3. Policy on ship. In 1926 P bought a yacht in Norway 'as she lies'. She was at the risk of the seller until she arrived in London. P effected a policy in respect of her, and claimed against the insurers in respect of damage which she had suffered by stranding in 1928. The insurers counterclaimed for £346 (which they had paid him for damage suffered by her on her voyage from Norway to London in 1926) on the ground that he had no insurable interest in her at the time of the loss. *Held*, the counterclaim succeeded.[9]

1 *Rhind v Wilkinson* (1810) 2 Taunt at 243; *Anderson v Morice* (1876) 1 App Cas 713, HL.
2 *Sutherland v Pratt* (1843) 11 M & W 296, and Sch I, r 1.
3 *Anderson v Morice* (1876) 1 App Cas 713, IIL.
4 See s 50 (1); *Sparkes v Marshall* (1836) 2 Bing NC 761; and see further, Sch I, r 1.
5 See *Chalmers' Sale of Goods Act 1979* (18th ed, 1981) pp 96–97.
6 As to when the risk passes from seller to buyer, see s 20 of the Sale of Goods Act 1979, and as to the seller's duty to insure, see s 32 of that Act, set out, post, Appendix I, pp 158–159.
7 *Anderson v Morice* (1875) LR 10 CP 609, Ex Ch; affd (1876) 1 App Cas 713, HL.
8 *Colonial Insurance Co of New Zealand v Adelaide Marine Insurance Co* (1886) 12 App Cas 128, PC.
9 *Piper v Royal Exchange Assurance* (1932) 44 Ll L Rep 103. As to the passing of property under the Sale of Goods Act 1979, see Appendix I, p 158, post.

7. Defeasible or contingent interest

(1) A defeasible interest is insurable, as also is a contingent interest.
(2) In particular, where the buyer of goods has insured them, he has an insurable interest, notwithstanding that he might, at his election, have rejected the goods, or have treated them as at the seller's risk, by reason of the latter's delay in making delivery or otherwise.[1]

Note

As regards contingent interests, the main difficulty is to determine, not whether there is an interest but whether the interest has attached at the time of the loss.[2]

Where captors of a ship insured her, but the Prize Court afterwards restored her to her owners, it was *held* that the premium was not returnable, for the risk had attached. The interest in this case may be regarded either as defeasible or contingent.³

In *Lucena v Craufurd* (1806) 2 Bos & P NR at 294, 295, seven of the Judges, in their opinion to the House of Lords, said, 'Inchoate rights founded on subsisting titles, unless prohibited by positive laws, are insurable. Freight, respondentia, and bottomry are of this description.' And then, after discussing various old definitions of insurance, they said (at 295): 'These definitions clearly embrace a contingent interest, which is subject to the perils of the sea, and for the loss of which a compensation may be made.'

Reinsurance is a good example of a contingent interest.

In the case provided for by sub-s (2), the assured has an actual interest, defeasible only at his own option.

Suppose A buys goods by sample, to be shipped from abroad, and insures them. Goods which are inferior to sample are shipped, and then partially sea damaged on the voyage. A may accept the goods and claim on the policy for he has an insurable interest since he has not rejected them. If A rejects the goods, presumably he could not claim on the policy; but could he assign the policy to the seller, and then reject the goods? Presumably not; but various complications may be suggested which still await decision.

1 *Sparkes v Marshall* (1836) 2 Bing NC 761, as explained in *Anderson v Morice* (1875) LR 10 CP at p 620; *Colonial Insurance Co of New Zealand v Adelaide Marine Insurance Co* (1886) 12 App Cas 128 at 140, PC.
2 Cf *Barber v Fleming* (1869) LR 5 QB at 73.
3 *Boehm v Bell* (1799) 8 Term Rep 154.

8. Partial interest

A partial interest of any nature is insurable.

Note

An undivided interest in a parcel of goods shipped f.o.b. is insurable.¹ So, too, a shareholder may insure his interest in the adventure of a company engaged in laying a submarine cable;² and a 'hotchpot' interest in cargo may be insured.³ 'I do not see,' said Heath J, 'why a joint tenant or tenant in common has not such an interest in the entirety as will entitle him to insure.'⁴

By s 5 of the Merchant Shipping Act 1894 ships are divided into sixty-four shares, and any number of persons not exceeding five may be registered as joint owners of a ship or any share in her. But a part owner, it seems, has no *implied* authority to insure on behalf of the other part owners.⁵

1 *Inglis v Stock* (1885) 10 App Cas 263 at 274 (390 tons of sugar sent off to satisfy two contracts, for 200 tons each, without any appropriation to either contract).
2 *Wilson v Jones* (1867) LR 2 Ex Ch 139, Ex Ch.
3 *Ebsworth v Alliance Marine Insurance Co* (1873) LR 8 CP at 613.
4 *Page v Fry* (1800) 2 Bos & P 240 at 243 (cargo).
5 *Bell v Humphries* (1818) 2 Stark 345; *Arnould*, para 213, but note s 14 (2); and see *Robinson v Gleadow* (1835) 2 Bing NC 156 (insurance by managing owner on behalf of all).

9. Reinsurance

(1) The insurer under a contract of marine insurance has an insurable interest in his risk, and may reinsure in respect of it.[1]

(2) Unless the policy otherwise provides, the original assured has no right or interest in respect of such reinsurance.[2]

Note

'Reinsurance,' that is to say, an insurance effected by an insurer to cover wholly or in part the risk he has undertaken, must be distinguished from 'double insurance,' ie a second insurance effected by or on behalf of an assured on a risk already covered; as to which, see s 32.

At Common Law reinsurance was valid, but it was prohibited in 1745 by the Marine Insurance Act, s 4, unless the insurer was dead or insolvent. The prohibition was removed in 1864 by the Revenue (No 2) Act, s 1 (since repealed), and reinsurance is now expressly recognised by the Marine Insurance Act 1906.

The usual form of a reinsurance policy runs thus—'being a reinsurance subject to all clauses and conditions of the original policy or policies, and to pay as may be paid thereon,' and then follow the exceptions, if any.[3]

A policy of reinsurance need not specify that it is a reinsurance, see s 26, and no notice of abandonment need be given to the reinsurer, see s 62(9). The modern practice in effecting reinsurance was detailed by Scrutton J, in a case where it was held that, in the absence of inquiry, the broker effecting a policy of reinsurance is not bound to disclose the name of the reassured (original insurer).[4]

Reinsurance treaties. The Marine Insurance Act 1906 does not deal with treaties of reinsurance. A treaty of reinsurance is a contract sui generis whereby the reinsurer agrees to reinsure the whole or a portion of a specified class or classes of risk to be underwritten by the reassured (original insurer). Schedules giving particulars of the risks underwritten are usually forwarded periodically to the reinsurers.

1 *Uzielli v Boston Marine Insurance Co* (1884) 15 QBD at 16; and cf *Bradford v Symondson* (1881) 7 QBD at 463, CA. Reinsurance is a contract of indemnity; see note to s 1.
2 *Arnould*, para 397. Cf *Nelson v Empress Assurance Corpn* [1905] 2 KB 281, CA (reinsurer not liable as third party in action by original assured). Contracts of reinsurance are not affected by the Third Parties (Rights against Insurers) Act 1930; see s 1 (5).
3 As to construction of this provision, see *Uzielli v Boston Marine Insurance Co* (1884) 15 QBD 11, CA (reinsurer not liable for expenses under sue and labour clauses), criticising *British Dominions General Insurance Co v Duder* [1915] 2 KB 394, CA; *Re Eddystone Insurance Co, ex p Western Insurance Co* [1892] 2 Ch 423 ('pay as paid'—payment by original insurer not condition precedent); *Chippendale v Holt* (1895) 65 LJQB 104 (reinsurer not bound by improper payment by original insurer); *Crocker v Sturge* [1897] 1 QB 330 (reinsurance of portion of risk—construction of 'final port'); *China Traders' Insurance v Royal Exchange* [1898] 2 QB 187, CA; *Sir William Garthwaite Insurance Ltd v Port of Manchester Insurance Co* (1930) 37 Ll L Rep 194 (right of reinsurer to discovery of ship's papers); *Lower Rhine Insurance Association v Sedgwick* [1899] 1 QB 179, CA (lapse of original policy, and issue of new one); *Charlesworth v Faber* (1900) 5 Com Cas 408 (continuation clause exceeding twelve months' limit for time policy); *Maritime Insurance Co v Stearns* [1901] 2 KB 912, 6 Com Cas 182 (variation of risk from summer to winter); *Marten v SS Owners' Underwriting Association Ltd* (1902) 7 Com Cas 195; *Fireman's Fund Insurance Co*

v Western Australian Assurance Co (1927) 33 Com Cas 36 ('pay as may be paid' = pay as reassured may be compelled to pay); *Western Assurance Co of Toronto v Poole* [1903] 1 KB 376 (reinsurance against total loss, salvage charges excluded); *South British Fire and Marine Insurance Co v Da Costa* [1906] 1 KB 456, 11 Com Cas 81 (reinsurance for £1,000 in excess of £500); *Assicurazioni Generali de Trieste v Empress Assurance Corporation Ltd* [1907] 2 KB 814 (subrogation, costs of action in which damages are recovered); *Home Insurance Co of New York v Victoria Fire Insurance Co* [1907] AC 59, PC (rejection of inapplicable terms); *Baker v Adam* (1910) 15 Com Cas 227 (set-off against assignee); *Scottish National Insurance Co v Poole* (1912) 18 Com Cas 9 (effect of two slips); *Property Insurance Co v Protector Insurance Co* (1913) 18 Com Cas 119 (subject *without notice* to same clauses and conditions as original policy); *Street v Royal Exchange* (1913) 18 Com Cas 284; affd (1914) 19 Com Cas 339, CA (to follow hull underwriters in event of a compromise being arranged); *Bergens Dampskibs Assurance v Sun Insurance* (1930) 46 TLR 543 ('arranged total loss'); *Emanuel v Andrew Weir & Co* (1914) 30 TLR 518 (two slips, rectification of policy issued on wrong slip); *British Dominions General Insurance Co Ltd v Duder* [1915] 2 KB 394, CA (compromise by original insurer, extent of reinsurer's right of indemnity); *London General Insurance Co v General Marine Underwriters' Association* [1921] 1 KB 104, CA (reassured's duty to consult casualty list); *Norwich Union Insurance Co v Colonial Mutual Insurance Co* [1922] 2 KB 461 (variation of head policy without reinsurer's consent); *Scottish Metropolitan Assurance Co Ltd v Groom* (1924) 41 TLR 35, CA (reinsurance, costs of original insurers in resisting a claim cannot be recovered from their reinsurers); *Young v Merchants' Marine Insurance Co Ltd* [1932] 2 KB 705, CA (insurance against total loss and collision liability, reinsurance of liability for total loss only, claim by reinsurer to benefit in respect of claim under running down clause); *Gurney v Grimmer* (1932) 44 Ll L Rep 189, CA 'total constructive compromised and/or arranged total loss of the vessel'); *Versicherungs Und Transport AG Daugava v Henderson* (1934) 39 Com Cas 312, CA (reinsurance, fire policy, original insurance in foreign currency, reinsurance in London, at what date rate of exchange must be taken in calculating sum to be paid by reinsurers); *Marine Insurance Co Ltd v Grimmer* [1944] 2 All ER 197, CA (reinsurance, cargo on named ships 'and/or steamers held covered at premiums to be arranged'); *Oscar L Aronsen Inc v Compton, The Megara* [1974] 1 Lloyd's Rep 590, US Ct of Appeals, Second Circuit ('compromised constructive total loss'). See generally, Ivamy, *Marine Insurance* (4th ed, 1985), pp 465–472.

4 *Glasgow Assurance Corpn v Symondson* (1911) 16 Com Cas 109.

10. Bottomry

The lender of money on bottomry or respondentia has an insurable interest in respect of the loan.[1]

Note

By the law of the sea the master may, in case of necessity, and under certain restrictions, raise money on the security of the ship, freight, and cargo. The condition of a loan on bottomry or respondentia is that the money is not repayable if the ship or cargo does not arrive. Consequently it is the lender who must insure. As to specifically describing the subject-matter insured in the policy, see s 26. As to the general law of bottomry and respondentia, see *Carver*, paras 1249–1252.

This section is now of no practical importance, for the practice of lending money on bottomry or respondentia is obsolete.

Illustrations

1. The master of a damaged British ship requires money for necessary repairs. A merchant abroad advances the money, taking a bond mortgaging the ship, and making the money repayable whether she arrives or not. The merchant has no insurable interest, for the master has no authority to give such a bond, or do more than hypothecate the ship for the advances[2] (sed quo now?).
2. Policy on bottomry bond in old form. The ship becomes a constructive total loss. The assured cannot recover, for the bond stands good unless there is an actual total loss.[3]

1 See note to s 7, and *Arnould*, para 372.
2 *Stainbank v Fenning* (1851) 11 CB 51; *Carver*, para 1250, but see *The Haabet* [1899] P 295, per Bucknill J; and *Price v Maritime Insurance Co* [1901] 2 KB 412, CA.
3 *Broomfield v Southern Insurance Co* (1870) LR 5 Ex 192. Some forms provide for constructive total loss. As to the requisites of a valid bottomry bond, see *The James W Elwell* [1921] P 351 at 365.

11. Master's and seamen's wages

The master or any member of the crew of a ship has an insurable interest in respect of his wages.

Note

The law as to the insurability of seamen's wages was doubtful. The master of a ship could always insure his wages, but formerly at any rate a seaman under the rank of master could not. 'Wages of seamen,' said the Judges in an old case, 'are in their nature insurable, though universally prohibited to be insured on principles of policy.'[1] But when this was laid down, the doctrine prevailed that 'freight was the mother of wages,' and if freight was not earned, the seaman was not entitled to his wages.

This doctrine was abandoned in 1854, and s 183 of the Merchant Shipping Act of that year provided that the right to wages should not be dependent on the earning of freight, but that in all cases of wreck or loss of the ship, proof that the seaman had not exerted himself to the utmost to save the ship and cargo should bar his claim to wages. This provision is now reproduced in s 15 of the Merchant Shipping Act 1970.

The master's effects were always insurable.[2]

1 *Lucena v Craufurd* (1806) 2 Bos & PNR at 294, HL.
2 *Duff v Mackenzie* (1857) 3 CBNS 16; *Anstey v Ocean Marine Insurance Co* (1913) 19 Com Cas 8 (small part of captain's effects not on board when ship lost). Cf Sch I, r 17.

12. Advance freight

In the case of advance freight, the person advancing the freight has an insurable interest, in so far as such freight is not repayable in case of loss.[1]

Note

By English law, advance freight, as such, is not repayable in case of loss. The shipowner therefore has not an insurable interest in it, but the person advancing it has.[2] But by special contract it may be repayable,[3] and then the positions are reversed.

Though advance freight may not be repayable in case of loss, the shipowner may be liable in damages to the cargo owner if the loss is occasioned by his negligence or fault, and in estimating the damages the amount advanced for freight must be taken into account.[4]

An advance to a shipowner by a shipper or charterer in respect of a voyage may fall into three categories: (*a*) it may be advance freight not repayable in case of loss; (*b*) it may be advance freight specially repayable in case of loss; or, (*c*) it may be a mere loan repayable in any event. In the last case it is not at risk, and therefore not insurable.[5]

As to the tests for determining within which category a given advance falls, see *Carver*, paras 1696–1697.

By the law of most foreign countries, advance freight is repayable in case of loss.[6]

Illustration

Policy by shipowner on freight. Under the charter-party, half the freight is to be paid in advance and half is to be paid on delivery of the cargo. The ship is lost, but half the cargo is saved and delivered. No further freight is payable in respect of the half so delivered, in as much as it is covered by the advance payment of half the freight. This is a total loss of half the shipowner's freight, the advance freight being at the charterer's and not at the shipowner's risk.[7]

1 Cf *Smith v Pyman* [1891] 1 QB at 744, 745, CA.
2 *Allison v Bristol Marine Insurance Co* (1876) 1 App Cas 209 at 238, HL reviewing the cases.
3 Ibid, at 221, citing *Hall v Janson* (1855) 4 E & B 500.
4 *Dufourcet v Bishop* (1886) 18 QBD 373.
5 *The Salacia* (1862) Lush 578 at 582.
6 *Byrne v Schiller* (1871) LR 6 Ex Ch at 325, Ex Ch.
7 *Allison v Bristol Marine Insurance Co* (1876) 1 App Cas 209, see at 235, 238; cf *The Main* [1894] P 320.

13. Charges of insurance

The assured has an insurable interest in the charges of any insurance which he may effect.[1]

Note

Ordinarily the charges of insurance consist of the premium and the brokerage (if paid by the assured). Cf s 16 as to insurable value. In practice, the broker's commission is paid, or rather allowed in account, by the insurer.[2]

1 *Usher v Noble* (1810) 12 East 639.
2 *United States Shipping Co v Empress Assurance Corpn* [1907] 1 KB at 262; *Glasgow Assurance Corpn v Symondson* (1911) 16 Com Cas 109.

14. Quantum of interest

(1) Where the subject-matter insured is mortgaged, the mortgagor has an insurable interest in the full value thereof, and the mortgagee has an insurable interest in respect of any sum due or to become due under the mortgage.[1]

(2) A mortgagee, consignee, or other person having an interest in the subject-matter insured may insure on behalf and for the benefit of other persons interested as well as for his own benefit.[2]

(3) The owner of insurable property has an insurable interest in respect of the full value thereof, notwithstanding that some third person may have agreed, or be liable, to indemnify him in case of loss.[3]

Note

In a case[4] where a policy was effected by ship's husbands for the mortgagee, at the instance of the mortgagor, who was part owner and master, the mortgagee was *held* entitled to recover, although the loss was occasioned by the barratry of the mortgagor.

'A person,' said Bowen LJ, 'with a limited interest may insure either for himself and to cover his own interest only, or he may insure so as to cover not merely his own limited interest, but the interest of all others who are interested in the property,' and he then proceeded to discuss various instances.[5]

Where two or more persons insure the same subject-matter, so as to exceed the insurable value, the equities are worked out by the principle of subrogation, and contribution between insurers; see note to s 32 (double insurance).

Sub-section (3) generalises a case where the charterer has agreed to indemnify the shipowner. Obviously a cargo owner may insure his cargo, though if it is lost through the negligence of the shipowner, he may have his remedy in damages.[6]

1 *Irving v Richardson* (1831) 2 B & Ad 193; *North British and Mercantile Insurance Co v London, Liverpool and Globe Insurance Co* (1877) 5 Ch D at 583, 584, CA.
2 *Ebsworth v Alliance Marine Insurance Co* (1873) LR 8 CP 596 at 608 and 641; *Castellain v Preston* (1883) 11 QBD at 398, CA. This sub-section was inserted in the Commons Committee. As to a 'bare' consignee, see *Seagrave v Union Marine Insurance Co* (1866) LR 1 CP at 319, 320.
3 *Hobbs v Hannam* (1811) 3 Camp 93 (guarantee by charterer).
4 *Small v United Kingdom Marine Mutual Insurance Association* [1897] 2 QB 311, CA.
5 *Castellain v Preston* (1883) 11 QBD at 398, CA.
6 Cf *Dufourcet v Bishop* (1886) 18 QBD 373, and *Yates v Whyte* (1838) 4 Bing NC 272. As to the insurer's right of subrogation consequent on payment, see s 79.

15. Assignment of interest

Where the assured assigns or otherwise parts with his interest in the subject-matter insured, he does not thereby transfer to the assignee his rights under the contract of insurance, unless there be an express or implied agreement with the assignee to that effect.[1]

But the provisions of this section do not affect a transmission of interest by operation of law.

Note

This section is supplemented by s 51 (assured not having interest cannot assign). As to assignment of policy, see s 50. As to ratification where one person insures on behalf of another without previous authority, see s 86.

In *Rayner v Preston*,[2] Lord Esher said: '. . . where the subject-matter of the insurance is sold during the running of the policy, no interest under the policy passes unless it is made part of the contract of purchase and sale, so that it would be considered in a Court of Equity as assigned.'

Where there is such an agreement, it may be given effect to either by an assignment of the policy, or by the assignor holding the policy as trustee for the assignee.

The ordinary cases of transmission of interest by act of law are death and bankruptcy, but the subrogation of the insurer to the rights of the assured on payment of the claim may perhaps be regarded as coming under this category; see s 79.

Illustration

Policy on a cargo of logs covering risk of craft, effected by B who sells part of the logs 'ex ship, cash against documents'. The logs are lost in transit from ship to shore. The buyer acquires no interest under this policy.[3]

1 *Powles v Innes* (1843) 11 M & W 10 (sale of shares in a ship); *North of England Pure Oil Cake Co v Archangel Maritime Insurance Co* (1875) LR 10 QB 249 (sale of cargo).
2 (1881) 18 Ch D at 12, CA (fire insurance). As to the converse case of an assignee insuring for his assignor, see s 14. As to partial transfers of interest, see *Hibbert v Carter* (1787) 1 Term Rep 745, and as to the right of a seller under a c.i.f. contract to retain 'increased value policies,' see *Strass v Spillers and Bakers Ltd*, [1911] 2 KB 759, 16 Com Cas 166.
3 *Yangtze Insurance Association v Lukmanjee* [1918] AC 585, 23 Com Cas 302, PC (ex ship and c.i.f. contracts contrasted).

INSURABLE VALUE

16. Measure of insurable value

Subject to any express provision or valuation in the policy, the insurable value of the subject-matter insured must be ascertained as follows:
(1) In insurance on ship, the insurable value is the value at the commencement of the risk,[1] of the ship, including her outfit, provisions and stores for the officers and crew, money advanced for seamen's wages, and other disbursements (if any) incurred to make the ship fit for the voyage or adventure contemplated by the policy, plus the charges of insurance upon the whole:[2]

The insurable value, in the case of a steamship, includes also the machinery, boilers, and coals and engine stores if owned by the assured,

22 Insurable value

and, in the case of a ship engaged in a special trade, the ordinary fittings requisite for that trade:[3]

(2) In insurance on freight, whether paid in advance or otherwise,[4] the insurable value is the gross amount of the freight at the risk of the assured, plus the charges of insurance:[5]

(3) In insurance on goods or merchandise, the insurable value is the prime cost of the property insured, plus the expenses of and incidental to shipping and the charges of insurance upon the whole:[6]

(4) In insurance on any other subject-matter, the insurable value is the amount at the risk of the assured when the policy attaches, plus the charges of insurance.[7]

Note

A clear delimitation of insurable value is necessary, (a) to fix the measure of indemnity in the case of an unvalued policy; (b) to fix the measure of indemnity in the few cases in which the valuation in a valued policy can be set aside; and (c) to furnish an approximate standard for fixing the value in a valued policy.

Though marine insurance is universally admitted to be a contract of indemnity (see note to s 1), there are two opposing theories as to what is the nature of the indemnity to be aimed at. According to some, the assured ought to be put in the same position as if he had not undertaken the adventure. According to others, he ought to be put in the same position as if the adventure had been carried to a successful issue.[8] English law steers a halting course between these two theories, but with a strong leaning towards the former.

According to modern practice, unvalued policies are very rare, being practically confined to goods and in a few instances to freight payable on arrival. Other interests are almost invariably insured by valued policies. When the amount to be insured on goods cannot be fixed until the receipt of what are known as 'closing particulars,' provision is usually made that, in the event of loss before declaration, the declaration shall be on the basis of invoice cost and charges, plus a certain agreed percentage for anticipated profits.

The words 'if owned by the assured,' are inserted in the second paragraph of sub-s (1) because it may happen that the fuel oil and engine stores are the property of the charterer and not of the shipowner.

It appears that a policy on 'hull and machinery' covers less than a policy on 'ship,' eg it may not cover fuel oil and stores.[9]

As regards 'goods,' a voyage policy on goods is an insurance of the adventure, as well as an insurance on the goods themselves.[10] Hence the doctrine of loss of voyage or frustration of the adventure; see s 60, and notes thereto.

As to measure of indemnity, see further, ss 67–68. As to charges of insurance, see s 13. As to the scope of the terms 'ship' and 'freight', see Sch I, rr 15, 16.

Illustrations

1. Time policy on ship in usual form, the ship being generally engaged in the grain trade. This policy covers separation cloths and dunnage mats as part of

the ship's outfit, even though at the time of loss the cloths and mats were not in use.[11]

2. Policy on freight effected by charterer. In case of total loss he is entitled to the gross freight without any deduction for the time it would have taken him to discharge the cargo, but he is not entitled to recover the commission he paid in getting a sub-charter.[12]

---

1 These words give rise to a difficulty in the case of an 'at and from' policy. Perhaps they may be construed as applying to the successive stages, ie as the risk progressively attaches; see *Halsbury's Laws of England*, 4th ed, vol 25, para 261. In practice, policies on ship are always valued policies.
2 *Brough v Whitmore* (1791) 4 Term Rep 206 (stores and provisions for crew); *Moran, Galloway & Co v Uzielli* [1905] 2 KB at 558 (disbursements); cf Sch I, r 1.
3 As to fittings, see *Hogarth v Walker* [1900] 2 QB 283, CA. The final words perhaps overrule *Hoskins v Pickersgill* (1783) 3 Doug 222, where it was held that a policy on ship did not cover fishing tackle for the whaling trade.
4 See 'freight' defined by s 90, and as to 'advance freight' see s 12.
5 *Palmer v Blackburn* (1822) 1 Bing 61; *United States Shipping Co v Empress Assurance Corpn* [1907] 1 KB 259 and [1908] 1 KB 115, CA (gross not net freight); Report of Commission on Unseaworthy Ships, 1874, vol 2, p xvi. As to the purpose of this rule, see *Thames and Mersey Marine Insurance Co Ltd v Gunford Ship Co Ltd* [1911] AC at 549, per Lord Robson.
6 *Usher v Noble* (1810) 12 East 639. As to charges of insurance, see ibid, at 646. The invoice price is prima facie evidence of prime cost. But the insurable value must be the value at the commencement of the risk, so as to ensure that the assured shall obtain neither more nor less than an indemnity in case of loss. If, therefore, the value of the goods has altered since the assured acquired them, the prime cost to the assured (as evidenced by the invoice price) does not necessarily represent their insurable value; the court must determine what the value was at the commencement of the risk: *Williams v Atlantic Assurance Co Ltd* [1933] 1 KB 81 at 92, 102, CA. See further, *Berger and Light Diffusers Pty Ltd v Pollock* [1973] 2 Lloyd's Rep 442, QBD (Commercial Court), where it was held that the insurable value of some steel injection moulds was their value on board at the place of loading and the insurance premium and commission, and amounted to £5,316.20 (see the judgment of Kerr J, ibid, at 456). As to floating policy effected by canal carriers, see *Crowley v Cohen* (1832) 3 B & Ad 478.
7 Commenting on this rule, *Arnould*, para 448, note 35 states: 'The application of this rule to a policy on profits may have a curious result when the amount to be earned depends on fluctuating market prices. Thus, if goods could only have been sold at a loss at the time of shipment, but would have realised a profit if sold at the time of the loss or of their expected arrival, can the assured recover nothing on an unvalued policy on profits? Moreover, the rule also seems inapplicable to a policy on commissions, when the amount thereof will depend on the sale of the goods during the voyage or upon arrival.'
8 C McArthur, *The Contract of Marine Insurance* (2nd ed, 1890), p 67, citing W Benecke, *Treatise on the Principles of Indemnity in Marine Insurance*, 1824.
9 *Roddick v Indemnity Mutual Marine Insurance Co* [1895] 2 QB at 386, CA.
10 *British and Foreign Marine Insurance v Samuel Sanday & Co* [1916] 1 AC 650 at 672, 21 Com Cas 154, HL. But this rule does not extend to non-marine policies: *Moore v Evans* [1918] AC 185, HL, affg [1917] 1 KB 458, CA (policy on jewellery detained in enemy occupied country).
11 *Hogarth v Walker* [1900] 2 QB 283, CA.
12 *United States Shipping Co v Empress Assurance Corpn* [1907] 1 KB 259, affd on another ground, [1908] 1 KB 115.

DISCLOSURE AND REPRESENTATIONS

17. Insurance is uberrimæ fidei

A contract of marine insurance is a contract based upon the utmost good faith, and, if the utmost good faith be not observed by either party, the contract may be avoided by the other party.[1]

Note

Section 17 'restates the long established duty of the utmost good faith in contracts of marine insurance. It is not necessary, even if it were possible to go into degrees of good faith, or the question what degree of good faith may apply to other contracts. It is enough that much more than an absence of bad faith is required of both parties to all contracts of insurance.'[2]

The general principle is stated in this section because the special sections which follow are not exhaustive.[3] 'Sections 17 and 18,' said Fletcher Moulton LJ, 'apply to policies of every kind, whatever risk be insured against. They apply to every policy by reason of the nature of the contract of insurance.'[4] 'The importance of the principle enshrined in the Marine Insurance Act 1906, s 17 that a contract of marine insurance is a contract based on the utmost good faith is not in question. Nothing I say is intended to diminish in any way that fundamental principle.'[5]

Insurance is a contract *uberrimæ fidei*, and the obligation is binding on both parties alike, though necessarily the question usually arises with reference to the conduct of the assured. 'Good faith,' said Lord Mansfield, 'forbids either party, by concealing what he privately knows, to draw the other into a bargain from his ignorance of that fact, and from his believing the contrary . . . The policy would be equally [void] against the underwriter if he concealed; as if he insured a ship on her voyage which he privately knew to be arrived, an action would lie to recover the premium.'[6]

'It seems to me essential to bear in mind two things, each of which stems from the need for equality between those bargaining in the marine insurance market. . . The first is that the insured is the one who knows most of what the underwriter needs to know but does not know; the second that, though the underwriter must trust the insured to give it him, he in his turn must be trusted not to abuse the help and protection given him by the duty the law imposes on the insured to disclose and represent truly all that a prudent underwriter needs to know, and so turn the duty into a means of avoiding a contractual liability which he ought in fairness to honour. This the [Act of 1906] recognises by making the duty to observe the utmost good faith mutual in s 17 and by providing the exceptions of circumstances which need not be disclosed that are to be found particularly in s 18(3)(b) and (c).'[7]

Where underwriters allege non-disclosure, they must adduce evidence in support of their plea. In one case, Scrutton LJ said: 'The underwriters have not taken the course, which in my view should always be pursued, of going into the box and saying what they knew and what was the material fact which they did not know. In my view an underwriter pleading concealment must come and say what he was or was not told.'[8]

The contract is often said to be rendered void by non-disclosure or misrepresentation, but it is clear that it is only voidable at the option of the party prejudiced, and that the ordinary rules of law as to voidable contracts apply to insurance.[9]

A breach of the duty of good faith does not sound in damages. The only remedy open to the insured is to rescind the policy and recover the premium.[10]

Ship's papers. It follows from the nature of the contract that both parties must play with their cards on the table;[11] hence the full and complete discovery allowed as to ship's papers and other material documents.[12]

The power of the Court to order the production of ship's papers is set out in RSC Order 72.[13]

An order for ship's papers may be made in Form No 94 in Appendix K[14] to the Rules of the Supreme Court or in such other form as the Court thinks fit.[15]

The order is in the discretion of the Court and will not be made automatically.[16]

It is also in the discretion of the Court whether to order a stay pending compliance with an order for ship's papers.[17]

1 *Brownlie v Campbell* (1880) 5 App Cas at 954, per Lord Blackburn; cf *Seaton v Heath* [1899] 1 QB at 792, CA. See further, Ivamy, *Marine Insurance* (4th ed, 1985), p 39.
2 *Container Transport International Inc and Reliance Group Inc v Oceanus Mutual Underwriting Association (Bermuda) Ltd* [1984] 1 Lloyd's Rep 476, at 525, CA (per Stephenson LJ).
3 This sentence was approved by Stephenson LJ in *Container Transport International Inc and Reliance Group Inc v Oceanus Mutual Underwriting Association (Bermuda) Ltd* [1984] 1 Lloyd's Rep 476, at 525, CA.
4 *Cantiere Meccanico v Janson* [1912] 3 KB 452 at 467, CA (policy on floating dock, 'seaworthiness admitted'). Further, in *Australia and New Zealand Bank Ltd v Colonial and Eagle Wharves Ltd: Boag (Third Party)* ([1960] 2 Lloyd's Rep 241, QB (Commercial Court) (all risks insurance) McNair J, said (ibid, at 251) that for the moment he was prepared to assume (though he must not be taken as finally accepting) that the law as stated in s 18 of the Marine Insurance Act 1906 did apply to non-marine insurance, though he had been referred to no case in which it has been so applied.
5 *Container Transport International Inc and Reliance Group Inc v Oceanus Mutual Underwriting Association (Bermuda) Ltd* [1982] 2 Lloyd's Rep 178 at 187 (per Lloyd J). In *Black King Shipping Corpn v Massie, The Litsion Pride* [1985] 1 Lloyd's Rep 437 at 508, QB (Commercial Court) both counsel adopted the view that s 17 was equally applicable to events after as well as before the conclusion of the contract of insurance. This view was approved by Hirst J, ibid, at 511. It may, however, be argued that since s 17 appears in the Act under the heading of 'Disclosure and Representations,' it is intended to apply only to the pre-contract situation.
6 *Carter v Boehm* (1766) 3 Burr 1905.
7 *Container Transport International Inc and Reliance Group Inc v Oceanus Mutual Underwriting Association (Bermuda) Ltd* [1984] 1 Lloyd's Rep 476, at 529, CA (per Stephenson LJ).
8 *Williams v Atlantic Assurance Co Ltd* [1933] 1 KB 81 at 94, CA. See also *Visscherij Maatschappij Nieuw Onderneming v Scottish Metropolitan Assurance Co* (1922) 27 Com Cas 198, CA.
9 *Morrison v Universal Marine Insurance Co* (1873) LR 8 Ex Ch 197, Ex Ch. As to cancellation of avoided policy, see *Brooking v Maudslay* (1888) 36 Ch D 636 at 643. See further, Ivamy, *General Principles of Insurance Law* (6th ed, 1993), pp 255–256.
10 *Banque Financière la Cité SA v Westgate Insurance Co Ltd* [1990] 2 All ER 947 at 959, HL (per Lord Templeman).

11 This sentence was approved by Hirst J in *Black King Shipping Corpn v Massie, The Litsion Pride* (supra) at 511.
12 *China Traders' Insurance Co v Royal Exchange* [1898] 2 QB 187, CA; *Boulton v Houlder Bros* [1904] 1 KB 784, CA (ship's papers—action by underwriters for misrepresentation); *Harding v Bussell* [1905] 2 KB 83, CA (ship's papers—mixed sea and land risk); *Sir William Garthwaite Insurance Ltd v Port of Manchester Insurance Co* (1930) 37 Ll L Rep 194 (ships' papers—order must be made ex debito justitiæ); *Leon v Casey* [1932] 2 KB 576, 48 LQR 464, CA (ship's papers—order may be made even where the alleged loss took place in course of land transit provided that policy is substantially one of marine insurance); *North British Rubber Co Ltd v Cheetham* (1938) 61 Ll L Rep 337, CA (another case where the alleged loss took place in course of land transit); *Keevil and Keevil Ltd v Boag* [1940] 3 All ER 346, CA (eggs found to be defective on delivery). But this special right of discovery is strictly confined to marine insurance: *Tannenbaum v Heath* (1908) 13 Com Cas 264, CA (fire insurance). The whole of the ship's papers must be disclosed in the affidavit of documents, even though not specifically asked for: *Graham Joint Stock Shipping Co v Motor Union Insurance Co* [1922] 2 KB 563, 27 Com Cas 130, CA; overruling *Fraser v Burrows* (1877) 2 QBD 624. But documents subsequent to the inception of litigation are privileged: *Adam SS Co v London Assurance Corpn* (1914) 20 Com Cas 37, CA (correspondence with salvage association after agreed date of writ). See further, *Arnould*, paras 1347–1350, and Ivamy, *Marine Insurance* (4th ed, 1985), pp 397–401.
13 See Appendix VI, p 304, post.
14 See Appendix VI, p 304, post.
15 RSC Ord 72, r 10 (2).
16 *Probatina Shipping Co Ltd v Sun Insurance Office Ltd, The Sageorge* [1974] QB 635, [1974] 2 All ER at 493, CA, where no order was made.
17 Ibid.

18. Disclosure by assured

(1) Subject to the provisions of this section, the assured must disclose to the insurer, before the contract is concluded,[1] every material circumstance which is known to the assured, and the assured is deemed to know every circumstance which, in the ordinary course of business, ought to be known by him. If the assured fails to make such disclosure, the insurer may avoid the contract.[2]

(2) Every circumstance is material which would influence the judgment of a prudent insurer in fixing the premium, or determining whether he will take the risk.[3]

(3) In the absence of inquiry the following circumstances need not be disclosed, namely:
   (a) Any circumstance which diminishes the risk;[4]
   (b) Any circumstance which is known or presumed to be known to the insurer. The insurer is presumed to know matters of common notoriety or knowledge, and matters which an insurer in the ordinary course of his business, as such, ought to know;[5]
   (c) Any circumstance as to which information is waived by the insurer;[6]

(d) Any circumstance which it is superfluous to disclose by reason of any express or implied warranty.[7]

(4) Whether any particular circumstance, which is not disclosed, be material or not is, in each case, a question of fact.[8]

(5) The term 'circumstance' includes any communication made to, or information received by, the assured.[9]

Note

'The duty of disclosure, as defined or circumscribed by ss 18 and 19, is one aspect of the overriding duty of the utmost good faith mentioned in s 17.'[10]

Non-disclosure by the assured is sometimes referred to as 'concealment,' but the expression 'non-disclosure' is preferable. *Aliud est celare, aliud tacere.* The duty of the assured to disclose material facts is a positive, not a negative duty. Mere silence, and even innocent silence, as to a material fact entitles the insurer to avoid the contract.[11] The duty of disclosure is confined to questions of fact; 'a question of opinion is not a material circumstance within the Act.'[12]

It is important to notice that the assured is deemed to know every circumstance which in the ordinary course of business ought to be known by him. Consequently, where the assured effects an insurance policy himself, knowledge of a material fact by his agent will be imputed to the assured.[13]

If insurance is undertaken by an agent for the insurer, the ordinary rules of agency apply, but special rules apply to the agent of the assured quoad the insurer; see s 19.[14]

The word 'influence' means that the disclosure is one which would have had an impact on the formation of the insurer's opinion and on his decision-making process in relation to the matters concerned.[15]

In determining whether there has been a non-disclosure the yardstick is the prudent insurer and not the particular insurer.[16] There is no requirement that the particular insurer should have been induced to take the risk or charge a lower premium than he would otherwise have done as a result of the non-disclosure.[17]

The Court cannot choose one prudent insurer rather than another. The very choice of a prudent insurer as a yardstick indicates that the test intended is one which can be sensibly answered in relation to prudent insurers in general. It is possible to say that prudent insurers in general would consider a particular circumstance as bearing on the risk and exercising an influence on their judgment towards declining the risk or loading the premium.[18]

It is to be emphasised that, as stated in s 18 (4), whether a particular circumstance be material or not is a question of fact. Consequently the illustrations set out below are not to be regarded as precedents but relate solely to the cases in question. It does not necessarily follow that because a fact has been held immaterial in one case, a similar fact is not material in another.[19]

Rivaz v Gerussi (illustration 3) was a case of fraud, but it was laid down generally that a circumstance might be material, though it had no direct bearing on the particular risk.

An apparently well-founded rumour, though it turns out afterwards to be incorrect, must be disclosed (*Arnould*, para 653).

If the assured knows of any peculiar risk attaching to the adventure, which the insurer does not know, the assured is bound to disclose it, even though it may be covered by the terms of the policy.[20]

28 Disclosure and representations

The rule which exempts the assured from disclosing circumstances covered by an implied warranty appears to be of doubtful value,[21] but it is an old one. As there is no implied warranty of seaworthiness in a time policy, facts bearing on the seaworthiness of the ship must be disclosed.[22]

The omission to make inquiry is no waiver, if the insurers are not put on inquiry. Waiver is not to be easily presumed.[23]

'There can, in my opinion, be no waiver of material information unless it would and should have been disclosed by an inquiry by the underwriter which common prudence demanded, and no affirmation of a contract unless the underwriter enters into it or carries it out after he has full knowledge of the information.'[24]

Even when the insurer has full knowledge of the facts, he is still entitled to a reasonable time in which to decide whether to affirm the contract. Where the insurer has taken no action to affirm or repudiate the contract and a reasonable time for making up his mind has elapsed, he will be deemed to have affirmed the contract if either so much time has elapsed that the necessary inference is one of affirmation or the assured has been prejudiced by the delay in making an election or rights of third parties have intervened.[25]

Expert evidence is admissible to prove or disprove the materiality of a fact which has not been disclosed.[26]

The existence of an open cover between the assured's brokers and the insurers does not relieve the assured of his duty under s 18 (1) to disclose material circumstances which are known to him.[27]

Illustrations

1. Insurance on ship *Cambria*. Lloyd's List contains an entry that a ship of this name had stranded. The broker, after inquiry, comes to the conclusion that the entry must relate to another ship, and does not disclose the information to the insurer. The insurer, not having seen the entry, may avoid the contract.[28]
2. Policy for £2,800 on goods valued at £2,800, the real value being £970. The assured does not disclose the over-valuation. The insurer may avoid the contract.[29]
3. Assured effects a series of consecutive policies on shipments to be declared. The goods declared on the earlier policies are systematically undervalued, and the earlier policies are thus more exhausted than they appear to be. The insurer may avoid the later policies on the ground of non-disclosure.[30]
4. Insurance on chartered freight. If the charter-party contains a cancelling clause, this must be disclosed.[31]
5. Insurance on goods, including risk of craft. The assured does not disclose that he gets his lighterage done on cheaper terms in consideration of the lighterman limiting his liability as a common carrier. The insurer may avoid the contract.[32]
6. Insurance on chartered freight, one-third diminishing each month. The 'slip' shows that this is a time charter-party, which may contain the usual 'off-hire' clause.[33] The assured need not disclose that it does, in fact, contain such a clause.
7. Policy on goods. The plaintiff's shipping agent at Smyrna hears that the vessel on which the goods were shipped has stranded. Instead of telegraphing, he informs plaintiff of this by letter, so that plaintiff may have

time to insure. Before receipt of the letter the plaintiff insures the goods. The insurer may avoid the contract.[34]
8. Policy for £18,500 on hull valued at £18,500, the real value being £9,000. At the same time freight is insured for £5,500, and 'honour' policies on disbursements to the amount of £11,000 are taken out. If this gross over-insurance is not disclosed, the policy on hull may be avoided.[35]
9. Voyage policy on ship. The master had not been at sea for twenty years, and had then lost a ship. It is not necessary to disclose these facts.[36]
10. Voyage policy on floating dock sent from England to Brindisi, 'seaworthiness admitted'. The dock had not been specially strengthened for the voyage, but the assured did not know or think that this was necessary. In the absence of inquiry, this need not be disclosed.[37]
11. Policy (against war risks) on freight from Portland to Kustendji. The ship had been chartered to a German. The insurance was effected on 31 July 1914. War breaks out on 4 August. The ship is stopped at Gibraltar, and subsequently is requisitioned by the Admiralty. It is not necessary to disclose that the charterer was a German.[38]
12. Reinsurance of cargo in the afternoon of 25 September. The cargo had been damaged by fire, and the news reached Lloyd's on the night of 24 September. The casualty was posted at Lloyd's, and casualty slips early on the morning of the 25th were sent to the reassured and the reinsurer. Neither party noticed them before the reinsurance was effected. The reinsurer may avoid the contract.[39]
13. Policy on wooden ship from America to France and back again. Part of the cargo she had contracted to carry from America consisted of petrol. This is not disclosed. The absence of inquiry by the insurer as to the nature of the cargo waives disclosure.[40]
14. Time policy on wooden ship. Assured did not disclose that vessel's gasoline carrying capacity had been increased from 3000 to 8000 gallons, and that the altered method of handling gasoline was not in common usage. These facts are material and the insurer is entitled to avoid the contract.[41]
15. Policy on goods. The assured's shipping agents knew that a bill of lading in respect of some steel injection moulds was 'claused' in that it stated that the moulds were 'unprotected,' 'secondhand' and 'insufficiently packed'. This fact was held to be deemed to be known by the assured.[42]
16. Policy on ship. The assured did not disclose: (i) that the master had reported to him that the vessel had unusual rhythmic vibrations and leaked excessively; (ii) that after a period in a shipyard she again leaked excessively; and (iii) that a marine surveyor had reported that she was unfit for any use off shore. These facts were held to be material. The insurers had not waived information of them and could avoid liability on the policy.[43]
17. Builders' risk policy. The assured failed to disclose: (i) the fact that a local authority had refused to give him permission to use his boatyard for any industrial purpose because it was a high hazard risk; and (ii) the fact that he was in financial difficulties and would be less able to maintain the equipment used in the yard and thereby would increase the hazard. These facts were material and the insurers were entitled to avoid liability.[44]
18. Policy on goods. Cargo described as 'enamelware (cups and plates) in

wooden cases'. The assured did not disclose that (i) the cargo included 823 cartons as contrasted with wooden cases; (ii) a significant part of the enamelware had been touched up by overpainting; and (iii) the cargo was an end of stock or job lot purchase and had been bought at a cheap rate.[45] The facts were material, and the insurers could avoid liability.

19. Policy on goods. Cargo of soya beans arrived in heated condition. The assured did not disclose that a similar cargo loaded on another vessel had arrived earlier also in a heated condition. The insurers could not avoid liability on the ground of non-disclosure of a material fact because they had been informed that there was damage to the other cargo but that it was insignificant and negligible.[46]

20. Policy on goods. Non-disclosure of claims experience of previous insurers of containers used in ocean transport. These facts were material and the present insurers had not waived information as to that experience.[47]

21. Policy on yacht. Non-disclosure by assured that he had been previously convicted of handling a stolen dinghy, and that yacht had been built from a kit. These facts were material and the insurers could avoid liability for there had been no waiver.[48]

1 See s 21, as to conclusion of contract.
2 *Ionides v Pender* (1874) LR 9 QB at 537, per Blackburn J. As to facts which the assured ought to know, see *Proudfoot v Montefiore* (1867) LR 2 QB 511 at 519; *Blackburn v Vigors* (1887) 12 App Cas at 537, 541. As to Lloyd's agents abroad, see *Wilson v Salamandra Assurance Co* (1903) 8 Com Cas 129 (knowledge of Lloyd's agent at Gibraltar does not affect a member of Lloyd's who reinsures).
3 *Rivaz v Gerussi* (1880) 6 QBD at 229, per Lord Esher; *Tate v Hyslop* (1885) 15 QBD at 379, per Bowen LJ. Cf *Republic of Bolivia v Indemnity Mutual Marine Assurance Co* (1908) 14 Com Cas at 167 (open cover which may be used for goods of different assured); *Associated Oil Carriers Ltd v Union Insurance Society of Canton Ltd* [1917] 2 KB 184 at 192 (per Atkin J) (for the facts of the case, see illustration 11, p 29, ante); *Berger and Light Diffusers Pty Ltd v Pollock* [1973] 2 Lloyd's Rep 442, QBD (Commercial Court) at 463 (per Kerr J); *Container Transport International Inc and Reliance Group Inc v Oceanus Mutual Underwriting Association (Bermuda) Ltd* [1984] 1 Lloyd's Rep 476, CA.
4 *Carter v Boehm* (1766) 3 Burr at 1910, per Lord Mansfield.
5 *Carter v Boehm* (1766) 3 Burr at 1910; *Vallance v Dewar* (1808) 1 Camp at 108 (trade usages); *Harrower v Hutchinson* (1870) LR 5 QB at 590. Cf *British and Foreign Marine Insurance Co v Gaunt* [1921] 2 AC 41 at 59–62 (usage as to deck cargo).
6 *Carter v Boehm* (1766) 3 Burr at 1910, 1911; cf *Laing v Union Marine Insurance Co* (1895) 1 Com Cas at 15. Cf *Property Insurance Co v Protector Insurance Co* (1913) 18 Com Cas 119 (reinsurance, special terms in contract); *Hewitt Bros v Wilson* [1915] 2 KB 739, CA (second-hand machinery described as machinery. Effect of 'held covered' clause); *Mann, MacNeal and Steeves Ltd v General Marine Underwriters Ltd* [1921] 2 KB 300, 26 Com Cas 132, CA (policy on ship, absence of inquiry as to cargo); *Greenhill v Federal Insurance Co* [1927] 1 KB 65, CA (previous history of goods); *G Cohen, Sons & Co v Standard Marine Insurance Co Ltd* (1925) 30 Com Cas 139 (absence of steam power on old battleship being towed to scrapyard); *Pacific Queen Fisheries v L Symes, The Pacific Queen* [1963] 2 Lloyd's Rep 201, US Ct of Appeals, Ninth Circuit (increase of vessel's gasoline carrying capacity); *Gulfstream Cargo Ltd v Reliance Insurance Co, The Papoose* [1971] 1 Lloyd's Rep 178, US Ct of Appeals, Fifth Circuit; *Container Transport International Inc and Reliance Group Inc v Oceanus Mutual Underwriting Association (Bermuda) Ltd* [1984] 1 Lloyd's Rep 476, CA (claims experience of previous insurers of containers used in ocean transport).

7 *Shoolbred v Nutt* (1782); *Arnould*, paras 611, 670; *Haywood v Rodgers* (1804) 4 East 590; *The Gunford Ship Co Ltd v Thames and Mersey Marine Insurance Co Ltd* 1910 SC 1072, Ct of Session; revsd by HL on another point: [1911] AC 529.
8 *Ionides v Pender* (1874) LR 9 QB 531.
9 *Blackburn v Haslam* (1888) 21 QBD 144.
10 *Container Transport International Inc and Reliance Group Inc v Oceanus Mutual Underwriting Association (Bermuda) Ltd* [1984] 1 Lloyd's Rep 476, at 492, CA (per Kerr LJ).
11 See *Bates v Hewitt* (1867) LR 2 QB 595 at 607 (failure to disclose that a merchant ship had formerly been a Confederate cruiser).
12 *Cantiere Meccanico v Janson* [1912] 3 KB at 472, per Buckley LJ.
13 *Berger and Light Diffusers Pty Ltd v Pollock* [1973] 2 Lloyd's Rep 442, QBD (Commercial Court), the facts of which are stated in illustration 15, p 29, ante.
14 As to agency in marine insurance, see *Arnould*, paras 211–235, and Ivamy, *Marine Insurance* (4th ed, 1985), pp 41–44, and note the special rule as to ratification in s 86 of the Act.
15 *Container Transport International Inc and Reliance Group Inc v Oceanus Mutual Underwriting Association (Bermuda) Ltd* [1984] 1 Lloyd's Rep 476 at 492, CA (per Kerr LJ).
16 Ibid, at 510 (per Parker LJ).
17 Ibid, at 510 (per Parker LJ).
18 Ibid, at 511 (per Parker LJ).
19 See Ivamy, *Marine Insurance* (4th ed, 1985) p 54.
20 *Cheshire & Co v Thompson* (1919) 24 Com Cas 198 CA.
21 See *Greenhill v Federal Insurance Co* [1927] 1 KB at 81.
22 *Russell v Thornton* (1859) 29 L J Ex 9; affd (1860) 6 H & N 140 (ship had been aground for three hours).
23 *Greenhill v Federal Insurance Co* [1927] 1 KB 65, CA.
24 *Container Transport International Inc and Reliance Inc v Oceanus Mutual Underwriting Association (Bermuda) Ltd* [1984] 1 Lloyd's Rep 476, at 529, CA (per Stephenson LJ).
25 *Liberian Agency Inc v Mosse* [1977] 2 Lloyd's Rep 560 at 565 (per Donaldson J). In that case it was held that a reasonable time had not elapsed. (See the judgment of Donaldson J, ibid, at 565–566.)
26 *Scottish Shire Line v London and Provincial Marine Insurance Co* [1912] 3 KB 51 at 70, 17 Com Cas at 269, and Ivamy, *General Principles of Insurance Law* (6th ed, 1993), pp 167–169), and cf *Associated Oil Carriers Ltd v Union Insurance Society of Canton Ltd* [1917] 2 KB 184.
27 *Berger and Light Diffusers Pty Ltd v Pollock* (supra). (See the judgment of Kerr J, ibid, at 460.)
28 *Morrison v Universal Marine Insurance Co* (1873) LR 8 Ex Ch 197, Ex Ch.
29 *Ionides v Pender* (1874) LR 9 QB 531; cf illustration 8 as to 'honour' policies, and see *Gooding v White* (1913) 29 TLR 312 (over-valued cargo); *Visscherij Maatschappij etc v Scottish Metropolitan Assurance Co* (1922), 27 Com Cas 198, CA (over-valued trawler); *Piper v Royal Exchange Assurance* (1932) 44 Ll L Rep 103, KB (over-valued yacht); *Slattery v Mance* [1962] 1 Lloyd's Rep 60 (over-valued yacht). Cf *Berger and Light Diffusers Pty Ltd v Pollock* [1973] 2 Lloyd's Rep 442, QBD (Commercial Court), where the assured had stated that some steel injection moulds were worth £20,000 and it was held that the insurers had failed to prove that the alleged over-valuation was material. (See the judgment of Kerr J ibid, at 465.)
30 *Rivaz v Gerussi* (1880) 6 QBD 222 CA (fraud).
31 *Mercantile SS Co v Tyser* (1881) 7 QBD 73, cf illustration 6.
32 *Tate v Hyslop* (1885) 15 QBD 368, CA. A common carrier is prima facie responsible as an insurer, and not merely for negligence.
33 *The Bedouin* [1894] P 1, CA; cf *Charlesworth v Faber* (1900) 5 Com Cas 408 (continuation clause). Distinguished in *Scottish Shire Line v London and Provincial Marine Insurance Co* [1912] 3 KB 51 (policy on freight 'chartered or as if chartered'—nondisclosure of agreement that ship should be at Hobart by March 28).
34 *Proudfoot v Montefiore* (1867) LR 2 QB 511.

32 *Disclosure and representations*

35 *Thames and Mersey Marine Insurance Co v Gunford Ship Co* [1911] AC 529, HL. Cf *Pickersgill v London and Provincial Marine Insurance Co* [1912] 3 KB 614 (action by innocent assignee of policy). But what if the 'honour' policies had been effected after the conclusion of the contract, instead of contemporaneously?
36 *Thames and Mersey Marine Insurance Co Ltd v Gunford Ship Co Ltd* (supra).
37 *Cantiere Meccanico v Janson* [1912] 3 KB 452, CA.
38 *Associated Oil Carriers Ltd v Union Insurance Society of Canton Ltd* [1917] 2 KB 184, 22 Com Cas 346.
39 *London General Insurance Co v General Marine Underwriters' Association Ltd* [1921] 1 KB 104, 26 Com Cas 52, CA.
40 *Mann, MacNeal and Steeves Ltd v General Marine Underwriters Ltd* [1921] 2 KB 300, 26 Com Cas 132, CA (ship burnt on return voyage).
41 *Pacific Queen Fisheries v L Symes, The Pacific Queen* [1963] 2 Lloyd's Rep 201, US Ct of Appeals, Ninth Circuit.
42 *Berger and Light Diffusers Pty Ltd v Pollock* [1973] 2 Lloyd's Rep 442, QBD (Commercial Court). (See the judgment of Kerr J, ibid, at 461.)
43 *Gulfstream Cargo Ltd v Reliance Insurance Co, The Papoose*, [1971] 1 Lloyd's Rep 178, US Ct of Appeals, Fifth Ciruit. (See the judgment of Brown Ch J, ibid, at 183.) The evidence of the alleged waiver is set out ibid at 209–210.
44 *James Yachts Ltd v Thames and Mersey Marine Insurance Co Ltd* [1977] 1 Lloyd's Rep 206, Supreme Court, British Columbia. (See the judgment of Ruttan J, ibid, at 212.)
45 *Liberian Insurance Agency Inc v Mosse* [1977] 2 Lloyd's Rep 560. (See the judgment of Donaldson J, ibid at 565).
46 *Soya GmbH Mainz Kommanditgesellschaft v White* [1982] 1 Lloyd's Rep 136, CA.
47 *Container Transport International Inc and Reliance Group Inc v Oceanus Mutual Underwriting Association (Bermuda) Ltd* [1984] 1 Lloyd's Rep 476, CA.
48 *Allden v Raven, The Kylie* [1983] 2 Lloyd's Rep 444. (See the judgment of Parker J, ibid, at 445–448.) See also *Inversiones Manria SA v Sphere Drake Insurance Co plc: The Dora* [1989] 1 Lloyd's Rep 69, where the skipper of a yacht had a criminal record.

19. Disclosure by agent effecting insurance

Subject to the provisions of the preceding section as to circumstances which need not be disclosed where an insurance is effected for the assured by an agent, the agent must disclose to the insurer—
  (a) Every material circumstance which is known to himself, and an agent to insure is deemed to know every circumstance which in the ordinary course of business ought to be known by, or to have been communicated to, him;[1] and
  (b) Every material circumstance which the assured is bound to disclose, unless it comes to his knowledge too late to communicate it to the agent.[2]

Note

The knowledge of an agent to insure, who does not effect the particular insurance, is immaterial,[3] but if an agent to insure employs a sub-agent, all material facts known to the agent must be communicated to the sub-agent.[4]

If, before the contract is made, the assured hears of a loss, but has not time to communicate with his agent, the contract would stand. The assured must use 'due diligence' to communicate with his agent.[5]

Whether the material circumstance comes to the assured's knowledge too late to communicate it to the agent, is a question of fact.[6]

Illustrations

1. Time policy on ship. The broker, who effects the insurance, omits to disclose a letter in his possession from the captain saying that the ship has been ashore, and that she is being repaired. This is not done dishonestly. The insurer may avoid the contract.[7]
2. A, who has insured an overdue ship, instructs his Glasgow brokers to reinsure it. The Glasgow brokers effect an insurance with B through their London agents, having received some material information about the ship which they do not disclose. Afterwards A effects another policy with B through R, his London agent, who knows nothing of the news about the ship, so that both parties act honestly. A can recover on the latter policy from B.[8]
3. Plaintiff in Glasgow employs a broker there to reinsure an overdue ship. The Glasgow broker employs a broker in London to effect the reinsurance. The Glasgow broker does not communicate either to the plaintiff or to the London broker information which he has received tending to show that the ship was lost. The insurer may avoid the contract.[9]
4. A in Bolivia, acting for the government, instructs his agent in London to effect a voyage policy on goods up the Amazon. The underwriters know that the country is disturbed, but A and the government further know that an expedition is being prepared by revolutionaries to attack the ship. If this is not disclosed, and the goods are captured, the underwriters may avoid the contract.[10]

1 *Blackburn v Vigors* (1887) 12 App Cas at 541; *Blackburn v Haslam* (1888) 21 QBD 144.
2 *Blackburn v Vigors* (1887) 12 App Cas at 537.
3 *Blackburn v Vigors* (1887) 12 App Cas 531.
4 *Blackburn v Haslam* (1888) 21 QBD 144.
5 *Cory v Patton* (1872) LR 7 QB at 308.
6 *Container Transport Inc and Reliance Group Inc v Oceanus Mutual Underwriting Association (Bermuda) Ltd* [1984] 1 Lloyd's Rep 476, CA, where it was held that it was not too late for the assured to have communicated their knowledge of the figures relating to a previous claim. (See the judgment of Parker LJ, ibid, at 518.)
7 *Russell v Thornton* (1859) 4 H & N 788; affd (1860) 6 H & N 140, Ex Ch.
8 *Blackburn v Vigors* (1887) 12 App Cas 531.
9 *Blackburn v Haslam* (1888) 21 QBD 144.
10 *Republic of Bolivia v Indemnity Mutual Assurance Co* (1908) 14 Com Cas at 166 (second policy).

20. Representations pending negotiation of contract

(1) Every material representation made by the assured or his agent to the insurer during the negotiations for the contract, and before the contract is concluded, must be true. If it be untrue the insurer may avoid the contract.[1]

(2) A representation is material which would influence the judgment of a prudent insurer in fixing the premium, or determining whether he will take the risk.[2]

(3) A representation may be either a representation as to a matter of fact, or as to a matter of expectation or belief.

(4) A representation as to a matter of fact is true, if it be substantially correct,[3] that is to say, if the difference between what is represented and what is actually correct would not be considered material by a prudent insurer.[4]

(5) A representation as to a matter of expectation or belief is true if it be made in good faith.[5]

(6) A representation may be withdrawn or corrected before the contract is concluded.[6]

(7) Whether a particular representation be material or not is, in each case, a question of fact.[7]

Note

Sibbald v Hill,[8] where the contract was avoided, though the representation had no direct bearing on the particular risk, was a case of fraud, but according to *Rivaz v Gerussi*,[9] it seems that the rule would apply whether there was fraud or not. Lord Esher in a later case, said: 'The assured is not bound to tell the insurer what the law is. He is bound to tell him, not every fact, but every material fact. His other obligation is this, that if he is asked a question— whether a material fact or not—by the underwriters, he must answer it truly. If he answers it falsely, with intent to deceive, though it may not be a material fact, it will vitiate the policy.'[10]

The cases seem generally to assume that it is sufficient if a representation as to expectation or belief is made in good faith, but there was an obiter dictum by Blackburn J, that the assured must have reasonable ground for his belief.[11] Having regard to the terms of sub-ss (3), (4) and (5), it may be that promissory representations, i e representations as to future events, now fall exclusively under sub-s (5).[12]

This section deals with representations made during the negotiations for the contract. They may be either oral or in writing, as, for instance, when letters are shown to the underwriter. A representation expressed in, or implied from the terms of, the policy itself, constitutes a warranty.[13] The policy is the final expression of the contract, and extrinsic evidence is inadmissible to contradict its terms. A representation differs from a warranty in this—a warranty must be exactly complied with, while it is sufficient if a representation is substantially correct. See ss 33–41 as to warranties.

It is to be emphasised that, as stated in s 20 (7), whether a particular representation be material or not is a question of fact. Consequently the illustrations set out above are not to be regarded as precedents, but relate solely to the cases in question.

As to the rule, or supposed rule, that a misrepresentation made to the first underwriter is presumed to be made to subsequent underwriters, see *Arnould*, paras 623–624 and Ivamy, *Marine Insurance* (4th ed, 1985), p 78.

The assured, or his agent, is not bound to give his opinion to the insurer on any matter relating to the adventure.[14] The assured is bound to disclose facts within his knowledge, and not the opinions which he forms on those facts. For example, the assured may think that war between two States is imminent; but unless he has special information, he may leave the insurer to form his own judgment on the matter. If the assured chooses to give his opinion, he must, of course, give it honestly.[15]

Illustrations

1. Insurance on ship. The assured falsely informs the insurer that he has partially insured the ship elsewhere on certain specified terms. The insurer, relying on this, issues a policy on similar terms. The insurer may avoid the contract.[16]
2. Policy on goods at sea. The assured represents to the insurer that the ship sailed from Baltimore for London on 12 January. In fact, she sailed on 1 January. The insurer may avoid the contract.[17]
3. Policy on goods to be shipped from abroad. The assured mistaking the old ship *Socrates* for a new ship called the *Socrate*, informs the insurer that the goods are to be shipped on the new ship. The insurer may avoid the contract.[18]
4. Policy on yacht. Assured during the negotiations for the contract stated that her value was £4,500, but a month beforehand had said he would be willing to accept an offer of £2,250 for her from a prospective buyer. The insurer could avoid the contract, for such a representation was a material one.[19]
5. Policy on goods. Assured made representations as to state of insured cargo of 'enamelware (cups and plates) in wooden cases,' whereas (i) the cargo included 823 cartons as contrasted with wooden cases; (ii) a significant proportion of the enamelware had been touched up by overpainting; and (iii) the cargo was an end of stock or job lot purchase and had been bought at a cheap rate. The representations were material, and the insurer could avoid liability.[20]
6. Policy on containers. The assured made an untrue statement concerning their previous claims record. *Held*, the statement was material, and the insurers were entitled to avoid liability.[21]
7. Policy on yacht. Assured made representation that they were producing yachts at the rate of about four per annum. Representation was intended to indicate to the insurers the scale of their business. *Held*, the representation was untrue, and was material, and, therefore, the insurers could avoid liability.[22]

1 *Anderson v Pacific Fire and Marine Insurance Co* (1872) LR 7 CP at 68, per Willes J; *Ionides v Pacific Fire and Marine Insurance Co* (1871) LR 6 QB at 683, per Blackburn J; *Williams v Atlantic Assurance Co Ltd* [1933] 1 KB 81, CA (see per Slesser LJ at 108, gross over-valuation, underwriter entitled to avoid contract for untrue material representation; but see per Greer LJ at 102).
2 *Rivaz v Gerussi* (1880) 6 QBD at 229, CA.
3 *Pawson v Watson* (1778) 2 Cowp 785. As to a warranty, see s 33(2).
4 *Macdowall v Frazer* (1779) 1 Doug 260, 261.
5 *Anderson v Pacific Fire and Marine Insurance Co* (1872) LR 7 CP at 69 (honest but wrong opinion given by master).

6 *Edwards v Footner* (1808) 1 Camp 530.
7 *Rivaz v Gerussi* (1880) 6 QBD at 229, CA.
8 *Sibbald v Hill* (1814) 2 Dow 263, HL.
9 *Rivaz v Gerussi* (1880) 6 QBD 222 at 229.
10 *The Bedouin* [1894] P at 12, CA.
11 *Ionides v Pacific Fire and Marine Insurance Co* (1871) LR 6 QB at 683, 684.
12 *Arnould*, paras 598–599; *Halsbury's Laws of England*, 4th edn, vol 25, para 240, but note the language of *Dennistoun v Lillie* (1821) 3 Bligh 202 at 210, HL.
13 *Behn v Burness* (1863) 32 LJQB 204 at 205, Ex Ch and s 33.
14 *Anderson v Pacific and Fire Marine Insurance Co* (1872) LR 7 CP 65 at 69.
15 Cf *The Bedouin* [1894] P at 12, per Lord Esher. As to special information concerning hostilities, see *Republic of Bolivia v Indemnity Mutual Marine Assurance Co* (1908) 14 Com Cas at 166.
16 *Sibbald v Hill* (1814) 2 Dow 263, HL.
17 *Anderson v Thornton* (1853) 8 Exch 425.
18 *Ionides v Pacific Fire and Marine Insurance Co* (1871) LR 6 QB 674 at 683.
19 *Slattery v Mance* [1962] 1 Lloyd's Rep 60. The evidence as to the overvaluation is set out ibid, at 67–70. The jury found that the representation had not been made fraudulently. In *Wilmott v General Accident Fire and Life Assurance Corpn Ltd* (1935) 53 Ll L Rep 156 the insurers contended that the assured had made a material misrepresentation of the value of a motor boat, and it was held that the plea failed because the incorrect answer given by him as to her value was probably due to the fact that he was incorrectly questioned by the insurers' agent, who had himself completed the proposal form. (See the judgment of Branson J, ibid, at 159.)
20 *Liberian Insurance Agency Inc v Mosse* [1977] 2 Lloyd's Rep 560. (See the judgment of Donaldson J, ibid, at 565.)
21 *Container Transport International Inc and Reliance Group Inc v Oceanus Mutual Underwriting Association (Bermuda) Ltd* [1984] 1 Lloyd's Rep 476, CA. (See the judgment of Kerr LJ, ibid, at 500.)
22 *Inversiones Manria SA v Sphere Drake Insurance plc, The Dora* [1989] 1 Lloyd's Rep 69, QB (Commercial Court). (See the judgment of Phillips J, ibid, at 90.)

21. When contract is deemed to be concluded[1]

A contract of marine insurance is deemed to be concluded when the proposal of the assured is accepted by the insurer, whether the policy be then issued or not; and for the purpose of showing when the proposal was accepted, reference may be made to the slip or covering note or other customary memorandum of the contract...

Note

'In effecting marine insurance,' said the Court of Exchequer Chamber, 'the matter is considered merely as negotiation till the slip is initialled, but, when that is done, the contract is considered to be concluded. It was proved to be the usage of underwriters to issue a stamped policy in accordance with the slip, notwithstanding anything that might happen after the initialling of the slip.'[2]

In *Cory v Patton*,[3] the proposal of the agent of the assured was accepted by the insurer subject to the ratification by the assured of the payment of an increased premium, and it was held that a material fact which came to the knowledge of the assured after the acceptance, but before the ratification, need not be disclosed, for the ratification related back to the acceptance. As to ratification by the assured, see s 86, and see further, notes to ss 22, 23 (policy) and s 89 ('slip' as evidence).

Where a contract concluded by means of a 'cross-slip' is only of a preliminary nature and is intended to be supplemented by a 'signing slip' when further information results in a greater definition of the contractual terms, there is a continuing duty of disclosure between the date of the 'cross-slip' and that of the 'signing slip'.[4]

Illustrations

1. A policy insuring goods from the United Kingdom to Africa and from Africa to the United Kingdom was effected in January 1916. The goods were stored at Burutu because it was difficult to get shipping space, and a lot of other goods were accumulated there after the date of the policy. The insurers could not avoid liability for non-disclosure of the accumulation of the goods, for once the contract was concluded, no further disclosure was necessary.[5]
2. A policy relating to a motor boat was effected at a time when the assured had no intention that she should be moored anywhere except in Knightstone Harbour. She was moved to Anchor Head near Weston-super-Mare two months later. Subsequently she was lost in a gale. The insurer was held not to be entitled to repudiate liability on the ground that the assured had not disclosed the fact that she would be habitually moored off Anchor Head, for his intention to moor her there was only formed after the conclusion of the contract.[6]

1 This section is printed as amended by the Finance Act 1959, 8th Sch, Pt II. See further, s 89, as to 'slip' as evidence.
2 *Morrison v Universal Marine Insurance Co* (1873) LR 8 Ex Ch at 199. As to unreasonable refusal to issue policy, see *Genforsikrings & Co v Da Costa* [1911] 1 KB 137.
3 (1874) LR 9 QB 577, Ex Ch.
4 *Berger and Light Diffusers Pty Ltd v Pollock* [1973] 2 Lloyd's Rep 442, QBD (Commercial Court). (See the judgment of Kerr J, ibid, at 461.)
5 *Niger Co Ltd v Guardian Assurance Co* (1922) 12 Ll L Rep 75, HL.
6 *Willmott v General Accident Fire and Life Assurance Corpn* (1935) 53 Ll L Rep 156.

THE POLICY

22. Contract must be embodied in policy

Subject to the provisions of any statute, a contract of marine insurance is inadmissible in evidence unless it is embodied in a marine policy in accordance with this Act.[1] The policy may be executed and issued either at the time when the contract is concluded or afterwards.

Note

No action can be maintained in the United Kingdom on the implied promise to grant a policy when the 'slip' is initialled.[2] If the insurers go into liquidation, the liquidator cannot issue policies on outstanding 'slips'.[3] It is otherwise in countries where revenue laws do not interpose.[4] But the section will apply to policies issued abroad which are sued on in England.[5]

38 The policy

When a policy has been duly issued, reference may be made to the 'slip' for the purpose of showing when the contract was concluded (s 21), or for the purpose of rectifying or avoiding the policy, see s 89.

An action on a marine policy is an action for unliquidated damages.[6]

Subject to rules of court in proceedings before the High Court for the recovery of a debt or damages there may be included in any sum for which judgment is given simple interest at such rate as the court thinks fit or as rules of court may provide on all or any part of the debt or damages in respect of which judgment is given or payment is made before judgment, for all or any part of the period between the date when the cause of action arose (a) in the case of any sum paid before judgment, the date of the payment; and (b) in the case of the sum for which judgment is given, the date of the judgment[7]. As to pleadings, see *Atkin's Encyclopaedia of Court Forms in Civil Proceedings* (2nd ed, 1992), vol 32, pp 5–116.

Illustration

Policy on ship insured with a mutual insurance association. The ship is accepted as insured in February, and after this a loss occurs. The policy may be issued in October, taking effect from February, although, when the policy is executed, it is known to both parties that the loss has occurred.[8]

1. Certain contracts entered into by the Secretary of State are exempt from this provision by Marine and Aviation Insurance (War Risks) Act 1952, s 7. For a case where a 'participation agreement' or reinsurance treaty was invalid because no marine policy was issued, see *Re National Benefit Assurance Co Ltd* [1931] 1 Ch 46; also *Motor Union Insurance Co Ltd v Mannheimer Versicherungs Gesellschaft* [1933] 1 KB 812, KB (another reinsurance case).
2. *Fisher v Liverpool Marine Insurance Co* (1874) LR 9 QB 418, Ex Ch; *Genforsikrings & Co v Da Costa* [1911] 1 KB 137 (open covers of reinsurance).
3. *Re Clyde Marine Insurance Co* 1924 SC 113, 17 Ll L Rep 287; *Re City Equitable Fire Insurance Co* [1930] 2 Ch 293.
4. *Bhugwandass v Netherlands Sea Insurance Co* (1888) 14 App Cas 83, PC (Rangoon foreign policy); *Arnould*, para 14.
5. *Royal Exchange Assurance Corpn v Vega* [1901] 2 KB 567, [1902] 2 KB 384, CA. See, however, *Norske Atlas Insurance Co v London General Insurance Co Ltd* (1927) 43 TLR 541 (action on foreign award).
6. *Baker v Adam* (1910) 15 Com Cas 227; *Pickersgill v London and Provincial Marine Insurance Co* [1912] 3 KB 614 at 622.
7. Supreme Court Act 1981, s 35A. For a similar provision in the County Court, see County Courts Act 1984, s 69.
8. *Mead v Davison* (1835) 3 A & El 303, 42 RR 401.

23. What policy must specify[1]

A marine policy must specify—
(1) The name of the assured, or of some person who effects the insurance on his behalf:[2] . . .

Note

The Marine Insurance Act 1788, now repealed as to marine insurance, was construed as merely prohibiting insurances in blank or to bearer, and is, therefore, sufficiently reproduced by this section.

Where different interests are concerned, it is a common practice, as Blackburn J, pointed out, for the broker to enter into the policy in his own name 'but on behalf of and to protect the interests of different constituents'.[3]

But this will only cover the interests of the persons whose interests are intended to be covered by the person who causes the insurance to be effected.[4]

For example, A & Co charter a ship from the owners. The owners' broker effects a policy on the ship including a 'running-down' clause. A & Co have to pay damages to another ship for collision. There being no evidence of any intention by the owners to insure on A & Co's behalf, A & Co cannot recover on the policy.

1 This section is printed as amended by the Finance Act 1959, Sch 8, Pt II.
2 As to ratification by assured, see s 86.
3 *Ionides v Pacific Fire and Marine Insurance Co* (1871) LR 6 QB at 678; cf *Ocean Iron SS Association v Leslie* (1887) 22 QBD 722n, as to scope of the term 'assured'.
4 *Boston Fruit Co v British and Foreign Marine Insurance Co* [1905] 1 KB 637, CA; affd [1906] AC 336 HL; cf *Reliance Marine Insurance Co v Duder* (1912) 17 Com Cas 227 at 237, [1913] 1 KB 265, CA; *Graham Joint Stock Shipping Co v Merchants' Marine Insurance Co* (1923) 28 Com Cas 151 at 157; *Samuel (P) & Co Ltd v Dumas* (1924) 29 Com Cas 239 at 246.

24. Signature of insurer

(1) A marine policy must be signed by or on behalf of the insurer, provided that in the case of a corporation the corporate seal may be sufficient, but nothing in this section shall be construed as requiring the subscription of a corporation to be under seal.[1]

(2) Where a policy is subscribed by or on behalf of two or more insurers, each subscription, unless the contrary be expressed, constitutes a distinct contract with the assured.[2]

Note

Underwriters formed a syndicate, and a Lloyd's policy was subscribed 'The S Syndicate, C Manager'; afterwards followed the names of the members and the amounts of their subscriptions. *Held*, that the contract of the members was several, and not joint.[3]

But when a policy is subscribed by several underwriters, one underwriter may sue for premiums for himself and for the others.[4]

A marine policy, like every other instrument, is incomplete and revocable until delivery to, or for the benefit of, the person entitled to hold it. In the case of an insurance company's policy delivery is presumed on very slight evidence.[5] In the case of Lloyd's policies the assured's broker formerly obtained the underwriters' signatures direct. They are now affixed by Lloyd's Policy Signing Office.

1 Cf Bills of Exchange Act 1882, s 91.
2 *Arnould*, para 45; Lloyd's Act 1871, Rule 4 in Schedule; and see per Walton J, in *Anglo-Californian Bank v London and Provincial Marine Insurance Co* (1904) 10 Com Cas at 8.
3 *Tyser v Shipowners' Syndicate* [1896] 1 QB 135.
4 *Janson v Property Insurance Co* (1913) 19 Com Cas 36.

5 *Xenos v Wickham* (1866) LR 2 HL 296 (policy executed by two directors, and ordered to lie in the office until assured called for it); see to like effect, *Roberts v Security Co Ltd* [1897] 1 QB 111, CA (burglary policy).

25. Voyage and time policies[1]

(1) Where the contract is to insure the subject-matter 'at and from,' or from one place to another or others, the policy is called a 'voyage policy,' and where the contract is to insure the subject-matter for a definite period of time the policy is called a 'time policy.' A contract for both voyage and time may be included in the same policy.[2]

Note

Thus, a ship may be insured eg (i) 'from London to Hong Kong'; (ii) 'for 12 months from June 15 1993'; or (iii) 'from London to New York, and thirty days after arrival'.

The word 'definite' in s 25(1) means that the period must be specified. It is sufficiently specified if it specifies a stated period even though that period is determinable on notice and even though the insurance will be renewed or continued automatically at the end of the period unless determined.[3]

Time policies sometimes give rise to difficult questions where the cause of loss comes into operation before the policy expires, but the actual loss occurs after it expires.[4] As to calculating time when ship's time differs from English time, see note to s 91.

As to the voyage insured, change of voyage, and deviation, see ss 42–49. The voyage insured (viaggium) must be distinguished from the course actually taken by the ship (iter navis); see *Arnould*, para 461.

1 This section is printed as amended by the Finance Act 1959, Sch 8, Pt II.
2 As to these 'mixed policies,' see *Gambles v Ocean Insurance Co* (1876) 1 Ex D 141, CA; *Maritime Insurance Co v Alianza Insurance Co of Santander* (1907) 13 Com Cas 46; *M Almojil Establishment v Malayan Motor and General Underwriters (Private) Ltd, The Al-Jubail IV* [1982] 2 Lloyd's Rep 637, Singapore Court of Appeal; *Halsbury's Laws of England*, 4th edn, vol 25, para 39. For a case where a motor launch was insured for 4½ months while used within a limited radius and a loss was sustained within the limits while on a voyage to a port outside the limits, and it was held to be a 'time' policy and not a 'mixed' policy, see *Wilson v Boag* [1956] 2 Lloyd's Rep 564 (Supreme Court of New South Wales). See especially, ibid, at 565.
3 *Compania Maritime San Basilio SA v Oceanus Mutual Underwriting Association (Bermuda) Ltd, The Eurysthenes* [1976] 2 Lloyd's Rep 171 at 177, CA (per Lord Denning MR).
4 See the cases reviewed in *Lidgett v Secretan* (1870) LR 5 CP 190; and see Rule 5 of First Sch.

26. Designation of subject-matter

(1) The subject-matter insured must be designated in a marine policy with reasonable certainty.[1]

(2) The nature and extent of the interest of the assured in the subject-matter insured need not be specified in the policy.[2]
(3) Where the policy designates the subject-matter insured in general terms, it shall be construed to apply to the interest intended by the assured to be covered.[3]
(4) In the application of this section regard shall be had to any usage regulating the designation of the subject-matter insured.

Note

In *Mackenzie v Whitworth*[4] in 1875, a policy of reinsurance was effected, simply as a policy 'on cotton'. It was *held* that this was sufficient, and that it was not necessary to specify that it was a reinsurance.

The decision at the time was supposed to be opposed to the ordinary understanding and practice, and the Lords Select Committee in 1896 proposed to alter the rule there laid down. But having regard to the length of time during which this decision had been unquestioned law, it was thought better not to disturb it. Though a reinsurance policy need not specify that it is a reinsurance, that leaves untouched the question whether the assured must not disclose the fact that he is effecting a reinsurance.

The quantum of the assured's interest need not be specified in the policy. Thus, it is not necessary to specify whether the assured insures for himself or as trustee for another, as full owner, or as mortgagor or mortgagee.

The subject-matter is usually very briefly described as being 'on ship,' 'on goods,' 'on freight,' and so on; but the description must not be misleading. Thus, a policy on 'piece goods' will not cover a loss on hats;[5] so, too, a policy 'on freight', will not cover passage money.[6]

In the absence of any usage an insurance on 'goods' will not cover deck cargo or live animals. (See Sch I, r 17.)

Prospective profits may be insured apart from the goods out of which they are expected to arise, but in that case they must be specifically described as profits. 'The subject-matter of this insurance is on "rice",' said Blackburn J, 'and though that is to be construed liberally as covering any interest in the rice, it cannot be construed as covering an interest in profits that might arise collaterally from a contract relating to the rice.'[7]

'In some cases,' said Blackburn J, 'the nature of the interest in the thing insured is such as to vary the nature of the risk, and then it should be stated . . . in all cases when the peculiar nature of the interest alters the risk, it may probably be said that such interest is the subject-matter of the insurance,' and he then went on to instance a case of profits dependent on various contingencies.[8]

But it is difficult to see how the nature of the interest of the assured in the subject-matter can vary the risk. The true question seems to be whether, having regard to usage, the subject-matter is sufficiently described. Loans on bottomry and respondentia must, it seems, be insured as such.[9]

Sub-section (3) is perhaps unfortunately worded. It was intended to protect the assured against technical objections to the description of the interest insured, and to give effect to the real intention of the contract where the wording was ambiguous.

But an unsuccessful attempt has been made to put it to the opposite use. Where a policy of reinsurance according to its natural construction covered risks under

42 The policy

three original policies, the reinsurer maintained that only the risk under the third policy was intended to be covered. But this claim was disallowed.[10]

Illustration

Cases of tinned pork were insured against all risks, each case having to be marked 'L 26 MS'. Some of them were not so marked. *Held*, the marking 'L 26 MS' was a term of description, and the policy attached only to such of the cases as complied with that description.[11]

1 *Mackenzie v Whitworth* (1875) 1 Ex D 36 at 40, CA.
2 Ibid, at 41.
3 *Allison v Bristol Marine Insurance Co* (1876) 1 App Cas at 216, 235; cf *Kynance Sailing Ship Co Ltd v Young* (1911) 16 Com Cas at 131; *Reliance Marine Insurance Co v Duder* (1912) 17 Com Cas 227 at 235, [1913] 1 KB 265, CA; distinguished in *Janson v Poole* (1915) 20 Com Cas 232 at 239; *Dunlop Bros v Townend* [1919] 2 KB 127, 24 Com Cas 201, (floating policy).
4 (1875) 1 Ex D 36.
5 *Mackenzie v Whitworth* (1875) 1 Ex D at 40.
6 *Denoon v Home and Colonial Assurance Co* (1872) LR 7 CP 341. As to what is covered by the term 'disbursements,' see *Buchanan v Faber* (1899) 4 Com Cas 223; *Lawther v Black* (1901) 6 Com Cas 5; affd by CA, ibid, p 197.
7 *Anderson v Morice* (1875) LR 10 CP at 621, Ex Ch, but cf *Reliance Marine Insurance Co v Duder* (1912) 17 Com Cas at 236, CA.
8 *Mackenzie v Whitworth* (1875) 1 Ex D at 41; cf *Wilson v Jones* (1867) LR 2 Ex Ch at 151 (submarine cable).
9 *Mackenzie v Whitworth* (1875) 1 Ex D at 43, citing *Glover v Black* (1763) 3 Burr 1394.
10 *Reliance Marine Insurance Co v Duder* [1913] 1 KB 265, 17 Com Cas 227, CA; see a useful explanation of the sub section by Bailhache J, in *Dunlop Bros v Townend* [1919] 2 KB 127.
11 *Overseas Commodities Ltd v Style* [1958] 1 Lloyd's Rep 546.

27. Valued policy

(1) A policy may be either valued or unvalued.[1]
(2) A valued policy is a policy which specifies the agreed value of the subject-matter insured.[2]
(3) Subject to the provisions of this Act,[3] and in the absence of fraud, the value fixed by the policy is, as between the insurer and assured, conclusive of the insurable value of the subject intended to be insured, whether the loss be total or partial.[4]
(4) Unless the policy otherwise provides, the value fixed by the policy is not conclusive for the purpose of determining whether there has been a constructive total loss.[5]

Note

An unvalued policy is sometimes spoken of as an 'open policy,' but as that term is applied in business language to a floating policy,[6] the Act uniformly uses the term 'unvalued policy'.

In 1761 the validity of valued policies was contested on the ground that in substance they were wagering policies. Lord Mansfield disposed of this contention, and the validity of valued policies has never since been questioned. He pointed out that the effect of the valuation was merely to fix the insurable value of the goods or other subject-matter insured, 'just as if the parties admitted it at the trial'.[7]

Speaking of a total loss, the judges in *Irving v Manning* said 'In an open policy the compensation must be ascertained by evidence; in a valued policy the agreed total value is conclusive.'[8]

It is often said that the valuation is conclusive 'for the purposes of the policy'. It is probably more correct to say that it is conclusive for all purposes relating to the insurable value of the subject-matter insured by a given policy.[9] For other purposes it is not conclusive, and in some cases not even relevant.

Notwithstanding the valuation, the interest of the assured may be disproved, or short interest may be shown, or it may be shown that the whole or part of the subject-matter insured was not at risk; see s 75(2), and illustration 7, post.

Over-valuation made in good faith is not a ground for avoiding the policy or reducing the amount payable under it,[10] but gross over-valuation, if not disclosed, is evidence of fraud,[11] and apart from fraud, gross over-insurance, even by collateral 'honour' policies, unless disclosed, will enable the insurer to avoid the contract; see s 18 and notes thereto.

Illustrations

1. A ship is insured with one insurance company for £1,700, and with another insurance company for £2,000. In both policies she is valued at £3,000. The assured, in case of total loss, is not entitled to recover more than £3,000 in all.[12]
2. Ship and freight valued at £3,000, with running-down clause under which insurers were to pay such proportion of three-fourths of any damages paid by the assured as the sum insured bore to the value of the ship insured and freight. The assured had to pay £2,110 damages for running down another ship. His ship was sold under a decree of the Admiralty Court to satisfy these damages. *Held*, that an underwriter who has insured the ship and freight for £100 must pay £52 15s.,[13] ie

    $$\frac{100}{3000} \times 2110 \times \tfrac{3}{4}$$

3. Ship valued at £9,000 is insured under one policy for £2,000. By another policy the same ship is valued at £8,000 and insured for £8,000. The insurer on the second policy pays for a total loss. The insurer on the first policy is liable to pay £1,000.[14]
4. A ship at sea is insured by time policy for £6,000, and valued at £8,000. When the policy is effected, the ship has been sea-damaged to the extent of £5,000, but the assured is not aware of the fact. Afterwards, during the currency of the policy, she is totally lost. The assured can recover the full £6,000.[15]
5. A ship valued at £6,000 is insured for £6,000. Her real value is £9,000. She is run down by another ship and lost. The insurers pay for a total loss. Afterwards the assured recovers £5,000 damages from the owners of the ship at fault. The insurers are entitled to the whole of this sum as salvage.[16]

44 The policy

6. Ship insured by same insurer by two successive valued policies. The first policy covers her to Calcutta and for 30 days after arrival. The second policy covers her at and from Calcutta to London. On the voyage out she is damaged by storms. While she is being repaired at Calcutta, and after the 30 days have expired, she is destroyed by fire. The insurer must pay on the first policy for the partially repaired loss,[17] and on the second policy for the total loss, without deducting what was paid on the first policy.[18]
7. A policy for £1,000 is effected on freight valued at £2,000. Only half the intended cargo is put on board, the rest of the ship being used for emigrants. The ship is lost. The insurer is only liable for £500.[19]
8. Policy on freight valued at £5,500. The ship is detained by an accident, and, during this delay, there is a great fall in freight rates. When a full cargo is loaded, the freight comes to £3,250, of which £925 is paid in advance. The ship is lost. The valuation stands, and the assured is entitled to receive £5,500, less £1,611, which is the proportion of the advance freight to the gross freight.[20]
9. Policy for £1,000 on ship valued at £3,750, with warranty that one-fifth shall remain uninsured. The real value of the ship is £5,000. For the purpose of determining whether the warranty has been broken by a subsequent insurance, regard must be had to the agreed value, and not to the real value.[21]
10. A ship is insured against fire by a valued time policy. During the currency of the policy she is so damaged by stranding that the cost of repairing her would exceed her repaired value. After this she is destroyed by fire. The insurer must pay the full amount insured.[22]
11. Policy on ship valued at £33,000. Her real value is £40,000. The ship incurs certain general average and salvage expenses, which are adjusted abroad on her real value. The assured can only recover 33/40ths of the adjustment from the insurer.[23]
12. Policy on ship valued at £17,500. The ship suffers storm damage, and it is shown that it would cost £10,500 to repair her, and that her market value when repaired would be £9,000. The assured, notwithstanding the valuation, is entitled to abandon the ship and claim for a total loss.[24]

1 *Irving v Manning* (1847) 1 HL Cas 305 at 307.
2 Ibid; and as to distinctly specifying the valuation, see *Wilson v Nelson* (1864) 33 LJQB 220. As to rectifying a defective valuation, see *Rankin v Potter* (1873) LR 6 HL at 114.
3 See s 29(4) (declaration on floating policy after loss or arrival); s 75 (2) (short interest), and cf *Reliance Marine Insurance Co v Duder* (1912) 17 Com Cas at 236, CA.
4 *Barker v Janson* (1868) LR 3 CP 303; *The Main* [1894] P at 325; *Irvin v Hine* [1949] 2 All ER 1089, KB. As to non-disclosure of over-valuation, see s 18 and notes.
5 *Irving v Manning* (1847) 1 HL Cas at 305; but it is now usual to provide that the insured value is to be taken as the repaired value; see Clause 19 of the Institute Time Clauses (Hulls), Appendix III, p 187, post and Clause 17 of the Institute Voyage Clauses, Appendix III, p 205, post; *Helmville Ltd v Yorkshire Insurance Co Ltd, The Medina Princess* [1965] 1 Lloyd's Rep 361, QB (Commercial Court), where the assured failed to prove that the vessel was a constructive total loss, and was held to be entitled to claim for a partial loss only.
6 See s 29.
7 *Lewis v Rucker* (1761) 2 Burr 1167, see p 1171 (partial loss); cf *Irving v Manning* (1847) 1 HL Cas at 305; *Lidgett v Secretan* (1871) LR 6 CP at 627, per Willes J.

8 *Irving v Manning* (1847) 1 HL Cas at 307. The same principle applies to a partial loss (see eg *Goole and Hull Steam Towing Co v Ocean Marine Insurance Co* [1928] 1 KB 589), but in an insurance on goods evidence of the real value must be given in order to fix the percentage of damage suffered by the subject-matter insured, *Arnould*, para 435.
9 Cf *Burnand v Rodocanachi* (1882) 7 App Cas at 335, per Lord Selborne.
10 *Herring v Janson* (1895) 1 Com Cas at 177, 178; cf *The Main* [1894] P 320 at 325; and see Report of Commission on Unseaworthy Ships 1874, vol 2, p xvi, and Memorandum by Willes J, p 426.
11 *Ionides v Pender* (1874) LR 9 QB 531.
12 *Irving v Richardson* (1831) 2 B & Ad 193.
13 *Thompson v Reynolds* (1857) 26 LJQB 93; cf *Xenos v Fox* (1868) LR 3 CP at 636 to like effect.
14 *Bruce v Jones* (1863) 32 LJ Ex 132; *Arnould*, para 435; and see s 32 (double insurance).
15 *Barker v Janson* (1868) LR 3 CP 303; cf *The Main* [1894] P 320 (freight).
16 *North of England Iron SS Insurance Association v Armstrong* (1870) LR 5 QB 244; doubted, *Burnand v Rodocanachi* (1882) 7 App Cas at 342, and see at 335, and also *Yorkshire Insurance Co Ltd v Nisbet Shipping Co Ltd* [1961] 2 All ER 487 at 494. But see *Thames and Mersey Marine Insurance Co v British and Chilian SS Co* [1916] 1 KB 30, 21 Com Cas 150, CA, and cf s 81 as to under-insurance, and note to s 79 (subrogation).
17 See s 77 (2).
18 *Lidgett v Secretan* (1871) LR 6 CP 616; cf *Arnould*, para 1117.
19 *Denoon v Home and Colonial Assurance Co* (1872) LR 7 CP 341.
20 *The Main* [1894] P 320. See also *Papadimitriou v Henderson* [1939] 3 All ER 908, KB ('anticipated freight' insured for £3,500, plaintiff entitled to recover).
21 *Muirhead v Forth Mutual Insurance Association* [1894] AC 72, HL.
22 *Woodside v Globe Marine Insurance Co Ltd* [1896] 1 QB 105.
23 *SS Balmoral v Marten* [1900] 2 KB 748; affd [1902] AC 511, HL.
24 *Irving v Manning* (1847) 1 HL Cas 287.

28. Unvalued policy

An unvalued policy is a policy which does not specify the value of the subject-matter insured, but, subject to the limit of the sum insured, leaves the insurable value to be subsequently ascertained, in the manner hereinbefore specified.[1]

Note

As to insurable value, see s 16 and as to the measure of indemnity, see ss 68–71, and as to under-insurance, see s 81.

Unvalued policies are found only rarely.[2]

1 *Irving v Manning* (1847) 1 HL Cas at 307.
2 For an example see *Berger and Light Diffusers Pty Ltd v Pollock* [1973] 2 Lloyd's Rep 442, QBD (Commercial Court), which concerned some steel injection moulds. (See the judgment of Kerr J, ibid, at 459.)

29. Floating policy by ship or ships

(1) A floating policy is a policy which describes the insurance in general terms, and leaves the name of the ship or ships and other particulars to be defined by subsequent declaration.[1]

(2) The subsequent declaration or declarations may be made by endorsement on the policy, or in other customary manner.

(3) Unless the policy otherwise provides, the declarations must be made in the order of despatch or shipment. They must, in the case of goods, comprise all consignments within the terms of the policy,[2] and the value of the goods or other property must be honestly stated, but an omission or erroneous declaration may be rectified even after loss or arrival, provided the omission or declaration was made in good faith.[3]

(4) Unless the policy otherwise provides, where a declaration of value is not made until after notice of loss or arrival, the policy must be treated as an unvalued policy as regards the subject-matter of that declaration.[4]

Note

The legality of the practice of effecting floating policies was affirmed in England in 1794.[5]

When two or more floating policies effected with different insurers are open, it was formerly held that the assured had a right to declare on any of the policies a loss on board any ship he pleased that came within the terms of that policy, but sub-s (3) apparently negatives this rule.[6]

Floating policies are now commonly effected 'to follow and succeed,' ie, the prior policy must be exhausted before the next policy is declared on.[7]

As to open covers,[8] see W Gow, *Marine Insurance: A Handbook*, (5th ed, 1931) p 233; *Arnould*, para 165.

Illustration

Floating policy on goods, declarations of interest to be made to insurers' agents 'as soon as possible'. The ship sailed from Liverpool on 21 August, and was destroyed by fire on 12 September. The declaration was made on 13 September. *Held*, that this was too late and that the assured could not recover under the policy.[9]

1 As to the practice in effecting floating policies, see *Arnould*, paras 274–278.
2 *Dunlop Bros v Townend* [1919] 2 KB 127 (omission to declare consignments covered by government insurance).
3 *Stephens v Australasian Insurance Co* (1872) LR 8 CP 18; *Imperial Marine Insurance Co v Fire Insurance Corpn* (1879) 4 CPD 166; cf *Davies v National Insurance Co of New Zealand* [1891] AC at 491 (form of policy requiring double declaration). Cf *Halsbury's Laws of England*, 4th edn, vol 25, para 108; and see *Scott v Globe Marine Insurance Co* (1896), 1 Com Cas 370 (declaration of goods not intended to be covered by policy).
4 *Gledstanes v Royal Exchange Assurance Corpn* (1864) 34 LJQB 30, 35. Special clauses as to valuation in event of loss or arrival before declaration are now usually inserted.
5 *Kewley v Ryan* (1794) 2 Hy Bl 345, 3 RR 400.
6 Cf *Arnould*, para 278.
7 *Arnould*, para 274; cf *Inglis v Stock* (1885) 10 App Cas at 269.
8 For an example, see *Reinhart Co v Joshua Hoyle & Sons Ltd* [1961] 1 Lloyd's Rep 346, QB (Commercial Court) (insurance of cotton against all risks).
9 *Union Insurance Society of Canton Ltd v Wills & Co* [1916] 1 AC 281 at 287, 21 Com Cas 169, PC.

30. Construction of terms in policy

(1) A policy may be in the form in the First Schedule to this Act.[1]
(2) Subject to the provisions of this Act, and unless the context of the policy otherwise requires, the terms and expressions mentioned in the First Schedule to this Act shall be construed as having the scope and meaning in that schedule assigned by them.[2]

Note

The policy which is set out in Sch 1 is the old form of Lloyd's policy. It has now been replaced by a new form[3] which is intended to be used with the relevant Institute Clauses.[4]

A new form of policy has also been adopted by marine insurance companies,[5] and to it are attached the relevant Institute Clauses.[6]

It would be beyond the scope of an Act of Parliament to attempt to reproduce the many decisions which interpret particular terms in particular policies.

But the rules in the Schedule record the interpretation which has been put on the more important terms and expressions in the old form of Lloyd's policy. This may assist the parties to see the scope and effect of any policy, and to add or alter its terms to meet their special requirements.

In sub-s (2) the words 'Subject to the provisions of this Act' were added in the Commons Committee, and the word 'may' was altered into 'shall'. The object of the first amendment was to make the provisions of the Act prevail in case of discrepancy.

1 For a case where the policy was not in the Lloyd's form, but was the company's own form, see *Russell v Provincial Insurance Co Ltd* [1959] 2 Lloyd's Rep 275, QB (Commercial Court).
2 See the main rules for the policy's construction in Sch I, post. See the section discussed by Lord Sumner, *British and Foreign Marine Insurance Co v Gaunt* [1921] 2 AC 41 at 59, 26 Com Cas 247 at 261, HL.
3 See Appendix II, pp 160–162, post.
4 See Appendix III, pp 166–276, post.
5 See Appendix II, pp 163–165, post.
6 See Appendix III, pp 166–276, post.

31. Premium to be arranged

(1) Where an insurance is effected at a premium to be arranged, and no arrangement is made, a reasonable premium is payable.
(2) Where an insurance is effected on the terms that an additional premium is to be arranged in a given event, and that event happens but no arrangement is made, then a reasonable additional premium is payable.

Note

This section was not really covered by any express decision, but it accords with business understanding, and follows the analogy of 'reasonable price' in the case of contracts of sale.[1] What is a reasonable premium, or an additional premium, is a question of fact; see s 88.

48 The policy

Policies are often effected on the terms that a deviation or a change of voyage or an error in description or a breach of a warranty shall be 'held covered at a premium to be arranged'.[2] 'Arranged' means 'agreed to, or in default of arrangement, fixed by an arbitrator or by the Court'.[3]

Notice of the deviation must be given within a reasonable time after the assured has knowledge of it.[4] Notice need not be given before loss and delay may be excused if earlier notice would have been of no benefit to the insurers.[5] The deviation clause will not cover a deviation altering the risk which was intended at the time the insurance was effected and was not disclosed.[6]

The Institute Cargo Clauses (A), Clause 10 provides for an additional premium to be payable where there is a change of voyage.[7]

The Institute Time Clauses (Hulls), Clause 1 concerns the payment of an additional premium in case of any breach of warranty as to cargo, trade locality, towage, salvage services or date of sailing.[8] The Institute Time Clauses (Freight), Clause 4,[9] and the Institute Voyage Clauses (Freight), Clause 3[10] are in the same terms.

Under the Institute Voyage Clauses (Hulls), Clause 2 an additional premium is payable where there is a deviation, a change of voyage or any breach of warranty as to towage or salvage services.[11]

1 *Chalmers' Sale of Goods Act 1979*, (18th ed, 1982), pp 101–103.
2 Cf *Hyderabad (Deccan) Co v Willoughby* [1899] 2 QB at 235 (deviation); *Greenock SS Co v Maritime Insurance Co* [1903] 1 KB 367 at 374 (any breach of warranty or unprovided risk); *Hewitt Bros v Wilson* [1914] 3 KB 1131: affd (1915) 20 Com Cas 241, CA ('any incorrect definition of the interest insured,' second-hand machinery described as 'machinery'); *Liberian Insurance Agency Inc v Mosse* [1977] 2 Lloyd's Rep 560 ('omission or error in description of interest vessel or voyage': enamelware). For deviation, see s 46. For change of voyage, see s 45. For description of subject-matter, see s 26. For warranties, see ss 33–41.
3 *Liberian Insurance Agency Inc v Mosse* [1977] 2 Lloyd's Rep 560 at 569 (per Donaldson J).
4 *Thames and Mersey Marine Insurance Co v Van Laun & Co* (1905), [1917] 2 KB 48n, 23 Com Cas 104, HL; *Hood v West End Motor Car Packing Co* [1917] 2 KB 38, 23 Com Cas 112, CA.
5 *Mentz, Decker & Co v Maritime Insurance Co* (1909); 15 Com Cas 17 (clause provided for due notice to *be given*); *Hewitt v London General Insurance Co* (1925) 23 Ll L Rep 243.
6 *Laing v Union Marine Insurance Co* (1895) 1 Com Cas 11.
7 See Appendix III, p 245, post. The Institute Cargo Clauses (B), Clause 10 (see Appendix III, p 253, post) and the Institute Cargo Clauses (C), Clause 10 are in the same terms.
8 See Appendix III, p 167, post.
9 See Appendix III, p 216, post.
10 See Appendix III, p 226, post.
11 See Appendix III, p 196, post.

DOUBLE INSURANCE

32. Double insurance

(1) Where two or more policies are effected by or on behalf of the assured on the same adventure and interest or any part thereof, and the sums

insured exceed the indemnity allowed by this Act, the assured is said to be over-insured by double insurance.¹

(2) Where the assured is over-insured by double insurance—
   (a) The assured, unless the policy otherwise provides, may claim payment from the insurers in such order as he may think fit, provided that he is not entitled to receive any sum in excess of the indemnity allowed by this Act;²
   (b) Where the policy under which the assured claims is a valued policy, the assured must give credit as against the valuation, for any sum received by him under any other policy without regard to the actual value of the subject-matter insured;³
   (c) Where the policy under which the assured claims is an unvalued policy he must give credit, as against the full insurable value, for any sum received by him under any other policy;⁴
   (d) Where the assured receives any sum in excess of the indemnity allowed by this Act, he is deemed to hold such sum in trust for the insurers, according to their right of contribution among themselves.⁵

Note

As regards valued policies, see the illustrations to s 27, and see s 80, as to contribution between insurers. As to under-insurance, see s 81.

As regards unvalued policies the following case may be put in illustration. Suppose a merchant to have effected insurance for £30,000 by one policy, and £20,000 by another, on cotton, and that the insurable value of the cotton on board is £40,000, and the loss on it £4000. He can recover the whole £4000, and a return of premium on £10,000, just as if he had one policy for £50,000; but he may at his option claim under one policy three-fifths and under the other policy two-fifths of this total; or he may claim the whole sum under either policy as if the other did not exist.

There is very little English authority on the rules relating to 'double insurance,' but the subject is clearly discussed in W Gow, *Marine Insurance: A Handbook* (5th ed 1931), pp 90–3.

Insurance is a contract of indemnity, and the assured is entitled to indemnity, but not to a gambling profit. Correlatively, the insurer must not make a profit where he runs no risk. Hence, the rules as to return of premium detailed in s 84. The English rule that the same subject-matter may be differently valued in different policies, while the valuation in a policy is conclusive for the purposes of that policy, gives rise to curious anomalies in working out the rules of double insurance under valued policies; see s 27.

There appears to be no decision as to overlapping policies. Suppose a ship is insured from A to B, and thirty days while there after arrival, and is also insured at and from B to C. If she is lost at B during the thirty days, she is doubly covered.⁶

Different assured. The question which arises when the same subject-matter is fully insured by persons who have different interests in it, eg mortgagor and mortgagee, or bailor and bailee, was discussed by Mellish LJ, in a case on a fire policy, where both the merchant and the wharfinger insured the same goods against fire. The goods were destroyed by fire, and it was held that the loss must be wholly borne by the wharfinger's insurers, as the wharfinger was liable to the merchant.

The Lord Justice said: 'The rule is perfectly established in the case of a marine policy that contribution only applies where it is an insurance by the same person having the same rights, and does not apply where different persons insure in respect of different rights. The reason of that is obvious enough. Where different persons insure the same property in respect of their different rights, they may be divided into two classes. It may be that the interest of the two between them makes up the whole property, as in the case of tenant for life and remainderman. Then if each insures, although they may use words apparently insuring the whole property, yet they would recover from their respective insurance companies the value of their own interests, and, of course, those values added together would make up the value of the whole property. Therefore it would not be a case either of subrogation or contribution, because the loss would be divided between the two companies in proportion to the interests which the respective persons assured had in the property. But then there may be cases where, although two different persons insured in respect of different rights, each of them can recover the whole, as in the case of a mortgagor and mortgagee. But wherever that is the case, it will necessarily follow that one of these two has a remedy over against the other, because the same property cannot in value belong at the same time to two different persons. Each of them may have an interest which entitles him to insure for the full value, because in certain events—for instance, if the other person become insolvent—it may be he would lose the full value of the property, and therefore would have in law an insurable interest; but yet it must be that if each recover the full value of the property from their respective offices with whom they insure, one office must have a remedy against the other. I think whenever that is the case, the company which has insured the person who has the remedy over succeeds to his right of remedy over, and then it is a case of subrogation.'[7]

1 Cf *North British and Mercantile Insurance Co v London, Liverpool and Globe Insurance Co* (1877) 5 Ch D at p 583, CA; *Arnould*, para 409.
2 *Newby v Reed* (1763) 1 WM Bl 416 (Lord Mansfield); *Morgan v Price* (1849) 4 Exch 615.
3 *Bruce v Jones* (1863) 1 H & C 769; *Halsbury's Laws of England*, 4th edn, vol 25, para 335.
4 As to insurable value, see s 16.
5 This is consequential. See s 80 supplementing this provision, and *Arnould*, para 433.
6 See the point raised in argument in *Union Marine Insurance Co v Martin* (1866) 35 LJCP 181, where the second policy superseded the first.
7 *North British and Mercantile Insurance Co v London, Liverpool and Globe Insurance Co* (1877) 5 Ch D at 583; *American Surety Co of New York v Wrightson* (1910) 16 Com Cas at 45–46. See further Ivamy, *General Principles of Insurance Law* (6th ed, 1993), pp 518–522, and see s 79, as to subrogation, and s 80, as to contribution.

WARRANTIES ETC

33. Nature of warranty

(1) A warranty, in the following sections relating to warranties,[1] means a promissory warranty, that is to say, a warranty by which the assured

undertakes that some particular thing shall or shall not be done, or that some condition shall be fulfilled, or whereby he affirms or negatives the existence of a particular state of facts.

(2) A warranty may be express or implied.[2]

(3) A warranty, as above defined, is a condition which must be exactly complied with, whether it be material to the risk or not. If it be not so complied with, then, subject to any express provision in the policy, the insurer is discharged from liability as from the date of the breach of warranty, but without prejudice to any liability incurred by him before that date.[3]

Note

The use of the term 'warranty' as signifying a condition precedent is inveterate in marine insurance, but it is unfortunate because in other branches of the law of contract the term has a different meaning. For example, in relation to the law of sale of goods it signifies a collateral stipulation, the breach of which gives rise merely to a claim for damages and not to a right to avoid the contract.

Again, in marine insurance the term is used to denote two wholly different kinds of stipulations. First, it is used to denote a condition to be fulfilled by the assured. Secondly, it is used to denote a mere limitation on, or an exception from, the general words of the policy. Thus, in the case of the warranty 'free from capture and seizure' the assured does not undertake that the ship or cargo shall not be captured. There is merely a stipulation that the policy shall not apply to such a loss, and the provisions of ss 33(3) and 34 are inapplicable. In the case of a promissory warranty, exact compliance is necessary. Substantial compliance is insufficient.[4]

It is often said that breach of a warranty makes the policy void. But this is not so. A void contract cannot be ratified, but a breach of warranty may be waived.[5] When a breach of warranty is proved, the insurer is discharged from further liability, unless the assured proved that the breach has been waived.

Discharge from liability is automatic: it is not dependent on any decision by the insurer to treat the policy as at an end.[6]

The Institute Clauses contain provisions which hold the assured covered in the event of a breach of warranty at a premium to be arranged.[7]

Thus, the Institute Time Clauses (Hulls), Clause 3[8] states: 'Held covered in case of any breach of warranty as to cargo, trade, locality, towage, salvage services or date of sailing, provided notice be given to the Underwriters immediately after receipt of advices and any amended terms of cover and any additional premium required by them be agreed.'

The Institute Voyage Clauses (Hulls), Clause 2[9] states: 'Held covered in case of . . . any breach of warranty as to towage or salvage services, provided notice be given to the Underwriters immediately after receipt of advices and any amended terms of cover and any additional premium required by them be agreed.'

The onus of proving a breach of warranty lies on the insurer.[10]

Illustrations

1. A ship is warranted to sail from L with 'fifty hands or upwards'. She sails from L with a crew of forty-six only, but afterwards takes on six more hands. The insurer is not liable.[11]

52 Warranties etc

2. A ship is insured from New York to Quebec, whilst there, and thence to London, and is warranted to sail from Quebec on or before 1 November. The ship sails from New York too late to arrive at Quebec by 1 November, and is lost before reaching that port. The insurer is liable.[12]
3. Policy on ship, with warranty not to be in Gulf of St. Lawrence after 15 November. After 15 November the ship is wrecked in the Gulf. The assured gives notice of abandonment, and the insurer with knowledge of the facts, accepts the notice. The insurer is liable, having waived the breach of warranty.[13]
4. Policy on ship with warranty that 'all arrangements for the conversion of the vessel so that she could carry cattle have been made at the inception of this insurance.' The insurance had been effected on 13 December, but only a tentative undertaking had been given by the ship repairers for the work of conversion. The insurers were discharged from liability because the warranty had not been exactly complied with, for 'all arrangements' meant that the ship repairers were *contractually* bound to carry out the work.[14]
5. Policy on tins of canned pork with warranty that all tins were marked by manufacturers with a code for verification of date of manufacture. A large number of tins were incorrectly marked. The insurer was held to be discharged from liability on the ground of breach of warranty.[15]
6. Policy on ship. 'Warranted German flag, ownership and management.' In fact, the ship was owned by a Panamanian corporation and its beneficial owner was a French national. Vessel struck by Exocet missile in war between Iraq and Iran in 1984. *Held*, the insurers were not liable for the damage because there had been a breach of warranty.[16]
7. Policy on ship. 'Warranted no other insurance is or shall be expected to operate during currency of policy.' A managing owners' interest insurance policy was effected. The vessel was subsequently lost. *Held*, a breach of warranty discharging the insurers from liability.[17]

1 See ss 34–41 as to warranties. The warranty may be either a condition precedent or a condition subsequent: *Union Insurance Society of Canton Ltd v Wills & Co* [1916] 1 AC 281, 21 Com Cas 169, PC.
2 *Quebec Marine Insurance Co v Commercial Bank of Canada* (1870) LR 3 PC 234.
3 *Pawson v Watson* (1778) 2 Cowp 785; *De Hahn v Hartley* (1786) 1 Term Rep 343; *Blackhurst v Cockell* (1789) 3 Term Rep 360, Buller J. As to the final words of proviso, see *Simpson SS Co v Premier Underwriting Association* (1905) 10 Com Cas 198 (intention to break warranty no breach). Cf s 20 (4) as to 'representations' which need only be 'substantially' complied with. Cf *Yorkshire Insurance Co v Campbell* [1917] AC 218 (misdescription in policy of insured horse's pedigree).
4 In the cases it is often said that a warranty must be 'literally' complied with. The Lords Committee substituted 'exactly' for 'literally' in the Bill.
5 Cf s 34(3) as to waiver.
6 *Bank of Nova Scotia v Hellenic Mutual War Risk Association (Bermuda) Ltd, The Good Luck* [1991] 3 All ER 1, HL.
7 As to the payment of an additional premium, see s 31(2).
8 See Appendix III, p 169, post.
9 See Appendix III, p 196, post.
10 *Simons v Gale, The Cap Tarifa* [1957] 2 Lloyd's Rep 485, Supreme Court of New South Wales; affd [1958] 2 All ER 504, PC.
11 *De Hahn v Hartley* (1786) 1 Term Rep 343, 1 RR 221.
12 *Baines v Holland* (1855) 10 Exch 802.

13 *Provincial Insurance Co v Leduc* (1874) LR 6 PC 224. See s 34 (3) as to waiver.
14 *Simons (trading as Acme Credit Services) v Gale* [1958] 2 All ER 504, PC.
15 *Overseas Commodities Ltd v Style* [1958] 1 Lloyd's Rep 546, QB (Commercial Court).
16 *Seavision Investment SA v Evennett and Clarkson Puckle Ltd, The Tiburon* [1990] 2 Lloyd's Rep 418, QB (Commercial Court).
17 *Outhwaite v Commercial Bank of Greece SA, The Sea Breeze* [1987] 1 Lloyd's Rep 372, QB (Commercial Court).

34. When breach of warranty excused

(1) Non-compliance with a warranty is excused when, by reason of a change of circumstances, the warranty ceases to be applicable to the circumstances of the contract, or when compliance with the warranty is rendered unlawful by any subsequent law.[1]

(2) Where a warranty is broken, the assured cannot avail himself of the defence that the breach has been remedied, and the warranty complied with, before loss.[2]

(3) A breach of warranty may be waived by the insurer.[3]

Note

The reported cases assume that there is no distinction between the effects of an express and an implied warranty. But an implied warranty may, of course, be negatived by the terms of the policy e g the implied warranty of seaworthiness in a voyage policy may be negatived by the 'unseaworthiness and unfitness exclusion' clause.[4]

As to a change of circumstances excusing compliance with a warranty, suppose a ship is warranted to sail on or before a particular day, but owing to the outbreak of war she has to wait for a convoy. Probably in that case the policy never attaches.[5] On the other hand, a ship may be warranted to sail with convoy, but if peace is made, the warranty becomes inapplicable.

Compliance with a warranty will be rendered unlawful if there is a declaration of war by England for this operates as an Act of Parliament prohibiting all trading with the enemy.[6]

The implied warranty set out in s 41[7] that the adventure insured is a lawful one and that, so far as the assured can control the matter, the adventure shall be carried out in a lawful manner, is a warranty which an insurer cannot waive.[8]

Illustrations

1. Policy on ship. Ship insured 'at and from Montreal to Halifax'. She sailed from Montreal with a defective boiler which was only discovered when she reached salt water. She had to return to Montreal for repairs which were effected. She then sailed again from Montreal, and was lost at the mouth of the river St Lawrence. The insurers were not liable for the assured could not avail himself of the defence that the breach of warranty of seaworthiness on sailing from Montreal on the first occasion had been remedied.[9]
2. Policy on ship. Warranty that she should be laid up between 16 November and 30 April. She subsequently became a total loss, and the insurers repudiated liability on the ground of breach of warranty. *Held* that, on the evidence, the breach had been waived and the insurers were liable.[10]

3. Policy on ship. Warranty that 'Captain C T Chism shall be the master except in the event of emergency.' The ship was a total loss at a time when he was not her master. *Held*, there was then no emergency. The insurers successfully pleaded that the warranty had been breached. On the evidence, the breach had not been waived.[11]

1 See *Arnould*, para 677; and see notes to s 41.
2 *De Hahn v Hartley* (1786) 1 Term Rep 343 (express warranty); *Quebec Marine Insurance Co v Commercial Bank of Canada* (1870) LR 3 PC 234 (implied warranty).
3 See *Quebec Marine Insurance Co v Commercial Bank of Canada* (1870) LR 3 PC at 244; *Provincial Insurance Co v Leduc* (1874) LR 6 PC at 243; *Daneau v Laurent Gendron Ltée: Union Insurance Society of Canton Ltd (Third Party)* [1964] 1 Lloyd's Rep 220, Exchequer Ct, Quebec Admiralty District; *Capital Coastal Shipping Corpn and Bulk Towing Corpn v Hartford Fire Insurance Co (United States of America, Third Party), The Cristie* [1975] 2 Lloyd's Rep 100, Dist Ct for the Eastern Dist of Virginia, Norfolk Division. The maxim of the law is *cuilibet licet renunciare juri pro se introducto*.
4 As to this clause, see p 242, post.
5 See *Hore v Whitmore* (1778) 2 Cowp 784 (effect of embargo). *Union Insurance Society of Canton Ltd v Wills & Co* [1916] 1 AC 281, 287, 21 Com Cas 169, PC: *Yorkshire Insurance Co v Campbell* [1917] AC 218, PC (policy on horse from Sydney to Fremantle— misdescription of horse's pedigree).
6 *Esposito v Bowden* (1857) 7 E & B 763, 779, Ex Ch; cf *Horlock v Beal* (1916) 21 Com Cas 201 at 216, HL; and notes to s 91.
7 See p 63, post.
8 *Gedge v Royal Exchange Assurance Corpn* [1900] 2 QB 214.
9 *Quebec Marine Insurance Co v Commercial Bank of Canada* (1870) LR 3 PC 234.
10 *Daneau v Laurent Gendron Ltée: Union Insurance Society of Canton Ltd (Third Party)* [1964] 1 Lloyd's Rep 220, Exchequer Ct, Quebec Admiralty District. (See the judgment of Arthur I Smith J, ibid, at p 223.)
11 *Capital Coastal Shipping Corpn and Bulk Towing Corpn v Hartford Fire Insurance Co (United States of America, Third Party), The Cristie* [1975] 2 Lloyd's Rep 100, Dist Ct for the Eastern Dist of Virginia, Norfolk Division. (See the judgment of Hoffman DJ, ibid, at 107.)

35. Express warranties

(1) An express warranty may be in any form of words from which the intention to warrant is to be inferred.[1]

(2) An express warranty must be included in, or written upon, the policy, or must be contained in some document incorporated by reference into the policy.[2]

(3) An express warranty does not exclude an implied warranty, unless it be inconsistent therewith.[3]

Note

The following are instances of express warranties which have been the subject of judicial interpretation:
'Warranted [50] per cent, uninsured.'[4]
'Warranted no other insurance which includes total loss of vessel.'[5]
'Warranted, no iron or ore in excess of registered tonnage.'[6]

'Warranted not to sail for North America after 15 August.'[7]
'Warranted no St Lawrence between 1 October and 1 April.'[8]
'Warranted not to proceed east of Singapore.'[9]
'Sailing on or after 1 March.'[10]
'Warranted all tins marked by manufacturers with a code for verification of date of manufacture.'[11]
'Warranted all arrangements for conversion [of vessel] made at inception of this insurance.'[12]
'Warranted German flag, ownership and management.'[13]
'Period of Lay-up—Warranted that the vessel is to be laid up and out of commission between 16 November and 30 April.'[14]
'Warranted no contraband of war.'[15]
'No mining timber carried.'[16]
'Warranted the master of the insured vessel shall be Captain C T Chism.'[17]
'Warranted subject to satisfactory survey by approved surveyors.'[18]
'Warranted class maintained.'[19]

Various express warranties are contained in the Institute Clauses.

Thus, by the Institute Time Clauses (Hulls), Clause 1,[20] the Institute Voyage Clauses (Hulls), Clause 1,[21] and the Institute Time Clauses (Freight), Clause 1[22] and the Institute Voyage Clauses (Freight), Clause 1:[23] 'It is warranted that the Vessel shall not be towed, except as is customary or when in need of assistance or undertake towage or salvage services under a contract previously arranged by the Assured and/or Owners and/or Managers and/or Charterers . . .'

The Institute Time Clauses (Hulls), Clause 21[24] contains a disbursements warranty.

1 *De Hahn v Hartley* (1786) 1 Term Rep 343; *Behn v Burness* (1863) 32 LJQB 204, 205; *Bentsen v Taylor* [1893] 2 QB at 281, CA. In *F B Walker & Sons Inc v Valentine* [1970] 2 Lloyd's Rep 429, US Ct of Appeals, Fifth Circuit, the Court found it unnecessary to decide whether or not a clause stating: 'It is agreed that when this vessel is tied up and moored, it shall be at all times in charge of a watchman in the employ of the assured, whose duty it shall be to make careful examination of the vessel throughout at reasonable intervals, including inspection of the bilges,' had the status of a warranty under Mississippi law, but held that, on the facts, there had been no compliance with the clause. (See the judgment of Brown Ch J, ibid, at pp 432–433.)
2 *Bean v Stupart* (1778) 1 Doug KB 11, 12n.
3 *Quebec Marine Insurance Co v Commercial Bank of Canada* (1870) LR 3 PC 234; *Sleigh v Tyser* [1900] 2 QB 333 (seaworthiness); approved and followed in *Petrofina SA of Brussels v Compagnia Italiana Transporto Olii Minerali of Genoa* (1937) 42 Com Cas 286, CA. As to the implied warranty of seaworthiness, see s 39.
4 *Roddick v Indemnity Mutual Marine Insurance Co Ltd* [1895] 2 QB 380 (subsequent 'honour' policy); *General Insurance Co of Trieste v Cory* [1897] 1 QB 335 (insolvency of insurer).
5 *Outhwaite v Commercial Bank of Greece SA, The Sea Breeze* [1987] 1 Lloyd's Rep 372, QB (Commercial Court).
6 *Hart v Standard Marine Insurance Co Ltd* (1889) 22 QBD 499, CA ('iron' includes steel).
7 *Cochrane v Fisher* (1835) 1 Cr M & R 809, Ex Ch (time policy).
8 *Birrell v Dryer* (1884) 9 App Cas 345, HL.
9 *Simpson SS Co v Premier Underwriting Association* (1905) 10 Com Cas 198.
10 *Sea Insurance Co v Blogg* [1898] 1 QB 27; affd [1898] 2 QB 398, CA (what is a 'sailing'?). As to sailing warranties, see further, *Arnould*, paras 694–696, and Ivamy, *Marine Insurance* (4th ed, 1985), pp 282–285.

56 *Warranties etc*

11 *Overseas Commodities Ltd v Style* [1958] 1 Lloyd's Rep 546, QB (Commercial Court).
12 *Simons (trading as Acme Credit Services) v Gale* [1958] 2 All ER 504, PC.
13 *Seavision Investment SA v Evennett and Clarkson Puckle Ltd, The Tiburon* [1990] 2 Lloyd's Rep 418, QB (Commercial Court).
14 *Daneau v Laurent Gendron Ltée: Union Insurance Society of Canton Ltd (Third Party)* [1964] 1 Lloyd's Rep 220, Exchequer Court, Quebec Admiralty District.
15 *Yangtze Insurance Association v Indemnity Mutual Marine Assurance Co* [1908] 2 KB 504, CA (applies only to goods, not to persons such as belligerent officers). As to the 'analogues of contraband', ie belligerent passengers or despatches, see W E Hall, *A Treatise on International Law* (8th ed), 1924, by A P Higgins, Pt IV, Ch VI.
16 *Aktieselskabet Grenland v Janson* (1918) 35 TLR 135.
17 *Capital Coastal Shipping Corpn and Bulk Towing Corpn v Hartford Fire Insurance Co (United States of America, Third Party), The Cristie* [1975] 2 Lloyd's Rep 100, Dist Ct for the Eastern Dist of Virginia, Norfolk Division.
18 *M Almojil Establishment v Malayan Motor and General Underwriters (Private) Ltd, The Al-Jubail IV*, [1982] 2 Lloyd's Rep 637, Singapore Court of Appeal.
19 *Pindos Shipping Corpn v Raven, The Mata Hari* [1983] 2 Lloyd's Rep 449.
20 See Appendix III, p 167, post.
21 See Appendix III, p 196, post.
22 See Appendix III, p 215, post.
23 See Appendix III, p 225, post.
24 See Appendix III, p 188, post.

36. Warranty of neutrality

(1) Where insurable property, whether ship or goods, is expressly warranted neutral, there is an implied condition that the property shall have a neutral character at the commencement of the risk, and that, so far as the assured can control the matter, its neutral character shall be preserved during the risk.[1]

(2) Where a ship is expressly warranted 'neutral' there is also an implied condition that, so far as the assured can control the matter, she shall be properly documented, that is to say, that she shall carry the necessary papers to establish her neutrality, and that she shall not falsify or suppress her papers, or use simulated papers. If any loss occurs through breach of this condition the insurer may avoid the contract.[2]

Note

The implied conditions may, of course, be negatived or varied by the terms of the particular express warranty.

The conditions of maritime commerce and war have altered so much that it would be misleading to attempt to deduce any rule from the numerous decisions at the beginning of the last century as to the effect of the warranty to sail with convoy.[3] As to carrying contraband of war, see note to s 41.

Illustrations

1. Policy on a Dutch ship warranted neutral, at and from A to B. After the ship sails war breaks out between England and Holland, and the ship is captured by the English. There is no breach of the warranty of neutrality.[4]

2. Policy on goods. Ship and goods belong to the same owner, and are both warranted Danish (ie neutral). The master commits a breach of the laws of neutrality by forcibly resisting search, and the ship and goods are captured and condemned as prize. The assured cannot recover under the policy.[5]
3. Policy on goods from America to England with leave to carry simulated papers. The ship and goods are, in fact, American, but she carries irregularly simulated British papers, and is captured by a privateer belonging to a State at war with England, and is condemned on the ground of having false papers. The insurer is liable.[6]

1 *Arnould*, paras 699–701, and Ivamy, *Marine Insurance* (4th ed, 1985), pp 287–288.
2 *Arnould*, paras 699–701. As to documents, see *Trinder v Thames and Mersey Marine Insurance Co* [1898] 2 QB at 128 per Collins LJ; and as to simulated papers, see *Arnould*, para 700.
3 See *Arnould*, para 695, and Ivamy, *Marine Insurance* (4th ed, 1985), p 286.
4 *Eden v Parkison* (1781) 2 Doug KB 732, per Lord Mansfield.
5 *Garrels v Kensington* (1799) 8 Term Rep 230.
6 *Bell v Bromfield* (1812) 15 East 364.

37. No implied warranty of nationality

There is no implied warranty as to the nationality of a ship, or that her nationality shall not be changed during the risk.[1]

Note

But suppose the assured changes the nationality of his ship, and thereby exposes her to risk of hostile capture? Possibly in that case the loss would be attributed to the act of the assured rather than to the capture.

As to express warranty of neutrality, see s 36.

1 *Dent v Smith* (1869) LR 4 QB 414, 449 (policy on goods, nationality of ship changed on day after insurance); cf *Clapham v Cologan* (1813) 3 Camp 382 (Spanish ship, *Tres Hermanas* described by broker as the *Three Sisters*). Cf *Associated Oil Carriers Ltd v Union Insurance Society of Canton Ltd* [1917] 2 KB 184 (policy on freight just before war, ship had been chartered to a German).

38. Warranty of good safety

Where the subject-matter insured is warranted 'well' or 'in good safety' on a particular day, it is sufficient if it be safe at any time during that day.[1]

Note

This section must obviously be read subject to s 18 as to disclosure of facts known to the assured before the contract is concluded. Cf Sch I, r 1 ('lost or not lost').

1 *Blackhurst v Cockell* (1789) 3 Term Rep 360 (ship).

39. Warranty of seaworthiness of ship

(1) In a voyage policy there is an implied warranty that at the commencement of the voyage the ship shall be seaworthy for the purpose of the particular adventure insured.[1]

(2) Where the policy attaches while the ship is in port, there is also an implied warranty that she shall, at the commencement of the risk, be reasonably fit to encounter the ordinary perils of the port.[2]

(3) Where the policy relates to a voyage which is performed in different stages, during which the ship requires different kinds of or further preparation or equipment, there is an implied warranty that at the commencement of each stage the ship is seaworthy in respect of such preparation or equipment for the purposes of that stage.[3]

(4) A ship is deemed to be seaworthy when she is reasonably fit in all respects to encounter the ordinary perils of the seas of the adventure insured.[4]

(5) In a time policy there is no implied warranty that the ship shall be seaworthy at any stage of the adventure, but where, with the privity of the assured, the ship is sent to sea in an unseaworthy state, the insurer is not liable for any loss attributable to unseaworthiness.[5]

Note

The implied warranty that the ship is seaworthy, attaches to every voyage policy, whether on ship, freight, cargo, profits, commission, or any other interest.[6] It may, of course, be negatived by the terms of the policy, eg by the 'unseaworthiness and unfitness exclusion' clause;[7] and it is usual to pay 'innocent shippers' as a matter of honour.[8]

The warranty applies only to the commencement of the voyage, or, as the case may be, of each distinct 'stage' of the voyage. At one time it was thought that the omission to employ a pilot, at any 'stage' of the voyage where pilotage was compulsory, constituted unseaworthiness, but that doctrine was subsequently disapproved.[9]

Lord Wensleydale, speaking of a voyage policy, said that a ship was seaworthy when she was in a fit state, 'as to repairs, equipment, and crew, and in all other respects, to encounter the ordinary perils of the voyage insured at the time of sailing upon it'.[10]

The state of seaworthiness is a relative and not an absolute one. It must be determined with reference to the particular voyage and adventure in contemplation. As the Privy Council said, 'There is seaworthiness for the port, seaworthiness in some cases for the river, and seaworthiness in some cases (as in a case which has been put forward of a whaling voyage) for some definite, well-recognised, and distinctly separate stage of the voyage.'[11]

So, too, a ship may be seaworthy in herself, but not seaworthy for the purpose of the particular adventure eg, carrying deck cargo.[12] On the other hand, if the insurer knows the nature of the risk, it is sufficient if every reasonable precaution is taken.[13]

Sub-section (3) was redrafted in the Commons Committee. It originally provided, in accordance with the older *dicta*, that the ship must be seaworthy, ie, seaworthy in all respects, at the commencement of each 'stage,' but having regard to the implied coaling warranty in the case of round voyages, it was narrowed to its present form.

There is no implied warranty that the lighters in which the goods are landed shall be seaworthy.[14]

Sub-section (5) is declaratory of the Common Law. 'Where a ship is sent to sea in a state of unseaworthiness in two respects, the assured being privy to the one and not privy to the other, the insurer is only protected if the loss was attributable to the particular unseaworthiness to which the assured was privy.'[15]

The words 'with the privity of the assured' in this subsection mean 'with his knowledge and consent'.[16]

Evidence of unseaworthiness. The burden of proving unseaworthiness ordinarily lies on the insurer,[17] but cases may arise where the maxim *res ipsa loquitur* would apply.[18]

In *Anderson v Morice*[19] the insurance was on a cargo of rice. The ship sank while loading at her moorings in the river near Rangoon in ordinary weather. Evidence was given that the ship had been recently overhauled and repaired. The jury found that she was seaworthy, and the court refused to disturb the verdict.

In *Pickup v Thames Insurance Co*[20] the insurance was on freight. The vessel left Rangoon and met with heavy weather. Eleven days after sailing she had to put back, and was then found to be strained and unseaworthy. *Held*, that these facts did not establish the presumption of unseaworthiness when she sailed. It was a question for the jury.

In *Ajum Goolam Hossen & Co v Union Marine Insurance Co*[21] the insurance was on cargo. The ship capsized and sank twenty-four hours after leaving Port Louis, but there was no evidence to explain why she did so. Some evidence was given tending to show that the ship was seaworthy when she started. *Held*, that unseaworthiness was not made out.

In *Capital Coastal Shipping Corpn and Bulk Towing Corpn v Hartford Fire Insurance Co (United States of America, Third Party), The Cristie*,[22] where a tug was insured under a time policy and sank in port in calm water, the District Court for the Eastern District of Virginia, Norfolk Division, held that the presumption that she was unseaworthy had not been satisfactorily rebutted by the assured.

Mixed policy. The warranty of seaworthiness implied by s 39 also applies in the case of a 'mixed policy'.[23]

Illustrations

1. **Ship.** Policy on ship from Montreal to Halifax. At the time the ship sailed there was a defect in her boiler. The defect did not appear in the river, but disabled her when she got out to sea. She put back to port, and the defect was repaired. Afterwards she proceeded on her voyage, and was lost in bad weather. She was unseaworthy at the commencement of the voyage, and the insurer is not liable.[24]
2. Voyage policy on ship. Steamer, built for inland navigation in Trinidad, is insured from the Clyde to Trinidad. In a heavy sea in the Atlantic she is lost. With the exercise of reasonable care she might have been made fit for the ocean voyage. The insurer is not liable.[25]

3. Policy on ship on *round voyage* from England to port or ports in South America, with liberty to call at any ports, and back again to England. The ship calls at Montevideo, but neglects to take on sufficient coal to bring her to St. Vincent, her next port, so that some of her fittings and cargo have to be burnt as fuel. For coaling purposes this voyage is necessarily divided into 'stages'. When she leaves Montevideo, she is not seaworthy as to her coaling equipment, and the loss incurred by burning the fittings and cargo cannot be recovered under the policy.[26]
4. Time policy on ship. As she is nearing port the master imprudently, and through bad seamanship, throws his ballast overboard, thus making her unseaworthy. Before the ship reaches port she is struck by a squall and capsizes. The insurer is liable.[27]
5. Time policy on ship, 'lost or not lost,' is effected in London in November, but to take effect from 25 September. On 24 September the ship was in the Indian Ocean badly damaged, but the assured did not know this when he effected the policy. The insurer is liable.[28]
6. Time policy on ship lying in her owner's yard. She is sent to sea in an unseaworthy condition, and lost. The owner did not know she was unseaworthy. The insurer is liable.[29]
7. Time policy on ship. Wooden-hulled vessel sent to sea in an unseaworthy state by reason of the hazardous condition by an increase in her gasoline carrying capacity from 3,000 to 8,000 gallons, and by reason of an alteration in the method of discharging the gasoline. The assured were privy to her being sent to sea in such a condition. She was subsequently lost as a result of an explosion and a fire. The insurers were held to be entitled to avoid liability.[30]
8. Time policy on profits, disbursements, etc, in respect of ship. She is sent to sea with an insufficient crew, with the knowledge of the managing owner who effects the policy. She is lost at sea owing to previous damage to her hull which the assured did not know of. The assured can recover, as he was not privy to the unseaworthiness which caused the loss.[31]
9. **Goods.** Voyage policy on 'wine in casks on or under deck'. The wine is all stowed on deck. The effect of this is to endanger the safety of the ship in rough weather, unless the wine is jettisoned, but the wine is so stowed as to be easily jettisoned. The ship meets with bad weather in the Bay of Biscay, and the wine is jettisoned. The ship was not seaworthy at the time of sailing, and the insurer is not liable.[32]
10. Policy on copper at and from port H and port N to S. At H 150 tons are loaded, and at N 250 tons more are loaded. The additional load is too heavy for the ship, she sinks, and the copper is lost. The insurers are liable for the first 150 tons, but not for the second load of 250 tons.[33]
11. **Freight.** Voyage policy on freight. The ship, being badly damaged, has to put into a port of distress, and the cargo is sent on in a substituted ship which is lost. There is, it seems, no implied warranty that the substituted ship is seaworthy.[34]

---

1 *Biccard v Shepherd* (1861) 14 Moo PCC at 493. As to the foundation of the rule, see *Christie v Secretan* (1799) 8 Term Rep 192 at 198, per Lawrence J.
2 *Quebec Marine Insurance Co v Commercial Bank of Canada* (1870) LR 3 PC at 241; cf *Haughton v Empire Marine Insurance Co* (1866) LR 1 Ex Ch 206 (overlapping policies).

3 *Bouillon v Lupton* (1863) 33 LJCP at 43; *Quebec Marine Insurance Co v Commercial Bank of Canada* (1870) LR 3 PC at 241; *The Vortigern* [1899] P 140, CA (coals); *Greenock SS Co v Maritime Insurance Co* [1903] 2 KB 657, CA (insufficient coal); *Northumbrian Shipping Co Ltd v E Timm & Son Ltd* [1939] 2 All ER 648, 56 LQR 9, HL (same doctrine applied in an affreightment case). As to damage to cargo by bad stowage, see *The Thorsa* (1916) 22 Com Cas 218, 221, CA (affreightment).
4 *Dixon v Sadler* (1839) 5 M & W at 414; *Bouillon v Lupton* (1864) 33 LJCP at 43. This includes manning, equipment, and stowage. As to 'perils of the seas,' see Sch I, r 7.
5 *Fawcus v Sarsfield* (1856) 6 E & B 192; *Dudgeon v Pembroke* (1877) 2 App Cas 284, HL; *Mountain v Whittle* [1921] 1 AC 615, HL (house-boat dragged by too powerful tug to dock for repair). As to the proviso, see *Thomas v Tyne and Wear Insurance Association* [1917] 1 KB 938 at 941.
6 *Daniels v Harris* (1874) LR 10 CP at 5; cf *Knill v Hooper* (1857) 26 LJ Ex 377, 379 (policy on salvage of abandoned ship); *Biccard v Shepherd* (1861) 14 Moo PCC at 494 (goods). As to the additional warranty in case of goods, see s 40 (2).
7 *Cantiere Meccanico v Janson* [1912] 3 KB 452, CA. For the clause, see p 242, post.
8 But cf *Sleigh v Tyser* [1900] 2 QB at 336, where the shipper was partly to blame.
9 *Law v Hollingworth* (1797) 7 Term Rep 160; disapproved, *Dixon v Sadler* (1839) 5 M & W at 408; *Sadler v Dixon* (1841) 8 M & W at 900, Ex Ch. See also *Phillips v Headlam* (1831) 2 B & Ad at 383.
10 *Dixon v Sadler* (1839) 5 M & W at 414.
11 *Quebec Marine Insurance Co v Commercial Bank of Canada* (1870) LR 3 PC at 241. And see per Collins MR, in *The Vortigern* [1899] P at 160, CA.
12 *Daniels v Harris* (1874) LR 10 CP 1 (policy on wine stowed on deck).
13 *Burges v Wickham* (1863) 33 LJQB 17 (river steamer sent across the sea to her destination); *Cantiere Meccanico v Janson* [1912] 3 KB 452, CA (floating dock sent to Brindisi, seaworthiness admitted).
14 *Lane v Nixon* (1866) LR 1 CP 412.
15 *Thomas v Tyne and Wear Insurance Association* [1917] 1 KB 938 at 941, per Atkin J; and see *George Cohen, Sons & Co v Standard Marine Insurance Co Ltd* (1925) 30 Com Cas 139 at 158.
16 *Compania Maritima San Basillo SA v Oceanus Mutual Underwriting Association (Bermuda) Ltd, The Eurysthenes* [1976] 2 Lloyd's Rep 171 at 179, CA (per Lord Denning). (See also the judgment of Roskill LJ, ibid at 184, and that of Geoffrey Lane LJ ibid, at 188.)
17 *Pickup v Thames Insurance Co* (1878) 3 QBD 594, CA. See further, Ivamy, *Marine Insurance* (4th ed, 1985), p 298.
18 *Pickup v Thames Insurance Co* (1878) 3 QBD at 600, per Lord Esher; *Lindsay v Klein* [1911] AC at 204, HL (general average).
19 (1875) LR 10 CP 58, 609; affd on this point (1876) 1 App Cas at 752.
20 (1878) 3 QBD 594, CA; distinguished in *R Silcock & Sons Ltd v Maritime Lighterage Co Ltd* (1937) 57 Ll L Rep 78, CA.
21 [1901] AC 362, PC.
22 [1975] 2 Lloyd's Rep 100. (See the judgment of Hoffman DJ, ibid, at 105.)
23 *M Almojil Establishment v Malayan Motor and General Underwriters (Private) Ltd, The Al-Jubail IV* [1982] 2 Lloyds Rep 637, Singapore Court of Appeal (see the judgment of Lai J, ibid, at 640). As to 'mixed policies,' see p 40, ante.
24 *Quebec Marine Insurance Co v Commercial Bank of Canada* (1870) LR 3 PC 234. See p 52, ante.
25 *Turnbull v Janson* (1877) 3 Asp Mar Cas 433, CA. *Aliter*, if all reasonable means had been used, *Burges v Wickham* (1863) 3 B & S 669; *Clapham v Langton* (1864) 5 B & S 729, Ex Ch.
26 *Greenock SS Co v Maritime Insurance Co* [1903] 1 KB 367; affd [1903] 2 KB 657, CA and following *The Vortigern* [1899] P 140 (contract of affreightment). See also *Northumbrian Shipping Co Ltd v E Timm & Son Ltd* [1939] 2 All ER 648 HL (the 'stage' of the voyage

must be determined before sailing; the availability of coal at some intermediate port cannot be taken into account). As to insurance of round voyage, see *Kynance Sailing Ship Co Ltd v Young* (1911) 16 Com Cas at 128.
27 *Dixon v Sadler* (1839) 5 M & W 414; affd (1841) 8 M & W 895. This would equally apply to a voyage policy: ibid.
28 *Gibson v Small* (1853) 4 HL Cas 353.
29 *Dudgeon v Pembroke* (1877) 2 App Cas 284.
30 *Pacific Queen Fisheries v L Symes, The Pacific Queen* [1963] 2 Lloyd's Rep 201, US Ct of Appeals, Ninth Circuit.
31 *Thomas v Tyne and Wear Insurance Association* [1917] 1 KB 938, 22 Com Cas 239, 241; cf *Thomas v London and Provincial Marine Insurance Co* (1914) 30 TLR 595, CA as to insufficient crew.
32 *Daniels v Harris* (1874) LR 10 CP 1.
33 *Biccard v Shepherd* (1861) 14 Moo PCC 471.
34 *De Cuadra v Swann* (1864) 16 CBNS 772, 3rd plea.

40. No implied warranty that goods are seaworthy

(1) In a policy on goods or other moveables there is no implied warranty that the goods or moveables are seaworthy.[1]

(2) In a voyage policy on goods or other moveables there is an implied warranty that at the commencement of the voyage the ship is not only seaworthy as a ship, but also that she is reasonably fit to carry the goods or other moveables to the destination contemplated by the policy.[2]

Note

Under a voyage policy the shipper, equally with the shipowner, is responsible for the seaworthiness of the ship. See note to last section, and for definition of 'moveables,' see s 90.

Questions of unseaworthiness frequently arise in cases between shipper and shipowner; but such cases must be applied with caution in insurance law. A ship may be seaworthy as between shipowner and insurer on ship, though unseaworthy as between shipowner and shipper of a particular cargo, eg frozen meat, which requires special freezing apparatus, but does not affect the safety of the ship.[3] Again, the warranty as to goods may apply at a different time from the warranty as to ship, eg where goods are shipped at an intermediate port.

Suppose a ship is insured from Malta to London. She calls at Gibraltar, and there takes on board a consignment of apes for the London Zoological Gardens. If the apes are insured, the ship must, for the purposes of the policy on apes, be reasonably fit (ie, in the matter of appliances) to carry the animals safely to their destination, ie she must be 'ape-worthy' as well as being seaworthy qua ship. This implied warranty is usually included in the warranty of seaworthiness, but that seems rather a strain upon language, and it is better to regard the warranty as an additional warranty by the assured on goods.

In practice, the policy usually contains an 'unseaworthiness and unfitness exclusion' clause nullifying the effect of s 40(2). The clause states: 'The underwriters waive any breach of the implied warranties of seaworthiness of the ship and fitness of the ship to carry the subject-matter insured to destination, unless the assured or their servants are privy to such unseaworthiness or unfitness.'[4]

Illustration

Policy on goods. Cotton was insured 'at and from Liverpool to Oporto'. Some of the cargo was lost overboard by perils insured against. The insurers repudiated liability on the ground that the vessel had sailed in an unseaworthy condition in that she was improperly stowed with all the light cargo in the hold and the heavy cargo on deck, thus tending to make her top-heavy. On the evidence, however, the vessel was not unseaworthy and the insurers were liable.[5]

1 *Koebel v Saunders* (1864) 33 LJCP 310 (coconut oil); cf *Boyd v Dubois* (1811) 3 Camp 133.
2 Cf *The Maori King* [1895] 2 QB 550, 558, CA (frozen meat); *Stanton v Richardson* (1874) LR 9 CP 390 (affreightment).
3 Cf *The Maori King* [1895] 2 QB 550, 558, CA.
4 See Institute Cargo Clauses (A), Clause 5, Appendix III, p 242, post; Institute Cargo Clauses (B), Clause 5, Appendix III, p 251 post; Institute Cargo Clauses (C), Clause 5, Appendix III, p 258, post.
5 *Blackett, Magalhaes and Colombie v National Benefit Assurance Co* (1921) 8 Ll L Rep 293, CA.

41. Warranty of legality

There is an implied warranty that the adventure insured is a lawful one, and that, so far as the assured can control the matter, the adventure shall be carried out in a lawful manner.[1]

Note

'Where a voyage is illegal, an insurance upon such a voyage is invalid. Thus, during the [Peninsular] War policies on vessels sailing in contravention of the Convoy Acts were held void, so too when the voyage was against the East India Company Acts, or the general Navigation Act, which statutes were made with reference to the general policy of the realm.'[2]

A contract to do a thing which cannot be done without a violation of the law is void, whether the parties know the law or not. But if a contract is capable of being performed in a legal manner, it is necessary to show clearly the intention to perform it in an illegal manner to enable the insurer to avoid it.[3]

An insurance on enemies' goods or against British capture is illegal. See notes to s 91(2), and see further, notes to s 3 (lawfulness of adventure) and s 4 (wager policies).

Contraband of war. The term 'contraband of war' in a marine policy applies only to goods. It does not extend to persons, e g officers of a belligerent power, though carrying them exposes the ship to capture.[4] 'It is well settled,' said Farwell LJ, 'that the carrying of contraband in time of war between two belligerents, both of whom are at peace with this country, is legitimate trading, although the trader runs the risk of capture, and of the condemnation of the contraband store, and in many (if not all) cases of his ship also.'[5]

If, in a policy on goods, there is a warranty, 'no contraband,' the whole policy may be avoided if any part of the goods are contraband.[6]

Illustrations

1. Time policy on ship. The master, with the connivance of the owner, engages in smuggling. The ship is arrested in England. The insurer is not liable.[7]
2. Policy on freight, from a British port abroad to Liverpool. The master, unknown to the owner, stows a part of the cargo (timber) on deck, and sails without a certificate from the clearing office, thereby contravening the Customs Consolidation Act 1853. The timber is lost by perils of the seas. The assured can recover under the policy.[8]
3. Policy on a French ship, effected in England, capture and seizure being among the perils insured against. After the policy is effected war breaks out between France and England, and the ship is captured by a British cruiser. The assured cannot recover under the policy.[9]
4. Builders' risk policy. The assured operates an unlawful business in carrying on boat building at his yard when forbidden to do so pursuant to the byelaws and regulations of the local authority. He cannot recover under the policy.[10]

---

1 *Arnould*, para 743, and Ivamy, *Marine Insurance* (4th ed, 1985), pp 308–310. *Dudgeon v Pembroke* (1874) LR 9 QB at 586; *Pacific Queen Fisheries v L Symes, The Pacific Queen* [1963] 2 Lloyd's Rep 201, US Ct of Appeals, Ninth Circuit, where the Court declined to express a view as to whether the violation of the Tanker Act (US Code Sect 391a) rendered the voyage illegal. 'Warranty' is not an apt term in this context, in as much as a warranty can be waived, but illegality cannot.
2 *Redmond v Smith* (1844) 7 Man & Gr at 474, per Tindal CJ.
3 *Waugh v Morris* (1873) LR 8 QB 202. The maxim is '*In ambigua voce accipienda est significatio quae vitio caret.*'
4 *Yangtze Insurance Association v Indemnity Mutual Marine Assurance* [1908] 2 KB 504, CA (warranty, no contraband). As to the 'analogues of contraband,' ie belligerent passengers or despatches, see W E Hall, *A Treatise on International Law*, 8th ed, 1924, by A P Higgins, Pt IV, ch VI; and as to contraband generally, whether absolute or conditional, ibid, ch V; and such cases as *The Kronprins Gustaf* [1919] P 182 (conditional contraband, coffee).
5 *Caine v Palace Shipping Co* (1906) 12 Com Cas at 109, CA; cf *Andersen v Marten* [1908] AC 334 at 338, HL.
6 *Seymour v London and Provincial Marine Insurance Co* (1872) 41 LJCP 193 (part of the goods consisted of artillery harness. They were shipped to a neutral port, but with a further hostile destination). As to necessity of disclosure of the risk to insurer, see *Arnould*, para 627 and the terms of s 18. As to contract of affreightment, see *Carver*, paras 807–808.
7 *Pipon v Cope* (1808) 1 Camp 434, as explained, *Trinder v Thames and Mersey Marine Insurance Co* [1898] 2 QB at 129, CA. If the master smuggles without the owners' connivance, it is barratry: *Cory v Burr* (1883) 8 App Cas at 399.
8 *Wilson v Rankin* (1865) LR 1 QB 162, Ex Ch. *Aliter*, if the owner was privy to the illegality: *Cunard v Hyde* (1859) 29 LJQB 6 (policy on goods).
9 *Kellner v Le Mesurier* (1803) 4 East 396, and *Gamba v Le Mesurier* (1803) 4 East 407. See note to s 91(2).
10 *James Yachts Ltd v Thames and Mersey Marine Insurance Co Ltd* [1977] 1 Lloyd's Rep 206, British Columbia, Supreme Court. (See the judgment of Rittan J, ibid, at 212.) The implied warranty of legality in this case was set out in the Marine Insurance Act of British Columbia (RSC c 231), s 43 (which corresponds to the (English) Marine Insurance Act 1906, s 41).

THE VOYAGE

42. Implied condition as to commencement of risk

(1) Where the subject-matter is insured by a voyage policy 'at and from' or 'from' a particular place, it is not necessary that the ship should be at that place when the contract is concluded, but there is an implied condition that the adventure shall be commenced within a reasonable time, and that if the adventure be not so commenced the insurer may avoid the contract.[1]

(2) The implied condition may be negatived by showing that the delay was caused by circumstances known to the insurer before the contract was concluded, or by showing that he waived the condition.[2]

Note

As to the attachment of a policy in the case of 'from' and 'at and from' risks, see Rules 2 and 3 in Sch I. Reasonable time is a question of fact; see s 88.

Where the assured abandons the adventure insured, the contract of marine insurance is determined.[3]

The requirement under s 42 that the adventure must be commenced within a reasonable time appears to be distinct from the requirement under s 48 that the voyage insured must be prosecuted throughout its course with reasonable dispatch.[4]

As to frustration of the adventure, see note to s 60 (constructive total loss).

Illustrations

1. Floating policy on cargo by a particular ship for twelve months from 11 May. A declaration of a cargo of coal having been made under this policy, the insurers, on 2 August, effected a reinsurance of the coal by that ship from the Tyne to Lulea. The vessel did not sail on the insured voyage till 25 September, and was lost with her cargo on 2 October. The reinsurer is not liable on the reinsurance policy, for the delay alters the risk from a summer risk to a winter risk.[5]
2. Policy on goods. 1916–17 tobacco crop insured in June 1917 at and from Sumatra to London and/or ports in Holland, the risk of fire before shipment being included. On 18 July part of the crop was destroyed by fire whilst in store in Sumatra. The insurers repudiated liability on the ground that there had been unreasonable delay in the commencement of the adventure. The claim, however, succeeded for they had accepted an additional premium to cover a period during which the loss occurred, and so were precluded from raising the defence of unreasonable delay.[6]

1 *De Wolf v Archangel Insurance Co* (1874) LR 9 QB 451, 457 (summer risk turned into winter risk), but cf *Halsbury's Laws of England*, 4th edn, vol 25, para 134. For a case where a motor launch was insured for 4½ months while used within a limited radius and a loss was sustained within the limits, and it was held to be a time policy, and not a voyage policy attaching only to voyages to begin and end within the radius and to remain wholly within it, see *Wilson v Boag* [1956] 2 Lloyd's Rep 564, Supreme Court of New South Wales.

2 Before the Act this was a somewhat doubtful proposition.
3 *Grant v King* (1802) 4 Esp 175 (delay of six months, policy not avoided); *Palmer v Fenning* (1833) 9 Bing 460 (delay of four months in case of a yacht, policy avoided); cf *Parkin v Tunno* (1809) 11 East 22 (abandonment of voyage in consequence of war perils); *Nickels v London and Provincial Marine Insurance Co* (1900) 6 Com Cas 15 (abandonment of voyage under apprehension of hostilities); and see illustrations to s 60.
4 As to s 48, see p 70, post.
5 *Maritime Insurance Co v Stearns* [1901] 2 KB 912, 6 Com Cas 182.
6 *Bah Lias Tobacco and Rubber Estates v Volga Insurance Co Ltd* (1920) 3 Ll L Rep 155, 202.

43. Alteration of port of departure

Where the place of departure is specified by the policy, and the ship instead of sailing from that place sails from any other place, the risk does not attach.[1]

Note

By usage, it is said, an intermediate voyage may be interposed, but the evidence of such a usage would have to be very clear.[2] Suppose a ship is insured from London to New York. If she starts from Southampton or Liverpool, it is a wholly different risk. Unless the ship starts from the terminus a quo, it is clear that the risk cannot attach.

1 *Way v Modigliani* (1787) 2 Term Rep 30.
2 Cf *Vallance v Dewar* (1808) 1 Camp 503, 10 RR 738; *Mount v Larkins* (1831) 8 Bing at 121.

44. Sailing for different destination

Where the destination is specified in the policy, and the ship, instead of sailing for that destination, sails for any other destination, the risk does not attach.[1]

Illustrations

1. Policy on ship from Maryland to Cadiz. She cleared from Maryland to Falmouth, and was captured in Chesapeake Bay. The insurers were not liable, for the policy never attached because the voyage which had been commenced was not the one insured.[2]
2. Policy on ship from the Mersey to any port or ports west of Gibraltar. The ship sails from Liverpool for Cartagena, which is east of Gibraltar. The policy does not attach, and a clause authorising a change of voyage does not come into operation.[3]

1 *Sellar v McVicar* (1804) 1 Bos & P NR 23, 8 RR 744; *Simon, Israel & Co v Sedgwick* [1893] 1 QB 303, CA: *Halsbury's Laws of England*, 4th edn, vol 25, para 142.
2 *Woolridge v Boydell* (1778) 1 Doug KB 16.

3 *Simon, Israel & Co v Sedgwick* [1893] 1 QB 303, CA; distinguished in the case of a warranty, *Simpson SS Co v Premier Underwriting Association* (1905) 10 Com Cas 198. As to change of voyage, see s 45.

45. Change of voyage

(1) Where, after the commencement of the risk, the destination of the ship is voluntarily changed from the destination contemplated by the policy, there is said to be a change of voyage.[1]

(2) Unless the policy otherwise provides, where there is a change of voyage the insurer is discharged from liability as from the time of change, that is to say, as from the time when the determination to change it is manifested; and it is immaterial that the ship may not in fact have left the course of voyage contemplated by the policy when the loss occurs.[2]

Note

Three different states of fact must be distinguished. First, the ship may sail on a voyage not contemplated by the policy. In that case the risk does not attach (ss 43 and 44). Secondly, a ship may commence the adventure insured, but afterwards change her destination. There is then a 'change of voyage'. In that case the risk attaches, but is afterwards avoided (s 45). Thirdly, a ship may proceed from the terminus a quo to the terminus ad quem, but sail there by an unauthorised route. In that case there is a deviation (s 46).[3]

A change of voyage must be voluntary, but very clear evidence of force majeure is required in order to continue the insurer's liability when the destination is altered. For instance, 'if the master of the ship of his own accord, or in obedience to the orders of the officers of the Queen, abstains from entering a blockaded port, the causa proxima is, not the blockade, but the voluntary act of the master.'[4] But if a voyage, legal in its inception, becomes illegal by English law before its termination, the assured is justified in changing his destination.[5]

In relation to the insurance of a ship for a voyage the Institute Voyage Clauses (Hulls), Clause 2 states: 'Held covered in a case of . . . change of voyage . . . provided notice be given to the underwriters immediately after receipt of advices and any amended terms of cover and any additional premium required by them be agreed.'[6]

In relation to the insurance of cargo the Institute Cargo Clauses (A), Clause 10 states: 'Where after attachment of this insurance, the destination is changed by the Assured, held covered at a premium and conditions to be arranged subject to prompt notice being given to the Underwriters.'[7]

Illustrations

1. Policy on ship at and from Cadiz to Liverpool. Afterwards, without the consent of the insurer, the destination of the ship is changed to Newfoundland. The ship is stranded and burnt in the Bay of Cadiz. The insurer is discharged from liability.[8]

2. Policy on goods. Cargo insured for carriage by German vessel from South American ports to Hong Kong and Shanghai. The vessel arrived at Rio de Janeiro on 25 August, 1939. War was declared on 3 September. The master sailed from Rio on 6 September in compliance with an order from the German Government to seek refuge in neutral ports or to return to Germany or as a last resort to scuttle themselves. Subsequently she was scuttled off the Faroe Islands to avoid capture by a British warship. The shipowners repudiated liability on the ground that there had been a change of voyage. This defence, however, failed, for the destination contemplated by the policy had not been voluntarily changed.[9]

1 Tudor Mar Cas Ed 3 p 125; *Bottomley v Bovill* (1826) 5 B & C 210; *Simon, Israel & Co v Sedgwick* [1893] 1 QB 303, CA.
2 Ibid; and *Tasker v Cunninghame* (1819) 1 Bligh 87, HL, 20 RR 33.
3 As to the distinction between deviation and change of voyage, see further, *Halsbury's Laws of England*, 4th edn, vol 25, para 143; *Thames and Mersey Marine Insurance Co v Van Laun & Co* (1905), (1917) 23 Com Cas at 110, 111, HL.
4 Per Brett J, in *Rodocanachi v Elliott* (1873) LR 8 CP 649 at 670, cited by Stirling LJ, in *Miller v Law Accident Insurance Co* [1903] 1 KB at 720, 8 Com Cas at 168, CA (restraint of princes); distinguishing cases like *Hadkinson v Robinson* (1803) 3 Bos & P 388; *Nickels v London and Provincial Marine Insurance Co* (1900) 6 Com Cas 15 (abandonment under apprehension of hostilities). But as to blockade, see *Geipel v Smith* (1872) LR 7 QB 404, which, however, was a contract of affreightment where the rule of causa proxima is not so strictly applied (cf *Russian Bank for Foreign Trade v Excess Insurance Co Ltd* (1918) 23 Com Cas at 327).
5 *British and Foreign Marine Insurance Co v Samuel Sanday & Co* [1916] 1 AC 650 (voyage from America to Hamburg—declaration of war with Germany); *Rickards v Forestal Land, Timber and Rlys Co Ltd* [1942] AC 50, [1941] 3 All ER 62, HL.
6 See Appendix III, p 196, post.
7 See Appendix III, p 245. The Institute Cargo Clauses (B), Clause 10 (see Appendix III, p 253, post) and the Institute Cargo Clauses (C), Clause 10 (see Appendix III, p 261, post) are in the same terms.
8 *Tasker v Cunninghame* (1819) 1 Bligh 87, HL, 102.
9 *Rickards v Forestal Land, Timber and Rlys Co Ltd* [1942] AC, 50, [1941] 3 All ER 62, HL. (See the judgment of Lord Wright, ibid, at p 78 and that of Lord Porter, ibid, at p 96).

46. Deviation

(1) Where a ship, without lawful excuse, deviates from the voyage contemplated by the policy, the insurer is discharged from liability as from the time of deviation, and it is immaterial that the ship may have regained her route before any loss occurs.[1]
(2) There is a deviation from the voyage contemplated by the policy—
  (a) Where the course of the voyage is specifically designated by the policy, and that course is departed from;[2] or
  (b) Where the course of the voyage is not specifically designated by the policy, but the usual and customary course is departed from.[3]
(3) The intention to deviate is immaterial; there must be a deviation in fact to discharge the insurer from his liability under the contract.[4]

Note

It is immaterial that the insurer may not be prejudiced by the deviation. As to causes which justify deviation, see s 49. As to liberty to 'touch and stay,' see Sch I, r 6; as to clause authorising deviation at a premium to be arranged, see s 31. Apart from the authority to deviate, a deviation may be waived by the insurer.

In relation to an insurance on a ship the Institute Voyage Clauses (Hulls), Clause 2 states: 'Held covered in case of deviation . . . provided notice be given to the Underwriters immediately after receipt of advices and any amended terms of cover and any additional premium required by them be agreed.'[5]

But no additional premium is required in the case of cargo insurance, for the Institute Cargo Clauses (A), Clause 8 states: 'This insurance shall remain in force . . . during . . . any deviation.'[6]

Illustrations

1. Policy on ship from L to J. There are two routes to J, one going north and the other south of the island of D. Sometimes one route and sometimes the other is the better, and the master ought to exercise his own discretion in each case. The owners direct him to call at a port in the north of the island of D. He therefore takes the northern route, and his ship is captured. This is a deviation.[7]
2. Policy on ship from her 'port of lading in North America to Liverpool'. She loads part of her cargo at K, proceeds to B, which is seven miles away to complete her cargo, and returns to K for provisions, and then sails for England, and is lost on the voyage. The proceeding to B and back again is a deviation, and the insurer is not liable.[8]
3. Insurance on salvage pumps from A to the *SS Alexandra* ashore in the neighbourhood of D, 'and while *there* engaged at the wreck and until again returned to A'. The pumps are lost on the wreck while it is being towed to N, a port of safety. This is a deviation.[9]
4. A vessel bound from Poti in the Black Sea to Sparrows' Point in the USA puts in to Constanza, which is not on her direct geographical route, to take in oil fuel. She strands at Constanza. There is evidence that about a quarter of the oil-burning vessels proceeding from Black Sea ports to the Bosphorus bunker at Constanza. This is not a deviation. Evidence is admissible to show what is the usual, or a usual, route, and if the evidence adduced is sufficient to establish a practice to follow a particular route, proceeding by that route is not a deviation.[10]

1 Cf *Hartley v Buggin* (1781) 3 Doug KB 39, 40, per Lord Mansfield.
2 *Phyn v Royal Exchange Assurance Co* (1798) 7 Term Rep 505; *Tait v Levi* (1811) 14 East 481.
3 *Davis v Garrett* (1830) 6 Bing 716; *Thompson v Hopper* (1856) 26 LJQB at 22; *Morrison v Shaw, Savill and Albion Co* [1916] 2 KB 783, CA. And it may be a deviation to go to a place authorised by the policy, but for a purpose unconnected with the voyage insured: *Hammond v Reid* (1820) 4 B & Ald 72.
4 Cf *Middlewood v Blakes* (1797) 7 Term Rep at 168, 4 RR 409; *Hewitt v London General Insurance Co* (1925) 23 Ll L Rep 243.
5 See Appendix III, p 242, post.
6 See Appendix III, p 245, post. The Institute Cargo Clauses (B), Clause 8 (see Appendix III, p 252, post) and the Institute Cargo Clauses (C), Clause 8 (see Appendix III, p 259, post) are in the same terms.

7 *Middlewood v Blakes* (1797) 7 Term Rep 162.
8 *Brown v Tayleur* (1835) 4 Ad & El 241, 43 RR 331.
9 *Wingate v Foster* (1878) 3 QBD 582; followed in *Difiori v Adams* (1884) 53 LJQB 437.
10 *Reardon Smith Lines Ltd v Black Sea and Baltic General Insurance Co Ltd, The Indian City* [1939] 3 All ER 444, HL. See also *Evans, Sons & Co v Cunard SS Co Ltd* (1902) 18 TLR 374; *Frenkel v MacAndrews & Co Ltd* [1929] AC 545, HL.

47. Several ports of discharge

(1) Where several ports of discharge[1] are specified by the policy, the ship may proceed to all or any of them, but, in the absence of any usage or sufficient cause to the contrary, she must proceed to them, or such of them as she goes to, in the order designated by the policy. If she does not, there is a deviation.[2]

(2) Where the policy is to 'ports of discharge,' within a given area, which are not named, the ship must, in the absence of any usage or sufficient cause to the contrary, proceed to them, or such of them as she goes to, in their geographical order. If she does not there is a deviation.[3]

Note

In a case where three ports of discharge were specified in the policy, Lord Ellenborough said, 'I think that the voyage insured to Palermo, Messina, and Naples meant a voyage to all or any of the places named; with this reserve only, that if the ship went to more than one place, she must visit them in the order described in the policy.'[4]

Illustration

Voyage policy on ship from River Plate 'to any port or ports in France and/or United Kingdom (final port)'. The ship discharges her cargo at St Nazaire and Le Havre, and then sails for Barry and is lost. 'Final port' means the final port of discharge, and when she leaves Le Havre, she is no longer covered by the policy.[5]

1 As to the meaning of 'port' in a policy, see *Hunter v Northern Marine Insurance Co* (1888) 13 App Cas 717, HL; *Kynance Sailing Ship Co Ltd v Young* (1911) 16 Com Cas at 130.
2 *Marsden v Reid* (1803) 3 East 572.
3 Cf *Metcalfe v Parry* (1814) 4 Camp 123; distinguish *Kynance Sailing Ship Co Ltd v Young* (1911) 16 Com Cas 123 (variation of chartered voyage justified by wide terms of policy).
4 *Marsden v Reid* (1803) 3 East at 576.
5 *Marten v Vestey Bros* [1920] AC 307, 25 Com Cas 175, HL (reversing court below).

48. Delay in voyage

In the case of a voyage policy, the adventure insured must be prosecuted throughout its course with reasonable despatch, and, if without lawful excuse it is not so prosecuted, the insurer is discharged from liability as from the time when the delay became unreasonable.[1]

Note

Unjustifiable delay in prosecuting the voyage is sometimes classed under the heading of deviation; but it seems clearer to draw a distinction between time and locality. Reasonable despatch is a question of fact; see s 88.

The Institute Cargo Clauses (A), Clause 8 states: 'This insurance shall remain in force . . . during delay beyond the control of the Assured.'[2]

A positive duty of reasonable dispatch is imposed by Clause 18 which states: 'It is a condition of this insurance that the Assured shall act with reasonable dispatch in all circumstances within their control.'[3]

Illustrations

1. A ship is insured from England to the coast of West Africa, and 'during her stay and trade there,' and back to England. After loading her cargo for the homeward voyage, she delays sailing for a month to salve the cargo of another ship which has been wrecked. On the voyage home she is lost. The assured cannot recover under the policy.[4]
2. Policy on goods. Twine insured against a number of risks including fire for voyage from London to Kavella, Greece. Under normal conditions the goods would have been transhipped at Piraeus to a coasting steamer for carriage to Kavella. Owing to war conditions the only means of forwarding the goods was to consign them to the British Consul at Piraeus, and request him to forward them. The goods were delayed at Piraeus for 3 months whilst awaiting a permit from the British Government. On arrival off Kavella the coasting steamer on which they were loaded was refused permission to land them, so the master decided to take them back to Piraeus to await instructions. On the return voyage they were destroyed by fire. The insurers repudiated liability on the ground that there had been unreasonable delay at Piraeus. The claim, however, succeeded because, on the evidence, the delay was not unreasonable.[5]
3. Policy on goods. Goods insured from interior of Africa and whilst awaiting shipment at Burutu for overseas ports. Owing to war conditions they were stored for 8 months, and were then lost by fire. The insurers repudiated liability on the ground that the delay at Burutu was unreasonable. This defence however failed because, on the evidence, the delay was not unreasonable, in the circumstances prevailing at the time.[6]
4. Mixed policy on ship for 12 months from Singapore to Damman, Saudi Arabia. Vessel encountering heavy weather and putting into Colombo where she was delayed for 79 days to complete non-essential repairs. *Held*, the time spent there was reasonable and there had not been an unreasonable delay.[7]

1 *Company of African Merchants v British Insurance Co* (1873) LR 8 Ex Ch 154, Ex Ch; cf *Schroder v Thompson* (1817) 7 Taunt 462 (delay justified by embargo); *Samuel v Royal Exchange Assurance Co* (1828) 8 B & C 119 (delay in entering port of destination caused by ice *held* justified). Cf *Arnould*, para 490.
2 See Appendix III, p 243, post. The Institute Cargo Clauses ((B), Clause 8 (see Appendix III, p 252, post) and the Institute Cargo Clauses (C), Clause 8 (see Appendix III, p 259, post) are in the same terms.
3 See Appendix III, p 248, post. The Institute Cargo Clauses (B), Clause 16 (see Appendix III, p 256, post) and the Institute Cargo Clauses (C), Clause 16 (see Appendix III, p 263, post) are in the same terms.

4 *Company of African Merchants v British Insurance Co* (1873) LR 8 Ex Ch 154, Ex Ch; and cf *Pearson v Commercial Union Assurance Co* (1876) 1 App Cas 498.
5 *British American Tobacco v Poland* (1921) 7 Ll L Rep 108, CA. (See the judgment of Bankes LJ, ibid, at p 109.)
6 *Niger Co Ltd v Guardian Assurance Co and Yorkshire Insurance Co* (1922) 13 Ll L Rep 75, HL. (See the judgment of Lord Buckmaster, ibid at 76, that of Lord Atkinson, ibid, at 81, and that of Lord Sumner, ibid, at 82.)
7 *M Almojil Establishment v Malayan Motor and General Underwriters (Private) Ltd, The Al-Jubail IV* [1982] 2 Lloyd's Rep 637, Singapore Court of Appeal. (See the judgment of Lai J, ibid, at p 641.) As to 'mixed policies,' see p 40, ante.

49. Excuses for deviation or delay

(1) Deviation or delay in prosecuting the voyage contemplated by the policy is excused—
  (a) Where authorised by any special term in the policy;[1] or
  (b) Where caused by circumstances beyond the control of the master and his employer;[2] or
  (c) Where reasonably necessary in order to comply with an express or implied warranty;[3] or
  (d) Where reasonably necessary for the safety of the ship or subject-matter insured;[4] or
  (e) For the purpose of saving human life, or aiding a ship in distress where human life may be in danger;[5] or
  (f) Where reasonably necessary for the purpose of obtaining medical or surgical aid for any person on board the ship; or
  (g) Where caused by the barratrous conduct of the master or crew, if barratry be one of the perils insured against.[6]

(2) When the cause excusing the deviation or delay ceases to operate, the ship must resume her course, and prosecute her voyage, with reasonable despatch.[7]

Note

In the case of a policy on a ship the Institute Voyage Clauses (Hulls), Clause 2 states: 'Held covered in case of deviation . . . provided notice be given to the Underwriters immediately after receipt of advices and amended terms of cover and any additional premium required by them be agreed.'[8]

In the case of a policy on goods no additional premium is required, for the Institute Cargo Clauses (A), Clause 8 states: 'This insurance shall remain in force . . . during any deviation . . .'[9]

Illustrations

1. Ship insured from Lyons to Galatz. She starts from Lyons on 24 July, properly equipped for the river voyage. She is detained for three weeks at Marseilles to equip herself for the open sea voyage. The delay is justifiable.[10]

2. Ship warranted 'free from capture in port'. To avoid capture she slips her cable before she is ready for sea, and then proceeds to a port out of her direct course to load. She is afterwards wrecked. The insurer is not liable.[11] Sed quo since the Act?
3. Policy on goods. Cargo insured for carriage by German vessel from South American ports to Hong Kong and Shanghai. At the outbreak of the Second World War the German Government ordered her to seek refuge, and her master did so. The deviation was excused under s 49(1)(b) as being beyond the control of the master and his employer.[12]

1 *Puller v Glover* (1810) 12 East 124; *Naylor v Taylor* (1829) 9 B & C 718; *Hyderabad (Deccan) Co v Willoughby* [1899] 2 QB 530.
2 *Elton v Brogden* (1747) 2 Stra 1264 (master forced out of his course by crew); *Delany v Stoddart* (1785) 1 Term Rep 22 (stress of weather); *Rickards v Forestal Land, Timber and Rlys Co Ltd* [1941] 3 All ER 62, HL.
3 Generalised from *Bouillon v Lupton* (1863) 15 CBNS 113 (delay to make ship seaworthy for a particular 'stage' of the voyage).
4 *Arnould*, para 149; *Halsbury's Laws of England*, 4th edn, vol 25, para 149.
5 *Scaramanga v Stamp* (1880) 5 CPD 295, CA. As to master's statutory duty to render salvage services where life is in danger, see Maritime Conventions Act 1911, s 6.
6 *Ross v Hunter* (1790) 4 Term Rep 33. As to barratry, see Sch I, r 11.
7 *Delany v Stoddart* (1785) 1 Term Rep 22, and see s 48.
8 See Appendix III, p 196, post. As to additional premium, see s 31.
9 See Appendix III, p 243, post. The Institute Cargo Clauses (B), Clause 8 (see Appendix III, p 252, post) and the Institute Cargo Clauses (C), Clause 8 (see Appendix III, p 259, post) are in the same terms.
10 *Bouillon v Lupton* (1863) 15 CBNS 113.
11 *O'Reilly v Royal Exchange Assurance Co* (1815) 4 Camp 246, criticised in *Arnould*, para 501. Sub-paragraph (d) perhaps overrules this decision.
12 *Rickards v Forestal Land, Timber and Rlys Co Ltd* (1941) 70 Ll L Rep 173, HL. (See the judgment of Lord Wright, ibid, at 189 and that of Lord Porter, ibid, at 201.)

ASSIGNMENT OF POLICY

50. When and how policy is assignable

(1) A marine policy is assignable unless it contains terms expressly prohibiting assignment.[1] It may be assigned either before or after loss.[2]
(2) Where a marine policy has been assigned so as to pass the beneficial interest in such policy, the assignee of the policy is entitled to sue thereon in his own name; and the defendant is entitled to make any defence arising out of the contract which he would have been entitled to make if the action had been brought in the name of the person by or on behalf of whom the policy was effected.[3]
(3) A marine policy may be assigned by indorsement thereon or in other customary manner.

Note

In practice, policies on goods do not contain clauses prohibiting assignment, for, if they did, international trade would be hampered.

In the case of insurance on a ship the Institute Time Clauses (Hulls), Clause 5 states: 'No assignment of or interest in this insurance or in any moneys which may be or become payable thereunder is to be binding on or recognised by the Underwriters unless a dated notice of such assignment or interest signed by the assured and by the assignor in case of a subsequent assignment is endorsed on the Policy and the Policy assignment is produced before payment of any claim or return of premium thereunder.'[4]

In the case of insurance on freight the same provision is to be found in the Institute Time Clauses (Freight)[5] and the Institute Voyage Clauses (Freight).[6]

Sub-section (2) reproduces the effect of the Policies of Marine Insurance Act 1868, s 1, which is repealed by this Act. That Act in terms only applied to policies on ship, freight, or goods; but it would probably have been held to extend to all marine policies.

Where a policy was effected by an agent in his own name, the person for whose benefit it was effected could always sue on it in his own name.[7] The difficulty arose in the case of an assignee.

Sub-section (3) reproduces the effect of s 2 of the Act of 1868, which, in addition, prescribed an optional form of indorsement. The subsection is permissive in its terms, and a marine policy may be assigned in any way by which an ordinary chose in action may be assigned.[8] It seems that it is not now customary to assign a policy by mere delivery.[9]

Illustrations

1. Action on policy by the assignee under a deed of assignment. The defendant (insurer) cannot set-off a claim against the assignor under another policy.[10]
2. Action on policy on ship by innocent assignee. The defendant (the insurer) may plead non-disclosure of a material fact by the assured (the assignor).[11]

---

1 As to policy prohibiting assignment, see *Arnould*, paras 253, 258; *Laurie v West Hartlepool Indemnity Association* (1899) 15 TLR 486 (mutual insurance association); cf *Pyman v Marten* (1906) 13 Com Cas 64, CA (cancellation of policy if ship transferred to new management).
2 *Sparkes v Marshall* (1836) 2 Bing NC 761; *Lloyd v Fleming* (1872) LR 7 QB 299 (action by executor of assignee); *J Aron & Co Inc v Miall* (1928) 34 Com Cas 18, CA.
3 As to the words 'arising out of the contract,' see *Pellas v Neptune Insurance Co* (1879) 5 CPD 34, CA (set-off no defence); *Pickersgill v London and Provincial Marine Insurance Co* [1912] 3 KB 614 at 621 (non-disclosure); *Black King Shipping Corpn v Massie, The Litsion Pride* [1985] 1 Lloyd's Rep 437, QB (Commercial Court) (fraudulent claim by mortgagee). (See the judgment of Hirst J, ibid, at 519.) As to action by mortgagor in respect of his residuary interest, when mortgagee is satisfied, see *Swan v Maritime Insurance Co* [1907] 1 KB 116, 12 Com Cas at 79, 80. It was held by Greer and Slesser LJJ in *Williams v Atlantic Assurance Co Ltd* [1933] 1 KB 81 at 100, 105 CA, that the words 'the beneficial interest' mean the whole beneficial interest; contra, Scrutton LJ at 97–8.
4 See Appendix III, p 170, post. The Institute Voyage Clauses, Clause 3 (see Appendix III, p 197, post) is in the same terms. As to return of premium, see ss 82–84.
5 Clause 6. (See Appendix III, p 217, post.)
6 Clause 4. (See Appendix III, p 226, post.)
7 *Browning v Provincial Insurance Co of Canada* (1873) LR 5 PC at 272.
8 See Law of Property Act 1925, s 136. For a discussion of this section in its application to policies of marine insurance, see *Williams v Atlantic Assurance Co Ltd*, supra, and *Compania Colombiana de Seguros v Pacific Steam Navigation Co* [1964] 1 All ER 216;

Amalgamated General Finance Co Ltd v C E Golding & Co Ltd [1964] 2 Lloyd's Rep 163, QB (Commercial Court).
9 *Baker v Adam* (1910) 15 Com Cas 227 at 230. See further, *J Aron & Co Inc v Miall* (1928) 34 Com Cas 18. 'On the policy there is an assignment in the ordinary form in which policies are assigned in England, that is to say, the brokers who effected the policy have signed their name and the agent of the first seller has signed his name; and that indorsement in blank according to the custom of marine insurance in England assigns all claims on the policy to the holder of the policy,' per Scrutton LJ at 20.
10 *Baker v Adam* (1910) 15 Com Cas 227. But as to mutual credit in bankruptcy, see the Insolvency Act 1986, s 323.
11 *Pickersgill v London and Provincial Marine Insurance Co* [1912] 3 KB 614.

51. Assured who has no interest cannot assign

Where the assured has parted with or lost his interest in the subject-matter insured, and has not, before or at the time of so doing, expressly or impliedly agreed to assign the policy, any subsequent assignment of the policy is inoperative:[1]

Provided that nothing in this section affects the assignment of a policy after loss.[2]

Note

This section supplements s 15 (assignment of interest).

After loss, the right to indemnity accrues and is fixed, and this right can be assigned. 'It is every day's practice, where a ship has sustained damage, to sell the injured hull for the benefit of whom it concerns, and then sue on the policy. If it can be made out that the loss is total, the sale is for the benefit of the underwriters who pay the total loss. If the loss proves partial only, it is for the benefit of the assured, but no one ever thought of saying that the sale of the damaged hull put an end to the right to recover an indemnity for the partial loss.'[3]

As to the time at which the risk passes from seller to buyer under a contract of sale, see Sale of Goods Act 1979, s 20 (risk) and s 32 (seller's duty to insure).[4] Prima facie, property and risk pass together.

Illustrations

1. A, B, and C each own a third share of a ship. A and B jointly insure their shares under a policy for £500. Afterwards B sells his share to C, but no arrangement is made as to the policy. The ship is lost. Only A's share (£250) can be recovered from the insurer.[5]
2. A, who is abroad, insures a cargo being carried to London, including all risk of craft. While the cargo is afloat, A's agent sells the cargo to B, but A retains the policy, as the cargo is not to be paid for until arrival. Part of the cargo is damaged while being landed in B's lighters. After A's interest has ceased, he assigns the policy to B. B cannot recover under the policy.[6]

1 *North of England Pure Oil Cake Co v Archangel Maritime Insurance Co* (1875) LR 10 QB 249, and cases cited for s 15 as to assignment of interest. As to partial transfers, see *Hibbert v Carter* (1787) 1 Term Rep 745; and as to right of assignors to retain 'increased value policies,' see *Strass v Spillers and Bakers Ltd* [1911] 2 KB 759, 16 Com Cas 166.

76 *Assignment of policy*

2 *Lloyd v Fleming* (1872) LR 7 QB 299, and s 50 (1).
3 *Lloyd v Fleming* (1872) LR 7 QB at 302, per Blackburn J.
4 See Appendix I, pp 158–159, post.
5 *Powles v Innes* (1843) 11 M & W 10.
6 *North of England Pure Oil Cake Co v Archangel Maritime Insurance Co* (1875) LR 10 QB 249.

THE PREMIUM

52. When premium payable

Unless otherwise agreed, the duty of the assured or his agent to pay the premium, and the duty of the insurer to issue the policy to the assured or his agent, are concurrent conditions, and the insurer is not bound to issue the policy until payment or tender of the premium.[1]

Note

The term 'agreed' includes a binding usage, for usage is binding as being an implied term of the agreement: see s 87(1).

Payment, it is to be noted, is not a technical term. It includes a settlement in account when that is the agreed way of doing business. See also note to s 53.

1 Cf *Burges v Wickham* (1863) 33 LJCP at 18, per Blackburn J. As to correcting error in premium by subsequent indorsement on policy, see *Mildred v Maspons* (1883) 8 App Cas at 878. As to issue of policy, see note s 24.

53. Policy effected through broker

(1) Unless otherwise agreed,[1] where a marine policy is effected on behalf of the assured by a broker, the broker is directly responsible to the insurer for the premium, and the insurer is directly responsible to the assured for the amount which may be payable in respect of losses, or in respect of returnable premium.[2]

(2) Unless otherwise agreed,[3] the broker has, as against the assured, a lien upon the policy for the amount of the premium and his charges in respect of effecting the policy;[4] and where he has dealt with the person who employs him as a principal, he has also a lien on the policy in respect of any balance on any insurance account which may be due to him from such person, unless when the debt was incurred he had reason to believe that such person was only an agent.[5]

Note

In a case on an insurance company's policy which, instead of reciting payment of the premium contained a promise by the assured to pay it, it was held that the ordinary custom applied, and the broker, not the assured, was liable to the insurer for the premium.[6]

Collins J, there said, 'A Lloyd's policy contains a recital that the premium has been paid; but supposing that the recital were made in a policy not under seal, so as not to amount to an estoppel; then upon the contract of insurance there would be an obligation upon the person insured to pay the premium. But that obligation is treated as discharged, although it is not discharged in fact; it is considered to be discharged by reason of a fiction based upon a custom which has received judicial sanction. It is a well-recognised practice in marine insurance for the broker to treat himself as responsible to the underwriter for the premium; by a fiction he is deemed to have paid the underwriter, and to have borrowed from him the money with which he pays.'

As to the practice in settling claims and losses, see *Arnould*, para 170.

Illustration

A instructs B, a broker at Hartlepool, to insure his ships. B employs C, another broker at Liverpool, to effect the insurances. C has a lien on the policies for the premiums and charges, even though A may have paid B.[7]

1 See eg *Black King Shipping Corpn v Massie, The Litsion Pride* [1985] 1 Lloyd's Rep 437, QB (Commercial Court), where it was held that, by virtue of the broker's cancelling clause in the policy, the brokers were specifically authorised to receive ordinary premiums on behalf of the insurers, and, by implication, any additional premium. (See the judgment of Hirst J, ibid, at 512.)
2 *Universo Insurance Co of Milan v Merchants' Marine Insurance Co* [1897] 2 QB at 97, 98 (premium); cf *Hine Bros v SS Insurance Syndicate* (1895) 7 Asp MLC 558, CA; *Sweeting v Pearce* (1859) 29 LJCP 265 (losses); *Matveieff v Crossfield* (1903) 8 Com Cas 120. Cf *Arnould*, paras 170–175.
3 *Fairfield Shipping Co v Gardner* (1911) 27 TLR 281 (lien restricted by agreement).
4 *Arnould*, para 162; *Fisher v Smith* (1878) 4 App Cas 1, HL; and cf *Mildred v Maspons* (1883) 8 App Cas at 879; *Hunter v Leathley* (1830) 10 B & C 858 (broker's duty to produce policy at trial).
5 As to lien for general balance, see *Westwood v Bell* (1815) 4 Camp 349; cf *Cahill v Dawson* (1857) 3 CBNS 106; *Juarez v Williams* (3 Feb, 1903), Shipping Gazette. The lien is confined to insurance business, *Dixon v Stansfield* (1850) 10 CB 398; and cf *Elgood v Harris* [1896] 2 QB 491, as to effect of bankruptcy on a set-off. As to loss and revival of lien, see *Near East Relief v King, Chasseur & Co Ltd* [1930] 2 KB 40, 35 Com Cas 104.
6 *Universo Insurance Co of Milan v Merchants' Marine Insurance Co*; affd [1897] 2 QB 93, CA. *Halsbury's Laws of England*, 4th edn, vol 25, para 89 doubts this case since the Act.
7 *Fisher v Smith* (1878) 4 App Cas 1, HL. As to del credere brokerage, see *Caruthers v Graham* (1811) 14 East 578: 'Del Credere' by R S T Chorley (1929) 45 LQR 221.

54. Effect of receipt on policy

Where a marine policy effected on behalf of the assured by a broker acknowledges the receipt of the premium, such acknowledgment is, in the absence of fraud, conclusive as between the insurer and the assured, but not as between the insurer and broker.[1]

Note

The acknowledgment is not conclusive as between the insurer and the broker. Probably then it is not conclusive as between insurer and assured, where the latter effects the policy directly. But it ought to be conclusive in favour of an assignee for value without notice.[2]

1 *Arnould*, para 170, and note to s 53.
2 See further, note to last section, and cf *Roberts v Security Co Ltd* [1897] 1 QB 111 (burglary policy).

LOSS AND ABANDONMENT

55. Included and excluded losses

(1) Subject to the provisions of this Act,[1] and unless the policy otherwise provides, the insurer is liable for any loss proximately caused by a peril insured against, but, subject as aforesaid, he is not liable for any loss which is not proximately caused by a peril insured against.[2]

(2) In particular,—
  (a) The insurer is not liable for any loss attributable to the wilful misconduct of the assured, but, unless the policy otherwise provides, he is liable for any loss proximately caused by a peril insured against, even though the loss would not have happened but for the misconduct or negligence of the master or crew;[3]
  (b) Unless the policy otherwise provides, the insurer on ship or goods is not liable for any loss proximately caused by delay, although the delay be caused by a peril insured against;[4]
  (c) Unless the policy otherwise provides,[5] the insurer is not liable for ordinary wear and tear, ordinary leakage and breakage, inherent vice or nature of the subject-matter insured, or for any loss proximately caused by rats or vermin,[6] or for any injury to machinery not proximately caused by maritime perils.[7]

Note

Proximate Cause Rule. No principle of marine insurance law is better established than the rule *causa proxima, non remota, spectatur*. 'It were infinite,' said Lord Bacon, 'for the law to judge the causes of causes, and their impulsion one of another; therefore it contenteth itself with the immediate cause.'[8]

But though the rule is universally admitted, lawyers have never attempted to work out any philosophical theory of cause and effect, and probably it is as well for commerce that they should not have made the attempt.[9] The numerous decisions on the rule are rough and ready applications of it to particular facts. As might be expected, many of the decisions are difficult to reconcile. But the apparent inconsistencies may be regarded as depending rather on inferences of fact than on matters of law. When there are inter-acting causes of loss, the efficient or 'dominant' cause is deemed to be the proximate cause.[10]

There may be more than one proximate (in the sense of effective or direct) cause of a loss. If one of those causes is insured against under the policy and none of the others is expressly excluded by it, the assured is entitled to recover.[11]

But if the loss is caused by two perils operating at the time of the loss and one is excluded by the policy the insurer is not liable.[12]

Sub-section (2) embodies the more important deductions from the general rule of proximate cause laid down in sub-s (1).

Negligence. As Collins LJ, pointed out, a man may lawfully stipulate against the consequences of his own negligence,[13] and he may stipulate against the consequences of his employees' negligence or misconduct. In the case of negligent or unskilful navigation, it now appears to be settled that the loss is regarded as caused proximately by perils of the seas, and only remotely by the negligence or unskilfulness of the master or crew. But when the loss is consequent on the wilful act or default of the assured, that act or default must be regarded as proximately causing the loss: *Dolus circuitu non purgatur*.[14]

Where, however, a ship is lost through the barratry of the master, who is a part owner, the innocent co-owners are entitled to recover.[15]

Scuttling. Where the insurers allege that a vessel has been scuttled, the matter must be pleaded with particularity so that the assured may know what case he has to meet.[16] But this does not mean that he is entitled to know what evidence will be adduced against him, nor is he entitled to particulars of circumstantial matters from which inferences will be sought to be drawn.[17] He is entitled to have the best particulars available of those circumstances which the insurers will, by direct evidence or by inference, attempt to establish as constituting scuttling.[18]

Delay. As a rule, the insurer is not liable for damage caused by delay, though the delay results from a peril insured against. But difficult cases arise with regard to freight, especially as regards time charters. Where the adventure is frustrated by a peril insured against, and freight is thereby lost, the insurer is liable.[19]

Thus, where a ship was delayed by the operation of perils of the seas, and the charterer justifiably refused to load, it was held to be a loss of freight by perils of the seas.[20]

On the other hand, in another case, a policy was effected 'on freight outstanding'. The ship was hired to the Admiralty, and the charter-party provided that if the ship became inefficient, the charterers might make such abatement out of the freight as they thought fit. The ship struck a rock and became inefficient for a time. The charterers made an abatement from the freight. *Held*, that the insurers were not liable, as the loss was not proximately caused by the perils of the seas, but by the action of the Admiralty.[21]

The line between the principles laid down by these cases is difficult to draw with certainty, and, as a result, special clauses are often inserted to protect the insurer or the assured, as the case may be, from the consequences of delay.[22]

Loss of time freight, resulting from detention for repair of general average damage, is not allowed in general average.[23]

Contracting out of the Act. The parties are entitled to contract out of the provisions of s 55(2)(b) and (c) by inserting appropriate words in the policy. Whether they have effectively done so is a matter of construction.[24]

Apprehended peril. A distinction must be drawn between the actual operation of a peril insured against, and the apprehension of its operation. As Willes J, said

80   Loss and abandonment

in one case, the insurer is not liable for a loss caused by the prudence of the master or owner.[25]

Sale by master. 'It has often been observed,' said Blackburn J, 'that a sale by the master is not one of the underwriter's perils, and is only material as showing that there is no longer anything which can be done to save the thing sold for whom it may concern.'[26]

Illustrations

Goods.—1. Policy on goods, which consist of hides and tobacco. Sea-water is shipped during a storm, which wets the hides. The hides become putrid, and the fumes from them spoil the flavour of the tobacco. The damage to the tobacco is proximately caused by perils of the seas.[27]
2. Policy on cargo warranted 'free from all consequences of hostilities'. During the American Civil War the Confederates extinguish the light on Cape Hatteras. Owing to the absence of the light, the ship runs on to the rocks and is wrecked. The proximate cause of loss is the perils of the seas, and the insurer is liable.[28]
3. Policy on living animals 'warranted free from mortality and jettison.' In a storm some of the animals are so injured as to cause their death. The insurer is liable notwithstanding the warranty.[29]
4. Voyage policy on goods at and from K to Y. While the ship is loading at K, the weight of the cargo brings the discharge pipe below water. In consequence of a valve being negligently left open, water from the discharge pipe gets into the hold and damages the cargo. This is a loss proximately caused by perils of the seas, or other perils of a like kind, for which the insurer is liable.[30]
5. Policy on a parcel of gold shipped by a Russian ship to Turkey. The ship is stranded in Turkey, and the gold taken charge of by the Russian Consul. As the ship is Russian, the Russian Consular Court has jurisdiction, and that court awards salvage charges against the gold which would not be payable by English law. The assured has to pay these charges to get his gold. This is a loss by perils of the seas, for which the insurer is liable.[31]
6. Policy on goods shipped in a French ship. The ship is damaged in a collision, and the master, not having the funds requisite for the necessary repairs, gives a bottomry bond on ship, freight and cargo. The ship and freight not being sufficient to satisfy the bond, the assured has to pay the balance to get his goods. The insurer is not liable. The loss is not caused by perils of the seas, but by the lack of funds on the part of the master.[32]
7. Policy on cargo of fruit warranted free from average 'unless damage be consequent on collision'. The ship is involved in a collision and has to go into port for repairs. The cargo has to be landed and re-shipped, and it is damaged partly by handling and partly by the delay. The collision is not the proximate cause of the damage, and the insurer is not liable.[33]
8. Policy on cargo of rice. Rats gnaw a hole in a pipe which passes through the cargo, and sea-water enters through the hole and damages the rice. The sea damage is the proximate cause of the loss, not the rats.[34]

9. Policy on goods. Soya beans insured for voyage from Surabaja, Indonesia, to Belgium and the Netherlands 'against the risks of heat, sweat and combustion only'. When shipped in bulk it was a natural characteristic that soya beans would deteriorate if the moisture content exceeded 14 per cent. Beans, in fact, shipped with moisture content of between 12 and 13 per cent, thus exposing them to risk of deterioration. Cargo deteriorated and insurers repudiated liability on ground of inherent vice. *Held*, insurers were liable because the policy 'otherwise provided'.[35]
10. Policy on goods. Industrial leather gloves shipped from Calcutta to Rotterdam and on discharge found to be wet, stained, mouldy and discoloured. When they were shipped, they contained excessive moisture. *Held*, the insurers were not liable because the loss was due to inherent vice.[36]

Freight.—11. Policy on freight from New South Wales to Valparaiso. The cargo consists of coal. The coal heats, and is in imminent danger of catching fire. Half of it has to be landed at Sydney. The rest is carried on and delivered. This is a partial loss of freight caused by fire (or other like perils) within the meaning of the policy.[37]
12. Policy on chartered freight for £3,000. The master signs bills of lading without reserving a lien on the cargo as a whole. Part of the goods are jettisoned, and, in consequence, the actual freight received is only £2,400. The assured cannot recover the difference, viz £600, from the insurer, for the proximate cause of this loss was not the perils of the seas, but the form in which the bills of lading were given.[38]

Ship.—13. Policy on ship, with F C & S clause. The master engages in smuggling, and in consequence she is seized by the Spanish revenue authorities. The proximate cause of the loss is the seizure, not the barratry of the master. The insurer is not liable.[39]
14. Time policy on ship. The ship starts on a voyage with insufficient coal, and engages the services of a trawler to tow her to her port of discharge. The owner of the trawler gets judgment for salvage services, which assured has to pay. The steamer met with no extraordinary weather, and might in time have proceeded to her port under sail. The loss is not due to the perils of the seas, but to the insufficiency of coal.[40]
15. Neutral ship carrying contraband of war is damaged by ice. She is captured, and while in charge of a prize crew becomes a total loss. The ship and cargo are afterwards condemned by a Japanese prize court. This is a loss by capture and not by perils of the seas, and if there is an F C & S clause, the insurer is not liable.[41]
16. Policy on ship, 'warranted free from all consequences of hostilities'. She is struck by an enemy torpedo, and badly damaged. She gets into port, but in consequence of bad weather there she strands and is lost. The proximate cause of loss is the torpedo, and the insurer is not liable.[42]
17. Ships sailing in convoy without lights on voyages which are not themselves warlike operations. One ship, *The Petersham*, comes into collision with another ship in the convoy and is lost. Another ship, *The Matiana*, obeying the naval officer's directions, takes a zig-zag course and strikes a hidden reef. These losses are attributable to perils of the seas. The marine, and not the war risk insurers, are liable.[43]

18. Ships sailing without lights under Admiralty orders. One ship comes into collision with a destroyer hunting for submarines. Another ship comes into collision with a warship going to take up escort duty for another convoy. Both losses are attributable to warlike operations, and the war risk, and not the marine, insurers are liable.[44]

19. *The Brendonia* is at anchor. A second ship, requisitioned by the Government, is ordered to go to Southampton for orders. It is the intention of the Government (not yet communicated to the owners of the second ship) to employ her after arrival at Southampton for Army transport purposes. The second ship collides with *The Brendonia*, and the latter becomes a total loss. *Held*, that the second ship is not engaged in a warlike operation; thus the loss of *The Brendonia* falls on the marine, and not the war risk, insurers.[45]

20. *The Coxwold* is sailing in convoy with a cargo of petrol for H.M. forces engaged in the Norwegian campaign. An alteration is ordered in the course of the convoy for half-an-hour to avoid a submarine. No subsequent correction is made for this considerable deviation. Later, an unexpected tidal set carries the ship some miles off her course. She is then damaged by stranding. There is no improper or negligent navigation of the vessel. *Held*, that the loss is the consequence of warlike operations.[46]

21. *The Priam* is requisitioned by the Government and is sailing with a cargo consisting mainly of war material, some of it being deck cargo. She maintains a zig-zag course at high speed to avoid submarines. Heavy weather is encountered. Both ship and cargo are damaged. Some of the damage occurs owing to war-stores carried on deck breaking loose, the remainder being directly caused by the force of wind and sea. *Held*, by the Court of Appeal that all the damage was the consequence of warlike operations. The House of Lords, however, varied this order. Such damage as was caused by the force of wind and sea was not a consequence of warlike operations, even though it would not have occurred if the vessel had not zig-zagged or kept her speed. Thus, some of the damage was, and some was not, a consequence of warlike operations.[47]

22. A ship is intentionally sunk by the master who opens a valve. The proximate cause of the loss is the act of the master, and not the inrush of the water. This is not a loss by perils of the seas.[48]

23. Ketch placed on mud berth. She slipped over and filled with water, and was later raised. No further steps were taken and she gradually deteriorated. *Held*, the assured was not entitled to an indemnity for her eventual deterioration resulted from delay.[49]

24. Defect in vessel consisted of fatigue cracks in a wedge-shaped nozzle joined to the vessel's plate. Defect was one of design. *Held*, loss of vessel not attributable to ordinary wear and tear, and the insurers were liable.[50]

25. Policy on ship. Ship deliberately run aground and set on fire by the master. Insurers proved that the assignees of the policy were privy to these acts. *Held*, that the insurers were not liable for her loss.[51]

---

1 See s 66 as to general average and s 78 ('sue and labour' clause).
2 *De Vaux v Salvador* (1836) 4 Ad & El at 431 (collision); *Jackson v Union Marine Insurance Co* (1874) LR 10 CP at 148, Ex Ch (freight); *Cory v Burr* (1883) 8 App Cas at 398 (barratry); *Reischer v Borwick* [1894] 2 QB at 550, CA (collision); *Trinder v Thames and*

Mersey Marine Insurance Co [1898] 2 QB at 124, CA (negligent navigation); *Brankelow v Canton Insurance Office* [1899] 2 QB 178, 186, CA (loss of freight due to form in which bills of lading were given); *Canada Rice Mills Ltd v Union Marine and General Insurance Co Ltd* [1940] 4 All ER 169, PC (see illustration 2, Sch I, r 7); *Kuehne and Nagel Inc v F W Baiden* [1975] 1 Lloyd's Rep 331, New York Supreme Court (Appellate Division), where a charterer's liability policy did not cover on-deck stowage and damage to cargo. (See the judgment of Judge Steuer, ibid, at 332.)

3 *Thompson v Hopper* (1858) E B & E at 1047, Ex Ch (act of assured himself); *Dixon v Sadler* (1839) 5 M & W 405 (bad seamanship of master); *Lind v Mitchell* (1928) 34 Com Cas 81, CA (insured vessel negligently abandoned by master and crew); *Trinder v Thames and Mersey Insurance Co* [1898] 2 QB 114, CA (negligent navigation by master and co-owner); cf *Price v Union Lighterage Co* (1903) 8 Com Cas at 157 (negligence of lighterman); *The Lapwing* [1940] P 112 (yacht negligently docked so as to be allowed to sit on a dangerous bottom; *held*, that the intervention of those responsible for the docking provided the fortuitous circumstances which entitled the assured to recover for a loss due to a peril ejusdem generis with a peril of the sea, namely, stranding); *Rosa v Insurance Co of the State of Pennsylvania, The Belle of Portugal* [1970] 2 Lloyd's Rep 386, US Ct of Appeals, Ninth Circuit (fire caused by electrician's negligence). This subsection is not qualified by s 78(4) as to 'sue and labour' clause: *British and Foreign Marine Insurance Co v Gaunt* [1921] 2 AC 41 at 65, followed in *Lind v Mitchell* (1928) 34 Com Cas 81 at 91, CA; *Astrovlanis Compania Naviera SA v Linard, The Gold Sky* [1972] 2 Lloyd's Rep 187, QBD (Commercial Court), where the relation between s 55(2)(a) and s 78(4) was considered by Mocatta J, ibid, at 221. See p 128, post.

4 *Tatham v Hodgson* (1796) 6 Term Rep 656 (mortality among slaves); *Taylor v Dunbar* (1869) LR 4 CP 206 (cargo of meat); *Pink v Fleming* (1890) 25 QBD 396 (cargo of fruit); cf *Shelbourne v Law Investment Corpn* [1898] 2 QB at 629 (collision, delay during repairs). See note, post, as to freight. And cf *Hudson v British and Foreign Marine Insurance Co* (1902) 8 Com Cas 6 at 15 (general average).

5 See *E D Sassoon & Co Ltd v Yorkshire Insurance Co* (1923) 16 Ll L Rep 129; *Dodwell & Co Ltd v British Dominion General Insurance Co Ltd* (1918), [1955] 2 Lloyd's Rep 391n; *F W Berk & Co Ltd v Style* [1955] 3 All ER 625; *Biddle, Sawyer & Co Ltd v Walter Peters (Trading as Burose and Peters)* [1957] 2 Lloyd's Rep 339, QB (Commercial Court); *Overseas Commodities Ltd v Style* [1958] 1 Lloyd's Rep 546, QB (Commercial Court); where tins of canned pork were insured under an all risks policy including 'inherent vice,' but the Court held that, having regard to the peculiar nature of the subject-matter, ie a pasteurised and not wholly sterilised pig product, it was inconceivable that the underwriters should, with their eyes open, have accepted liability for loss by inherent vice developing at any time in the future, since such a product must inevitably, if not consumed within a limited period, suffer loss from inherent vice, for, being perishable, it necessarily contained the seeds of its own ultimate destruction (see the judgment of McNair J, ibid, at 560); *Robert A Parente v Bayville Marine Inc and General Insurance Co of America* [1975] 1 Lloyd's Rep 333, New York Supreme Court (Appellate Division), where a boat was insured against 'latent defect,' which was defined by Acting President Judge Hopkins (ibid, at 333) as 'a defect or flaw which could not be discovered by any known or customary test'; *Soya GmbH Mainz Kommanditgesellschaft v White* [1983] 1 Lloyd's Rep 122, HL, where a policy against the risks of heat, sweat and spontaneous combustion only was held to cover the risk of deterioration of soya beans.

6 *The Xantho* (1887) 12 App Cas at 509 (wear and tear, sea damage): *Sassoon v Western Assurance Co* [1912] AC 561, PC (ibid); *Koebel v Saunders* (1864) 33 LJCP 310 (vice propre); *Grant Smith & Co v Seattle Dry Dock Co* [1920] AC 162, PC (dry dock capsizing in port owing to faulty construction); *Wadsworth Lighterage Co v Sea Insurance Co* (1929) 35 Com Cas 1 (barge sinking through general debility); *The Stranna* [1938] 1 All ER 458, CA (loss of deck cargo owing to ship heeling over *held* to be due to a peril of the sea). But note *Greenshields, Cowie & Co v Stephens & Sons* [1908] AC at 435, HL (general average arising out of spontaneous combustion). As to rats, see *Hunter v Potts* (1815) 4 Camp

203; *Laveroni v Drury* (1852) 22 L J Ex 2; but see *Hamilton v Pandorf* (1887) 12 App Cas 518, where the action of the rats was not the proximate cause of the loss.
7   See *Thames and Mersey Marine Insurance Co v Hamilton, Fraser & Co* (1887) 12 App Cas 484, HL; *Stott (Baltic) Steamers v Marten* [1916] 1 AC 304, HL (crane breaking and dropping boiler into hold of ship, damaging the hull).
8   Maxims of the Law, cited *De Vaux v Salvador* (1836) 4 Ad & E 1 at p 431, 43 RR at p 383; *Thompson v Hopper* (1856) 26 LJQB at 22, 23; cf *Greenock SS Co v Maritime Insurance Co* [1903] 1 KB at 374, distinguishing the *causa causans* from the *causa sine qua non*.
9   *Inman SS Co Ltd v Bischoff* (1882) 7 App Cas at 683.
10 *Leyland Shipping Co v Norwich Union Insurance Co* [1918] AC 350 at 363, HL. In *CCR Fishing Ltd v Tomenson, The La Pointe* [1991] 1 Lloyd's Rep 89, Supreme Court of Canada, McLachlin J suggested a different test when she said (at 94): 'It is my view that in determining whether a loss falls within the policy, the cause of the loss should be determined by looking at all the events which gave rise to it and asking whether it is fortuitous in the sense that the accident would not have occurred "but for" or without an act or event which is fortuitous in the sense that it was not to be expected in the ordinary course of things. This approach is preferable, in my view, to the artificial exercise of segregating the causes of the loss with a view to labelling one as proximate and the others as remote, an exercise on which the best of minds may differ.'
11 *JJ Lloyd Instruments Ltd v Northern Star Insurance Co Ltd, The Miss Jay Jay* [1987] 1 Lloyd's Rep 32, CA, where the question was whether damage suffered by a yacht was caused by external accidental means (which were insured against) and also by a faulty design (which was *not* insured against), and it was held that the assured could claim under the policy. (See the judgment of Slade LJ ibid, at 41.)
12 Ibid, at 41 (per Slade LJ); *P Samuel & Co Ltd v Dumas* [1924] AC 431 at 467, HL (per Lord Sumner).
13 *Westport Coal Co v McPhail* [1898] 2 QB at 132.
14 Cf *Trinder v Thames and Mersey Marine Insurance Co* [1898] 2 QB at 127, CA.
15 *Westport Coal Co v McPhail* [1898] 2 QB at 132; and see *Small v United Kingdom Marine Mutual Insurance Association* [1897] 2 QB 311, CA (mortgagor and mortgagee).
16 *Palamisto General Enterprises SA v Ocean Marine Insurance Co Ltd, The Dias* [1972] 2 Lloyd's Rep 60 at 73, CA (per Buckley LJ).
17 Ibid, at 73 (per Buckley LJ).
18 Ibid, at 73 (per Buckley LJ). See also *Astrovlanis Compania Naviera SA v Linard, The Gold Sky* [1972] 1 Lloyd's Rep 331, CA, where, however, an order for particulars of scuttling was not made because the application had been made too late. (See the judgment of Lord Denning MR, ibid, at 333, that of Edmund Davies LJ, ibid, at 338, and that of Stephenson, LJ, ibid, at 339.)
19 See *Re Jamieson* [1895] 2 QB at 95.
20 *Jackson v Union Marine Insurance Co* (1874) LR 10 CP 125, Ex Ch; see, too, *The Alps* [1893] P 109; and *The Bedouin* [1894] P 1, CA, also cases of chartered freight.
21 *Inman SS Co v Bischoff* (1882) 7 App Cas 670. See, to like effect, *Manchester Liners v British and Foreign Marine Insurance Co* (1901) 7 Com Cas 26.
22 See, e g *Bensaude v Thames and Mersey Marine Insurance Co Ltd* [1897] AC 609, HL; *Turnbull, Martin & Co v Hull Underwriters' Association* [1900] 2 QB 402 (warranty, 'free from any claim consequent on loss of time'); *Russian Bank for Foreign Trade v Excess Insurance Co Ltd* [1918] 2 KB 123 ('excluding all claims due to delay'); *Federation Insurance Co of Canada v Coret Accessories Inc and Hirsch (Trading as SA Hirsch & Co)* [1968] 2 Lloyd's Rep 109, Quebec Superior Court, District of Montreal ('warranted free of claim for loss, damage or deterioration arising from delay'); *Naviera de Canarias SA v Nacional Hispanica Aseguradora SA, The Playa de las Nieves* [1977] 1 Lloyd's Rep 457, HL ('warranted free from any claim consequent on loss of time whether arising from a peril of the sea or otherwise'); and clause 14 of the Institute Time Clauses (Freight), Appendix III, p 222, post.

23 *The Leitrim* [1902] P 256; followed and explained in *J H Wetherall & Co Ltd v London Assurance* [1931] 2 KB 448.
24 *Overseas Commodities Ltd v Style* [1958] 1 Lloyd's Rep 546; *Soya GmbH Mainz Kommanditgesellschaft v White* [1983] 1 Lloyd's Rep 122, HL.
25 *Philpott v Swann* (1861) 11 CBNS at 282; *Nickels v London and Provincial Marine Insurance Co* (1900) 6 Com Cas 15; *Kacianoff & Co v China Traders' Insurance Co* [1914] 3 KB 1121, CA (war risk policy, notice by insurer to assured not to continue the contemplated voyage); *Becker, Gray & Co v London Assurance Corpn* [1918] AC 101, 23 Com Cas 205, HL (German captain putting into neutral port, and landing goods there to avoid chance of capture); cf *Watts & Co Ltd v Mitsui & Co Ltd* [1917] AC 227, 22 Com Cas 242, 253, HL (charter-party, apprehended restraint of princes); *Joseph Watson & Co v Fireman's Fund Insurance Co* [1922] 2 KB 355 (imaginary peril, general average).
26 *Rankin v Potter* (1873) LR 6 HL at 122. But the facts justifying the sale may, of course, show a total loss by perils insured against. They must amount to 'stringent necessity': *Cobequid Marine Insurance Co v Barteaux* (1875) LR 6 PC 319, 323. Obviously if a person sells his ship because he gets a good offer for it, or wants ready money, it is no concern of the underwriters. Cf *McCarthy v Abel* (1804) 7 RR 711, 719 (policy on freight, abandonment of ship to insurers). As to assignment of policy after loss, see s 51.
27 *Montoya v London Assurance* (1851) 6 Exch 451.
28 *Ionides v Universal Marine Insurance Association* (1863) 32 LJCP 170. Most of the cargo was destroyed by the sea, but a small part was saved, and a further part could have been saved but for the action of the Confederates, who prevented its being landed. *Held*, as to this part, that the warranty exempted the insurers from liability. Cf *Le Quellec v Thomson* (1916) 115 LT 224 (extinguished light).
29 *Lawrence v Aberdein* (1821) 5 B & Ald 107, 24 RR 299. Mortality = mortality from natural causes; cf *St. Paul Fire and Marine Insurance Co v Morice* (1906) 11 Com Cas 153.
30 *Davidson v Burnand* (1868) LR 4 CP 117.
31 *Dent v Smith* (1869) LR 4 QB 414.
32 *Greer v Poole* (1880) 5 QBD 272; cf *Powell v Gudgeon* (1816) 5 M & S 431 (loss on sale of goods to pay for repairs).
33 *Pink v Fleming* (1890) 25 QBD 396, CA; cf *Field SS Co v Burr* [1899] 1 QB 579, CA. And distinguish *Schloss Bros v Stevens* [1906] 2 KB 665 (insurance against all risks).
34 *Hamilton v Pandorf* (1887) 12 App Cas 518 (bill of lading case, but the principle applies to insurance).
35 *Soya GmbH Mainz Kommanditgesellschaft v White* [1983] 1 Lloyd's Rep 122, HL. (See the judgment of Lord Diplock, ibid, at 126.)
36 *TM Noten BV v Harding* [1990] 2 Lloyd's Rep 283, CA. (See the judgment of Bingham LJ, ibid, at 286–287.)
37 *The Knight of St. Michael* [1898] P 30; cf *Iredale v China Traders' Insurance Co* [1900] 2 QB at 518, CA.
38 *Williams & Co v Canton Insurance Office Ltd* [1901] AC 462.
39 *Cory v Burr* (1883) 8 App Cas 393.
40 *Ballantyne v Mackinnon* [1896] 2 QB 455, CA; see at 461 as to 'inherent vice'.
41 *Anderson v Marten* [1908] AC 334, HL (policy on disbursements, but treated as policy on ship). For converse case, i e ship driven on to sandbank by perils of the seas, and then captured, see *Hahn v Corbett* (1824) 2 Bing 205.
42 *Leyland Shipping Co v Norwich Union Insurance Co* [1918] AC 350, HL, see at 363, per Lord Dunedin, as to the 'dominant cause'; affirming ibid, 22 Com Cas 256, CA (*The Ikaria*); cf *Stoomvart Maatschappij Sophie H v Merchants' Marine Insurance Co* (1919) 36 TLR 73, [1919] WN 307, HL (ship striking drifting mine).
43 *Britain SS Co v R* [1921] 1 AC 99, HL; affg [1919] 2 KB 670, CA; cf *France, Fenwick & Co Ltd v North of England Protecting Association* [1917] 2 KB 522 (collision with ship sunk by submarine in shallow water).

44 *A-G v Ard Coasters Ltd* [1921] 2 AC 141, 26 Com Cas 352, HL; affg sub nom *Richard de Larrinaga SS (Owners) v Admiralty Comrs* [1920] 3 KB 65, CA; cf *Adelaide SS Co v R* (1922) 27 Com Cas 234, 239 (scope of term 'warlike operations').

45 *J Wharton (Shipping) Ltd v Mortleman* [1941] 2 All ER 261, 58 LQR 13, CA. It was likewise held in *Larrinaga SS Co Ltd v R* [1945] 1 All ER 329, HL, that a requisitioned merchant ship proceeding in ballast to a port of discharge after completion of her war services was not on a warlike operation. In this latter case, Lord Porter said (at p 335) that *J Wharton (Shipping) Ltd v Mortleman*, supra, was not free from complications, and that he preferred not to express any opinion on it. See also *Clan Line Steamers Ltd v Liverpool and London War Risks Insurance Association Ltd* [1942] 2 All ER 367, KB (ship carrying raw material for armaments from England to France not engaged in a warlike operation); *Athel Line Ltd v Liverpool and London War Risks Insurance Association Ltd* [1945] 2 All ER 694, CA (warlike operation may continue although ship is riding at anchor and not 'proceeding through the water').

46 *Yorkshire Dale SS Co Ltd v Minister of War Transport, The Coxwold* [1942] 2 All ER 6, HL. It is not easy at first sight to distinguish *The Matiana* (see illustration 17) from *The Coxwold*. Lord Wright said that *The Matiana* 'is to be distinguished . . . from the present case, because of the nature of the cargo of *The Matiana*, which was cotton, and because neither her port of departure nor her port of arrival was a "war base"': [1942] 2 All ER at 16. It is said that the decision in *The Coxwold* took the market by surprise, because it was felt that stranding was pre-eminently a maritime peril. Steps were at once taken to alter the F C & S clause. See *Arnould*, para 903.

47 *Liverpool and London War Risks Insurance Association Ltd v Ocean SS Co Ltd* [1947] 2 All ER 586, HL.

48 *Samuel (P) & Co Ltd v Dumas* [1924] AC 431, 29 Com Cas 239, HL.

49 *St. Margaret's Trust Ltd v Navigators and General Insurance Co Ltd* (1949) 82 Ll L Rep 752.

50 *Prudent Tankers Ltd SA v Dominion Insurance Co Ltd, The Caribbean Sea* [1980] 1 Lloyd's Rep 338.

51 *Continental Illinois National Bank v Alliance Assurance Co Ltd, The Captain Panagos DP* [1989] 1 Lloyd's Rep 33, CA. (See the judgment of O'Connor LJ, ibid, at 46.)

56. Partial and total loss

(1) A loss may be either total or partial. Any loss other than a total loss, as hereinafter defined, is a partial loss.

(2) A total loss may be either an actual total loss, or a constructive total loss.[1]

(3) Unless a different intention appears from the terms of the policy, an insurance against total loss includes a constructive, as well as an actual, total loss.[2]

(4) Where the assured brings an action for a total loss and the evidence proves only a partial loss, he may, unless the policy otherwise provides, recover for a partial loss.[3]

(5) Where goods reach their destination in specie, but by reason of obliteration of marks, or otherwise, they are incapable of identification, the loss, if any, is partial and not total.[4]

Note

A loss must be either total or partial. A total loss of part is a partial loss. For example, if 100 bags of seed are insured, and 10 are destroyed by perils insured against, this is a partial loss.

An apparent, but not a real, exception to this rule occurs when two or more distinct interests are covered by a single valuation. This is provided for by ss 71, 72, and 76 (1).

For actual total loss, see s 57; for constructive total loss, see s 60.

1 *Roux v Salvador* (1836) 3 Bing N C at 285, Ex Ch. These two sub-sections are exhaustive; see *Sanday & Co v British and Foreign Marine Insurance Co* [1915] 2 KB 781, CA.
2 *Adams v Mackenzie* (1863) 13 CBNS 442; *Sailing Ship Blairmore v Macredie* [1898] AC at 598; and see *Forwood v North Wales Insurance Co* (1880) 9 QBD 732, CA as to by-laws of a mutual insurance association; cf *Montreal Light, Heat and Power Co v Sedgwick* [1910] AC 598, PC (goods insured against total loss by total loss of vessel).
3 *Benson v Chapman* (1849) 2 HLC at 696; *King v Walker* (1864) 2 H & C 384. As to the FPA warranty, see s 76.
4 *Spence v Union Marine Insurance Co* (1868) LR 3 CP 427.

57. Actual total loss

(1) Where the subject-matter insured is destroyed, or so damaged as to cease to be a thing of the kind insured, or where the assured is irretrievably deprived thereof, there is an actual total loss.[1]

(2) In the case of an actual total loss no notice of abandonment need be given.[2]

Note

Where by a peril insured against the goods of different owners are damaged and become so inextricably mixed as to be incapable of identification (eg, marks obliterated), the loss is partial, not total. See s 56(5), and the note to s 60 (constructive total loss).

Before the Act the rule as to goods was that they were deemed to be an actual total loss where they were so damaged as to cease to exist in specie, or so damaged that they could not be rendered capable of arriving at their destination in specie. Goods ceased to exist in specie when they no longer answered to the commercial denomination under which they were insured.[3]

A sub-section to this effect was cut out in Committee, and the possible result may be that goods which still exist in specie, though they could not be rendered capable of arriving at their destination in specie, must now be regarded as a constructive total loss. If so, notice of abandonment must be given.

It is to be noticed that in determining whether there is an actual total loss the rule *de minimis non curat lex* might apply.[4]

For notice of abandonment, see s 62.

Illustrations

1. Hides are insured from Valparaiso to Bordeaux. In consequence of sea damage they arrive at Rio in a state of incipient putridity, and are sold there. Their state is such that they would be wholly putrid if carried on to Bordeaux. This is an actual total loss.[5] Sed quo now? (see note, infra).

2. Insurance on goods in barges, as interest may appear. A cargo of rice valued at £450 is declared. The barge is sunk, and the rice remains under water for two tides. The rice is so damaged that the consignee refuses to accept it. Afterwards it is kiln-dried at a cost of £60, and then sold for £110. The rice still remains in specie, so this is only a partial loss.[6]
3. A ship is deserted in a sinking condition. She is afterwards towed into port by salvors and sold, by order of the court, for less than the salvage costs. The sale creates an actual total loss.[7]
4. Insurance on 'profit on charter' warranted free from all average. The assured, having chartered a ship for a lump sum, employs her up as a general ship. The bill of lading freight exceeds the chartered freight, but in consequence of sea damage to cargo only a portion of it becomes payable, and the portion payable is less than the chartered freight which assured has to pay. This is a total loss of profit on charter.[8]
5. Policy on ship. Obsolete battleship being towed to German port for breaking up went ashore on Dutch coast. She could be got off but the operation would be expensive. The Dutch authorities would not allow her to be moved because of the danger to the sea defences, but their decision was subject to appeal to a higher tribunal. *Held*, not an actual loss because the assured had not been irretrievably deprived of the vessel.[9]
6. Policy on ship. Tug sank in shallow water after a collision but was quickly raised. *Held*, not an actual total loss.[10]
7. Policy on ship. Insured vessel was boarded by Vietnamese customs officials. Unmanifested goods were found on board, and she was escorted into port. A special military court ordered that she should be confiscated. *Held*, there was not actual total loss because it had not been shown that the assured was irretrievably deprived of her.[11]
8. Steel injection moulds were insured for a voyage from Australia to England. On arrival they were found to be damaged by rust due to being immersed in water after the fracture of a pipe in the vessel's hold. It was held that there was an actual total loss of the goods, for they had no value in their damaged state.[12]
9. 668 steel pipes were insured for a voyage from Prai to Brunei. All except 12 fell into the sea. The assured claimed for an actual total loss on the ground that the rule *de minimis non curat lex* applied. It was held that the claim failed because the 12 pipes were far too high a proportion of the whole consignment of 668 pipes to be capable of being dismissed as a matter *de minimis*.[13]
10. Policy on ketch. Ketch submerged at low tide, and subsequently raised. No further steps taken, and she gradually detriorated. *Held*, not an actual total loss because evidence showed only that when she was raised she could have been put into condition in which she was before she submerged, and the deterioration resulted from delay.[14]
11. Policy on freight in respect of dates. Vessel carrying them sank. Dates recovered and found to be unfit as human food, and sold for distilling purposes. *Held*, an actual total loss of freight because the dates were no longer dates in a commercial sense.[15]

1 *Fleming v Smith* (1848) 1 HL Cas at 535; *Lohre v Aitchison* (1878) 3 QBD at 562; *Cossman v West* (1887) 13 App Cas 160; *Rankin v Potter* (1873) LR 6 HL at 127; *Captain*

J A Cates Tug and Wharfage Co v Franklin Insurance Co [1927] AC 698; *Carras v London and Scottish Assurance Corpn Ltd* [1936] 1 KB 291 at 306, CA; *Marstrand Fishing Co Ltd v Beer* [1937] 1 All ER 158, KB (taking of a ship by barrators not in itself sufficient evidence of irretrievable deprivation to constitute an actual total loss); *Panamanian Oriental SS Corpn v Wright* [1970] 2 Lloyd's Rep 365.
2 *Kaltenbach v Mackenzie* (1878) 3 CPD at 471, CA; cf *Rankin v Potter* (1873) LR 6 HL at 106; *Associated Oil Carriers Ltd v Union Insurance Society of Canton Ltd* [1917] 2 KB 184, 22 Com Cas 346; cf s 4(2)(b) proviso, as to benefit of salvage.
3 *Arnould*, para 1142, and Ivamy, *Marine Insurance* (4th ed, 1985), p 352, *Roux v Salvador* (1836) 3 Bing NC 266, 287, Ex Ch; *Asfar v Blundell* [1896] 1 QB at 127, CA.
4 See illustration 9, supra.
5 *Roux v Salvador* (1836) 3 Bing NC 266, Ex Ch; cf *Farnworth v Hyde* (1865) 18 CBNS 835, as dealt with (1866) LR 2 CP at 226.
6 *Francis v Boulton* (1895) 65 LJQB 153.
7 *Cossman v West* (1887) 13 App Cas 160, PC, reviewing the cases; cf *Buchanan v London and Provincial Marine Insurance Co* (1895) 1 Com Cas at 168.
8 *Asfar v Blundell* [1896] 1 QB 123, CA. Semble an actual total loss. But distinguish *Williams v Canton Insurance Office Ltd* [1901] AC 462, HL and *Wyllie v Povah* (1907) 12 Com Cas 317 (profits on cargo, to pay on non-arrival of cargo at destination).
9 *George Cohen Sons & Co v Standard Marine Insurance Co Ltd* (1925) 21 Ll L Rep 30. (See the judgment of Roche, J, ibid, at 33.)
10 *Captain J A Cates Tug and Wharfage Co Ltd v Franklin Insurance Co* [1927] AC 698, 137 LT 709, PC.
11 *Panamanian Oriental SS Corpn v Wright* [1970] 2 Lloyd's Rep 365. (See the judgment of Mocatta J, ibid, at 383.) The decision in the case was later reversed on another ground: [1971] 1 Lloyd's Rep 487, CA.
12 *Berger and Light Diffusers Pty Ltd v Pollock* [1973] 2 Lloyd's Rep 442, QBD (Commercial Court). (See the judgment of Kerr J, ibid, at 456.)
13 *Boon and Cheah Steel Pipes Sdn Bhd v Asia Insurance Co Ltd* [1975] 1 Lloyd's Rep 452, Malaysia High Court. (See the judgment of Raja Azlan Shah J, ibid, at 460, where he said that it might be that in the case of a single pipe or two out of the whole consignment, the rule would apply.)
14 *St Margaret's Trust Ltd v Navigators and General Insurance Co Ltd* (1949) 82 Ll L Rep 752.
15 [1896] 1 QB 123, CA.

58. Missing ship

Where the ship concerned in the adventure is missing, and after the lapse of a reasonable time no news of her has been received, an actual total loss may be presumed.[1]

Note

Reasonable time is a question of fact; see s 88.

If the insurer pays for a missing ship as lost, and she afterwards turns up, she belongs to the insurer.[2]

When a ship is missing in wartime, the court must consider the probabilities, and determine as best it can whether the loss falls on the marine or the war risk underwriters.[3]

1 *Green v Brown* (1743) 2 Stra 1199.
2 *Houstman v Thornton* (1816) Holt NP 242, 17 RR 632.

3 *Munro, Brice & Co v War Risks Association* [1920] 3 KB 94, 25 Com Cas 112, CA; rvsg [1918] 2 KB 78, and reviewing the previous cases. For a strange case where a ship was holed, but did not sink for several hours, see *United Scottish Insurance Co Ltd v British Fishing Vessels Mutual War Risks Association Ltd* (1944) 78 Ll L Rep 70, KB (*held*, on a balance of probabilities, that the ship was holed by contact with an explosive float). See generally, Ivamy, *Marine Insurance* (4th ed, 1985), p 349.

59. Effect of transhipment etc

Where, by a peril insured against, the voyage is interrupted at an intermediate port or place, under such circumstances as, apart from any special stipulation in the contract of affreightment,[1] to justify the master in landing and re-shipping the goods or other moveables, or in transhipping them, and sending them on to their destination, the liability of the insurer continues, notwithstanding the landing or transhipment.[2]

Note

The English rules as to transhipment are not very well settled.[3] In the United States, and under some of the foreign codes, it is the duty of the master to tranship whenever it is reasonable to do so.

Concerning the master's authority of duty to tranship as between shipper and shipowner, see *Carver*, paras 1243–1245. The extent of his powers is determined by the law of the flag.[4]

Where the policy on goods contains a 'transit clause,' the risk continues during transhipment.[5]

When goods have to be landed and transhipped, the consequent expenses, according to the circumstances, are sometimes recoverable as general average[6] and sometimes as particular charges.[7] But to avoid difficulties of proof policies on goods now include a clause in which underwriters agree to pay landing, warehousing and forwarding charges.[8]

1 The insurer is not a party to the contract of affreightment, and is not concerned with it, unless and in so far as it is in some way expressly incorporated into the policy, eg by the clause 'all liberties as per contract of affreightment'.
2 Cf *Bold v Rotheram* (1846) 8 QB at 808; *Halsbury's Laws of England*, 4th edn, vol 25, para 131.
3 *Hansen v Dunn* (1906) 11 Com Cas 100 (general principles as to transhipment) is the most recent exposition.
4 *Carver*, para 974; and see *Cammell v Sewell* (1860) 29 LJ Ex 350, Ex Ch (power to sell).
5 See eg Institute Cargo Clauses (A), Clause 8. See Appendix III, p 243, post.
6 *Atwood v Sellar & Co* (1880) 5 QBD 286, CA.
7 *Kidston v Empire Insurance Co* (1866) LR 1 CP 535, and (1867) LR 2 CP 357, explaining *Booth v Gair* (1864) 33 LJCP 99, and *Great Indian Peninsular Rly Co v Saunders* (1862) 2 B & S 266.
8 See eg clause 12 of the Institute Cargo Clauses (A), Appendix III, p 246, post.

60. Constructive total loss defined

(1) Subject to any express provision in the policy,[1] there is a constructive total loss[2] where the subject-matter[3] insured is reasonably abandoned[4]

on account of its actual total loss appearing to be unavoidable, or because it could not be preserved from actual total loss without an expenditure which would exceed its value when the expenditure had been incurred.[5]

(2) In particular,[6] there is a constructive total loss—
  (i) Where the assured is deprived of the possession of his ship or goods by a peril insured against, and (a) it is unlikely[7] that he can recover the ship or goods as the case may be, or (b) the cost of recovering the ship or goods, as the case may be, would exceed their value when recovered;[8] or
  (ii) In the case of damage to a ship, where she is so damaged by a peril insured against, that the cost of repairing the damage would exceed the value of the ship when repaired.[9]

  In estimating the cost of repairs, no deduction is to be made in respect of general average contributions to those repairs payable by other interests, but account is to be taken of the expense of future salvage operations and of any future general average contributions to which the ship would be liable if repaired;[10] or
  (iii) In the case of damage to goods, where the cost of repairing the damage and forwarding the goods to their destination would exceed their value on arrival.[11]

Note

Sub-section (1) lays down the general rule. Sub-s (2) formulates certain of the more important deductions from it.

The Bill originally contained a sub-section dealing with freight, which was agreed to by the Lord Chancellor's Committee, but it was contended that it was too broadly expressed, and it was afterwards cut out. Constructive total loss of freight is, therefore, now governed by the general provision contained in sub-s (1) of this section.[12]

It is commonly said that, for the purpose of determining whether the assured is entitled to treat a loss as a constructive total loss, regard must be had to the course which would be pursued by a prudent uninsured owner in the circumstances of the case.[13] But as decisions multiply 'the prudent uninsured owner' test becomes of diminishing importance, because the decisions tend to settle as a matter of law the course which a prudent uninsured owner would be bound to take. This, perhaps, is fortunate, because the test is not an easy one to apply. When the test is applicable, the question is, not what the particular owner, if uninsured, would do, but what a man of average prudence ought to do in similar circumstances.[14]

Constructive total loss lies midway between actual total loss on the one hand and partial loss on the other. It is in effect a hybrid loss, and its dual character has complicated the decisions. In some instances notice of abandonment has been given as a matter of precaution, and a case is treated as one of constructive total loss when the facts would have justified its being treated as an actual total loss. In other instances due notice of abandonment has not been given, and the case has to be treated as a partial loss, though the facts show a constructive total loss. Again, when there was a warranty free of particular average, and the loss was heavy, juries sometimes struggled to bring the case within the line of constructive total loss. The result is that the outlines of the law are somewhat blurred.

In the majority of cases the distinction between actual total loss and constructive total loss corresponds with the distinction which has been drawn between physical impossibility and business impossibility.[15] A merchant trades for profit, not for pleasure, and the law will not compel him to carry on business at a loss. A commercial operation is regarded as impracticable, from the business point of view, when the cost of performing it is prohibitive.

As regards a ship, sub-s (2)(ii) settles a controverted point in favour of the insurer. After much doubt it had been decided by the Court of Appeal in 1903, that the value of the wreck could not be added to the cost of repairs for the purpose of determining whether there had been a constructive total loss.[16] But in a subsequent case, which was commenced before, but decided after the passing of the Act, the House of Lords in 1908 overruled this decision on the ground that a prudent uninsured owner would take the value of the wreck into account in considering whether he would repair or not.[17] The Act, however, re-establishes the rule which was in force when it was passed.[18]

In practice, a clause in the policy usually states 'In ascertaining whether the vessel is a constructive total loss the insured value shall be taken as the repaired value and nothing in respect of the damaged or break-up value or wreck shall be taken into account. . .'[19]

A usual clause in war risks policies in respect of a ship concerns constructive total loss due to her detention where the assured loses the free use and disposal of her for a continuous period of 12 months.[20] There is a similar clause as regards freight.[21]

The same general principle as to loss by frustration of the adventure seems to cover goods, freight and profits. 'It is well established,' said Lord Bramwell, 'that there may be a loss of the goods by a loss of the voyage in which the goods are being transported, if it amounts, to use the words of Lord Ellenborough, to a destruction of the contemplated adventure.'[22] But the doctrine of 'loss of voyage' has no application to a ship.[23]

With the object of avoiding the uncertainty and complication of the English rule, the laws of most foreign countries arbitrarily set out certain facts which authorise the assured to abandon and claim for a total loss. Thus, in the United States, unless the policy otherwise provides, there is a constructive total loss if the damage to a ship exceeds 50 per cent of her repaired value.[24]

The rules as to constructive total loss are peculiar to marine insurance, and do not apply to non-marine policies.[25]

Illustrations

Ship. 1. Policy on ship. The ship gets on a rock and the master bona fide comes to the opinion that she cannot be saved. He therefore sells her for £18. The buyer gets her off the rock and repairs her at a cost of £750, when she is worth £1,200. This is not a constructive total loss.[26]

2. Ship of a special class and size is valued at £17,000. In consequence of sea damage she puts into Mauritius, where she is sold for £1,400. Her value four years before the insurance was effected was £20,000. The cost of repairing her would have been £10,500, and her value when repaired would have been £7,500; but a ship of that class and size, fitted for the particular

trade, could not be built or bought for £10,500. The assured can only claim for a partial loss.[27]
3. Policy on ship with stipulation that if she is stranded for six months, during which time it is impracticable to save her, the assured may abandon her. The ship strands and remains stranded for more than six months, but it would be practicable to save her eventually. This is a constructive total loss.[28]
4. Policy on ship. The cost of repairing a vessel would have amounted to $30,500. Her value when repaired would have been $34,000. The assured sought to add the value of the wreck ($14,000) to the cost of the repairs in order to claim that she was a constructive total loss. *Held*, that he was not entitled to do so.[29]
5. Policy on ship on voyage from England to Constantinople. After she sails war breaks out between Greece and Turkey. The captain was not aware of this. The Greeks capture the ship, and confiscate the cargo (coal) as contraband. Notice of abandonment is given, but not accepted. Six weeks afterwards, on proof that the captain did not know of the state of war, the ship is released. This is not a constructive total loss. It was uncertain, but not 'unlikely' that the ship would be released.[30]
6 The *Lavington Court* is requisitioned by the Government. Whilst sailing in convoy on 18 July, 1942 she is struck by a torpedo. The master and crew leave her. Later the naval authorities attempt to save her by towing, but on 1 August she founders and sinks. There is a dispute as to when hire ceases to be payable. The owners say that there was no total loss of the ship, actual or constructive, before 1 August, and they claim hire under the charter-party up to that date. *Held*, by a majority that the action of the master in leaving the ship was not an 'abandonment' within s 60(1); nor was the recovery of the ship on 18 July 'unlikely' within s 60(2)(i). Hence the owners succeeded.[31]
7. Ship insured from 15 January to 15 July 1966 under time policy incorporating Institute War Clauses. Vessel seized by Vietnamese Customs authorities for carrying unmanifested goods and confiscated on order of Special Court. Attempts were made to obtain her release down to 29 August, 1967 (when writ was issued by assured) and a long time afterwards. *Held*, that she was a constructive total loss because her recovery was 'unlikely'.[32]
8. A vessel was detained in the Shatt-al-Arab roads by the Iraqi authorities during a war between Iraq and Iran, and was forbidden to leave. Notice of abandonment was given on 30 September and 14 October 1981. The assured was entitled to claim for a constructive total loss because it was unlikely that possession of the vessel would be recovered within 12 months of either of those dates.[33]

Goods. 9. Policy on goods. The ship becomes a constructive total loss, and the goods have to be landed in a damaged condition. There is a constructive total loss of the goods if the cost of landing, warehousing, reconditioning, reshipping, and forwarding them to their destination (*minus the original freight*) would exceed their value on arrival.[34]
10. Policy on cargo of salt. The ship meets with bad weather, and is towed into a port of refuge by salvors. The salt is landed in a damaged condition, and is sold under a decree of the court for salvage costs. This is a partial loss, not a constructive total loss.[35]

94 *Loss and abandonment*

11. Policy on two lots of goods from River Plate to Hamburg, shipped in two different ships. After the ships sail war breaks out with Germany. One ship is ordered by a French cruiser into an English port, and the other ship under Admiralty instructions is diverted by the owners into an English port. The cargoes are discharged in England. There is a constructive total loss by 'restraint of princes,' for the adventure is frustrated.[36]
12. Policy on goods, shipped by an English merchant from Calcutta to Hamburg on a German ship. War breaks out while the ship is in the Mediterranean. The captain to avoid risk of capture puts into Messina, and then goes on to Syracuse (neutral port) where he abandons the voyage. This is not a constructive total loss. The loss is due to the voluntary act of the captain and not to the operation of any peril insured against.[37]
13. Policy on 668 steel pipes insured for voyage from Prai to Brunei. All except 12 pipes fell into the sea. Claim for constructive total loss. No proof by assured that cost of reconditioning and forwarding the pipes to Brunei would exceed their value on arrival. *Held*, not a constructive total loss.[38]

Freight. 14. Policy on freight valued at £2,000. The ship strikes a rock. The master puts into Pernambuco, and instead of abandoning as he might have done, repairs the ship at a cost exceeding her repaired value, borrowing the money on bottomry. The ship arrives with her cargo. On arrival the ship is sold to satisfy the claim of the lender on bottomry, and the freight also is paid to him. The owner cannot repudiate the acts of the master, and, as freight has been earned, there is no loss of freight.[39]
15. Policy on freight. The ship becomes a constructive total loss at her port of destination, but freight is earned. On the abandonment of the ship by the assured, the freight passes to insurers on ship. The assured cannot claim for a loss of freight, for it has been earned.[40]
16. Policy on chartered freight from Chittagong to Dundee. The ship is wrecked fifty miles from Dundee, and notice of abandonment is properly given in respect of ship, cargo, and freight. Underwriters employ salvors, who bring the cargo into Dundee. This is a total loss of freight. No freight is earned, because the goods are brought to their destination under a salvage contract, and not under the contract of affreightment.[41]
17. Policy on chartered freight from M to N. The ship becomes a constructive total loss, and is bought by the underwriters on cargo with the right to collect freight. The underwriters receive a certain sum as freight, but the cost of towage exceeds what they receive. This (it seems) is a total loss of freight.[42]
18. Under a charter-party (which specifies a cancelling date) the plaintiffs' ship is proceeding to Valparaiso to load cargo. The assured take out a policy on freight and/or chartered freight and/or anticipated freight, subject to the Institute Voyage Clauses (Freight). The ship, while proceeding to Valparaiso, strands and is abandoned to hull underwriters. She is refloated and brought by salvors to M. The hull underwriters compromise for a total loss, the owners retaining the ship but remaining liable to the salvors. The ship is surrendered to the salvors in discharge of their claim. *Held*, that as, owing to perils of the sea, the ship could not make the cancelling date or be tendered to the charterers according to the charter-party, there was an actual loss of freight, and that it was not material to consider whether the ship was a constructive total loss.[43]

19. Under a charter-party the assured's ship proceeds to South America and loads a cargo for UK ports. Under the charter-party, the assured are to receive a lump sum freight of £8,000 payable concurrent with discharge. The assured take out a policy on 'freight and/or chartered freight,' subject to the Institute Voyage Clauses (Freight). The ship, after loading, strands. The assured form the opinion that to continue the voyage will be hopelessly unprofitable, so they abandon the ship and cargo to the salvors, and give notice of abandonment. The assured agree to accept a certain sum from hull underwriters who accept full liability for the ship. Cargo underwriters pay a total loss on cargo. After repairs the ship proceeds to Rotterdam with about half the original cargo. *Held*, for varying reasons, that there was a total loss of freight and that the assured were entitled to recover under the policy.[44]

20. The assured take out a policy, subject to the Institute Time Clauses (Freight), on the freight to be earned by their ship for twelve months. One of the clauses provides: 'In the event of the total loss whether absolute or constructive of the steamer, the amount underwritten by this policy shall be paid in full. . .' The assured charter the ship to a company to sail to V or A or C and there load oil for European ports. Before starting on her voyage and whilst undergoing repairs, she sustains damage from an explosion followed by a fire. The cost of the repairs is more than the insured value of the hull, but owing to the rise in the value of shipping, the assured have the repairs effected. The charter-party is never performed, and the assured receive no part of the freight payable thereunder. *Held*, that as there was a constructive total loss of the ship, the freight underwriters were liable under the policy on freight.[45]

1 See eg *Fowler v English and Scottish Marine Insurance Co* (1865) 18 CBNS 818 (to pay a total loss 30 days after official news of capture or embargo); *Rowland and Marwood's SS Co Ltd v Maritime Insurance Co* (1901) 6 Com Cas 160 (CTL if ship stranded for six months).

2 This section 'circumscribes completely the conception of constructive total loss': per Devlin J, in *Irvin v Hine* [1949] 2 All ER 1089 at 1091, KB. To the same effect, see Lord Porter's dictum in *Robertson v Petros M Nomikos Ltd* [1939] 2 All ER 723 at 734, HL.

3 See the expression 'subject-matter' discussed, *British and Foreign Marine Insurance Co v Samuel Sanday & Co* [1916] 1 AC 650, 657 (policy on goods).

4 'This word is used in one sense in relation to the first, and another in relation to the second limb of this subsection': per Scott LJ, and Stable J, in *Court Line Ltd v R, The Lavington Court* [1945] 2 All ER 357, CA. Contra per du Parcq LJ, ibid. In *Lind v Mitchell* (1928) 34 Com Cas 81, the Court was satisfied that the abandonment of a schooner was unreasonable, for she was 15 miles from her own port. She floated high in the water 7 or 8 hours after she was abandoned.

5 *Kaltenbach v Mackenzie* (1878) 3 CPD at 473 and 479, per Lord Esher; *Shepherd v Henderson* (1881) 7 App Cas at 70, per Lord Blackburn; cf *Moss v Smith* (1850) 19 LJCP at 228; *Robertson v Petros M Nomikos Ltd* [1939] 2 All ER 723, HL (notice of abandonment not an ingredient of a constructive total loss). As to the meaning of 'constructively lost' in the Merchant Shipping Act 1894, s 21, see *Manchester Ship Canal Co v Horlock* [1914] 2 Ch 199, CA (ships sunk in fairway).

6 'Sub-s (2), as compared with sub-s (1), is thus additional, and not merely illustrative': per Lord Wright in *Rickards v Forestal Land, Timber and Rlys Co Ltd* [1941] 3 All ER 62 at 79, HL. See also per Stable J, in *Court Line Ltd v R, The Lavington Court* [1945] 2 All ER 357 at 368, CA.

7 In the Bill as drafted the word used was 'uncertain,' but the word 'unlikely' was substituted at the suggestion of the Lord Chancellor's Committee. This alters the law, somewhat to the prejudice of the assured; see *Polurrian SS Co v Young* [1915] 1 KB 922, 20 Com Cas 152, 163, CA; *Marstrand Fishing Co Ltd v Beer* [1937] 1 All ER 158, KB (a case where it was 'uncertain,' but not 'unlikely,' that the ship would be recovered; it is the true facts, and not the facts as known at the time of abandonment, which provide the criterion); *C Czarnikow Ltd v Java Sea and Fire Insurance Co Ltd* [1941] 3 All ER 256, KB ('unlikely' that a cargo-owner would recover his goods on a German ship in a nominally neutral (Italian) port); *Court Line Ltd v R, The Lavington Court* [1945] 2 All ER 357, CA (see illustration 6, supra).

8 *Roux v Salvador* (1836) 3 Bing NC at 286 (goods); *Rodocanachi v Elliott* (1874) LR 9 CP 518, Ex Ch (goods in besieged town); *Sailing Ship Blairmore v Macredie* [1898] AC 593; *Rickards v Forestal Land, Timber and Rlys Co Ltd* [1941] 3 All ER 62, HL (for facts, see note to Sch I, r 10); and see illustrations to s 62 (notice of abandonment).

9 *Moss v Smith* (1850) 19 LJCP 225; *Lohre v Aitchison* (1878) 3 QBD at 562, 563; affd on this point, *Aitchison v Lohre* (1879) 4 App Cas at 762; *Rankin v Potter* (1873) LR 6 HL at 116. Apart from any special provision, in applying this test, the real value and not the policy valuation is to be regarded: *Irving v Manning* (1847) 1 HL Cas 287, and s 27 (4). As to construction of a special clause 'the insured value to be taken as the repaired value,' see *North Atlantic SS Co v Burr* (1904) 9 Com Cas 164, and *Hall v Hayman* [1912] 2 KB 5; *Helmville Ltd v Yorkshire Insurance Co Ltd, The Medina Princess* [1965] 1 Lloyd's Rep 361, QB (Commercial Court) where the assured failed to prove that the vessel was a constructive total loss, and was held to be entitled to claim for a partial loss only; and see Clause 19 of the Institute Time Clauses (Hulls), Appendix III, post, p 187. For a case where the insurers contended that the vessel was a partial loss only, and the assured proved that she was a constructive loss because the cost of the repairs exceeded the insured value, see *Bank of America National Trust and Savings Association v Chrismas, The Kyriaki* [1993] 1 Lloyd's Rep 137, QB (Commercial Court). (See the judgment of Hirst J, ibid, at 142.)

10 *Kemp v Halliday* (1866) LR 1 QB 520, Ex Ch. Conversely, freight which has been earned is not to be taken into account, *Parker v Budd* (1896) 2 Com Cas 47; see further, *Arnould*, para 1214.

11 *Arnould*, paras 1226–1231; *Farnworth v Hyde* (1866) LR 2 CP 204, Ex Ch (sea damage to goods).

12 See, as to freight, *Moss v Smith* (1850) 19 LJCP 225; *Rankin v Potter* (1873) LR 6 HL at 102, 104; *Jackson v Union Marine Insurance Co* (1873) LR 8 CP 572; *Re Jamieson* [1895] 2 QB at 95, CA; and the illustrations given below.

13 *Roux v Salvador* (1836) 3 Bing NC at 286 (goods); *Irving v Manning* (1847) 1 HL Cas at 306 (ship); *Rankin v Potter* (1873) LR 6 HL at 155; *Sailing Ship Blairmore v Macredie* [1898] AC 593, HL (ship); but perhaps the test did not apply to freight; see *Philpott v Swann* (1861) 11 CBNS at 282, per Willes J.

14 The prudent or reasonable man of English law corresponds with the *bonus paterfamilias* of Roman law. The standard is an objective one, and any personal equation must be excluded from consideration; cf *Angel v Merchants' Marine Insurance Co* [1903] 1 KB at 819, CA.

15 *Moss v Smith* (1850) 19 LJCP at 228, per Maule J; cf *Rankin v Potter* (1873) LR 6 HL at 104.

16 *Angel v Merchants' Marine Insurance Co* [1903] 1 KB 811, CA.

17 *Macbeth v Maritime Insurance Co* [1908] AC 144, HL.

18 *Hall v Hayman* [1912] 2 KB 5. (See the judgment of Bray J, ibid, at 15.) See *Arnould*, para 1198.

19 See Institute Time Clauses (Hulls), cl 19. See p 187, post, and cases cited in footnote 1, p 187, post.

20 See eg Institute War and Strikes Clauses (Hulls-Time), Clause 3 (see Appendix III, p 209, post); Institute War and Strikes Clauses (Hulls-Voyage), Clause 3 (see Appendix III, p 213, post); *The Bamburi* [1982] 1 Lloyd's 312, where the meaning of 'free use and disposal' is considered, ibid, at 321 (per Staughton J).

21 See Institute War and Strikes Clauses (Freight-Time) (see Appendix III, p 232, post); Institute War and Strikes Clauses (Freight-Voyage) (see Appendix III, p 236, post).
22 *Rodocanachi v Elliott* (1873) LR 9 CP at 522, Ex Ch; *British and Foreign Marine Insurance Co v Samuel Sanday & Co* [1916] 1 AC 650, HL (goods). As to freight, cf *Re Jamieson* [1895] 2 QB at 95; *Kulukundis v Norwich Union Fire Insurance Society* [1936] 2 All ER 242, 1488n, CA. As to frustration of adventure in relation to affreightment (where the rule of proximate cause is less strictly applied), see e g *Bank Line Ltd v Arthur Capel & Co* [1919] AC 435, HL; distinguished in *Court Line Ltd v R, The Lavington Court* [1945] 2 All ER 357, CA. See also *Joseph Constantine SS Line Ltd v Imperial Smelting Corpn Ltd, The Kingswood* [1941] 2 All ER 165, HL.
23 *Halsbury's Laws of England*, 4th edn, vol 25, para 310; *Arnould*, paras 1217–1219.
24 See *Arnould*, para 1212.
25 *Moore v Evans* [1918] AC 185, 194, 23 Com Cas 124, 129, HL; reviewing the cases, and discussing the origin of the marine insurance rules.
26 *Gardner v Salvador* (1831) 1 Mood & R 116, 42 RR 767.
27 *Grainger v Martin* (1862) 2 B & S 456; affd (1863) 4 B & S 9, Ex Ch.
28 *Rowland and Marwood's SS Co Ltd v Maritime Insurance Co* (1901) 6 Com Cas 160.
29 *Hall v Hayman* [1912] 2 KB 5. See p 92, ante.
30 *Polurrian SS Co v Young* [1915] 1 KB 922, 20 Com Cas 152, CA (discussed *Roura and Forgas v Townend* (1918) 24 Com Cas 71 at 81); *Marstrand Fishing Co Ltd v Beer* [1937] 1 All ER 158, KB; *C Czarnikow Ltd v Java Sea and Fire Insurance Co Ltd* [1941] 3 All ER 256, KB.
31 *Court Line Ltd v R, The Lavington Court* [1945] 2 All ER 357, CA. Scott and du Parcq LJJ, Stable J, dissenting.
32 *Panamanian Oriental SS Corpn v Wright* [1970] 2 Lloyd's Rep 365, QB (Commercial Court). See the judgment of Mocatta J, ibid, at 338. This decision was subsequently reversed on another ground: [1971] 1 Lloyd's Rep 487, CA.
33 *The Bamburi* [1982] 1 Lloyd's Rep 312, a case decided by Staughton J, sitting as a sole arbitrator. (As to the loss amounting to a constructive total loss, see the award ibid, at 322.) The loss of 'free use and disposal' of the vessel amounted to loss of possession within the meaning of the policy. (See ibid, at 321.)
34 *Farnworth v Hyde* (1866) LR 2 CP 204, Ex Ch. This decision has been the subject of much discussion. For criticisms and arguments in support, see *Arnould*, paras 1226–1231.
35 *De Mattos v Saunders* (1872) LR 7 CP 570; cf *Meyer v Ralli* (1876) 1 CPD 358.
36 *British and Foreign Marine Insurance Co v Samuel Sanday & Co* [1916] 1 AC 650, 21 Com Cas 154, HL; affg [1915] 2 KB 781, CA; cf *Rickards v Forestal Land, Timber and Rlys Co Ltd* [1941] 3 All ER 62, HL (for facts, see note to Sch I, r 10).
37 *Becker, Gray & Corpn v London Assurance Corpn* [1918] AC 101, 23 Com Cas 205, HL; affg [1916] 2 KB 156, CA. As to apprehended perils, see note, p 79, ante.
38 *Boon and Cheah Steel Pipes Sdn Bhd v Asia Insurance Co Ltd* [1975] 1 Lloyd's Rep 452, Malaysia High Court. (See the judgment of Raja Azlan Shah J, ibid, at 454.) The claim for an actual total loss by reason of the rule *de minimis non curat lex* also failed. (See ibid, at 460.)
39 *Benson v Chapman* (1849) 2 HLC at 696, 723.
40 *Scottish Marine Insurance Co of Glasgow v Turner* (1853) 1 Macq 334, HL.
41 *Guthrie v North China Insurance Co* (1902) 7 Com Cas 130, CA.
42 *Barque Robert S Besnard v Murton* (1909) 14 Com Cas 267. (The freight had not been earned at the date taken by consent as the date of the writ.)
43 *Carras v London and Scottish Assurance Corpn Ltd* [1936] 1 KB 291, CA. It is convenient to insert this case here because of the preceding illustrations, but, as Lord Wright MR, pointed out (ibid, at 306), 'it may indeed be that part of the definition of actual total loss in s 57(1), that is, the words "where the assured is irretrievably deprived" of the subject-matter insured, may apply to an actual total loss of freight such as the present.'

44 *Kulukundis v Norwich Union Fire Insurance Society Ltd* [1936] 2 All ER 242, 1488n, CA. Slesser and Greene LJJ, were chiefly influenced by the fact that the cost of temporary repairs to the ship would have exceeded the repaired value of the ship; Scott LJ, rejected this test, but held that the facts established a 'commercial loss' of the ship, judged by the charter-party criterion. See also *Vrondissis v Stevens* [1940] 3 All ER 74, KB (preliminary issue on a point of law as to interpretation of a policy which provided that loss of freight was not recoverable if 'arising from' total loss and/or constructive total loss of vessel).

45 *Robertson v Petros M Nomikos Ltd* [1939] 2 All ER 723, HL. See also *Continental Grain Co Inc v Twitchell* [1945] 1 All ER 357, KB; affd (1945) 61 TLR 291, CA (policy on 'anticipated earnings and/or interest, warranted free of all average. Only against total and/or constructive total loss of the vessel. . .' The assured failed to prove total loss of the estimated earnings).

61. Effect of constructive total loss

Where there is a constructive total loss the assured may either treat the loss as a partial loss, or abandon the subject-matter insured to the insurer and treat the loss as if it were an actual total loss.[1]

Notes

As Cotton LJ, put it, 'A constructive total loss is when the damage is of such a character that the assured is entitled, if he thinks fit, to treat it as a total loss.'[2]

The section, of course, would not apply to a case where, by the terms of the policy, the assured was only entitled to claim for an actual total loss; see s 56(3).

As to notice of abandonment, see s 62, and as to its effects, see s 63. The Act does not define 'abandonment,'[3] and the term is used in three different senses.

(1) First, and strictly, in the case of a constructive total loss, it denotes the voluntary cession by the assured to the insurer of whatever remains of the subject-matter insured, together with all proprietary rights and remedies in respect thereof. This is the meaning in which it is used in the Act.[4]

(2) Secondly, but incorrectly, it is used as equivalent to notice or tender of abandonment, that is to say, the act by which the assured signifies to the insurer his election to abandon what remains and claim for a total loss.[5]

(3) Thirdly, it denotes the cession or transfer, which takes place, by operation of law, of whatever remains of the subject-matter insured when the insurer pays for a total loss. In this sense, it is a corollary of the doctrine of subrogation, which is a necessary incident of every contract of indemnity.[6]

Date of cause of action. In a constructive total loss case the cause of action arises at the date of the casualty, so that the notice of abandonment is not an essential ingredient of that cause of action, but rather a notification of an election between two alternative quantums of damage.[7] Accordingly, where a vessel was a constructive total loss on 22 July 1985 and the notice of abandonment was given on 3 September 1985, the period of limitation under the Limitation Act 1980 began on 22 July 1985.[8]

Illustration

A ship is damaged by sea perils and puts into a foreign port. The master, after communicating with the owners, has her repaired at a cost exceeding her value when repaired. After her arrival in London the owners give notice of abandonment. This is ineffectual. There is only a partial loss.[9]

1 *Roux v Salvador* (1836) 3 Bing NC at 286, 287, Ex Ch; *Fleming v Smith* (1848) 1 HL Cas 513; *Rankin v Potter* (1873) LR 6 HL at 118, 131, 135; and *Kaltenbach v Mackenzie* (1878) 3 CPD 467, 479, CA, where abandonment and notice of abandonment are distinguished. As to election, see ibid, and *Browning v Provincial Insurance Co of Canada* (1873) LR 5 PC 263.
2 *Kaltenbach v Mackenzie* (1878) 3 CPD at 479.
3 From the French *abandonnement*, but the corresponding term in insurance law is *délaissement*.
4 *Rankin v Potter* (1873) LR 6 HL at 144; cf *Kaltenbach v Mackenzie* (1878) 3 CPD at 471.
5 *Rankin v Potter* (1873) LR 6 HL 83 at 118, 119, per Blackburn J, and at 156 (per Lord Chelmsford); cf *Kaltenbach v Mackenzie* (1878) 3 CPD at 479.
6 *Simpson v Thomson* (1877) 3 App Cas at 292, 293, per Lord Blackburn; cf *Rankin v Potter* (1873) LR 6 HL at 118; *Kaltenbach v Mackenzie* (1878) 3 CPD at 471, per Lord Esher; and see s 79 as to subrogation, and note to s 63.
7 *Bank of America National Trust and Savings Association v Chrismas, The Kyriaki* [1993] 1 Lloyd's Rep 137, QB (Commercial Court). (See the judgment of Hirst J, ibid, at 151.)
8 Ibid.
9 *Fleming v Smith* (1848) 1 HL Cas 513.

62. Notice of abandonment

(1) Subject to the provisions of this section, where the assured elects to abandon the subject-matter insured to the insurer he must give notice of abandonment. If he fails to do so the loss can only be treated as a partial loss.[1]

(2) Notice of abandonment may be given in writing, or by word of mouth, or partly in writing and partly by word of mouth, and may be given in any terms which indicate the intention of the assured to abandon his insured interest in the subject-matter insured unconditionally to the insurer.[2]

(3) Notice of abandonment must be given with reasonable diligence after the receipt of reliable information of the loss, but where the information is of a doubtful character the assured is entitled to a reasonable time to make inquiry.[3]

(4) Where notice of abandonment is properly given, the rights of the assured are not prejudiced by the fact that the insurer refuses to accept the abandonment.

(5) The acceptance of an abandonment may be either express or implied from the conduct of the insurer. The mere silence of the insurer after notice is not an acceptance.[4]

(6) Where notice of abandonment is accepted the abandonment is irrevocable. The acceptance of the notice conclusively admits liability for the loss and the sufficiency of the notice.[5]

(7) Notice of abandonment is unnecessary where at the time when the assured receives information of the loss there would be no possibility of benefit to the insurer if notice were given to him.[6]

(8) Notice of abandonment may be waived by the insurer.[7]
(9) Where an insurer has reinsured his risk, no notice of abandonment need be given by him.[8]

Note

As to definition of abandonment, see note to s 61; as to its effects, see s 63. As to under-insurance, see s 81 and the notes to s 79 (subrogation).

Suppose notice of abandonment is given, and the insurer does not accept it. Can the assured withdraw the notice? Atkinson J, answered this question by saying that 'by a notice of abandonment the assured merely makes an offer, which remains executory unless and until it is accepted. Until it is accepted the assured has the right to look to intervening events which may restore in whole or in part his former situation, and may limit his claim accordingly if it suits him better to claim as for a partial loss... Indeed if it were not so, s 62(6) of the Marine Insurance Act 1906 would be otherwise expressed.'[9]

It seems that where due notice of abandonment has not been given, the right to give notice of abandonment may revive on a change of circumstances.[10]

Before the Act it was an open question whether notice must be given if the subject-matter must inevitably perish before notice could be received and acted on, though the subject-matter exists when the election to abandon is made.[11]

Notice of abandonment is not excused simply because the insurers, if notified, could have done nothing more than was done by the assured. If the goods are there to be dealt with, and there is something useful which can be done, notice must be given.[12]

'Information of the loss' means information such that the assured is in a position to make up his mind that there is a constructive total loss.[13]

Notice of abandonment can only be given by or on behalf of the owner of the subject-matter insured, e g it cannot be given by a pledgee of the policy, but it can be given by a joint owner who manages the vessel for the rest.[14]

Sub-section (9) is rather ambiguously worded. It would be clearer if it ran: 'Where an insurer has reinsured his risk, no notice of abandonment need be given by him *to the reinsurer*.'

Ademption of loss. According to the law of Scotland and of most foreign countries, the validity of a notice of abandonment must be determined by reference to the state of facts at the time when notice is given, but in England, as Lord Herschell said, the rule is 'that if, in the interval between the notice of abandonment and the time when legal proceedings are commenced, there has been a change of circumstances reducing the loss from a total to a partial one, or, in other words, if at the time of action brought the circumstances are such that a notice of abandonment would not be justifiable, the assured can only recover for a partial loss,' but this rule does not extend to a change of circumstances when brought about by the action of the insurer.[15] The theory of ademption of loss, said Roche J, 'is that restoration precludes recovery, not because in such case there never was a constructive total loss, but because an assured cannot, under a contract of indemnity, although he may at one time have suffered a loss, recover in respect of such loss, if before action it has already been made good to him.'[16]

The issue of the writ is therefore all important in England. Until that is done, the notice of abandonment is liable to be defeated. A sub-section embodying the

English rule was cut out in Committee on objection taken by the Scottish members. It has not yet been decided whether the possible effect of the Act, as it stands, may be to abrogate the English in favour of the Scottish rule: *Halsbury's Laws of England*, 4th edn, vol 25, para 329.

Be that as it may, in modern practice the conflict between the English rule and the Scottish rule is negligible, because, as Pickford J, pointed out, when notice of abandonment is sent, 'the underwriters are asked in case they refuse to accept the abandonment to put the assured in the same position as if a writ had been issued. In nine cases out of ten, and probably a much larger proportion, the underwriters agree to do so, and, if they do not, the consequence is that the assured issues his writ immediately, and therefore the two dates in ordinary English insurance practice correspond.'[17]

Similarly, Staughton J, sitting as a sole arbitrator, said: 'If abandonment is declined, it is the usual practice, so far as my knowledge goes, to agree to place the assured in the same position as if a writ had been issued.'[18]

Illustrations

1. Policy on ship. On 7 February the assured is informed that the ship is a constructive total loss. On 23 February she is sold for what she will fetch. On 10 March notice of abandonment is given. This is too late.[19]
2. Policy on ship. Obsolete battleship left Chatham in December 1922 for Germany to be broken up. After 2 or 3 days she stranded on the Dutch coast and became a constructive total loss. In February 1923 the assured claimed for a total loss and in April 1923 gave formal notice of abandonment. *Held*, the claim made in February 1923 was a valid notice of abandonment and had been made within a reasonable time.[20]
3. A ship is captured by the enemy. The owner, hearing of the capture, gives notice of abandonment. The ship is recaptured and restored to her owner before action brought. The notice of abandonment is ineffectual. This is only a partial loss.[21]
4. A ship insured against war risks is captured, and the assured gives notice of abandonment. The insurer declines to accept it. The assured commences an action. After the issue of the writ, the Prize Court, on the termination of the war, decrees the restoration of the ship. This is a valid abandonment, and the assured can recover for a total loss.[22]
5. A ship is sunk in deep water in harbour. Notice of abandonment is given, but not accepted, and then the underwriter, on his own initiative, and at great expense, recovers the ship before action is brought. The notice is valid, and the assured can recover for a total loss.[23]
6. Chartered freight on homeward voyage is insured by policy covering prior outward voyage. On the outward voyage the ship becomes a constructive total loss, so freight on homeward voyage is lost. No notice of abandonment need be given.[24]
7. Policy on freight from New Zealand to San Francisco. The ship strands near Honolulu, and the cargo, which consists of coal, gets wetted. Ship and cargo are both sold at Honolulu. If the coal had been dried and sent on, the cost would have been more than its worth. There is a total loss of freight, and no notice of abandonment is necessary.[25]

Loss and abandonment

8. Policy on profit on charter. The ship becomes a constructive total loss, but no notice of abandonment is given by the shipowner. The assured (charterer) can recover, although no notice of abandonment has been given.[26]
9. Policy on goods. Cargo insured from Novorossisk to Falmouth. After the closing of the Dardanelles the assured telegraphed to their brokers saying: 'Agreeable release underwriters if underwriters will pay difference between present value in Novorossisk and insured value.' This telegram was shown to the underwriters. *Held*, there had been no effective notice of abandonment, for the telegram had not indicated the intention of the assured to abandon their interest unconditionally.[27]
10. Policy on goods. Some tins of petroleum were a constructive total loss. Notice of abandonment was given to a Lloyd's agent by a representative of the assured. The notice was invalid because a Lloyd's agent was not authorised to receive it on behalf of the insurers.[28]
11. Policy on ship. Tug was sunk in a collision and notice of abandonment was given to the insurers. As a result of salvage operations which they instituted the vessel was raised and towed inshore, and the notice was not accepted. Without the knowledge of the assured the salvors made an offer to purchase the vessel but withdrew it 3 weeks later. The assured contended that the negotiations between the insurers and the salvors constituted an acceptance of the notice. *Held*, that no acceptance could be implied from the conduct of the insurers.[29]
12. Policy on ship. Ship attacked and struck by missile in war between Iraq and Iran, and subsequently sank. Salvage was completely impracticable by reason of the place and the circumstances of the sinking. *Held*, notice of abandonment was unnecessary.[30]

1 *Gernon v Royal Exchange* (1815) 6 Taunt 383, 387. As to the origin of notice of abandonment, see *Kaltenbach v Mackenzie* (1878) 3 CPD at 471, CA, where the whole subject is discussed.
2 *Currie & Co v Bombay Native Insurance Co* (1869) LR 3 CP at 78; *Hall v Hayman* (1911) 17 Com Cas at 87; *Panamanian Oriental SS Corpn v Wright* [1970] 2 Lloyd's Rep 365, QB (Commercial Court). This decision was subsequently reversed on another ground: [1971] 1 Lloyd's Rep 487, CA; *Black King Shipping Corpn v Massie, The Litsion Pride* [1985] 1 Lloyd's Rep 475, QB (Commercial Court), where a number of telexes and the writ claiming an indemnity in respect of a total loss amounted to a notice of abandonment. (See the judgment of Hirst J, ibid, at 478.) A conditional notice of abandonment, suggesting a compromise, is insufficient: *Russian Bank for Foreign Trade v Excess Insurance Co* [1919] 1 KB 39, 24 Com Cas 55, 57, CA.
3 *Currie v Bombay Insurance Co* (1869) LR 3 PC at 79; *Rankin v Potter* (1873) LR 6 HL at 105; *Kaltenbach v Mackenzie* (1878) 3 CPD at 472, 478. Reasonable diligence, like reasonable time, is a question of fact: see s 88.
4 *Provincial Insurance Co of Canada v Leduc* (1874) LR 6 PC 224; *Shepherd v Henderson* (1881) 7 App Cas 49, HL (underwriters acting as salvors not an acceptance); *Captain J A Cates Tug and Wharfage Co Ltd v Franklin Insurance Co* [1927] AC 698.
5 *Smith v Robertson* (1814) 2 Dow 474, 14 RR 174; *Provincial Insurance Co v Leduc* (1874) LR 6 PC 224 (implied acceptance, waiver of breach of warranty). Semble, a notice of abandonment given and accepted under a mutual mistake of fact may be a nullity: *Norwich Union Fire Insurance Society Ltd v William H Price Ltd* [1934] AC 455, PC.

Section 62

6 *Farnworth v Hyde* (1865) 18 CBNS 835 (goods); *Rankin v Potter* (1873) LR 6 HL 83 (freight); *Kaltenbach v Mackenzie* (1878) 3 CPD 467, CA (ship); *Associated Oil Carriers Ltd v Union Insurance Society of Canton Ltd* [1917] 2 KB 184, 22 Com Cas 346, 350 (freight, chartered voyage becoming illegal by outbreak of war). As to constructive total loss developing into actual total loss, see *Levy v Merchants' Marine Insurance Co* (1885) 5 Asp MLC 407.

7 *Houstman v Thornton* (1816) Holt NP 242; *Black King Shipping Corpn v Massie, The Litsion Pride* (supra), where it was held that there was no evidence of a waiver. (See the judgment of Hirst J, ibid, at 478.) Notice was waived in *Rickards v Forestal Land, Timber and Rlys Co Ltd* [1941] 3 All ER 62, HL.

8 *Uzielli v Boston Marine Insurance Co* (1884) 15 QBD 11, CA. As to rights of reinsurer when original insurer effects a compromise, see *British Dominions' General Insurance Co Ltd v Duder* [1915] 2 KB 394, CA, criticising the *Uzielli* case.

9 *Pesquerias y Secaderos de Bacalao de Espana SA v Beer* (1946) 79 Ll L Rep 417, KB, per Atkinson J, p 433; rvsd on the facts (1947) 80 Ll L Rep 318, CA; [1949] 1 All ER 845n, HL. See also *Halsbury's Laws of England*, 4th edn, vol 25, para 324.

10 *Stringer v English and Scottish Marine Insurance Co* (1869) LR 4 QB 676, and (1870) LR 5 QB 599 at 604.

11 *Kaltenbach v Mackenzie* (1878) CPD at 475, per Brett LJ.

12 *Vacuum Oil Co v Union Insurance Society of Canton Ltd* (1926) 25 Ll L Rep 546 at 554.

13 Ibid, at 553.

14 *Jardine v Leathley* (1863) 32 LJQB 132.

15 *Sailing Ship Blairmore v Macredie* [1898] AC at 610. See at 606, 609 as to Scottish rule.

16 *Roura and Forgas v Townend* [1919] 1 KB 189 at 196, 24 Com Cas 71 at 81.

17 *Polurrian SS Co v Young* (1913) 19 Com Cas 143 at 153. See eg *Panamanian Oriental SS Corpn v Wright* [1970] 2 Lloyd's Rep 365, QB (Commercial Court), where the insurers agreed to put the assured in the same position as if they had issued a writ on 23 May 1966, when the constructive total loss of the vessel was alleged to have occurred. (See the judgment of Mocatta J, ibid, at 383.) This decision was subsequently reversed on another ground: [1971] 1 Lloyd's Rep 487, CA.

18 *The Bamburi* [1982] 1 Lloyd's Rep 312 at 321.

19 *Kaltenbach v Mackenzie* (1878) 3 CPD 467, CA.

20 *George Cohen Sons & Co v Standard Marine Insurance Co Ltd* (1925) 30 Com Cas 139.

21 *Bainbridge v Neilson* (1808) 10 East 329; cf *Dean v Hornby* (1854) 3 E & B 180, 190. See note, ante, as to ademption of loss.

22 *Ruys v Royal Exchange Assurance Corpn* [1897] 2 QB 135, reviewing previous cases. Aliter, it seems, in Scotland: *Sailing Ship Blairmore v Macredie* [1898] AC 593 at 606, 609. See, p 100 ante.

23 *Sailing Ship Blairmore v Macredie* [1898] AC 593.

24 *Rankin v Potter* (1873) LR 6 HL 83.

25 *Trinder v Thames and Mersey Marine Insurance Co* [1898] 2 QB at 119, CA.

26 *Roura and Forgas v Townend* [1919] 1 KB 189, 24 Com Cas 71 (ship captured by Germans but afterwards recovered).

27 *Russian Bank for Foreign Trade v Excess Insurance Co Ltd* [1919] 1 KB 39, CA.

28 *Vacuum Oil Co v Union Insurance Society of Canton Ltd* (1926) 25 Ll L Rep 546, CA. (See the judgment of Atkin LJ, ibid, at 554.)

29 *Captain J A Cates Tug and Wharfage Co Ltd v Franklin Insurance Co* (1927) 137 LT 709, PC. (See the judgment of Lord Sumner, ibid, at 711.)

30 *Black King Shipping Corpn v Massie, The Litsion Pride* (supra). (See the judgment of Hirst J, ibid, at 478.)

63. Effect of abandonment

(1) Where there is a valid abandonment, the insurer is entitled to take over the interest of the assured in whatever may remain of the subject-matter insured, and all proprietary rights incidental thereto.[1]

(2) Upon the abandonment of a ship the insurer thereof is entitled to any freight in course of being earned, and which is earned by her subsequent to the casualty causing the loss,[2] less the expenses of earning it incurred after the casualty; and where the ship is carrying the owner's goods the insurer is entitled to a reasonable remuneration for the carriage of them subsequent to the casualty causing the loss.[3]

Note

As to the effect of under-insurance, see s 81, and see s 79 as to subrogation. As to the various meanings of 'abandonment,' see note to s 61.

Scrutton LJ, explained the effect of abandonment thus:[4] 'What is the effect of abandonment under English or German law, which are assumed to be the same? When the total loss of a thing insured is not actual but constructive, that is, where the thing insured is in specie, but the cost of preserving and repairing it would be more than its value when preserved or repaired (see Marine Insurance Act 1906, s 60), the assured must give a notice of abandonment. This in itself does not pass any property or rights in the thing insured to the underwriter. If the underwriter then pays the assured a total loss, it used to be thought that the payment passed the property and rights incidental to it to the underwriter, as benefit of salvage. Lord Blackburn in 1877, before the Marine Insurance Act [1906], in *Simpson v Thomson* said:[5] 'I do not doubt at all that where the owners of an insured ship have claimed or been paid as for a total loss, the property in what remains of the ship, and all rights incident to the property, are transferred to the underwriters as from the time of the disaster in respect of which the total loss is claimed for and paid.' He distinguishes the case from subrogation to a right to recover damages against a third party in respect of the thing insured, which he says follows on payment for a total loss, but must be exercised in the name of the assured and in respect of his right. . .

'. . . But before the Marine Insurance Act was passed in 1906, circumstances arose which rendered it necessary to consider whether an underwriter, merely by paying, necessarily became the "owner" of the thing insured, for it might be a *damnosa hereditas*, whose ownership only imposed liabilities which the underwriter did not want. The owner of a ship wrecked in a harbour might be liable to the harbour authority for the costs of buoying and removing the wreck. The case of *River Wear Comrs v Adamson*,[6] as explained in *The Mostyn*,[7] shows the difficulties of deciding the liability of "the owner" in such a case, and in 1894, in *Arrow Shipping Co v Tyne Improvement Comrs*,[8] the question was raised whether underwriters, who had paid a total loss, were not "owners" liable for the expense of raising the wreck, and Lord Herschell declined to decide the question. Probably in consequence of this question having arisen when the Marine Insurance Act 1906 was passed, s 63 was worded thus: "Where there is a valid abandonment, the insurer is entitled to take over the interest of the assured in whatever may remain of the subject-matter insured, and all proprietary rights incidental thereto," thus apparently leaving it open to the underwriter not to "take over" the interest of the assured, though "entitled to take it over".'

A decision of Bailhache J, supports the view that if notice of abandonment is given, but not accepted, the property becomes *res nullius*.[9] But in a later case,[10] Greer LJ said: 'It does not follow that because notice of abandonment is given to an insurer, therefore, the vessel which may have some value, is abandoned to all the world, so that it has no owner at all, and becomes what lawyers prefer to describe, using the Latin language, as *res nullius*.' More recently,[11] Cohen LJ, said that his inclination was to prefer the opinion expressed by Greer LJ, to that of Bailhache J.

It has been suggested that, in case of abandonment, freight should be apportioned between the insurer on ship and the insurer on freight: see a curious case where this was done by consent.[12]

The provisions of this section may be modified by agreement;[13] they are modified, for example, by Clause 20 of the Institute Time Clauses (Hulls), which states: 'In the event of total or constructive total loss no claim to be made by the underwriters for freight whether notice of abandonment has been given or not.'[14] Clause 18 of the Institute Voyage Clauses (Hulls) is in the same terms.[15]

On abandonment, any act or thing done subsequent to the casualty causing the loss by the assured or his agents for the protection of the subject-matter insured, is at the risk of the insurer and for his benefit, provided such an act or thing is done in good faith and reasonably.[16]

Illustrations

1. Ship insured from Quebec to Liverpool. She is damaged first by an iceberg, and again damaged in entering the dock at Liverpool. The cargo is delivered and freight paid. After survey the ship is found to be not repairable, and the owner abandons her to the insurer. The freight belongs to the insurer on ship.[17]
2. Policy on ship. The ship halfway on the voyage becomes a total loss and is abandoned to the insurers, but the cargo is landed, and sent on by the master in another ship to its destination. The insurer on ship is not entitled to the freight so earned.[18]
3. Policy on ship, which has been chartered. The ship is damaged by collision and cannot earn freight. Her damage is such that she is abandoned to the insurer. The insurer on ship is not entitled to the damages which the assured may recover from the ship at fault for loss of freight.[19]
4. Policy on chartered freight from Pensacola to England. The ship gets into Havannah as a constructive total loss, and is abandoned. The cargo is brought home by the insurers. The adjustment is made at Liverpool, but by agreement in accordance with the law of Havannah. Under that law *pro rata* freight to Havannah is payable. The insurer is entitled to this freight.[20]
5. Policy on ship from Pensacola to Hartlepool. Part of the freight is paid in advance. The ship is stranded getting into Hartlepool, but the cargo is delivered, and freight earned. Assured abandons the ship. The insurer is not entitled to the advance freight, but only to the balance payable on arrival.[21]

1 *Stewart v Greenock Insurance Co* (1848) 2 HL Cas at 183; *Rankin v Potter* (1873) LR 6 HL at 118, 114; and cf s 79 (subrogation).

106 *Loss and abandonment*

2 *Sea Insurance Co v Hadden* (1884) 13 QBD 706, CA.
3 *Miller v Woodfall* (1857) 27 LJQB 120.
4 *Allgemeine Versicherungs-Gesellvetia v Administrator of German Property* [1931] 1 KB 672 at 687–8, CA (a case where abandonment involved the assignment of a chose in action by an enemy).
5 (1877) 3 App Cas 279 at 292.
6 (1877) 2 App Cas 743.
7 *Great Western Rly Co v SS Mostyn (owner)* [1928] AC 57.
8 [1894] AC 508.
9 *Boston Corpn v Fenwick & Co Ltd* (1923) 28 Com Cas 367.
10 *Oceanic Steam Navigation Co Ltd v Evans* (1934) 40 Com Cas 108 at 111, CA.
11 *Blane Steamships Ltd v Minister of Transport* [1951] 2 KB 965 at 991, CA.
12 *Sharp v Gladstone* (1805) 7 East 24.
13 *Coker v Bolton* [1912] 3 KB 315 (agreement that in case of CTL freight shall not go to insurer on ship). But note that a policy 'without benefit of abandonment' is a wager policy under s 4.
14 Appendix III, p 187, post.
15 Appendix III, p 205, post.
16 *Rankin v Potter* (1873) LR 6 HL at 119; cf the 'waiver' clause, p 248, post, and s 78 (4).
17 *Stewart v Greenock Insurance Co* (1848) 2 HL Cas 159; on these facts there is no loss of freight for which assured can claim against insurer on freight: *Scottish Marine Insurance Co of Glasgow v Turner* (1853) 1 Macq 334, HL.
18 *Hickie v Rodocanachi* (1859) 28 LJ Ex 273. But the insurer is entitled to *pro rata* freight earned under a foreign contract of affreightment; see *London Assurance v Williams* (1892) 9 TLR 96; affd 9 TLR 257, CA. See illustration 4, post.
19 *Sea Insurance Co v Hadden* (1884) 13 QBD 706, CA.
20 *London Assurance v Williams* (1892) 9 TLR 96; affd 9 TLR 257, CA.
21 *The Red Sea* [1896] P 20, CA.

PARTIAL LOSSES (INCLUDING SALVAGE AND GENERAL AVERAGE AND PARTICULAR CHARGES)

64. Particular average loss

(1) A particular average loss is a partial loss of the subject-matter insured, caused by a peril insured against, and which is not a general average loss.[1]

(2) Expenses incurred by or on behalf of the assured for the safety or preservation of the subject-matter insured, other than general average and salvage charges, are called particular charges. Particular charges are not included in particular average.[2]

Note

The expression 'particular average loss' involves a tautology, but the use of the term among lawyers is inveterate.

'A general average differs from a particular average in its nature and incidence. The former is a partial loss, voluntarily incurred for the common safety, and made good proportionably by all parties concerned in the adventure; the latter is a partial loss, fortuitously caused by a maritime peril, and which has to be borne by the party upon whom it falls.'[3]

As to particular charges, see further s 65(2), s 76(2) and s 78, and Sch I, r 13; and as to particular average warranties, see s 76. See further, the illustrations to ss 69, 71 and 76.

1 *Kidston v Empire Insurance Co* (1866) LR 1 CP at 544; *Lohre v Aitchison* (1878) 3 QBD at 566, per Brett LJ; *Price & Co v A1 Ships' Small Damage Insurance Association Ltd* (1889) 22 QBD at 590, CA.
2 Ibid.
3 C. McArthur, *The Contract of Marine Insurance* (2nd ed, 1890), p 163.

65. Salvage charges

(1) Subject to any express provision in the policy, salvage charges incurred in preventing a loss by perils insured against may be recovered as a loss by those perils.[1]

(2) 'Salvage charges' means the charges recoverable under maritime law by a salvor independently of contract. They do not include the expenses of services in the nature of salvage rendered by the assured or his agents, or any person employed for hire by them, for the purpose of averting a peril insured against. Such expenses, where properly incurred, may be recovered as particular charges or as a general average loss, according to the circumstances under which they were incurred.[2]

Note

The decision of the House of Lords in 1879 in *Aitchison v Lohre*[3] that an award paid to a salvor, who was not acting under a salvage contract, could not be recovered under the 'sue and labour' clause occasioned some surprise. The case proceeded on the ground that salvors, who intervene voluntarily and not under contract, are not the agents of the assured, for English law does not, as a rule, recognise the Continental doctrine of 'agent of necessity'.

The practical effect of the decision, now embodied in the Act, is this. As 'salvage charges' strictly so called, are recoverable under the policy, and not under the 'sue and labour' clause, they cannot be recovered in addition to the sum insured, but the total liability of the insurer is limited to the sum insured.[4]

The payment of salvage charges under a foreign adjustment is usually provided for by a special clause in the policy, a usual form of which runs:[5] General average and salvage to be adjusted 'according to the law and practice obtaining at the place where the adventure ends, as if the contract of affreightment contained no special terms upon the subject; but where the contract of affreightment so provides the adjustment shall be according to York-Antwerp Rules'.[6]

The expression 'salvage' requires definition, because it is used in various senses.

In maritime law it is applied alike to the salvor's service and the salvor's reward. It is used to denote the services of a salvor, who intervenes voluntarily, and whose rights are given him by maritime law, and also the services of a salvor, who is employed by the ship, and whose rights depend on contract.

In insurance law it is also used to denote the thing saved, as e g in the phrase 'without benefit of salvage,' or when a loss is referred to as a 'salvage loss'.

108 Partial losses

If the insurer voluntarily pays a salvage claim, without the assent of the assured, he does so at his own risk, and cannot set off the sum so paid against an assignee of the policy.[7]

Life salvage, apart from the salvage of property, is the creation of statute,[8] and the shipowner's liability therefore is not covered by the ordinary form of policy on ship. It must be covered by a special insurance.[9]

But a salvage award in so far as it reflects an element of life salvage gives rise to a charge incurred in preventing a loss by perils insured against within the meaning of s 65(1), for by the practice of the Admiralty Court an award made in these circumstances is treated as being an award for services rendered to the ship and cargo.[10]

In the present section, and throughout the Act, the term 'salvage' is used to denote salvage strictly so called, ie the salvor's reward, under maritime law, for saving property or property and life conjointly.

'With regard to salvage, general average, and contribution,' said Bowen LJ, 'the maritime law differs from the Common Law. That has been so from the time of the Roman law downwards. The maritime law, for the purposes of public policy, and for the advantage of trade, imposes in these cases a liability upon the thing saved—a liability which is a special consequence arising out of the character of mercantile enterprise, the nature of sea perils, and the fact that the thing saved was saved under great stress and exceptional circumstances.'[11]

As to the adjustment of salvage charges, see s 73(2). As to salvage generally, see W R Kennedy, *Law of Salvage*, 5th ed, 1985; and *Carver*, paras 1270–1334.

Military salvage, that is to say salvage by Her Majesty's ships, is necessarily regulated on different lines, because of the special duty of those ships to render protection and help to ships in distress.[12]

As to 'particular charges,' see s 64(2), and as to 'general average loss,' see s 66(1).

Illustrations

1. A ship valued at £2,600 is insured with D for £1,200. After encountering very bad weather, the ship is rescued by a steamer, with which no contract is made, and which afterwards obtains a salvage award of £800. The owner does not abandon the ship, but elects to repair her. D's proportion of the expenses of repair comes to £1,200; ie the full sum insured. He is not liable for any portion of the salvage or general average expenses in excess of the £1,200.[13]
2. Time policy on ship. The ship starts on a voyage with an insufficiency of coal, and engages the services of a trawler to tow her to her port of discharge. The owner of the trawler gets judgment for salvage services, which the assured has to pay. The steamer met with no extraordinary weather, and might in time have sailed to the port. The loss is not due to the perils of the seas, but to the insufficiency of coal, which is not a peril insured against, and accordingly the insurer is not liable.[14]

1 *Aitchison v Lohre* (1879) 4 App Cas at 765; cf *SS Balmoral v Marten* [1901] 2 KB at 904, CA.
2 *Australian Coastal Shipping Commission v Green* [1971] 1 All ER 353, CA, where

expenses incurred in defending an action brought by tugowners, who had rendered services to the insured vessel, were held to be general average expenditure and recoverable under the policy. Cf *Anderson v Ocean SS Co* (1884) 10 App Cas 107, 114; cf s 78 ('sue and labour' clause). As to the meaning of salvage and the history of the subject, see *Aitchison v Lohre* (1879) 4 App Cas 755 at 765–6; W R Kennedy, *Law of Salvage*, 5th ed, 1985, paras 71–130; *Carver*, paras 1270–1334.
3 (1879) 4 App Cas at 765; and cf *Uzielli v Boston Marine Insurance Co* (1884) 15 QBD 11, CA.
4 Cf *Montgomery v Indemnity Mutual Marine Insurance Co* [1902] 1 KB at 152, per Mathew J.
5 See Institute Time Clauses (Hulls) Clause 11 p 181, post. The Institute Voyage Clauses (Hulls) Clause 9 is in the same terms (see Appendix III, p 200, post).
6 For the York-Antwerp Rules 1974, see Appendix IV, pp 277–284, post.
7 *Swan v Maritime Insurance Co* [1907] 1 KB 116; cf *Buchanan v London and Provincial Marine Insurance Co* (1895) 1 Com Cas 165 (salvage expenses paid by insurers, who afterwards have to pay a total loss).
8 Merchant Shipping Act 1894, s 544.
9 *Nourse v Liverpool Sailing Ship Association* [1896] 2 QB 16, CA; W R Kennedy, *Law of Salvage*, 5th ed, 1985, paras 223–260. The assured's liability to pay life salvage may be insured with a mutual insurance association. See Ivamy, *Marine Insurance* (4th ed, 1985), p 217.
10 *Grand Union (Shipping) Ltd v London SS Owners' Mutual Insurnce Association Ltd, The Bosworth (No 3)* [1962] 1 Lloyd's Rep 483, QB (Commercial Court). See especially the judgment of McNair J, ibid, at 490–491.
11 *Falcke v Scottish Insurance Co* (1886) 34 Ch D at 248.
12 See Merchant Shipping Act 1894, ss 557–564 as amended by Merchant Shipping (Salvage) Act 1916, and the cases decided on these enactments.
13 *Aitchison v Lohre* (1879) 4 App Cas 755, discussed in *Montgomery v Indemnity Mutual Marine Insurance Co* [1902] 1 KB at 152; *Dixon v Sea Insurance Co* (1880) 4 Asp MLC 327, CA.
14 *Ballantyne v Mackinnon* [1896] 2 QB 455, CA.

66. General average loss

(1) A general average loss is a loss caused by or directly consequential on a general average act. It includes a general average expenditure as well as a general average sacrifice.[1]

(2) There is a general average act where any extraordinary sacrifice or expenditure is voluntarily and reasonably made or incurred in time of peril for the purpose of preserving the property imperilled in the common adventure.[2]

(3) Where there is a general average loss, the party on whom it falls is entitled, subject to the conditions imposed by maritime law,[3] to a rateable contribution from the other parties interested, and such contribution is called a general average contribution.[4]

(4) Subject to any express provision in the policy, where the assured has incurred a general average expenditure, he may recover from the insurer in respect of the proportion of the loss which falls upon him;[5] and in the case of a general average sacrifice he may recover from the insurer in

respect of the whole loss without having enforced his right of contribution from the other parties liable to contribute.[6]

(5) Subject to any express provision in the policy, where the assured has paid, or is liable to pay, a general average contribution in respect of the subject insured, he may recover therefor from the insurer.[7]

(6) In the absence of express stipulation, the insurer is not liable for any general average loss or contribution where the loss was not incurred for the purpose of avoiding, or in connection with the avoidance of, a peril insured against.[8]

(7) Where ship, freight, and cargo, or any two of those interests, are owned by the same assured, the liability of the insurer in respect of general average losses or contributions is to be determined as if those subjects were owned by different persons.[9]

Note

The definition of 'general average' given by Lawrence J, in 1801, still remains the standard definition. 'All loss,' he said, 'which arises in consequence of extraordinary sacrifices made, or expenses incurred, for the preservation of the ship and cargo comes within general average, and must be borne proportionably by all who are interested.'[10]

Where there is a general average loss, the period of limitation under the Limitation Act 1980 runs from the date of the loss, and not from the date when the general average statement prepared by the average adjusters is published to the insurers.[11]

But where the parties sign a general average bond, the period of limitation runs from the time when the general average statement has been completed by the average adjuster.[12]

Sub-sections (1) to (3) are merely explanatory, and perhaps belong more properly to the law of general average than to the law of marine insurance.[13] As Gorell Barnes J, said, '. . . the obligation to contribute in general average exists between the parties to the adventure, whether they are insured or not. The circumstances of a party being insured can have no influence on the adjustment of general average, the rules of which . . . are entirely independent of insurance. If a contributing party is insured, he can claim an indemnity against his underwriter in respect of the contribution which he has been compelled to pay in general average, but that is all. I do not forget that in some cases an assured may have a right to recover in full for the loss of sacrificed property, but the underwriters have the right to recover contribution from the various contributories, and, subject to certain differences of values, the result to the underwriters should be practically the same as if the assured had only claimed his contribution from them.'[14]

Sub-section (7) was twice altered during the passage of the Bill through Parliament, and is not very happily expressed. It was intended to affirm the recently established rule that there might be a claim on the insurer for a loss in the nature of a general average loss though there were no contributing interests, owing to single ownership.

But take this case. A mast is sacrificed for the benefit of ship and cargo. If they are owned by different owners, the assured on ship gets the full value of the mast from the underwriter on ship, but the latter then becomes entitled to contribution from the cargo owner.[15] But where the shipowner is the same person as the cargo owner, it seems absurd to pay him the full value of the mast and thereby become entitled to claim from him the cargo contribution. No doubt as a matter of adjustment the cargo contribution will have to be deducted.

The English law of general average is in a somewhat unsatisfactory condition.[16] The liability to contribute is a Common Law liability, independent of insurance, and consequently the liability of the assured under the contract of affreightment may differ from that of the insurer under the policy. For example, suppose goods are insured with a warranty 'free of capture and seizure'. General average expenses may be incurred in avoiding capture, but the insurer would not be liable for them.

The English rule of law, though not always logically carried out in details, is narrower than the consistent practice of average adjusters, and considerably narrower than the rule which prevails in nearly all foreign countries. In England, general average is only payable when the sacrifice was made, or the expenditure incurred, for the *preservation* of the ship and cargo. Foreign laws for the most part include in general average nearly all expenses incurred for the *benefit* of the common adventure. As to the place of adjustment, and the law to be followed, see note to s 91.

In practice, the normal English rule only applies in exceptional cases, because nearly every policy contains a foreign adjustment clause[17] which makes either some foreign laws or the York-Antwerp Rules applicable. A usual clause[18] states: General average and salvage to be adjusted 'according to the law and practice obtaining at the place where the adventure ends, as if the contract of affreightment contained no special terms upon the subject; but where the contract of affreightment so provides the adjustment shall be according to York-Antwerp Rules.' The York-Antwerp Rules of 1890 attempted to cover only a portion of the field, but those of 1924 were intended to provide a complete code.[19] The present Rules are those of 1974, reproduced in Appendix IV, pp 277–284.

It seems a moot point whether volunteer salvage charges can ever be recovered as general average. *Carver* contends that they cannot.[20]

Concerning general average as between ship, freight, and cargo, see R Lowndes and G R Rudolf, *The Law of General Average and the York-Antwerp Rules* 11th ed, 1990, by D J Wilson and J H S Cooke; *Carver*, paras 1345–1484; T E Scrutton, *Charterparties and Bills of Lading*, 19th ed, 1984, by Sir Alan Abraham Mocatta, Michael J Mustill and Stewart C Boyd, pp 276–288; K S Selmer, *The Survival of General Average* (2nd ed, 1985).

It is the duty of the shipowner and his agents to take such steps as may be reasonable to provide that all general average contributions (whether due to himself or others) are adjusted and collected, and he has a lien on the cargo until this be done.[21]

As to adjustment of general average loss, see s 73.

Illustrations

1. Policy on goods. Certain goods are jettisoned as a general average act. The insurer of these goods must pay the insured value of them as a loss under the policy, but he then stands in the place of the assured as regards claims for contribution from the other parties interested.[22]

112 Partial losses

2. Policy on ship from London to Liverpool and thence to Calcutta. The ship strands on a bank in Ireland. Half the cargo, consisting of salt, is jettisoned. The remainder is brought back much damaged to Liverpool. The amount to be made good in general average must be ascertained by valuing the jettisoned salt at the price it would have fetched in Liverpool, and the probability that it would have been damaged like the rest of the cargo must be taken into account.[23]

3. Policy on cargo of corn from Varna to Marseilles, general average 'as per foreign statement'. The ship springs a leak, part of the corn is sea-damaged, and the voyage has to be abandoned at Constantinople. Average is adjusted according to the law prevailing there, and the damage to the wheat is charged to general average though, according to English law, it would be particular average but excluded by the terms of the policy. The insurer is liable to pay this sum.[24]

4. Policy on goods. Both ship and goods belong to the same owner. In stormy weather the mast has to be cut away for the safety of ship and cargo. The shipowner is entitled to a general average contribution from the insurer on goods in respect of the general average sacrifice.[25]

5. Policy on ship. Under charter-party the ship sails in ballast for Savannah, where she is to load a cargo of cotton for England. On the voyage out the ship grounds, and a general average loss is incurred in respect of the ship's machinery. The chartered freight is liable to contribute, and the amount of the contribution can be deducted from the sum due under the policy on ship.[26]

6. Sailing ship in wartime engages a tug to tow her from Queenstown to Sheerness in order to lessen the danger from submarines. The cost of the tug is not a general average expenditure, for the vessel is not in immediate peril.[27]

7. Vessel insured under policy incorporating York-Antwerp Rules 1950 was in peril, and engaged a tug under United Kingdom Standard Towage Conditions, which stated that the shipowner must indemnify the tugowner for any damage to the tug. Tow line fouled the tug's propeller and she was damaged. The shipowner indemnified the tugowner and claimed that the expenditure was a general average expenditure. *Held*, the insurer was liable to reimburse him, for the expenditure was a 'direct consequence' of a general average act within the meaning of Rule C[28] of the York-Antwerp Rules 1950.[29]

---

1 *Ocean SS Co v Anderson* (1883) 13 QBD at 666, CA; *Svendsen v Wallace* (1884) 13 QBD at 84, CA; (1885) 10 App Cas at 419, HL. As to the words 'directly consequential,' see *Atwood v Sellar* (1880) 5 QBD 286, CA (landing and warehousing goods); cf *Greenshields, Cowie & Co v Stephens & Sons Ltd* [1908] AC 431, HL (damage to goods by water used to put out fire). As to 'substituted expenses,' see R Lowndes and G R Rudolf, *The Law of General Average and the York-Antwerp Rules*, 11th ed, 1990, paras F.01–F.39.

2 *Iredale v China Traders' Insurance Co* [1900] 2 QB at 519, CA. The usual phrase is 'ship and cargo' instead of 'common adventure,' but cases occur where there is a common adventure, but no cargo, eg ship in ballast going out to earn chartered freight.

3 As to the English conditions, see *Carver*, paras 1345/1484.

4 *Svendsen v Wallace* (1885) 10 App Cas at 415.

5 These words are wide enough to include the cargo's share of a general average expenditure incurred by the shipowner but irrecoverable from the cargo by reason of the diminution or extinction of its value before the adventure terminates: *Green Star Shipping Co Ltd v London Assurance* [1933] 1 KB 378, KB.

6 *Dickenson v Jardine* (1868) LR 3 CP 639; *The Mary Thomas* [1894] P at 125, CA. Where the York-Antwerp Rules apply, contributory values are to be assessed as at the termination of the adventure: *Green Star Shipping Co Ltd v London Assurance* (supra).
7 Cf *Henderson v Shankland* [1896] 1 QB 525, CA (general average sacrifice following particular average loss and ship then becoming CTL). The word 'subject' more correctly should be 'subject-matter' or 'interest'.
8 *Harris v Scaramanga* (1872) LR 7 CP at 496. Cf *Joseph Watson & Co v Fireman's Fund Insurance Co* [1922] 2 KB 355 (imaginary peril, no general average).
9 *Montgomery v Indemnity Mutual Marine Insurance Co* [1901] 1 KB 147; affd [1902] 1 KB 734, CA. Cf *Popham v St Petersburg Insurance Co* (1904) 10 Com Cas 31 (freight and goods both owned by charterer). The word 'subjects' more correctly should be 'interests'.
10 *Birkley v Presgrave* (1801) 1 East at 228, discussed in *Hudson v British and Foreign Marine Insurance Co* (1902) 8 Com Cas at 12 (loss of time freight, not general average). Cf *Austin Friars SS Co v Spillers and Bakers Ltd* [1915] 1 KB 833; affd [1915] 3 KB 586, CA (ship voluntarily running into dock pier, to escape stranding outside, general average).
11 *Chandris v Argo Insurance Co Ltd* [1963] 2 Lloyd's Rep 65, QB (Commercial Court).
12 *Castle Insurance Co Ltd v Hong Kong Islands Shipping Co Ltd, The Potoi Chau* [1983] 2 Lloyd's Rep 376, PC. (See the judgment of Lord Diplock, ibid, at 382–383.)
13 For a case where these sub-sections were considered in their relation to the York-Antwerp Rules 1924, see *Athel Line Ltd v Liverpool and London War Risks Insurance Association Ltd* [1944] KB 87, [1944] 1 All ER 46, KB.
14 *The Brigella* [1893] P at 195.
15 *Dickenson v Jardine* (1868) LR 3 CP 369.
16 See generally K S Selmer, *The Survival of General Average* (2nd ed, 1985).
17 *Vlassopoulos v British and Foreign Insurance Co* [1929] 1 KB 187; *Australian Coastal Shipping Commission v Green* [1971] QB 456, [1971] 1 All ER 353, CA.
18 See Institute Time Clauses (Hulls), Clause 11, p 181, post. The Institute Voyage Clauses (Hulls), Clause 9 is in similar terms (see Appendix III, p 200, post).
19 Cf *The Mary Thomas* [1894] P 108, CA (Dutch adjustment); *Brandeis Goldschmidt & Co v Economic Insurance Co Ltd* (1922) 38 TLR 609 (foreign adjustment clause, but no adjustment made).
20 See *Carver*, para 1402.
21 *Crooks v Allan* (1879) 5 QBD 38; approved in *Strang, Steel & Co v Scott* (1889) 14 App Cas at 607; R Lowndes and G R Rudolf, *The Law of General Average and the York-Antwerp Rules*, 11th ed, 1990, by D J Wilson and J H S Cooke, paras 30.01–30.30.
22 *Dickenson v Jardine* (1868) LR 3 CP 639 (London usage to hold insurer only liable for the assured's share of the loss of jettisoned goods *held* invalid).
23 *Fletcher v Alexander* (1868) LR 3 CP 375.
24 *Mavro v Ocean Marine Insurance Co* (1875) LR 10 CP 414, Ex Ch; cf *The Mary Thomas* [1894] P 108, CA; and *De Hart v Compania Anonima de Seguros Aurora* [1903] 2 KB 503 (general average payable as per foreign statement, special stipulation in charter-party as to general average). As to a new foreign adjustment clause framed with reference to this last case, see *Halsbury's Laws of England*, 4th ed, vol 25, para 258.
25 *Montgomery v Indemnity Mutual Marine Insurance Co* [1901] 1 KB 147; affd [1902] 1 KB 734, CA.
26 *SS Carisbrooke Co v London and Provincial Marine Insurance Co* (1901) 6 Com Cas 291.
27 *Société Nouvelle d'Armament v Spillers and Bakers Ltd* [1917] 1 KB 865, 870 (not an insurance case, but based on the definition of general average in s 66).
28 Which states: 'Only such losses, damages or expenses which are the direct consequence of the general average act shall be allowed as general average.' Rule C of the York-Antwerp Rules 1974 is in the same words. See Appendix IV, p 277, post.
29 *Australian Coastal Shipping Commission v Green* [1971] QB 456, [1971] 1 All ER 353, CA. (See the judgment of Lord Denning MR, ibid, at 360.)

MEASURE OF INDEMNITY[1]

67. Extent of liability of insurer for loss

(1) The sum which the assured can recover in respect of a loss on a policy by which he is insured, in the case of an unvalued policy, to the full extent of the insurable value, or, in the case of a valued policy, to the full extent of the value fixed by the policy, is called the measure of indemnity.[2]

(2) Where there is a loss recoverable under the policy, the insurer, or each insurer if there be more than one, is liable for such proportion of the measure of indemnity as the amount of his subscription bears to the value fixed by the policy, in the case of a valued policy, or to the insurable value, in the case of an unvalued policy.[3]

Note

Insurance is a contract of indemnity, but in marine insurance the amount of the indemnity is a matter of agreement between the parties, and the following sections supply the standard or measure for ascertaining it.

The adjustment of marine losses proceeds on the hypothesis that the subject-matter insured is fully covered by insurance. Suppose a ship valued at £1,000,000 is insured for £100,000 only. The shipowner is said to be 'his own insurer' for £900,000, and any loss which occurs must be adjusted on this basis; see s 81.[4] The following cases may be put in illustration of this principle:

(i) A cargo valued at £100,000 is insured for £10,000 by ten underwriters who each subscribe for £1,000. It is damaged by sea perils to the extent of £10,000. Each underwriter is liable for £100 only.

(ii) A ship valued at £500,000 is insured for £100,000. The ship is stranded, and the owner spends £100,000 in trying to get her off, but eventually she is a total loss. The insurer must pay £100,000 on the policy, and £20,000 (ie one-fifth) under the suing and labouring clause. It is immaterial whether the real value of the ship is £450,000 or £550,000.

As to 'insurable value,' see s 16. As to the 'sue and labour' clause, which is a distinct engagement in the policy, see s 78; and for a quasi-exception, see s 74 (liabilities to third parties).

Section 67, together with s 68 in total loss cases, is conclusively definite on the extent of the liability of the insurer for the loss of a vessel under a valued policy.[5]

---

1 The term has been criticised as unfamiliar. See this 'fasciculus of sections' and their construction discussed by Lord Sumner, *British and Foreign Insurance Co v Wilson Shipping Co Ltd* [1921] 1 AC 188, 26 Com Cas 13, 32, HL, pointing out that the words 'a policy' and 'the policy' are constantly used to denote not merely a single instrument, but also an entire insurance on the same subject-matter, though contained in two or more policies.
2 *Papadimitriou v Henderson* [1939] 3 All ER 908, KB ('anticipated freight' fixed by valuation).
3 Cf *Lohre v Aitchison* (1878) 3 QBD at 564, 565, CA, affd on this point, but reversed on another, (1879) 4 App Cas 755.
4 See principle explained by Walton J, in *Anglo-Californian Bank v London and Provincial Marine Insurance Co* (1904) 10 Com Cas at 8, 9.

5 *Ventouris v Mountain, The Italia Express (No 2)* [1992] 2 Lloyd's Rep 281, QB (Commercial Court) at 291 (per Hirst J).

68. Total loss

Subject to the provisions of this Act,[1] and to any express provision in the policy, where there is a total loss of the subject-matter insured,—
(1) If the policy be a valued policy, the measure of indemnity is the sum fixed by the policy:[2]
(2) If the policy be an unvalued policy, the measure of indemnity is the insurable value of the subject-matter insured.[3]

Note

As to 'valued' and 'unvalued' policies, see ss 27 and 28, and as to 'insurable value' and the rules of determining it, see s 16.

The Institute Clauses contain a special provision concerning the breaking up of the vessel.

Thus, the Institute Time Clauses (Hulls), Clause 1[4] states: 'In the event of the Vessel sailing (with or without cargo) with the intention of being (a) broken up, or (b) sold for breaking up, any claim for loss of or damage to the Vessel occurring subsequent to such sailing shall be limited to the market value of the Vessel as scrap at the time when the loss or damage is sustained, unless previous notice has been given to the Underwriters and any amendment to the terms of cover, insured value and premiums required by them have been agreed . . .'

In relation to the total loss of freight, the Institute Clauses[5] state that: 'In the event of the total loss (actual or constructive) of the vessel . . . the amount [of freight] insured shall be paid in full, whether the vessel be fully or partly loaded or in ballast, chartered or unchartered . . . Should the vessel be a constructive total loss but the claim on the insurances on hull and machinery be settled as a claim for partial loss,[6] no payment [for freight] shall be due.'

Section 68 is conclusive as to the extent of the insurer's liability in the case of a total loss.[7]

Illustration

A vessel was a total loss. As part of his claim the plaintiff contended that he was entitled to damages for loss of income, the increase in the capital value of a replacement vessel, inconvenience and mental distress. *Held*, by s 68, he could claim only for the value fixed by the policy.[8]

1 See s 77 as to successive losses, and s 78 as to 'sue and labour' clause.
2 *Irving v Manning* (1847) 1 HL Cas at 305, 307; *Sailing Ship Blairmore v Macredie* [1898] AC at 610; cf *Woodside v Globe Marine Insurance Co Ltd* [1896] 1 QB 105.
3 *Irving v Manning* (1847) 1 HL Cas at 305, 307.
4 See Appendix III, p 168, post.
5 Institute Time Clauses (Freight), Clause 15, Appendix III, p 222, post: Institute Voyage Clauses (Freight), Clause 13, Appendix III, p 230, post.

6 As to partial loss of ship, see s 69.
7 *Ventouris v Mountain, The Italia Express (No 2)* [1992] 2 Lloyd's Rep 281, QB (Commercial Court) at 291 (per Hirst J).
8 Ibid.

69. Partial loss of ship

Where a ship is damaged, but is not totally lost, the measure of indemnity, subject to any express provision in the policy, is as follows:
(1) Where the ship has been repaired, the assured is entitled to the reasonable cost of the repairs, less the customary deductions,[1] but not exceeding the sum insured in respect of any one casualty:[2]
(2) Where the ship has been only partially repaired, the assured is entitled to the reasonable cost of such repairs, computed as above, and also to be indemnified for the reasonable depreciation, if any, arising from the unrepaired damage, provided that the aggregate amount shall not exceed the cost of repairing the whole damage, computed as above:[3]
(3) Where the ship has not been repaired, and has not been sold in her damaged state during the risk, the assured is entitled to be indemnified for the reasonable depreciation arising from the unrepaired damage, but not exceeding the reasonable cost of repairing such damage computed as above.[4]

Note

In the case of wooden ships, except on a first voyage, the custom is to make an arbitrary deduction of 'one third new for old' from the cost of the repairs.[5] But this rule is inapplicable to iron ships, and the practice is to provide for them by special clauses.

Thus, Clause 14 of the Institute Time Clauses (Hulls) provides: 'Claims payable without deduction, new for old.'[6] Clause 8 of the Institute Yacht Clauses provides: 'Average irrespective of percentage. No deduction of things new for old shall be made except in respect of sails, protective covers and running rigging.'

The 'customary deductions' were originally set out as a schedule to the Bill, but the schedule was cut out afterwards as it was thought better to leave it to custom, which may alter from time to time to meet new needs. See Rules of Practice of the Association of Average Adjusters, rule D7.[7]

The Act does not provide for the case where the ship is not repaired, but *is* sold in her damaged state during the risk. In that case, according to the majority of the Court of Appeal in *Pitman v Universal Marine Insurance Co*,[8] the assured is entitled to the reasonable cost of repairing such damage, computed as above, but not exceeding the actual depreciation in the value of the ship as ascertained by the sale. Brett LJ, dissented, thinking the principle it laid down a dangerous innovation, and that the estimated cost of repairs, less the usual deductions, should be the sole measure of indemnity.

The decision is unsatisfactory, because the other Judges on appeal expressly refrained from deciding what was to be taken as the basis of depreciation. The sale price is one factor in the comparison, but what is the other factor? Is it the value of the ship at the commencement of the risk, or at the time of the casualty, or what other value?

In the case of a time policy the time at which the measure of indemnity under s 69(3) falls to be determined is the time when the policy expires.[9] 'It is only when the risk is ended that it can be predicted for certain that neither repair nor sale will take place during the risk.'[10]

Where a ship is not repaired or sold during the risk, the measure of indemnity is the depreciation (not exceeding the reasonable cost of repairs) arising from the unrepaired damage, as stated in s 69(3). But where the damaged value of a vessel is virtually nil, the indemnity is limited to the reasonable cost of the repairs.[11]

The term 'reasonable cost of repairs' is not confined to the reasonable cost of permanent repairs. It is a question of fact in each case as to what the phrase includes.[12]

Section 69 (3) requires the measure of indemnity to be quantified on the basis of what it would have cost to repair a vessel if the repairs had been carried out. Thus, if it would have been necessary for her to be towed to a port for repairs, the cost of towing, although not incurred, is recoverable as part of the partial loss claim.[13]

As to total loss following a partial loss, see s 77.

The Institute Clauses provide that in the case of a partial loss of a ship the claim is subject to a 'deductible,' ie it will not be paid if the damage does not exceed a specified percentage.[14]

Further, as regards claims for unrepaired damage, they state: 'The measure of indemnity in respect of claims for unrepaired damage shall be the reasonable depreciation in the market value of the Vessel at the time this insurance terminates arising from such unrepaired damage, but not exceeding the reasonable cost of repairs . . . The Underwriters shall not be liable in respect of unrepaired damage for more than the insured value at the time this insurance terminates.'[15]

Illustrations

1. Policy on hull and machinery. The ship is damaged in a collision, and has to put into dock for repairs. The cargo becomes putrid, and the shipowner incurs expenses in landing it. These expenses cannot be recovered under the policy on ship.[16]
2. Policy on ship. In consequence of damage the ship is put into dry dock for repairs. The owners take the opportunity to have her surveyed for Lloyd's classification, but this does not increase the time in dock. The insurer must pay the whole expenses of docking the ship.[17]
3. Policy on ship. Ship insured for £4,000 was involved in a collision. The cost of repairing her amounted to £5,000. Any expenditure over £4,000 cannot be recovered from the insurers.[18]
4. Whilst a trawler is being towed in January 1942 to a dry dock for refitting, she strands and is severely damaged. The assured gives notice of abandonment. After the ship is salvaged by the Admiralty, he refuses to have her put in dry dock for ascertainment of damage. He does not contest salvage proceedings after which the ship is sold under an order of the court. At all material times the assured was unlikely to obtain a licence to repair her or to place her in dry dock. *Held*, that there was no constructive total loss, because

118 Measure of indemnity

the claim did not fall under any of the heads specified in s 60. With regard to partial loss, the risk ended when the ship was abandoned, and so the case fell within s 69(3).[19]

1. As to reasonable cost of repairs, see *Agenoria SS Co v Merchants' Marine Insurance Co* (1903) 8 Com Cas 212 (costs of special surveyor from England, banker's overdraft, and scarfing stern-post); *Helmville Ltd v Yorkshire Insurance Co Ltd, The Medina Princess* [1965] 1 Lloyd's Rep 361 at 523 QB (Commercial Court) (reasonable fees for classification surveyors and other surveyors properly allowable as part of the cost of repairs); cf *Hall v Hayman* (1911) 17 Com Cas at pp 90–92 (scarfing, etc). As to the customary deductions, see Note supra.
2. *Arnould*, para 1115 et seq; *Aitchison v Lohre* (1879) 4 App Cas at 762; *Pitman v Universal Marine Insurance Co* (1882) 9 QBD at 208. As to successive losses, see s 77.
3. Cf *Stewart v Steele* (1842) 5 Scott NR 927 at 948; *British and Foreign Insurance Co Ltd v Wilson Shipping Co Ltd* [1921] 1 AC 188 at 194, 206.
4. Ibid.
5. See *Arnould*, para 1117; *Pitman v Universal Marine Insurance Co* (1882) 9 QBD at 215; cf *Henderson v Shankland* [1896] 1 QB at 530, CA.
6. See Appendix III, p 185, post. The Institute Voyage Clauses (Hulls), Clause 12 is in the same terms. (See Appendix III, p 203, post.)
7. See Appendix V, p 296, post.
8. (1882) 9 QBD 192 at 218, 219, CA; cf *Stewart v Steele* (1842) 5 Scott NR 927 at 948; *British Steam Navigation Co v Indemnity Mutual Marine Assurance Co* (1887) 6 Asp MLC 173. Cf *Arnould*, para 1116; W Gow, *Marine Insurance: A Handbook* (5th ed, 1931), p 220. See further, *Elcock v Thomson* [1949] 2 KB 755, 762 (fire insurance).
9. *Helmville Ltd v Yorkshire Insurance Co Ltd, The Medina Princess* [1965] 1 Lloyd's Rep 361, QBD (Commercial Court).
10. Ibid, at 516 (per Roskill J).
11. Ibid, at 515 (per Roskill J).
12. Ibid, at 518–520 (per Roskill J).
13. Ibid, at 521 (per Roskill J).
14. Institute Time Clauses (Hulls), Clause 12, Appendix III, p 183, post; Institute Voyage Clauses (Hulls), Clause 10, Appendix III, p 201, post.
15. Institute Time Clauses (Hulls), Clause 18, Appendix III, p 117, post; Institute Voyage Clauses (Hulls), Clause 16, Appendix III, p 204, post.
16. *Field SS Co v Burr* [1899] 1 QB 579, CA, followed in *Polurrian SS Co v Young* (1913) 19 Com Cas 143 at 159.
17. *Ruabon SS Co v London Assurance* [1900] AC 6, HL, distinguishing *Marine Insurance Co Ltd v China Transpacific SS Co Ltd* (1886) 11 App Cas 573.
18. *Goole and Hull Steam Towing Co Ltd v Ocean Marine Insurance Co Ltd* (1929) 29 Ll L Rep 242. (See the judgment of Mackinnon J, ibid, at 244.)
19. *Irvin v Hine* [1949] 2 All ER 1089, KB. 'In estimating the cost of repair for the purpose of a partial loss I think that the court has to get as near as possible to the actual figure which would have been expended had she been repaired, and, if it be proved to my satisfaction, as it is, that she could not have been repaired earlier than the early part of 1947, I think I ought to take the figures appropriate to that time.' Per Devlin J, at 1092–3. As to 'constructive total loss', see s 60, ante.

70. Partial loss of freight

Subject to any express provision in the policy, where there is a partial loss of freight, the measure of indemnity is such proportion of the sum fixed by the policy, in the case of a valued policy, or of the insurable value, in the case of an unvalued policy, as the proportion of freight lost by the assured bears to the whole freight at the risk of the assured under the policy.[1]

Note

As to valued policy, see s 27, and as to unvalued policy, see s 28.

The insurable value in the case of freight is the gross freight; see s 16(2). 'The rule for adjusting a partial loss on freight is very simple, ie, that where the sum insured is less than the insurable value of the interest at risk, the underwriter pays the same proportional part of the loss that the sum insured is of the insurable value of the freight; if the sum insured equals the insurable value of the interest, then he pays the whole of the loss.' *Arnould*, para 1133.

The Institute Time Clauses (Freight)[2] and the Institute Voyage Clauses (Freight)[3] set out a 'franchise' in respect of small losses (ie the insurer is not liable if the specified percentage of loss is not reached, but is liable for the whole of the loss once the percentage is reached) and state: 'The insurance does not cover partial loss other than general average loss,[4] under 3 per cent unless caused by fire, sinking, stranding or collision with another vessel. Each craft and/or lighter to be deemed a separate insurance if required by the Assured.'

Further, the Clauses also state that the amount recoverable for any partial loss of freight shall not exceed the gross freight actually lost.[5]

1 *Forbes v Aspinall* (1811) 13 East 323, 12 RR 352; *Denoon v Home and Colonial Assurance Co* (1872) LR 7 CP at 351; *The Main* [1894] P 320. As to the facts which constitute a partial, as distinguished from a total loss of freight, see *Rankin v Potter* (1873) LR 6 HL at 98–100, per Brett J. See W Gow, *Marine Insurance: A Handbook* (5th ed, 1931), pp 154–155.
2 Clause 12, Appendix III, p 221, post.
3 Clause 10, Appendix III, p 229, post.
4 As to 'general average loss,' see s 66.
5 Institute Time Clauses (Freight), Clause 13, p 221, post; Institute Voyage Clauses (Freight), Clause 11, p 230, post.

71. Partial loss of goods, merchandise etc

Where there is a partial loss of goods, merchandise, or other moveables, the measure of indemnity, subject to any express provision in the policy, is as follows:

(1) Where part of the goods, merchandise, or other moveables insured by a valued policy is totally lost, the measure of indemnity is such proportion of the sum fixed by the policy as the insurable value of the part lost bears to the insurable value of the whole, ascertained as in the case of an unvalued policy:[1]

(2) Where part of the goods, merchandise, or other moveables insured by an unvalued policy is totally lost, the measure of indemnity is the insurable value of the part lost, ascertained as in case of total loss:[2]

(3) Where the whole or any part of the goods or merchandise insured has been delivered damaged at its destination, the measure of indemnity is such proportion of the sum fixed by the policy, in the case of a valued policy, or of the insurable value in the case of an unvalued policy, as the difference between the gross sound and damaged values at the place of arrival bears to the gross sound value:[3]

(4) 'Gross value' means the wholesale price, or, if there be no such price, the estimated value, with, in either case, freight, landing charges, and duty paid beforehand; provided that in the case of goods or merchandise customarily sold in bond, the bonded price is deemed to be the gross value. 'Gross proceeds' means the actual price obtained at a sale where all charges on sale are paid by the sellers.[4]

Note

The policy of the rules contained in sub-ss (3) and (4) has often been criticised, but they are only prima facie rules, applicable to ordinary goods. There are many matters to which they could not apply, e g loss of part of a machine, rendering the whole valueless.[5] Such cases are usually provided for by special clauses. See further s 75, as to cases not specially provided for. As to insurable value, see s 16(3).

The insurers insure against actual damage to the goods but not against prejudice or suspicion of damage. 'However great the suspicion of damage and however strong the moral belief and conviction of the [assured], unless damage is proved on the balance of probabilities on the basis of legal evidence and material on record, there cannot be proof of damage.'[6]

Illustrations

1. Unvalued policy on coffee from Jamaica to London. The insurable value, ie, the invoice cost, plus shipping expenses and charges of insurance, is £200. Half the coffee is damaged on the voyage. The value of the damaged coffee in London is half that of the undamaged coffee. The selling price in London fixes the measure of percentage of depreciation, but not the amount the insurer has to pay. That must be determined by applying the depreciation to the insurable value, so that in this case the insurer has to pay £50.[7]
2. Policy on 40 bales of cotton, which are shipped as part of a cargo of 1,600 bales of cotton belonging to different owners. Owing to sea perils 200 bales have to be jettisoned, and the rest are damaged and the marks wholly obliterated. The 1,400 bales are sold for the benefit of whom it may concern. This is a partial loss, and the assured is entitled to recover as if five of his 40 bales had been jettisoned, and the rest damaged to the extent shown by the sale of the whole.[8]
3. Policy on 1,700 packages of tea, valued at £6,000. Part of the tea is sea-damaged, and the remainder, which arrives undamaged, is sold in consequence for a smaller price. The insurer is not liable for the depreciation so caused.[9]

4. Policy on cargo of sheet iron in separate packages, average payable 'on each package separately or on the whole'. Damage is sustained before the termination of the risk. The whole of the iron is unpacked and examined. The damaged iron is sold, and the rest is repacked and sent on. The insurer is not liable for the expenses incurred in examining and repacking the packages which were not damaged.[10]

1 *Arnould*, para 1102 et seq; *Lewis v Rucker* (1761) 2 Burr 1167; *Irving v Manning* (1847) 1 HL Cas at 305.
2 *Lewis v Rucker* (1761) 2 Burr 1167; *Irving v Manning* (1847) 1 HL Cas at 305; cf *Tobin v Harford* (1863) 32 LJCP 134, 136; see s 16(3) as to insurable value.
3 *Johnson v Sheddon* (1802) 2 East 581 (the 'brimstone case'). As to estimating the value of jettisoned goods, cf *Fletcher v Alexander* (1868) LR 3 CP 375 (general average). The values must, of course, be reduced to the same cash basis. 'Where the goods are sold by public auction the gross amount they realise is called the "damaged value," and the value they would have been sold for if sound, ie, the current price for sound articles of the same kind in the same market, is called the "sound value".' *Halsbury's Laws of England*, 4th edn, vol 25, para 284.
4 Rules of Practice of the Association of Average Adjusters, rule E2. (See Appendix V, p 297, post). Where any sale or other preliminary charges on damaged goods or merchandise are paid or payable by the buyers, such charges must be added to the gross proceeds before establishing the ratio of damage, as above provided, and in the event of a claim being established, such charges are subsequently recoverable from the insurers as 'extra charges': *Francis v Boulton* (1895) 65 LJQB 153 (conditioning charges).
5 Cf *British Columbia Sawmill Co v Nettleship* (1868) LR 3 CP 499 (measure of damage against shipowner); and see s 75.
6 *Boon and Cheah Steel Pipes Sdn Bhd v Asia Insurance Co Ltd* (supra) at 454 (per Raja Azlan, Shah J).
7 *Usher v Noble* (1810) 12 East 639, and s 16 (insurable value). The test adopted excludes the rise or fall of the London market.
8 *Spence v Union Marine Insurance Co* (1868) LR 3 CP 427.
9 *Cator v Great Western Insurance Co* (1873) LR 8 CP 552, 561. There was a special warranty as to sea-damage, but the judgment establishes the general principle. See this case distinguished, *Brown Bros v Fleming* (1902) 7 Com Cas 245 (policy on cases of whisky—damage to labels and packing by sea perils). *Cator v Great Western Insurance Co* was applied obiter by McNair J, in *Overseas Commodities Ltd v Style* [1958] 1 Lloyd's Rep 546 (all risks insurance) at pp 561–562, where he said that financial loss resulting from sound canned pork being suspect was not recoverable as a particular average loss. See also *Boon and Cheah Steel Pipes Sdn Bhd v Asia Insurance Co Ltd* [1975] 1 Lloyd's Rep 452, Malaysia High Court, where some steel pipes were thought to be damaged.
10 *Lysaght v Coleman* [1895] 1 QB 49, CA.

72. Apportionment of valuation

(1) Where different species of property are insured under a single valuation, the valuation must be apportioned over the different species in proportion to their respective insurable values, as in the case of an unvalued policy. The insured value of any part of a species is such proportion of the total insured value of the same as the insurable value of the part bears to the insurable value of the whole ascertained in both cases as provided by this Act.[1]

122 Measure of indemnity

(2) Where a valuation has to be apportioned, and particulars of the prime cost of each separate species, quality, or description of goods cannot be ascertained, the division of the valuation may be made over the net arrived sound values of the different species, qualities, or descriptions of goods.

Note

As to 'insurable value,' see s 16(3); and for the mode of ascertaining the value referred to in sub-s (1), see s 71, as read with s 16.

1 *Arnould*, para 444; Rules of Practice of the Association of Average Adjusters, rule E3 (see Appendix V, p 297, post); and see s 76, as to fpa warranties.

73. General average contributions and salvage charges

(1) Subject to any express provision in the policy, where the assured has paid, or is liable for, any general average contribution, the measure of indemnity is the full amount of such contribution if the subject-matter liable to contribution is insured for its full contributory value; but if such subject-matter be not insured for its full contributory value, or if only part of it be insured, the indemnity payable by the insurer must be reduced in proportion to the under-insurance, and where there has been a particular average loss which constitutes a deduction from the contributory value, and for which the insurer is liable, that amount must be deducted from the insured value in order to ascertain what the insurer is liable to contribute.[1]

(2) Where the insurer is liable for salvage charges the extent of his liability must be determined on the like principle.

Note

This section deals with adjustment. As to liability, see ss 65 and 66.

Suppose goods are insured for £1,500 by a valued policy. General average is incurred, of which £80 is found to be the proportion payable by the owner of the goods, their contributory value being taken at £1,600. The insurer is liable for 15-16ths of £80, viz, £75. But if the contributory value of the goods is taken at £1,500, the insurer is liable for the whole £80.

See s 81 as to under-insurance. As to assessment of contributory value in salvage cases, see W R Kennedy, *Law of Salvage*, 5th ed, 1985, by David W Steel and Francis D Rose, paras 1031–1096; *Carver*, paras 1330–1334.

Illustration

Policy on ship valued at £33,000, for that sum. Her real value is £40,000. The ship incurs certain general average and salvage expenses which are adjusted abroad on her real value. The assured can only recover 33/40ths of the amount so adjusted from the insurer.[2]

1 See *Arnould*, para 1107; Rules of Practice of the Association of Average Adjusters, rule E3. As to the effect to be given to the foreign general average clause, see *Greer v Poole* (1880) 5 QBD 272; *The Mary Thomas* [1894] P 108, CA. As to contribution by goods where ship is a constructive total loss, see *Henderson v Shankland* [1896] 1 QB 525, CA.
2 *SS Balmoral Co v Marten* [1901] 2 KB 896, CA; affd [1902] AC 511, HL.

74. Liabilities to third parties

Where the assured has effected an insurance in express terms against any liability to a third party, the measure of indemnity, subject to any express provision in the policy, is the amount paid or payable by him to such third party in respect of such liability.[1]

Note

A carrier may insure his liability to a cargo owner if the cargo is damaged by the carrier's negligence.

So, too, may a marina operator insure against his legal liability to a third party.[2]

Again, a shipowner may insure against liability for damage caused to another vessel by the negligent navigation of the insured vessel. This insurance cover is provided by the 'Collision Clause' contained in the Institute Time Clauses (Hulls)[3] and the Institute Voyage Clauses (Hulls).[4] The construction of such a clause depends entirely on the language used by the parties in the particular clause in question, for its wording has been modernised from time to time.[5]

As to distribution of liability in case of negligent collision, see ss 1–5 of the Maritime Conventions Act 1911. By the Third Parties (Rights against Insurers) Act 1930, s 1(1) if an assured incurs liability to a third party, and before making payment becomes bankrupt or goes into liquidation, the rights in the policy are transferred to the third party.

Illustration

A carrier insures his liability to a third party in respect of goods worth £40,000 for £20,000. If the goods are sea-damaged to the extent of £20,000, he can recover the whole £20,000.[6]

1 *The Niobe* [1891] AC 401, HL (collision); cf *Joyce v Kennard* (1871) LR 8 QB 78 (lighterman's liability); *Cunard SS Co v Marten* [1902] 2 KB 624, 629 (carriers' liability); *Holman & Sons v Merchants' Marine Insurance Co* [1919] 1 KB 383, 24 Com Cas 102 ('increased value' policy on ship is insurance on the res, not against liability).
2 *Pillgrem v Cliff Richardson Boats Ltd and Richardson (Switzerland General Insurance Co, Third Party)* [1977] 1 Lloyd's Rep 297, Supreme Court of Ontario, where there was a 'deductible' of $1,250.
3 See Clause 8, Appendix III, p 177, post.
4 See Clause 6, Appendix III, p 198, post.
5 *Davidson v Burnand* (1868) LR 4 CP at 121, per Willes J. As to the scope to be given to the term 'collision,' see *Chandler v Blogg* [1898] 1 QB 32 (collision with sunken barge); *The Niobe* [1891] AC 401 (collision with tug: tug and tow regarded as identical); *Arnould*, para 803; *The Munroe* [1893] P 248 (meaning of sunken wreck); *Union Marine Insurance Co v Borwick* [1895] 2 QB 279 ('piers or similar structures' include artificial bank); *Shelbourne v Law Investment Insurance Corpn* [1898] 2 QB 626 (loss by detention during repairs not

recoverable); *Tatham v Burr* [1898] AC 382 (removal of obstructions under statutory powers); *Burger v Indemnity Mutual Marine Assurance Co* [1900] 2 QB 348, CA (damage to ship or vessel herself); *Re Margetts and Ocean Accident and Guarantee Corpn Ltd* [1901] 2 KB 792 (collision with anchor of another vessel); *Bennett SS Co v Hull Mutual SS Protecting Society* [1913] 3 KB 372; affd [1914] 3 KB 57, CA (ship, running into fishing nets not within collision clause); *France, Fenwick & Co Ltd v Merchants' Marine Insurance Co Ltd* [1915] 3 KB 290, CA; affg [1914] 3 KB 827 (ship A colliding with ship B thereby causing ship B to run into ship C); *Furness Withy & Co Ltd v Duder* [1936] 2 All ER 119, KB (the words 'liable to pay . . . by way of damages' in a collision clause cover only liability arising by way of tort and not by way of contract); *Hall Bros SS Co Ltd v Young, The Trident* [1939] 1 All ER 809, CA (a payment by way of indemnity under French legislation to a French pilot-boat irrespective of negligence is not 'by way of damages'); *Polpen Shipping Co Ltd v Commercial Union Assurance Co Ltd* [1943] 1 All ER 162, KB (collision with a flying-boat, *held* not a 'ship or vessel'). See further Ivamy, *Marine Insurance*, (4th ed, 1985), pp 170–176.

6 *Cunard SS Co v Marten* [1902] 2 KB 624 at 629, 8 Com Cas at 22, per Walton J. Aliter if, as bailee, he insures the goods himself: *Crowley v Cohen* (1832) 3 B & Ad 478.

75. General provisions as to measure of indemnity

(1) Where there has been a loss in respect of any subject-matter not expressly provided for in the foregoing provisions of this Act, the measure of indemnity shall be ascertained, as nearly as may be, in accordance with those provisions, in so far as applicable to the particular case.[1]

(2) Nothing in the provisions of this Act relating to the measure of indemnity shall affect the rules relating to double insurance, or prohibit the insurer from disproving interest wholly or in part, or from showing that at the time of the loss the whole or any part of the subject-matter insured was not at risk under the policy.[2]

Note

If the provisions of sub-s (1) do not meet the case, recourse may be had to the common law (including the law merchant) under the saving provided by s 91(2).

1 See notes to ss 71 and 74 and such cases as *Baring Bros & Co v Marine Insurance Co* (1894) 10 TLR 276 (stock certificates sent abroad by registered letter).
2 See s 32 (double insurance). As to disproving interest entirely, see *Lewis v Rucker* (1761) 2 Burr at 1171 (colourable interest); *Seagrave v Union Marine Insurance Co* (1866) LR 1 CP 305, 316–320 (bare consignee); as to short interest, see *Forbes v Aspinall* (1811) 13 East 323; *Denoon v Home and Colonial Assurance Co* (1872) LR 7 CP 341; *Williams v North China Insurance Co* (1876) 1 CPD 757, CA; cf *Reliance Marine Insurance Co v Duder* (1912) 17 Com Cas at 236, Kennedy LJ, and as to part of the subject-matter not being at risk, see *Tobin v Harford* (1864) 34 LJCP 37, 57, Ex Ch; *The Main* [1894] P 320 (freight).

76. Particular average warranties

(1) Where the subject-matter insured is warranted free from particular average, the assured cannot recover for a loss of part, other than a loss

incurred by a general average sacrifice, unless the contract contained in the policy be apportionable; but, if the contract be apportionable, the assured may recover for a total loss of any apportionable part.[1]

(2) Where the subject-matter insured is warranted free from particular average, either wholly or under a certain percentage, the insurer is nevertheless liable for salvage charges, and for particular charges and other expenses properly incurred pursuant to the provisions of the suing and labouring clause in order to avert a loss insured against.[2]

(3) Unless the policy otherwise provides, where the subject-matter insured is warranted free from particular average under a specified percentage, a general average loss cannot be added to a particular average loss to make up the specified percentage.[3]

(4) For the purpose of ascertaining whether the specified percentage has been reached, regard shall be had only to the actual loss suffered by the subject-matter insured. Particular charges and the expenses of and incidental to ascertaining and proving the loss must be excluded.[4]

Note

As to 'general average sacrifice,' see s 66; as to 'salvage charges,' see s 65; as to 'particular charges', see s 64(2); as to 'suing and labouring clause', see s 78; and as to 'particular average loss', see s 64.

A policy, or rather the contract contained in it, is apportionable where the policy itself provides for apportionment, or where by usage it is treated as apportionable. Cf s 72 as to apportionment.

Illustrations

1. Policy on master's effects, 'free of all average'. The effects include articles of different species, eg feather-bed, chronometer, spy-glass, etc. Some of the effects are totally lost by perils of the seas, others are saved. The assured can recover in respect of those which are totally lost.[5]
2. Policy on iron rails, warranted 'free from particular average unless the ship be stranded'. The ship is not stranded, but becomes a constructive total loss. The rails are saved, landed, and sent on to their destination in another ship at an increased freight. The assured cannot recover the extra freight he has had to pay.[6]
3. Policy on 2,000 bags of linseed insured for (say) £2,000, 'warranted free from average, unless general, etc'. One thousand bags are so sea-damaged as to become rotten and valueless. The insurer is not liable. This is not a separate insurance of each bag, but of the whole of the linseed, and the warranty applies accordingly.[7]
4. Policy on disbursements and advances warranted 'free from all average'. The disbursements include outlay, before the ship sails, on provisions, stores, port dues, and insurance. The ship was chartered to take a cargo to South America, and the intention of the assured was to obtain a homeward cargo there. On the voyage out the ship catches fire, and the assured abandons the voyage and brings the ship home for repairs. This is an average and not a total loss, and the warranty applies.[8]

1 *Arnould*, para 853, and Ivamy, *Marine Insurance* (4th ed, 1985), p 430; *Ralli v Janson* (1856) 6 E & B 422 (bags of seed), read with *Duff v Mackenzie* (1857) 3 CBNS 16 (master's effects), and *Cator v Great Western Insurance Co* (1873) LR 8 CP at 559. And see *Fabrique de Produits Chimiques v Large* [1923] 1 KB 203, 28 Com Cas 248. In *Duff v Mackenzie* it was held that where the goods were different in specie, the contract was apportionable, but it is submitted that this is only one test of severability. For cases on the fpa warranty, see *Hagedorn v Whitmore* (1816) 1 Stark 157; *Navone v Haddon* (1850) 9 CB 30; *Kidston v Empire Insurance Co* (1866) LR 1 CP at 548 (reviewing cases); *De Mattos v Saunders* (1872) LR 7 CP 570.
2 *Kidston v Empire Insurance Co* (1866) LR 1 CP 535; and s 78 ('sue and labour' clause).
3 *Price & Co v A1 Ships' Small Damage Insurance Association Ltd* (1889) 22 QBD 580, CA; and cf *Oppenheim v Fry* (1863) 3 B & S at 884.
4 As to last two sub-sections, see *Arnould*, para 849 and Ivamy, *Marine Insurance* (4th ed, 1985), pp 416–417.
5 *Duff v Mackenzie* (1857) 3 CBNS 16; cf *Wilkinson v Hyde* (1858) 3 CBNS 30, 34 (iron castings, sheet glass, and other species of goods).
6 *Great Indian Peninsular Rly Co v Saunders* (1861) 1 B & S 41; affd (1862) 2 B & S 266; discussed and explained in *Kidston v Empire Insurance Co* (1866) LR 1 CP at 548; distinguished in *Wilson Bros Bobbin Co v Green* [1917] 1 KB 860, 863, 22 Com Cas 185.
7 *Ralli v Janson* (1856) 6 E & B 422, Ex Ch.
8 *Lawther v Black* (1900) 6 Com Cas 5; affd (1901) 6 Com Cas 196, CA; cf *Price v Maritime Insurance Co* [1901] 2 KB 412, CA, as to distance freight payable under Italian law.

77. Successive losses

(1) Unless the policy otherwise provides, and subject to the provisions of this Act, the insurer is liable for successive losses, even though the total amount of such losses may exceed the sum insured.[1]

(2) Where under the same policy, a partial loss, which has not been repaired or otherwise made good, is followed by a total loss, the assured can only recover in respect of the total loss:

Provided that nothing in this section shall affect the liability of the insurer under the suing and labouring clause.[2]

Note

In *Lidgett v Secretan*,[3] where the assured recovered for both a partial and total loss, the losses were covered by different and consecutive policies, and the fact that the insurer was the same person in both cases was held to be immaterial.

'It is clear,' said Lord Abinger, 'that whenever the underwriter adjusts a partial loss, he still remains liable on the policy, and may go on paying partial losses exceeding in the whole cent per cent, and may ultimately have to pay a total loss of cent per cent. Such a case is possible.'[4]

As to the 'sue and labour' clause, see s 78.

The Institute Clauses[5] state that: 'In no case shall the Underwriters be liable for unrepaired damage in the event of a subsequent total loss (whether or not covered under this insurance) sustained during the period covered by this insurance or any extension thereof.'

Illustrations

1. A ship is insured against perils of the seas, but not against fire. She is sea-damaged, but the sea-damage is not repaired. Afterwards she is destroyed by fire. The assured cannot recover anything on the policy.[6]
2. A ship is insured by her owners under a time policy. After insurance she is chartered. On the voyage out the ship is damaged, and the repairs are paid for by the charterers, and the cost specially insured by them. On the voyage home she is totally lost. The shipowner can only recover for the total loss.[7]
3. Ship insured by one insurer against marine perils, and by another insurer against war risks. She suffers marine damage, which is not repaired. She is afterwards totally lost by a war peril (torpedoed by submarine). The unrepaired partial loss is merged in the total loss, and cannot be recovered under the marine policy.[8]

1 *Le Cheminant v Pearson* (1812) 4 Taunt 367; cf *Aitchison v Lohre* (1879) 4 App Cas at 763.
2 *Livie v Janson* (1810) 12 East 648. As to proviso, see ibid, at 655; cf *British and Foreign Insurance Co v Wilson Shipping Co Ltd* [1921] 1 AC 188, HL. The words 'under the same policy' do not confine the rule to this case; see infra.
3 *Lidgett v Secretan* (1871) LR 6 CP 616; cf *Woodside v Globe Marine Insurance Co* [1896] 1 QB 105; *Lidgett v Secretan* was discussed in the *Wilson Shipping Case*, supra and was not disapproved, but is difficult to reconcile with the principle of the latter case; see especially Lord Sumner's speech.
4 *Brooks v MacDonnell* (1835) 1 Y & C Ex 500 at 515, 41 RR at 342.
5 Institute Time Clauses (Hulls), Clause 18, Appendix III, p 186, post; Institute Voyage Clauses (Hulls), Clause 16, Appendix III, p 204, post.
6 *Livie v Janson* (1810) 12 East 648 at 654, where this case is put.
7 *The Dora Forster* [1900] P 241.
8 *British and Foreign Insurance Co v Wilson Shipping Co Ltd* [1921] 1 AC 188, 26 Com Cas 13, HL. As Lord Shaw said in his judgment, at 206, 'The assured has no vested right of action when the injury is sustained.'

78. Suing and labouring clause

(1) Where the policy contains a suing and labouring clause, the engagement thereby entered into is deemed to be supplementary to the contract of insurance, and the assured may recover from the insurer any expenses properly incurred pursuant to the clause, notwithstanding that the insurer may have paid for a total loss, or that the subject-matter may have been warranted free from particular average, either wholly or under a certain percentage.[1]
(2) General average losses and contributions and salvage charges, as defined by this Act, are not recoverable under the suing and labouring clause.[2]
(3) Expenses incurred for the purpose of averting or diminishing any loss not covered by the policy are not recoverable under the suing and labouring clause.[3]
(4) It is the duty of the assured and his agents, in all cases, to take such measures as may be reasonable for the purpose of averting or minimising a loss.[4]

Note

The assured and his agents are bound by law to use all reasonable efforts to avert or minimise a loss.[5] The 'sue and labour' clause enables the assured to recover the expenditure involved in these efforts from the insurer. The continental codes embody the conditions of the 'sue and labour' clause so that under those codes the liability of the insurer is determined by law, whereas in England it rests on contract.[6]

The 'sue and labour' clause is usually supplemented by the 'waiver clause,' which provides that 'no acts of the insurer or insured in recovering, saving or preserving the property insured shall be considered as a waiver or acceptance of abandonment.'

Although the 'sue and labour' clause is a distinct engagement added to the policy, expenses incurred under it are apportioned according to the normal rule of marine insurance. The clause imports that 'whilst the underwriters are to bear their share of any suing and labouring expenses, they are to bear such share only in the proportion of the amount underwritten to the whole value of the property or interest insured.'[7]

Where there is no 'sue and labour' clause in the policy, particular charges incurred by the assured in preserving the subject-matter insured may be recoverable.[8]

Sub-section (4) relates only to suing and labouring, and does not qualify the provisions of s 55(2) as to insurance against negligence or the misconduct of the master and crew.[9]

The words 'his agents' in s 78(4) should be read as inapplicable to the master or crew unless expressly instructed by the assured in relation to what to do or not to do in respect of suing and labouring. Many persons other than the master or members of the crew may be agents of the assured with the duty to act on his behalf in relation to suing and labouring. A possible exception exists in the case of a master/owner. Negligent navigation by such an assured will not bar his claim under s 55(2)(a), whereas s 78(4) clearly seems to impose the statutory duty on him.[10]

Illustrations

1. Insurance on chartered freight, warranted free from particular average. The ship in consequence of sea-damage becomes a constructive total loss, but the cargo is landed and sent on in another ship. The expenses of landing, warehousing, and reloading the cargo can be recovered as particular charges under the 'sue and labour' clause.[11]
2. Policy on ship containing a 'collision' clause. The assured is sued for running down another ship, and incurs costs in defending the action. These costs are not recoverable from the insurer under the 'sue and labour' clause.[12]
3. Policy on freight. A ship bound for L is stranded at P. The cargo is landed, and, in order to earn freight, is sent on by rail to L at a cost of £200. It might have been sent on by ship at a cost of £70. The insurer on freight is liable for £70 only, under the 'sue and labour' clause.[13]
4. Policy for £1,000 on ship and cargo valued at £4,000. Expenses are incurred under the 'sue and labour' clause to the extent of £2,000. The insurer is liable to pay £500.[14]
5. Live cattle are insured against all risks. The ship, owing to sea perils, is detained in a port of refuge for some weeks. The cost of extra fodder supplied to the cattle during the detention is recoverable under the 'sue and labour' clause.[15]
6. A ship valued at £2,600 is insured with D for £1,200. After encountering very heavy weather the ship is rescued by a steamer with which no contract

is made, and which afterwards obtains an award of £800 for salvage. The owner, instead of abandoning, elects to repair the ship at a cost of £2,600. The insurer is only liable for £1,200. He is not liable under the 'sue and labour' clause for any additional sum for salvage charges, for the salving steamer is not the 'factor, servant, or assign' of the assured.[16]

7. A ship is insured by A (an underwriter) who reinsures with B, who again reinsures with C for £100. The ship becomes a constructive total loss. A pays the claim of the original assured, and then at great expense refloats the ship and sells her. His expenses amount to 112 per cent of the insured value. If B pays A, he can only recover £100 from C, for A (the first insurer) is not the 'factor, servant, or assign' of B within the meaning of the 'sue and labour' clause.[17]

8. Policy effected by shipowner 'to cover shipowner's liability of any kind to owners of mules and cargo up to £20,000 owing to the omission of the negligence clause in the contract'. The mules are worth £40,000. The ship is stranded, and expenses are incurred in landing some of the mules which were saved. The 'sue and labour' clause does not apply to a policy in this form, and the expenses so incurred cannot be recovered under the clause.[18]

9. A ship insured against total loss is stranded, and abandoned. The insurers employ a firm of ship repairers, who succeed in getting her off and saving her, and the assured fails in his claim for a total loss. The insurers cannot counter-claim under the 'sue and labour' clause, or otherwise, for the expenses of salving the ship.[19]

10. Policy on goods against war risks. The ship is stopped by a German cruiser, and has to put into a Norwegian port, where storage and re-shipment expenses are incurred. These expenses are recoverable under the 'sue and labour' clause.[20]

11. Policy on kieselguhr[21] packed in bags and insured against 'all risks'. The bags were defective and burst whilst being transferred from the ship's hold to a lighter. Assured incurred expenses in rebagging the goods. *Held*, insurer not liable under the 'sue and labour' clause for these expenses, as they were due to inherent vice of the goods, and not a peril insured against.[22]

12. Policy on intermodal freight containers. Containers were leased to a third party. The assured incurs costs in recovering them from the third party, who has been adjudged bankrupt. He is entitled to an indemnity under the 'sue and labour' clause in respect of such costs.[23]

13. Policy on ship. An accurate estimate of the damage to the vessel could not be obtained without a survey of her in dry dock, but this was never done. The insurers contended that the assured was in breach of duty under s 78 (4), and they were not liable on his claim under the policy. This argument was rejected by the Court, for a survey in dry dock would not avert or minimise the loss but would merely ascertain its extent. Consequently the assured had not committed a breach of duty under s 78(4).[24]

14. Policy on freight. The assured claimed sue and labour expenses. *Held*, on the evidence, no loss of freight had been proved, and therefore no sue and labour expenses were recoverable.[25]

---

1 *Lohre v Aitchison* (1878) 3 QBD at 567, CA (reversed on another point); and *Kidston v Empire Insurance Co* (1866) LR 1 CP 535; affd (1867) LR 2 CP 357, Ex Ch; cf *Duus Brown & Co v Binning* (1906) 11 Com Cas 190.

2 *Aitchison v Lohre* (1879) 4 App Cas 755, especially at 765, 768. As to 'salvage charges' see s 65, and as to 'general average,' see s 66. See e g *Australian Coastal Shipping Commission v Green* [1971] 1 All ER 353, CA, where it was held that expenditure incurred in indemnifying a tugowner for damage to the tug engaged under the United Kingdom Standard Towage Conditions was general average expenditure for which the insurer was liable, and the expenditure was not 'salvage charges' and therefore not recoverable under s 78(2), for the services were rendered under contract and not by a 'salvor independently of contract' within the meaning of s 65(2). (See the judgment of Lord Denning MR, ibid, at 360.)
3 *Kidston v Empire Insurance Co* (1866) LR 1 CP at 546, 547, per Willes J; *Meyer v Ralli* (1876) 1 CPD 358; *Lohre v Aitchison* (1878) 3 QBD at 566, per Brett LJ.
4 *Kidston v Empire Insurance Co* (1866) LR 1 CP at 544; *Currie & Co v Bombay Native Insurance Co* (1869) LR 3 PC 72; cf *Benson v Chapman* (1849) 2 HL Cas 696; *Notara v Henderson* (1872) LR 7 QB 225, Ex Ch (shipper v shipowner); *Irvin v Hine* [1950] 1 KB 555, [1949] 2 All ER 1089, KB (by refusing to have a survey in dry dock, owner not in breach of any duty laid on him by this provision); *Halsbury's Laws of England*, 4th edn, vol 25, para 266. This provision does not qualify s 55(2) as to insurance against negligence; see note 10, p 128, ante.
5 *Benson v Chapman* (1849) 2 HL Cas at 696; *Notara v Henderson* (1872) LR 7 QB 225, Ex Ch (shipper v shipowner).
6 The clause, it seems, may be excluded by agreement, e g by the term 'no s/c,' *Western Assurance Co of Toronto v Poole* [1903] 1 KB 376, 384, 8 Com Cas at 119 (reinsurance, expert evidence admitted to show that 'no salvage charges' meant 'no sue and labour charges').
7 *Cunard SS Co v Marten* [1902] 2 KB at 629, 8 Com Cas at p 23.
8 *Arnould*, para 914A. But see *Emperor Goldmining Co Ltd v Switzerland General Insurance Co Ltd* [1964] 1 Lloyd's Rep 348 (Supreme Ct of New South Wales), where Manning J, held that they were recoverable. This decision would not appear to be in accordance with principle, for if it is correct, no 'sue and labour' clause need ever be inserted in a policy. The assured could recover any expenses in any event, as long as they were reasonably incurred. See Ivamy, *Marine Insurance* (4th ed, 1985), pp 450–451.
9 *British and Foreign Marine Insurance Co Ltd v Gaunt* [1921] 2 AC 41 at 65, 26 Com Cas at 267, HL.
10 *Astrovlanis Compania Naviera SA v Linard, The Gold Sky* [1972] 2 Lloyd's Rep 187, QBD (Commercial Court) at 221 (per Mocatta J).
11 *Kidston v Empire Insurance Co* (1866) LR 1 CP 535; affd (1867) LR 2 CP 357, Ex Ch.
12 *Xenos v Fox* (1869) LR 4 CP 665, Ex Ch ('sue and labour' clause does not apply).
13 *Lee v Southern Insurance Co* (1870) LR 5 CP 397.
14 *Dixon v Whitworth* (1879) 4 CPD at 377, 378. The case is overruled only so far as it decided that salvage expenses were recoverable under the clause. See, too, *Cunard SS Co v Marten* [1902] 2 KB at 629.
15 *The Pomeranian* [1895] P 349.
16 *Aitchison v Lohre* (1879) 4 App Cas 755.
17 *Uzielli v Boston Marine Insurance Co* (1884) 15 QBD 11, CA; distinguished and discussed in *Western Assurance Co of Toronto v Poole* [1903] 1 KB 376, 384.
18 *Cunard SS Co v Marten* [1902] 2 KB 624; affd [1903] 2 KB 511, CA.
19 *Crouan v Stanier* [1904] 1 KB 87, distinguishing *The Pickwick* (1852) 16 Jur 669.
20 *Wilson Bros Bobbin Co v Green* [1917] 1 KB 860, 22 Com Cas 185, 191.
21 Ie a diatomaceous earth used as an absorbent of nitro-glycerine in the manufacture of dynamite.
22 *F W Berk & Co Ltd v Style* [1955] 2 Lloyd's Rep 382, QB. See the judgment of Sellers J, ibid, at 388.
23 *Integrated Container Service Inc v British Traders' Insurance Co Ltd* [1981] 2 Lloyd's Rep 460.
24 *Irvin v Hine* [1949] 2 All ER 1089. (See the judgment of Devlin J, ibid, at 1092.)

25 *Ikerigi Compania Naviera SA v Palmer, The Wondrous* [1992] 2 Lloyd's Rep 566, CA. (See the judgment of Lloyd LJ, ibid, at 576.)

RIGHTS OF INSURER ON PAYMENT

79. Right of subrogation

(1) Where the insurer pays for a total loss, either of the whole, or in the case of goods of any apportionable part, of the subject-matter insured,[1] he thereupon becomes entitled to take over the interest of the assured in whatever may remain of the subject-matter so paid for, and he is thereby subrogated to all the rights and remedies of the assured in and in respect of that subject-matter[2] as from the time of the casualty causing the loss.[3]

(2) Subject to the foregoing provisions, where the insurer pays for a partial loss, he acquires no title to the subject-matter insured, or such part of it as may remain, but he is thereupon subrogated to all rights and remedies of the assured in and in respect of the subject-matter insured as from the time of the casualty causing the loss, in so far as the assured has been indemnified, according to this Act, by such payment for the loss.[4]

Note

The right of subrogation is a necessary incident of a contract of indemnity, and it operates on every right and remedy 'by which the loss insured against can be or has been diminished'.[5] The assured is 'indemnified according to this Act' when he has received the indemnity agreed on, even though he may remain out of pocket.[6] If the assured is indemnified, the insurer cannot recover from a third party under the doctrine of subrogation more than he has paid to the assured.[7]

If a ship valued at £500,000 is insured for £400,000, the assured, being 'his own insurer' for £100,000, is entitled to a fifth of the salvage.[8] It is to be noted, however, that the rights of an insurer cannot be affected by any contract made by the assured with a later insurer, unless the assured reserves the right of making such other contract and the first insurer subscribes the policy under a condition that the assured may avail himself of such right.[9]

The question has been raised whether an insurer, merely by paying for a total loss, necessarily becomes the 'owner' of the thing insured.[10] It will be noticed that s 79(1) provides that the insurer becomes 'entitled to take over' the interest of the assured. The same words appear in s 63 (see note thereto), and the result would appear to be that it is left open to the insurer not to 'take over' the interest of the assured, although 'entitled to take it over'.

Speaking broadly, the insurer, in the absence of a special contract, must exercise all remedies arising from subrogation in the name of the assured.[11] It follows that the insurer is entitled to the use of the assured's name; but if the insurer wishes to bring an action, he must, of course, be prepared to indemnify the assured as regards costs.

The right of subrogation may be waived by agreement between the assured and the insurers.[12] Further, the policy may contain an implied term that the insurer will not exercise the right of subrogation.[13]

132 Rights of insurer on payment

As to under-insurance, see s 81, and as to the distinction between abandonment and subrogation, see note to s 63.

As to the effect of the rule of subrogation on the doctrine of contribution between insurers of the same property, see note to s 32.

Illustrations

1. Goods insured by a valued policy are captured and sold. The underwriters pay 50 per cent of the loss on account. Afterwards the assured receives half the proceeds of the goods from the captors. The insurers are not entitled to this or any part of it for they have not fully indemnified the assured.[14]
2. A ship is missing, and the insurer pays for a total loss. If the ship afterwards arrives, she belongs to the insurer.[15]
3. Policy on goods. The ship is captured by a Brazilian cruiser as a blockade-runner. The assured offers to abandon her. The insurer declines to accept the abandonment, but eventually compromises the claim by paying 35 per cent. Some years afterwards, the Brazilian Government, under a Convention with Great Britain, pays compensation. The insurer is not entitled to any part of the compensation so paid for the insurers have not fully indemnified the assured in respect of the loss.[16]
4. Insured goods are jettisoned. The insurer of these goods pays for a total loss, but he then stands in the place of the assured as regards claims for a general average contribution from the other interests involved in the adventure.[17]
5. A ship valued at £6,000 is insured for £6,000. Her real value is £9,000. She is run down by another ship, and the insurers pay for a total loss. Afterwards the assured recovers £5,000 damages from the owners of the ship at fault. The insurers are entitled to the whole of this sum as salvage for they have paid for a total loss.[18]
6. Cargo insured under a valued policy is destroyed by a Confederate cruiser in the American Civil War. The cargo is worth more than the valuation. After the war, compensation is paid to the cargo owner by the United States under an Act which expressly refuses to recognise claims made by or on behalf of insurers. The insurers, who have paid for a total loss, are not entitled to this compensation in view of the express provisions of the Act.[19]
7. Two ships belonging to the same owner come into collision. The insurers of the ship not at fault have no claim against the ship at fault, for they stand in the place of the assured, who cannot have a claim against himself.[20]
8. Goods, on which freight has been paid in advance by the shipper, are lost through the negligence of the shipowner. Subject to any special provision in the contract of affreightment, the shipper can recover as damages the advance freight for the benefit of the insurers on freight once they have paid the sum assured.[21]
9. A ship is run down, and the insurer pays for a total loss. The insurer on ship is not entitled to the damages recovered by the shipowner from the ship at fault for loss of freight.[22]
10. Wool is damaged in a collision between lighters. The insurers pay the claim, and the assured assigns to them his rights against the owner of the lighter at fault. That owner cannot set up the defence that the payment was outside the terms of the policy for the settlement of the loss concerns the assured and the insurers alone, and a third party plays no part in it.[23]

11. An insurer is induced by misrepresentation to pay a loss. He recovers the amount back in an action against the assured. The reinsurer, who had paid the original insurer before the fraud was discovered, is entitled to recover the sum he paid less the reasonable (not taxed) costs of the original insurer.[24]
12. Policy for £1,000 on ship valued in the policy at £1,350. The ship is run down and the insurer pays a total loss, ie £1,000. The shipowner afterwards recovers £1,000 and interest from the owners of the vessel which was to blame for the collision. The insurer is entitled to 1,000/1,350ths of the sum recovered, and the assured to 350/1,350ths.[25]
13. Neutral ship seized as prize. The owner had insured with enemy underwriters who paid for a total loss. The neutral assured's claim in the Prize Court is dismissed, and the ship is condemned, as the claim is made on behalf of the enemy underwriters.[26]
14. Policy for £4,000 on ship so valued. The ship is in collision and £5,000 is expended by the assured owners in repairing the damage. In an action against the colliding vessel both ships are found to blame and the assured owners recover £2,500. The amount required to indemnify the assured owners 'according to this Act' is £4,000 (ie the reasonable cost of repairs not exceeding the sum insured); the assured owners must give underwriters credit for £2,500 and can recover £1,500 only.[27]
15. Cargo is insured under a policy for its then value of £685. Later an 'increased value' policy is taken out with other insurers for £215. The cargo is jettisoned, and both insurers pay for a total loss. £532 becomes payable to cargo owners in general average. The first insurers are entitled to the whole amount because the rights of subrogation vest in them 'as from the time of the casualty causing the loss,' as stated in s 79(1), nothing being payable to the increased value insurers.[28]
16. Ship insured for £72,000. She became a total loss as a result of a collision with a Canadian Government vessel. The insurers paid the £72,000 to the assured, and then claimed damages from the Canadian Government. The action was successful, but meanwhile the Pound Sterling had been devalued in 1949 and the loss, when quantified and converted into English currency, came to nearly £127,000. The assured then repaid the £72,000 to the insurers, and claimed that they were entitled to keep the balance. *Held*, that this contention succeeded because the insurers could not recover under the doctrine of subrogation anything more than they had paid.[29]
17. Goods insured from Hong Kong to Scotland via Port of London, and lost in transit between London and Scotland on 16 December 1965 through negligence of carriers. Assured claimed against insurers who paid claim on 11 August 1966. Insurers brought action in assured's name against carriers, who on 12 November 1969 paid into Court sum representing full value of goods lost. *Held*, that (i) interest would be awarded from 17 January 1966 (ie date on which assured would have expected payment from their customers in respect of the goods) until 12 November 1969; and (ii) by subrogation, insurers were entitled to proportionate part of that interest from date of settlement of claim, ie 11 August 1966.[30]

---

1 The words as to total loss of part were added after some discussion by the Lord Chancellor's Committee. Before the Act the law was very doubtful.

2   A claim in respect of interest on the value of goods lost through the negligence of a third party is a right or remedy of the assured 'in or in respect of the subject-matter'. A judgment given in favour of the assured for their loss and a sum by way of interest is a single judgment based on a single cause of action, and the insurers are subrogated to the assured's right to sue for the loss of the goods and also interest: *H Cousins & Co Ltd v D and C Carriers Ltd* [1970] 2 Lloyd's Rep 397, CA. (See the judgment of Widgery LJ, ibid, at 400.) For the facts of the case, see illustration 17, p 133, ante.

3   *Rankin v Potter* (1873) LR 6 HL at 118, 119, 144; *Simpson v Thomson* (1877) 3 App Cas at 284, 292; *Burnand v Rodocanachi* (1882) 7 App Cas at 339; *Darrell v Tibbitts* (1880) 5 QBD at 563, CA, per Lord Esher; *Assicurazioni Generali de Trieste v Empress Assurance Corpn Ltd* [1907] 2 KB 814 at 820. But cf *John Edwards & Co v Motor Union Insurance Co* [1922] 2 KB 249 (no subrogation in case of wager policy).

4   *Simpson v Thomson* (1877) 3 App Cas at 292, HL; *Halsbury's Laws of England*, 4th edn, vol 25, paras 330–331; cf *Commercial Union Assurance Co v Lister* (1874) 9 Ch App 483 (fire policy, bona fide compromise of action by assured).

5   *Castellain v Preston* (1883) 11 QBD at 388, 404, CA; and cf *West of England Fire Insurance Co v Isaacs* [1896] 2 QB 377 (fire policy). As to ademption of loss, see note to s 62.

6   *Goole and Hull Steam Towing Co v Ocean Marine Insurance Co* [1928] 1 KB 589.

7   *Yorkshire Insurance Co Ltd v Nisbet Shipping Co Ltd* [1962] 2 QB 330, [1961] 2 All ER 487.

8   See s 81 (under-insurance) and illustration 12.

9   *Boag v Standard Marine Insurance Co Ltd* [1937] 1 All ER 714, CA, illustration 15.

10 *Eglinton v Norman* (1877) 3 Asp MLC 471, CA; and see *Arrow Shipping Co v Tyne Improvement Comrs* [1894] AC 508, HL; and *Barraclough v Brown* [1897] AC 615; *Boston Corpn v Fenwick & Co Ltd* (1923) 129 LT 766, 28 Com Cas 367.

11 *Simpson v Thomson* (1877) 3 App Cas 290 at 293; *The Charlotte* [1908] P 206, CA; *Oriental Fire and General Insurance Co Ltd v American President Lines Ltd and Cotton Trading Corpn of San Francisco* [1968] 2 Lloyd's Rep 372, High Court of Bombay, where it was held that an insurer who was subrogated to the rights of the assured under the Indian Transfer of Property Act (since repealed and re-enacted by the (Indian) Marine Insurance Act 1963) was not entitled to bring an action in his own name against the wrongdoer; and cf *Kruger & Co v Moel Tryvan Ship Co* (1907) 13 Com Cas at 4; but see *King v Victoria Insurance Co* [1896] AC 250 (special assignment of rights) and *Compania Colombiana de Seguros v Pacific Steam Navigation Co* [1964] 1 All ER 216, where consignees assigned to the insurer all their rights against the shipowners in respect of the damaged goods, and the insurer was held entitled to sue in his own name. As to the division of costs of unsuccessful action brought by an assured partly for his own benefit and partly for that of the insurer, see *Duus Brown & Co v Binning* (1906) 11 Com Cas 190.

12 *The Marine Sulphur Queen* [1970] 2 Lloyd's Rep 285, District Court of Southern District of New York, where the policy stated: 'These assurers hereby agree to waive all rights against the steamer and/or the assured and/or affiliated and/or associated and/or allied companies and/or corporations in the event that the carrying steamer is owned and/or chartered and/or operated by the assured and/or affiliated and/or associated and/or allied companies and/or corporations,' and it was held that the assured was not affiliated and/or associated with another company to which the vessel concerned had been let out under a demise charter, and that therefore the clause did not apply, and the insurers had not waived their right of subrogation (see the judgment of Cannella DJ ibid, at 299); *Tenneco Oil Co v Tug Tony and Coastal Towing Corpn* [1972] 1 Lloyd's Rep 514, Dist Ct for the Southern Dist of Texas (Houston Division), where it was held that a clause stating 'Privilege is granted the assured hereunder to waive subrogation prior to a loss against parties with whom the assured has a working agreement' was not void as being contrary to public policy, and that, on the evidence, the right of subrogation had been waived. (See the judgment of Carl O Bue Jr DJ, ibid, at 516–517.)

13 *The Yasin* [1979] 2 Lloyd's Rep 45, where, however, it was held that the policy did not contain an implied term (see the judgment of Lloyd J, ibid, at 56).

14 *Tunno v Edwards* (1810) 12 East 488, 11 RR 458.
15 *Houstman v Thornton* (1816) Holt NP 242.
16 *Brooks v MacDonnell* (1835) 41 RR 336.
17 *Dickenson v Jardine* (1868) LR 3 CP 639; and Rules of Practice of the Association of Average Adjusters rules B30/B31. See Appendix V, p 289, post.
18 *North of England Iron SS Insurance Association v Armstrong* (1870) LR 5 QB 244, doubted *Burnand v Rodocanachi* (1882) 7 App Cas at 342; and see *Arnould*, para 1304; but approved in *Thames and Mersey Marine Insurance Co v British and Chilian SS Co* [1915] 2 KB 214, per Scrutton J; not discussed on appeal, [1916] 1 KB 30, CA. *North of England Iron SS Insurance Association v Armstrong* (supra) was criticised and explained in *Yorkshire Insurance Co Ltd v Nisbet Shipping Co Ltd* [1961] 2 All ER at 492–493.
19 *Burnand v Rodocanachi* (1882) 7 App Cas 333, explained in *Castellain v Preston* (1883) 11 QBD at 404, per Bowen LJ; and *Stearns v Village Main Reef Co* (1904) 10 Com Cas 89, CA.
20 *Simpson v Thomson* (1877) 3 App Cas 279, HL; discussed in *Midland Insurance Co v Smith* (1881) 6 QBD at 565; *Arnould*, para 1309. A special clause known as the 'Sister Ship' clause has been framed to meet this case; see the Institute Time Clauses (Hulls), Clause 9 and the Institute Voyage Clauses (Hulls), Clause 7. See Appendix III, pp 180, 199, post.
21 *Dufourcet v Bishop* (1886) 18 QBD 373.
22 *Sea Insurance Co v Hadden* (1884) 13 QBD 706, CA.
23 *King v Victoria Insurance Co* [1896] AC 250, PC; distinguished in *John Edwards & Co v Motor Union Insurance Co* [1922] 2 KB 249 at 256 (ppi policy).
24 *Assicurazioni Generali de Trieste v Empress Assurance Corpn Ltd* [1907] 2 KB 814.
25 *The Commonwealth* [1907] P 216, CA; affg *The Welsh Girl* (1906) 22 TLR 475.
26 *The Palm Branch* [1916] P 230, but orders modified on appeal because a small percentage of the underwriters were neutrals: [1919] AC 272, PC.
27 *Goole and Hull Steam Towing Co Ltd v Ocean Marine Insurance Co Ltd* [1928] 1 KB 589.
28 *Boag v Standard Marine Insurance Co Ltd* [1937] 1 All ER 714, CA.
29 *Yorkshire Insurance Co Ltd v Nisbet Shipping Co Ltd* [1962] 2 QB 330, [1961] 2 All ER 487.
30 *H Cousins & Co Ltd v D and C Carriers Ltd* [1970] 2 Lloyd's Rep 397, CA. (See the judgment of Widgery LJ, ibid, at 401, and that of Davies LJ, ibid, at 402.)

80. Right of contribution

(1) Where the assured is over-insured by double insurance, each insurer is bound, as between himself and the other insurers, to contribute rateably to the loss in proportion to the amount for which he is liable under his contract.[1]

(2) If any insurer pays more than his proportion of the loss, he is entitled to maintain an action for contribution against the other insurers, and is entitled to the like remedies as a surety who has paid more than his proportion of the debt.[2]

Note

Co-insurers are not co-sureties, but in many respects they have similar relations inter se. As Martin B, said, when two or more policies are effected on the same subject-matter and interest, 'the policies are one insurance as between all the underwriters, but not one insurance for all purposes.'[3]

But for a qualification of this principle as regards return of premium, see s 84(3)(f) and note thereto.

1 *Newby v Reed* (1763) 1 Wm Bl 416; *North British and Mercantile Insurance Co v London, Liverpool and Globe Insurance Co* (1877) 5 Ch D at 583, CA; *American Surety Co of New York v Wrightson* (1910) 16 Com Cas at pp 54–56.
2 Sub-section (2) is consequential.
3 *Bruce v Jones* (1863) 32 LJ Ex at 135. Cf *British and Foreign Insurance Co v Wilson Shipping Co Ltd* (1920) 26 Com Cas at 35, per Lord Sumner [1921] 1 AC at 214.

81. Effect of under-insurance

Where the assured is insured for an amount less than the insurable value, or, in the case of a valued policy, for an amount less than the policy valuation, he is deemed to be his own insurer in respect of the uninsured balance.[1]

Note

The measure of indemnity rests on the hypothesis that the subject-matter insured is to be regarded as fully insured.

Suppose a ship, valued at £300,000, is insured with A for £100,000 and with B for £100,000. If she is damaged by perils of the seas to the extent of £30,000 A is liable for £10,000 and B is liable for £10,000. That being so, it is obviously immaterial to A and B whether the remaining £100,000 is uninsured or whether it is insured with C.[2]

For a quasi-exception, see s 74 as to insurance against liability to a third party. As to 'insurable value', see s 16.

1 *Whitworth v Shepherd* (1884) 12 R 204, Court of Session (abandonment); *Western Assurance Co of Toronto v Poole* (1903) 8 Com Cas at 119 ('sue and labour'); *The Commonwealth* [1907] P 216, CA (subrogation), and see ss 67–72 as to the measure of indemnity generally. See, further, the illustrations to s 79 (subrogation).
2 Cf *Anglo-Californian Bank v London and Provincial Marine Insurance Co* (1904) 10 Com Cas at 8, 9, per Walton J.

RETURN OF PREMIUM

82. Enforcement of return

Where the premium, or a proportionate part thereof, is, by this Act, declared to be returnable,—
   (a) If already paid, it may be recovered by the assured from the insurer; and,
   (b) If unpaid, it may be retained by the assured or his agent.[1]

Note

The broker is directly responsible to the insurer for the payment of the premium, but, when returnable, it is repayable to the assured; see ss 52 and 53.

1 *Shee v Clarkson* (1810) 12 East 507 11 RR 473, (broker); cf C McArthur, *The Contract of Marine Insurance* (2nd ed, 1890), p 40.

83. Return by agreement

Where the policy contains a stipulation for the return of the premium, or a proportionate part thereof, on the happening of a certain event, and that event happens, the premium, or, as the case may be, the proportionate part thereof, is thereupon returnable to the assured.[1]

Note

Express clauses may state that a proportionate part of the premium is returnable in the case of e g, the vessel being transferred to new management, the cancellation of the policy or the vessel being laid up in port. Thus, Clause 4 of the Institute Time Clauses (Hulls) states that a pro rata daily net return of premium is to be made on 'any change, voluntary or otherwise, in the ownership or flag, transfer to new management, or charter on a bareboat basis, or requisition . . .'.[2]

Further, cl 22 of the Institute Time Clauses (Hulls) states: 'To return as follows: . . . per cent net for each uncommenced month if this policy be cancelled by agreement, and for each period of 30 consecutive days the vessel may be laid up in port or in a lay-up area approved by the underwriters . . . : (a) . . . per cent net not under repair, (b) . . . per cent net under repair . . .'.[3]

Illustrations

1. Time policy on ship, providing for pro rata return of premium if she is sold, or 'transferred to new management'. She is captured and condemned for carrying contraband. This is not a 'transfer to new management', and the premium is not returnable.[4]
2. Time policy on ship. Proportionate part of premium to be returned 'for every thirty consecutive days vessel may be laid up in port.' The ship is employed for two months in port in coaling other ships under Admiralty orders. She is not 'laid up in port,' so no premium is returnable.[5]

1 *Kellner v Le Mesurier* (1803) 4 East 396, 7 RR 581; *Hunter v Wright* (1830) 10 B & C 714 (return if ship 'laid up'); *Gorsedd SS Co v Forbes* (1900) 5 Com Cas 413 (return after loss); *Dominion Coal Co v Maskinonge SS Co* (1918) 87 LJKB 459, HL (premium returnable if ship ordered into war zone).
2 See Appendix III, p 169, post.
3 See Appendix III, p 189, post.
4 *Pyman v Marten* (1906) 13 Com Cas 64, CA.
5 *North Shipping Co Ltd v Union Marine Insurance Co Ltd* (1918) 24 Com Cas 83; affd (1919) 24 Com Cas 161, CA.

84. Return for failure of consideration

(1) Where the consideration for the payment of the premium totally fails, and there has been no fraud or illegality on the part of the assured or his agents, the premium is thereupon returnable to the assured.[1]

(2) Where the consideration for the payment of the premium is apportionable and there is a total failure of any apportionable part of the consideration, a proportionate part of the premium is, under the like conditions, thereupon returnable to the assured.[2]

(3) In particular—

(a) Where the policy is void, or is avoided by the insurer as from the commencement of the risk, the premium is returnable, provided that there has been no fraud or illegality on the part of the assured; but if the risk is not apportionable, and has once attached, the premium is not returnable;[3]

(b) Where the subject-matter insured, or part thereof, has never been imperilled, the premium, or, as the case may be, a proportionate part thereof, is returnable:

Provided that where the subject-matter has been insured 'lost or not lost,' and has arrived in safety at the time when the contract is concluded, the premium is not returnable unless, at such time, the insurer knew of the safe arrival.[4]

(c) Where the assured has no insurable interest throughout the currency of the risk the premium is returnable, provided that this rule does not apply to a policy effected by way of gaming or wagering;[5]

(d) Where the assured has a defeasible interest which is terminated during the currency of the risk, the premium is not returnable;[6]

(e) Where the assured has over-insured under an unvalued policy, a proportionate part of the premium is returnable;[7]

(f) Subject to the foregoing provisions, where the assured has over-insured by double insurance, a proportionate part of the several premiums is returnable:[8]

Provided that, if the policies are effected at different times, and any earlier policy has at any time borne the entire risk, or if a claim has been paid on the policy in respect of the full sum insured thereby, no premium is returnable in respect of that policy, and when the double insurance is effected knowingly by the assured no premium is returnable.[9]

Note

Apart from agreement, the return of the premium seems to rest on the doctrine of failure of consideration.[10] The principle has been generalised in sub-ss (1) and (2), as the subordinate rules in sub-s (3) may not be exhaustive.

'The general rule of law,' said Bovill CJ, 'is that where a contract has been in part performed, no part of the money paid under such contract can be recovered back. There may be some cases of partial performance which form exceptions to this rule, as, for instance, if there were a contract to deliver ten sacks of wheat and six only were delivered, the price of the remaining four might be recovered back. But there the consideration is clearly severable.'[11]

The case of 'double insurance' gives rise to complications. 'The assured has the right to elect under which policy or set of policies he will claim for a loss, and under which policy or set of policies he will claim for a return of premium; but the underwriters, having settled with the assured, must proceed to readjust the entire claim among themselves, so that each underwriter shall ultimately bear his proportionate part both of the loss and of the return premium.'[12]

But as regards return of premium this rule is subject to qualification. When, as often happens, the risk under some of the policies attaches before the risk under later policies, so that under the earlier policies the entire risk is run for a time, then the premium is only returnable by the underwriter of the later policies.[13] This qualification is really a deduction from sub-s (3)(a).

To get rid of this complication and to discourage over-insurance, Lord Herschell proposed that in case of double insurance, the premium should not be returnable, but sub-s 3(f) stops somewhat short of this.

Illustrations

1. Goods are insured from London to a port in an enemy's country. The ship is captured. The insurance is void as trading with the enemy is illegal, and the premium is not returnable.[14]
2. A ship insured 'at and from A,' sails from A, with an insufficient crew, and is lost. The insurer is not liable, and the premium is not returnable.[15]
3. Cotton, at sea and overdue, valued at £30,000, is insured by policies effected on 12 April for £20,000, and by policies effected on 13 April for £16,000. In case of safe arrival, no premium is returnable on the policies effected on the 12th, for they bore the whole risk till the other policies were effected. But the premium on £6,000 (ie the extent of the over-insurance) is returnable on the policies effected on the 13th.[16]
4. Policy on goods at sea. The assured represents to the insurer that the ship sailed from Baltimore on 12 January. In fact, she sailed on 1 January. The insurer avoids liability on the policy. If the representation was an honest mistake, the premium is returnable. Aliter, if it was made dishonestly.[17]
5. Insurance on profits and commission 'without benefit of salvage'. The policy is void as being a wager policy, and the premium is not returnable.[18]
6. A, who has insured the cargo on a ship believed to be overdue, reinsures his risk with B 'lost or not lost'. At the time the reinsurance is effected the ship has safely arrived, but neither party knows this. The reinsurance policy attaches, and the premium is not returnable.[19]
7. Insurance on 500 bales of cotton to be shipped by a particular ship. Only 250 bales are shipped. Half the premium is returnable.

1 *Halsbury's Laws of England*, 4th edn, vol 25, para 345. As to fraud by insurer, see *Kettlewell v Refuge Assurance Co* [1908] 1 KB 545, CA; affd [1909] AC 243, HL (life insurance). As to illegality, see *Re National Benefit Assurance Co Ltd* [1931] 1 Ch 46 (reinsurance treaty).
2 Ibid; *Ionides v Harford* (1859) 29 LJ Ex 36.
3 *Halsbury's Laws of England*, 4th edn, vol 25, para 342, and see para 349, as to policy avoided by material alteration.
4 As to proviso, see *Bradford v Symondson* (1881) 7 QBD 456, CA.
5 See s 4(2), as to wager policies, and illustration 5.
6 *Boehm v Bell* (1799) 8 Term Rep 154.
7 *Arnould*, paras 1336–1337.
8 Ibid, and see s 32 as to 'double insurance'.

9 *Fisk v Masterman* (1841) 8 M & W 165.
10 *Tyrie v Fletcher* (1777) 2 Cowp 666, 668, per Lord Mansfield.
11 *Whincup v Hughes* (1871) LR 6 CP at 81. Different rules apply, in general, where a contract has become impossible of performance or has otherwise been frustrated. The Law Reform (Frustrated Contracts) Act 1943, s 1 permits the recovery of money paid on a contract which has been frustrated even where there has been no total failure of consideration, and makes provision for compensation in the case of partial performance before frustration. But s 2(5) provides that the Act does not apply to contracts of insurance. See *Halsbury's Laws of England*, 4th ed, vol 49, para 470.
12 C McArthur, *The Contract of Marine Insurance* (2nd ed, 1890), p 44. See, too, s 32.
13 *Fisk v Masterman* (1841) 8 M & W 165.
14 *Vandyck v Hewitt* (1800) 1 East 96, 5 RR 516; see, too, *Kellner v Le Mesurier* (1803) 4 East 396, 7 RR 581 (foreign ship, British capture), and *Palyart v Leckie* (1817) 6 M & S 290, where the voyage was abandoned.
15 *Annen v Woodman* (1810) 3 Taunt 299.
16 *Fisk v Masterman* (1841) 8 M & W 165.
17 *Anderson v Thornton* (1853) 8 Exch 425.
18 *Allkins v Jupe* (1877) 2 CPD 375, see at 388, as to possibility of salvage in such a case; cf s 4, as to wager policies. But see *Re London County Commercial Reinsurance Office Ltd* [1922] 2 Ch 67, 86 (ppi policy where there was bona fide interest).
19 *Bradford v Symondson* (1881) 7 QBD 456, CA.

MUTUAL INSURANCE

85. Modification of Act in case of mutual insurance

(1) Where two or more persons mutually agree to insure each other against marine losses there is said to be a mutual insurance.[1]
(2) The provisions of this Act relating to the premium do not apply to mutual insurance, but a guarantee, or such other arrangement as may be agreed upon, may be substituted for the premium.[2]
(3) The provisions of this Act in so far as they may be modified by the agreement of the parties, may in the case of mutual insurance be modified by the terms of the policies issued by the association, or by the rules and regulations of the association.[3]
(4) Subject to the exceptions mentioned in this section, the provisions of this Act apply to a mutual insurance.[4]

Note

Mutual insurance associations[5] consisting of more than twenty members must be registered under the Companies Act 1985,[6] and the insurances effected by them must be embodied in marine policies.[7]
    Mathew J, said: '... mutual insurance is the simplest thing in the world, if you have not to record it in written documents. It is a system by which every one insured is at once underwriter and assured.... This very simple principle was acted upon successfully for many years, until technical difficulties began to be interposed. The first technical difficulty was this: all mutual insurance associations were ordered by statute to be incorporated as joint stock companies. The

second technical difficulty was, that under statutes framed for different purposes, which were positive in their terms, every contract of insurance had to be recorded in a written document; there must be a policy of insurance. These two conditions having to be complied with, the mutual insurance associations set themselves to work, by various forms of rules, to endeavour to reconcile the rules of the law with the conduct of their business, and different regulations have been adopted to meet the decisions on the subject.'[8]

The policies issued by mutual insurance associations to members omit the ordinary provision as to premium. The omission is provided for by rules of the association which regulate members' contributions to losses.[9] Their policies therefore have to be construed together with the rules and regulations of the association.[10]

The risks[11] covered by mutual insurance associations cover (i) *risks of a general nature*, eg damages for loss of life or personal injury, repatriation, crew substitute expenses, life salvage, collision liability, liability under towage contracts, removal of wrecks,[12] quarantine expenses, and liability for loss of cargo;[13] (ii) *war risks*, eg detention of vessel and prolongation of voyage,[14] and diversion of vessel;[15] (iii) *freight and demurrage risks*; and (iv) *through transit risks*.

1 For the history of mutual insurance, see *Marine Mutual Insurance Association Ltd v Young* (1880) 4 Asp MLC at 358. The wording of this sub-section, although it represents the substance of the transaction, is technically inaccurate, because practically all mutual associations require to be incorporated, and then the assured is insured by the body corporate and not by the individual members.
2 *Arnould*, para 129; *Lion Insurance Association v Tucker* (1883) 12 QBD at 187, CA.
3 *Ocean Iron SS Insurance Association Ltd v Leslie* (1887) 22 QBD 722n; *British Marine Mutual Insurance Co v Jenkins* [1900] 1 QB 299; *North Eastern 100A SS Insurance Association v Red S SS Co Ltd* (1905) 10 Com Cas 245.
4 *British Marine Mutual Insurance Co v Jenkins* [1900] 1 QB 299.
5 See generally, Ivamy, *Marine Insurance* (4th ed, 1985), pp 475–479.
6 *Re Padstow Assurance Association* (1882) 20 Ch D 137, CA. See Companies Act 1985 s 716(1).
7 *Edwards v Aberayron Mutual Insurance Society* (1876) 1 QBD 563, Ex Ch.
8 *Ocean Iron SS Insurance Association v Leslie* (1889) 22 QBD at 724.
9 For a case where an association brought an action to enforce a call, see *West of Scotland Shipowners' Mutual Protection and Indemnity Association (Luxembourg) v Aifanourios Shipping SA, The Aifanourios* [1980] 2 Lloyd's Rep 403, Court of Session. For a case where the question was whether an association could set off an amount due in respect of calls against an amount due from the association, see *First National Bank of Chicago v West of England Shipowners' Mutual Protection and Indemnity Association (Luxembourg), The Evelpidis Era* [1981] 1 Lloyd's Rep 54.
10 See, further, *Arnould*, paras 129–135 and as to questions which arise when part owners of insured ships are not members of the association, see *Halsbury's Laws of England*, 4th edn, vol 25, para 361, and *Corfield v Buchanan* (1913) 29 TLR 258, HL (issue of fixed premium policies to non-members).
11 See generally Ivamy, *Marine Insurance* (4th ed, 1985), pp 215–224.
12 See eg *M J Rudolph Corpn v Lumber Mutual Fire Insurance Co (Luria International, Third Parties), The Cape Borer* [1975] 2 Lloyd's Rep 108, Dist Ct for the Eastern Dist of New York.
13 For a case where a fisherman was excluded from the coverage of a protection and indemnity policy and claimed that the insurers had no right to do so, see *Goulart v Trans-Atlantic Marine Inc and Enos* [1970] 2 Lloyd's Rep 389, Massachusetts Superior Court.

14 See, eg *Union Castle Mail SS Co Ltd v United Kingdom Mutual War Risks Association Ltd* [1958] 1 Lloyd's Rep 58, QB (Commercial Court), where the voyages of two vessels were changed due to the closure of the Suez Canal in 1956.
15 See eg *Atlantic Maritime Carriers SA v Hellenic Mutual War Risks Association Ltd; Capetandiamantis Compania Maritima SA; Eastern Seas Transport Corpn and Orient Shipping Corpn v Same* [1969] 1 Lloyd's Rep 359, CA, where three vessels were diverted due to the closure of the Suez Canal in 1967.

SUPPLEMENTAL

86. Ratification by assured

Where a contract of marine insurance is in good faith effected by one person on behalf of another, the person on whose behalf it is effected may ratify the contract even after he is aware of a loss.[1]

Note

This is an old rule of marine insurance law. 'I think,' said Cockburn CJ, 'that this is a legitimate exception from the general rule, because the case is not within the principle of that rule. Where an agent effects an insurance subject to ratification, the loss is very likely to happen before ratification, and it must be taken that the insurance so effected involves that possibility as the basis of the contract.'[2]

The insurance can only be ratified by the person on whose behalf it is effected.[3] Thus, if A takes out a policy in his own name on behalf of B, the transaction cannot be adopted by C.[4]

See further, the notes to ss 15 and 23(1).

1 *Williams v North China Insurance Co* (1876) 1 CPD 757 at 764, CA.
2 Ibid. As to the Common Law rule, to which this is an exception, see *Keighley, Maxsted & Co v Durant* [1901] AC 240, HL; and *Grover and Grover Ltd v Mathews* [1910] 2 KB 401 (fire insurance).
3 *Boston Fruit Co v British and Foreign Marine Insurance Co* [1905] 1 KB 637, CA; affd [1906] AC 336, HL (policy effected for shipowner cannot afterwards be adopted by charterer).
4 *Byas v Miller* (1897) 3 Com Cas 39, and last note.

87. Implied obligations varied by agreement or usage

(1) Where any right, duty, or liability would arise under a contract of marine insurance by implication of law, it may be negatived or varied by express agreement, or by usage, if the usage be such as to bind both parties to the contract.[1]

(2) The provisions of this section extend to any right, duty, or liability declared by this Act which may be lawfully modified by agreement.

Note

Marine insurance is a consensual contract, and in the absence of a positive legal prohibition, the parties may make any stipulation they please.

Express Agreement. As regards 'express agreement,' the maxims of the law are *Expressum facit cessare tacitum* and *Modus et conventio vincunt legem*. For example, it is a well-known rule of law that deviation is a ground for avoiding the insurance, but the parties may agree to a deviation clause being inserted in the policy.

On the other hand, the parties cannot by agreement dispense with the provisions against gaming and wagering which are prohibited in the public interest.

But, speaking generally, the main object of the Act is to declare the law, that is to say, to indicate to the parties the legal position if they do not make any express bargain, leaving them free to make any bargain they like to suit their own needs.

Usage. Speaking, in 1791, of a marine policy, Buller J, said, 'it is founded on usage and must be governed by usage.'[2] This proposition must now be taken with qualifications. A usage may be either a general usage of trade, or a particular usage, prevailing only among particular classes or in particular localities.

When a general usage has been affirmed by judicial decision, it becomes incorporated into the law merchant, and thenceforward evidence of any usages inconsistent therewith is inadmissible.[3]

A particular usage must be proved by evidence in each case, at any rate till it becomes so notorious that the Courts will take judicial notice of it.[4] It is only binding in so far as it forms an implied term of the contract between the parties concerned. Geographical terms used in a policy, eg the term 'Baltic,' may have a special meaning attached to them by usage.[5]

As a marine policy is an instrument in writing, evidence of usage is not admissible to contradict anything which is plainly expressed.[6] Such evidence is only admissible either to explain what is technical or ambiguous, or to annex incidents to the contract.[7]

1 *Arnould*, paras 64–79; *Hart v Standard Marine Insurance Co Ltd* (1889) 22 QBD at 501, CA; cf *Matveieff v Crossfield* (1903) 8 Com Cas 120 (settlement according to custom of Lloyd's not binding on person ignorant of custom).
2 *Brough v Whitmore* (1791) 4 Term Rep at 210.
3 *Goodwin v Robarts* (1875) LR 10 Ex at 357, Ex Ch.
4 Cf *Ex p Turquand* (1885) 14 QBD at 645.
5 *Uhde v Walters* (1811) 3 Camp 16; cf *Birrell v Dryer* (1884) 9 App Cas at 351.
6 *Parkinson v Collier* (1797) 2 Park's Marine Insurance 8th ed; *Blackett v Royal Exchange Assurance Co* (1832) 2 Cr & J at 250. As to usage in maritime law generally, see *Carver*, paras 905–930.
7 For illustrations of the part played by usage, see *Universo Insurance Co of Milan v Merchants' Marine Insurance Co* [1897] 2 QB 93 (liability of broker for premium); *Atwood v Sellar* (1880) 5 QBD 286, CA (practice of average adjusters to charge certain general average expenses to particular average, invalid); *Stephens v Australasian Insurance Co* (1872) LR 8 CP at 23 (declarations on floating policies); *Dickinson v Jardine* (1868) LR 3 CP 639 (special usage as to jettison, invalid); *Sweeting v Pearce* (1861) 30 LJCP 109 (usage of Lloyd's as to settlement of losses); *Blackett v Royal Exchange Assurance Co* (1832) 2 Cr & J 244 (usage not to pay for boat slung outside, invalid); *Palmer v Blackburn* (1822) 1 Bing 61, 64 (measure of indemnity, gross freight).

88. Reasonable time etc, a question of fact

Where by this Act any reference is made to reasonable time, reasonable premium, or reasonable diligence, the question what is reasonable is a question of fact.[1]

144 *Supplemental*

Note

This section is similar to the lines of the Sale of Goods Act 1979, s 56.

1 As to reasonable time, see *Carlton SS Co v Castle Mail Packets Co* [1898] AC at 491, per Lord Herschell; *Currie & Co v Bombay Native Insurance Co* (1869) LR 3 CP at 79; as to premium, see note to s 31.

89. Slip as evidence

Where there is a duly stamped policy, reference may be made, as heretofore, to the slip or covering note in any legal proceeding.[1]

Note

Lord Blackburn said, 'As the slip is clearly a contract for marine insurance, and is equally clearly not a policy, it is, by virtue of these enactments (the stamp laws), not valid, that is, not enforceable at law or in equity; but it may be given in evidence wherever it is, though not valid, material.' For example, the slip is evidence for the purpose of correcting an error in the name of the ship.[2] So, too, if the insurer seeks to avoid the policy on the ground of non-disclosure of a material fact, the date of the 'slip' would be material to show whether, when the fact came to the knowledge of the assured, the contract had or had not been concluded.[3]

The 'slip' cannot be used to contradict the terms of the policy[4] unless there is a clear case of common mistake. It may then be used for the purpose of rectifying the policy.[5]

1 *Ionides v Pacific Fire and Marine Insurance Co* (1872) LR 7 QB 517, Ex Ch. Cf *Scottish National Insurance Co v Poole* (1912) 18 Com Cas 9 (effect of two slips); *Janson v Poole* (1915) 20 Com Cas 232 at 239 (whether homeward voyage covered or not).
2 *Ionides v Pacific Marine Insurance Co* (1871) LR 6 QB at 685 (name of ship); cf *Western Assurance Co of Toronto v Poole* (1903) 8 Com Cas at 118 ('no s/c' to exclude 'sue and labour' clause in a policy of reinsurance).
3 *Cory v Patton* (1872) LR 7 QB 304; cf *Lishman v Northern Marine Insurance Co* (1875) LR 10 CP 179, Ex Ch. See s 21, as to conclusion of contract.
4 *British and Foreign Marine Insurance Co Ltd v Sturge* (1897) 2 Com Cas 244.
5 *Empress Assurance Corpn v Bowring* (1905) 11 Com Cas 107 at 114, per Kennedy J. Cf *Spalding v Crocker* (1897) 13 TLR 396, per Mathew J; *Symington v Union Insurance Society of Canton Ltd* (1928), 34 Com Cas 233. As to rectification of policy, see, further, *Arnould*, paras 49–50; *Halsbury's Laws of England*, 4th edn, vol 25, para 85; Ivamy, *Marine Insurance* (4th ed, 1985), pp 274–277.

90. Interpretation of terms

In this Act, unless the context or subject-matter otherwise requires,—
'Action' includes counter-claim and set-off:[1]
'Freight' includes the profit derivable by a shipowner from the employment of his ship to carry his own goods or moveables, as well as freight payable by a third party, but does not include passage money:[2]

'Moveables' means any moveable tangible property, other than the ship, and includes money, valuable securities, and other documents:[3]
'Policy' means a marine policy.

Note

'Action'. This definition is merely inclusive. For a substantive definition of 'action' see the Supreme Court Act 1981, s 151(1). See s 50(2), s 56(4), and s 80(2), which require this definition. As to actions on marine policies, see note to s 22.

'Freight'. In shipping law the term 'freight' is sometimes used to denote the goods or cargo laden on board ship. More usually it is used to denote the sum payable to a shipowner by a third person for the use of a ship as a vehicle for merchandise.[4]

In insurance law the term has a wider meaning. In a case where it was held that an insurance 'on freight' did not cover coolies' passage money, Willes J, after commenting on the different meanings of the word, said that it had been 'decided that "freight" sufficiently represents the interest of the shipowner in the carriage of his own goods, and includes the value of their carriage'.[5] It is immaterial to the insurer whether the ship is regarded as hired to an actual or to a hypothetical charterer.

As to 'advance freight,' see s 12. As to freight 'chartered or as if chartered' and the distinction between chartered and bill of lading freight, see Sch I, r 3.

See s 16(2), s 60, and s 71(4), which require this definition.

'Moveables'. In commercial law generally, the term 'goods' includes all moveable tangible property,[6] but in marine insurance law the term has a restricted meaning; see Sch I, r 17. See s 3, s 40 and s 71(1) and (2), which require this definition.

'Policy'. See ss 1, 2, and 22 which refer to a 'marine policy'.

1 Cf Sale of Goods Act 1979, s 61 (2).
2 *Flint v Flemyng* (1830) 1 B & Ad 45; see note to this section.
3 See *Baring Bros & Co v Marine Insurance Co* (1894) 10 TLR 276 (postal packet containing stock certificates); *The Pomeranian* [1895] P 349 (live cattle); *Sleigh v Tyser* [1900] 2 QB 333 (live cattle).
4 By English law, apart from special contract, freight is only payable on delivery of the cargo, and freight *pro rata itineris* is not recognised. Cf *Carver*, paras 1662, 1667.
5 *Denoon v Home and Colonial Assurance Co* (1872) LR 7 CP 341 at 349.
6 Cf Sale of Goods Act 1979, s 61(2), where the term 'goods,' however, expressly excludes money.

91. Savings

(1) Nothing in this Act, or in any repeal effected thereby, shall affect—
  (a) The provisions of the Stamp Act 1891, or any enactment for the time being in force relating to the revenue;
  (b) The provisions of the Companies Act 1862, or any enactment amending or substituted for the same;[1]
  (c) The provisions of any statute not expressly repealed by this Act.

(2) The rules of the Common Law, including the law merchant, save in so far as they are inconsistent with the express provisions of this Act, shall continue to apply to contracts of marine insurance.[2]

Note

The object of sub-s (2) is (i) to fill up lacunæ in the Act itself, and (ii) to preserve the operation of rules of law applicable to all contracts of insurance so far as consistent with the special provisions of the Act.

In Continental countries marine and commercial cases are relegated to special commercial tribunals. In England, as in the United States, they are dealt with by the ordinary courts.

The Law Merchant is part of the Common Law, and its special rules are enforced as part of the ordinary law of the land. Marine insurance is a contract, and in so far as the contract has not special incidents peculiar to itself, it is dealt with on the same footing as other contracts.

Conflict of Laws. An underwriter is bound by an average adjustment duly made according to the law of the place of adjustment, i e when the voyage is completed in due course, by the law of the port of destination, or, when the voyage is not completed, by the law of the place where the voyage is broken up and the ship and cargo part company. An English insurer of goods shipped by an English merchant on board a foreign ship is not affected by the law of the flag.[3]

As Lush J, said, an insurer under an English policy may, if he chooses, stipulate 'that such policy shall be construed and applied in whole or in part according to the law of any foreign state, as if it had been made in and by a subject of the foreign state, and the policy in question does so stipulate as regards general average; but, except when it is so stipulated, the policy must be construed according to our law, and without regard to the nationality of the vessel.'[4]

Foreign law. In the absence of evidence to the contrary, the law of a foreign country is presumed to be the same as English law. If the foreign law differs, and the difference is relied on, it must be proved as a question of fact by expert evidence.[5] But when the evidence has been given, its effect is a question for the Judge, and not for the jury, if any.[6]

Calculation of time. Suppose a ship is insured in London with A up to midnight of 31 December without any special provision as to time, and with B from 1 January. The ship founders in the West Indies on 31 December at 10 pm according to the ship's time. According to London time, A's policy would have expired, and the risk would be on B's policy. If the policy is made in Great Britain, Greenwich mean time applies,[7] except for any time during which the Summer Time Act 1972 is in operation.

The time for general purposes in Great Britain is, during the period of summer time, one hour in advance of Greenwich mean time.[8]

Effect on policy of subsequent hostilities. Subject to the provisions of any licence to trade,[9] the insurer is not liable for any loss suffered by an enemy alien during the continuance of hostilities, even though the policy may have been effected before the commencement of hostilities.[10] For example:

1. Policy on goods from London to Bayonne, effected on behalf of a Frenchman. War afterwards breaks out between England and France, and the goods are captured by a Spanish cruiser, ie by a British ally. The insurer is not liable, even though the action is brought after peace has been concluded.[11]

2. Policy on gold bullion from Johannesburg to London, effected by a company registered and carrying on business in the (Boer) South African Republic. On 2 October the gold is seized in transit by the Government of the South African Republic. On that day war with England was anticipated, but it did not break out until 11 October. The assured is entitled to recover.[12]

3. Policy effected in May on gold bullion from a mine in the Transvaal to London. In October war breaks out between the Transvaal Government and England, and the gold is seized. The assured is a company registered in Natal, though working the mine in the Transvaal. The gold is not enemy property, and the insurer is liable under the policy.[13]

'There are three rules,' said Lord Davey, 'which are established in our Common Law. The first is that the King's subjects cannot trade with an alien enemy, ie a person owing allegiance to a Government at war with the King, *without the King's licence*. Every contract made in violation of this principle is void, and goods which are the subject of such a contract are liable to confiscation.

'The second principle is a corollary from the first, but it is also rested on distinct grounds of public policy. It is that no action can be maintained against an insurer of an enemy's goods or ships against capture by the British Government. One of the most effectual instruments of war is the crippling of the enemy's commerce, and to permit such an insurance would be to relieve enemies from the loss they incur by the action of British arms, and would, therefore, be detrimental to the interests of the insurer's own country. The principle equally applies where the insurance is made previously to the commencement of hostilities, and was therefore legal in its inception, and whether the person claiming on the policy be a neutral or even a British subject, if the insurance be effected on behalf of an alien enemy.

'The third rule is that, if a loss has taken place before the commencement of hostilities, the right of action on a policy of insurance by which goods lost were insured is suspended during the continuance of war and revives on the restoration of peace.'[14]

The Common Law doctrines as to enemies and trading with the enemy have been considerably extended by legislation. At Common Law an alien enemy is a person who voluntarily resides, or carries on business, in enemy territory.[15] Locality and not nationality furnishes the test. But by statute enemy status may be imposed on enemy nationals and other persons having hostile associations outside enemy territory; see eg Trading with the Enemy Act 1939, s 2.

A declaration of war by this country operates as an Act of Parliament prohibiting all trading and business intercourse with the enemy.[16] If a contract made before the war involves intercourse with the enemy for its due fulfilment, the contract is dissolved, and a clause purporting to suspend its operation during war is null and void.[17]

If a British ship sails before the war for a port which, owing to the outbreak of war, becomes an enemy port, the voyage becomes illegal, and must be abandoned;[18] and if a neutral insures with an enemy underwriter who pays for a total loss, the subject-matter insured or whatever remains of it becomes enemy property, and may be dealt with accordingly.[19]

1 The principal Act is now the Companies Act 1985.
2 Cf *British and Foreign Insurance Co v Wilson Shipping Co Ltd* [1921] 1 AC 188 at 193, 211, HL.
3 A V Dicey and J H C Morris, *The Conflict of Laws* (11th ed, 1987), pp 1168–1182; cf *Wavertree Sailing Ship Co v Love* [1897] AC 373, PC.
4 *Greer v Poole* (1880) 5 QBD 272 at 274. (English policy with foreign general average clause). For the rules determining the 'proper law' of a contract, see generally *R v International Trustee for the Protection of Bondholders Akt* [1937] 2 All ER 164, HL; *Vita Food Products Inc v Unus Shipping Co Ltd* [1939] 1 All ER 513, PC; *Re United Rlys of Havana and Regla Warehouses Ltd* [1960] 2 All ER 332, HL; *Halsbury's Laws of England*, 4th edn, vol 8, para 581; Ivamy, *General Principles of Insurance Law* (6th ed, 1993), pp 615–620. As to appointment of salvage according to the national law in the case of a foreign ship, see the Maritime Conventions Act 1911, s 7.
5 *The Parchim* [1918] AC 157 at 160, 161, per Lord Parker. As to expert evidence, see S L Phipson *The Law of Evidence* (14th ed, 1990), paras 32-07–32-54.
6 Supreme Court Act 1981, s 69(5).
7 Interpretation Act 1978, ss 9, 23(3).
8 Summer Time Act 1972, s 1(2). The period of summer time is the period beginning at 2 o'clock, Greenwich mean time, in the morning of the day after the third Saturday in March, or, if that day is Easter Day, the day after the second Saturday in March, and ending at 2 o'clock, Greenwich mean time, in the morning after the fourth Saturday in October: ibid, s 1(2). But Her Majesty may by Order in Council direct that the period of summer time shall be such period as specified in the Order instead of the period mentioned above, and that the time for general purposes in Great Britain during any part of the period of summer time, be two hours instead of one hour in advance of Greenwich mean time: ibid, s 2 (1).
9 *Usparicha v Noble* (1811) 13 East 332, 12 RR 360. *Morgan v Oswald* (1812) 3 Taunt 554; W E Hall, *A Treatise on International Law* (8th ed, 1924); by A P Higgins, pp 668–671, para 196; George J Webber, *Effect of War on Contracts* (2nd ed, 1946), pp 149–151; Lord McNair and A D Watts, *Legal Effects of War* (4th ed, 1966), pp 356–363.
10 *Brandon v Curling* (1803) 4 East 410; *Arnould*, paras 141–142.
11 Ibid; and cf *Potts v Bell* (1800) 8 Term Rep 548, 5 RR 452, Ex Ch (goods purchased in enemy territory, shipped to this country in a neutral vessel).
12 *Driefontein Consolidated Mines v Janson* [1901] 2 KB 419, CA; affd [1902] AC 484, HL.
13 *Nigel Gold Mining Co v Hoade* [1901] 2 KB 849, 6 Com Cas 268.
14 *Janson v Driefontein Consolidated Mines* [1902] AC at 499, HL.
15 Ibid, at 505, HL, per Lord Lindley; *Porter v Freudenberg* [1915] 1 KB 857, CA. Speaking generally, an enemy cannot be the *actor* in any legal proceeding except under royal licence, but, as he may be sued, he can appeal. See also *V/O Sovfracht v Gebr Van Udens Scheepvaart en Agentuur Maatschappij* [1943] 1 All ER 76, HL (a company domiciled in Holland became an alien enemy during German occupation); distinguished in *Lubrafol Owners v Pamia SS Owners, The Pamia* [1943] 1 All ER 269, P (company transferred its business from enemy-occupied territory to neutral country); *Re The Anglo-International Bank Ltd* [1943] 2 All ER 88, CA (further discussion of enemy and enemy-occupied territory).
16 *Esposito v Bowden* (1857) 7 E & B 763, 781, Ex Ch, per Willes J.
17 *Ertel Bieber & Co v Rio Tinto Co* [1918] AC 260, HL; as to cif contracts, see *Arnhold Karberg & Co v Blythe, Green, Jourdain & Co* [1916] 1 KB 495, CA; as to contracts between banker and customer, see *Arab Bank Ltd v Barclays Bank (Dominion, Colonial and Overseas)* [1954] 2 All ER 226, HL.
18 *British and Foreign Marine Insurance Co Ltd v Samuel Sanday & Co* [1916] 1 AC 650, 673, HL. (See the judgment of Lord Wrenbury.)
19 *The Palm Branch* [1916] P 230, modified on appeal because it turned out that a small percentage of the insurers were not enemies, [1919] AC 272, PC. As regards enemy

property, the English or neutral pledgee or mortgagee has no claim cognisable by a British Prize Court, even though the security was given before war; see *The Odessa* [1916] 1 AC 145, PC.

92. *This section was repealed by the Statute Law Revision Act 1927.*

93. *This section was repealed by the Statute Law Revision Act 1927.*

94. Short title

This Act may be cited as the Marine Insurance Act 1906.

Note

This Act, like all Acts passed subsequent to 1889, must be read subject to the provisions of the Interpretation Act 1978.

A codifying Act, as Lord Herschell has pointed out, must be construed according to its natural meaning without regard to the previous state of the law. It is only in case of doubt that resort to the previous law is legitimate.[1]

Where an Act is divided into Parts or Headings, regard should be had to these divisions in construing the Act.[2]

1 *Vagliano v Bank of England* [1891] AC at 145, HL; *Hall v Hayman* [1912] 2 KB at 12; *The Anglo-Mexican* [1918] AC 422, PC, but later cases show an inclination to construe the Act as declaratory whenever possible; see eg *British and Foreign Marine Insurance Co Ltd v Sanday & Co* [1916] 1 AC 650 at 672, per Lord Wrenbury.
2 *Inglis v Robertson* [1898] AC at 630, HL.

SCHEDULES

FIRST SCHEDULE

Form of Policy (see s 30)

BE IT KNOWN THAT   as well in
                 own name as for and in the name and names of all and every other person or persons to whom the same doth, may, or shall appertain, in part or in all doth make assurance and cause
and them, and every of them, to be insured lost or not lost, at and from

Upon any kind of goods and merchandises, and also upon the body, tackle, apparel, ordnance, munition, artillery, boat, and other furniture, of and in the good ship or vessel called the
whereof is master under God, for this present voyage,   or whosoever else shall go for master in the said ship, or by whatsoever other name or names the said ship, or the master thereof, is or shall be named or called; beginning the adventure upon the said goods and merchandises from the loading thereof aboard the said ship,   upon the said ship, etc
and so shall continue and endure, during her abode there, upon the said ship, etc. And further, until the said ship, with all her ordnance, tackle, apparel, etc, and goods and merchandises whatsoever shall be arrived at
       upon the said ship, etc, until she hath moored at anchor twenty-four hours in good safety; and upon the goods and merchandises, until the same be there discharged and safely landed. And it shall be lawful for the said ship, etc, in this voyage, to proceed and sail to and touch and stay at any ports or places whatsoever   without prejudice to this insurance. The said ship, etc, goods and merchandises, etc, for so much as concerns the assured by agreement between the assured and assurers in this policy, are and shall be valued at
Touching the adventures and perils which we, the assurers, are contented to bear and do take upon us in this voyage: they are of the seas, men of war, fire, enemies, pirates, rovers, thieves, jettisons, letters of mart and countermart, surprisals, takings at sea, arrests, restraints, and

detainments of all kings, princes, and people, of what nation, condition, or quality soever, barratry of the master and mariners, and of all other perils, losses, and misfortunes, that have or shall come to the hurt, detriment, or damage of the said goods, and merchandises, and ship, etc, or any part thereof. And in case of any loss or misfortune it shall be lawful to the assured, their factors, servants and assigns, to sue, labour, and travel for, in and about the defence, safeguards, and recovery of the said goods and merchandises, and ship, etc, or any part thereof, without prejudice to this insurance; to the charges whereof we, the assurers, will contribute each one according to the rate and quantity of this sum herein assured. And it is especially declared and agreed that no acts of the insurer or insured in recovering, saving, or preserving the property insured shall be considered as a waiver, or acceptance of abandonment. And it is agreed by us, the insurers, that this writing or policy of assurance shall be of as much force and effect as the surest writing or policy of assurance heretofore made in Lombard Street, or in the Royal Exchange, or elsewhere in London. And so we, the assurers, are contented, and do hereby promise and bind ourselves, each one for his own part, our heirs, executors, and goods to the assured, their executors, administrators, and assigns, for the true performance of the premises, confessing ourselves paid the consideration due unto us for this assurance by the assured, at and after the rate of

IN WITNESS whereof we, the assurers, have subscribed our names and sums assured in London.

NB—Corn, fish, salt, fruit, flour, and seed are warranted free from average, unless general, or the ship be stranded—sugar, tobacco, hemp, flax, hides, and skins are warranted free from average, under five pounds per cent, and all other goods, also the ship and freight, are warranted free from average, under three pounds per cent, unless general, or the ship be stranded.

RULES FOR CONSTRUCTION OF POLICY

The following are the rules referred to by this Act for the construction of a policy in the above or other like form, where the context does not otherwise require:

1. Lost or not lost

Where the subject-matter is insured 'lost or not lost,' and the loss has occurred before the contract is concluded, the risk attaches unless, at such time, the assured was aware of the loss, and the insurer was not.

2. From

Where the subject-matter is insured 'from' a particular place, the risk does not attach until the ship starts on the voyage insured.

3. At and from

[**Ship**] (a) Where a ship is insured 'at and from' a particular place, and she is at that place in good safety when the contract is concluded, the risk attaches immediately.
(b) If she be not at that place when the contract is concluded, the risk attaches as soon as she arrives there in good safety, and, unless the policy otherwise provides, it is immaterial that she is covered by another policy for a specified time after arrival.
[**Freight**] (c) Where chartered freight is insured 'at and from' a particular place, and the ship is at that place in good safety when the contract is concluded, the risk attaches immediately. If she be not there when the contract is concluded, the risk attaches as soon as she arrives there in good safety.
(d) Where freight other than chartered freight, is payable without special conditions and is insured 'at and from' a particular place, the risk attaches pro rata as the goods or merchandise are shipped; provided that if there be cargo in readiness which belongs to the shipowner, or which some other person has contracted with him to ship, the risk attaches as soon as the ship is ready to receive such cargo.

4. From the loading thereof

Where goods or other moveables are insured 'from the loading thereof,' the risk does not attach until such goods or moveables are actually on board and the insurer is not liable for them while in transit from the shore to the ship.

5. Safely landed

Where the risk on goods or other moveables continues until they are 'safely landed,' they must be landed in the customary manner and within a reasonable time after arrival at the port of discharge, and if they are not so landed the risk ceases.

6. Touch and stay

In the absence of any further license or usage, the liberty to touch and stay 'at any port or place whatsoever' does not authorise the ship to depart from the course of her voyage from the port of departure to the port of destination.

7. Perils of the seas

The term 'perils of the seas' refers only to fortuitous accidents or casualties of the seas. It does not include the ordinary action of the winds and waves.

8. Pirates

The term 'pirates' includes passengers who mutiny and rioters who attack the ship from the shore.

9. Thieves

The term 'thieves' does not cover clandestine theft, or a theft committed by any one of the ship's company, whether crew or passengers.

10. Restraint of princes

The term 'arrests etc of kings, princes, and people' refers to political or executive acts, and does not include a loss caused by riot or by ordinary judicial process.

11. Barratry

The term 'barratry' includes every wrongful act wilfully committed by the master or crew to the prejudice of the owner, or, as the case may be, the charterer.

12. All other perils

The term 'all other perils' includes only perils similar in kind to the perils specifically mentioned in the policy.

13. Average unless general

The term 'average unless general' means a partial loss of the subject-matter insured other than a general average loss, and does not include 'particular charges'.

14. Stranded

Where the ship has stranded, the insurer is liable for the excepted losses, although the loss is not attributable to the stranding, provided that when the stranding takes place the risk has attached and, if the policy be on goods, that the damaged goods are on board.

15. Ship

The term 'ship' includes the hull, materials and outfit, stores and provisions for the officers and crew, and, in the case of vessels engaged in a special trade, the ordinary fittings requisite for the trade, and also, in the case of a steamship, the machinery, boilers, and coals and engine stores, if owned by the assured.

16. Freight

The term 'freight' includes the profit derivable by a shipowner from the employment of his ship to carry his own goods or moveables, as well as freight payable by a third party, but does not include passage money.

17. Goods

The term 'goods' means goods in the nature of merchandise, and does not include personal effects or provisions and stores for use on board.

In the absence of any usage to the contrary, deck cargo and living animals must be insured specifically, and not under the general denomination of goods.

SECOND SCHEDULE

[*This Schedule was repealed by the Statute Law Revision Act 1927*].

APPENDIX I—STATUTES

THE MARINE INSURANCE (GAMBLING POLICIES) ACT 1909
(9 Edw 7 c 12)
An Act to Prohibit Gambling on Loss by Maritime Perils

[20 October 1909]

1. Prohibition of gambling on loss by maritime perils
(1) If—
   (a) any person effects a contract of marine insurance without having any bona fide interest, direct or indirect, either in the safe arrival of the ship in relation to which the contract is made or in the safety or preservation of the subject-matter insured, or a bona fide expectation of acquiring such an interest; or
   (b) any person in the employment of the owner of a ship, not being a part owner of the ship, effects a contract of marine insurance in relation to the ship, and the contract is made 'interest or no interest,' or 'without further proof of interest than the policy itself,' or 'without benefit of salvage to the insurer,' or subject to any other like term,

the contract shall be deemed to be a contract by way of gambling on loss by maritime perils, and the person effecting it shall be guilty of an offence, and shall be liable, on summary conviction, to imprisonment, . . . for a term not exceeding six months or to a fine not exceeding level 3 on the standard scale, and in either case to forfeit to the Crown any money he may receive under the contract.

(2) Any broker or other person through whom, and any insurer with whom, any such contract is effected shall be guilty of an offence and liable on summary conviction to the like penalties if he acted knowing that the contract was by way of gambling on loss by maritime perils within the meaning of this Act.

(3) Proceedings under this Act shall not be instituted without the consent in England of the Attorney-General, in Scotland of the Lord Advocate, and in Ireland of the Attorney-General for Ireland.

(4) Proceedings shall not be instituted under this Act against a person (other than a person in the employment of the owner of the ship in relation to which the contract was made) alleged to have effected a contract by way of gambling on loss by maritime perils until an opportunity has been afforded him of showing that the contract was not such a contract as aforesaid, and any information given by that person for that purpose shall not be admissible in evidence against him in any prosecution under this Act.

(5) If proceedings under this Act are taken against any person (other than a person in the employment of the owner of the ship in relation to which the contract was made) for effecting such a contract, and the contract was made 'interest or no interest,' or 'without further proof of interest than the policy itself,' or 'without benefit of salvage to the insurer,' or subject to any other like term, the contract shall be deemed to be a contract by way of gambling on loss by maritime perils unless the contrary is proved.

(6) For the purpose of giving jurisdiction under this Act, every offence shall be deemed to have been committed either in the place in which the same actually was committed or in any place in which the offender may be.

(7) Any person aggrieved by an order or decision of a court of summary jurisdiction under this Act, may appeal to the Crown Court.

(8) For the purposes of this Act the expression 'owner' includes charterer.

(9) Subsection (7) of this section shall not apply to Scotland.

2. Short title

This Act may be cited as the Marine Insurance (Gambling Policies) Act 1909, and the Marine Insurance Act 1906, and this Act may be cited together as the Marine Insurance Acts 1906 and 1909.[1]

[1] As to the mischiefs at which this Act was aimed, see *Hansard* (1909), Vol III, pp 1676–1680. The Act supplements the Marine Insurance Act 1906, s 4 by penalising certain gambling insurances which the latter Act merely avoided.

THE SALE OF GOODS ACT 1979[1]
(1979 c 54)

20. Risk prima facie passes with property

(1) Unless otherwise agreed, the goods remain at the seller's risk until the property in them is transferred to the buyer, but when the property in them is transferred to the buyer the goods are at the buyer's risk whether delivery has been made or not.

(2) But where delivery has been delayed through the fault of either buyer or seller the goods are at the risk of the party at fault as regards any loss which might not have occurred but for such fault.

(3) Nothing in this section affects the duties or liabilities of either seller or buyer as a bailee or custodier of the goods of the other party.

32. Delivery to carrier
(1) Where, in pursuance of a contract of sale, the seller is authorised or required to send the goods to the buyer, delivery of the goods to a carrier (whether named by the buyer or not) for the purpose of transmission to the buyer is prima facie deemed to be a delivery of the goods to the buyer.
(2) Unless otherwise authorised by the buyer, the seller must make such contract with the carrier on behalf of the buyer as may be reasonable having regard to the nature of the goods and the other circumstances of the case; and if the seller omits to do so, and the goods are lost or damaged in course of transit, the buyer may decline to treat the delivery to the carrier as a delivery to himself or may hold the seller responsible in damages.
(3) Unless otherwise agreed, where goods are sent by the seller to the buyer by a route involving sea transit, under circumstances in which it is usual to insure, the seller must give such notice to the buyer as may enable him to insure them during their sea transit; and if the seller fails to do so, the goods are at his risk during such sea transit.

1 See notes to these provisions in *Chalmers' Sale of Goods Act 1979* (18th ed, 1981) pp 155–187, and notes to the Marine Insurance Act 1906, ss 6 and 14. (See pp 13 and 20, ante).

APPENDIX II—MARINE POLICY FORMS[1]

(1) Lloyd's Form

LLOYD'S MARINE POLICY

We, The Underwriters, hereby agree, in consideration of the payment to us by or on behalf of the Assured of the premium specified in the Schedule, to insure against loss damage liability or expense in the proportions and manner herinafter provided. Each Underwriting Member of a Syndicate whose definitive number and proportion is set out in the following Table shall be liable only for his own share of his respective Syndicate's proportion.

In Witness whereof the General Manager of Lloyd's Policy Signing Office has subscribed his Name on behalf of each of Us.

LLOYD'S POLICY SIGNING OFFICE
General Manager

(For embossment by Lloyds Policy Signing Office)

This insurance is subject to English jurisdiction.

---

[1] These forms were introduced in 1982 and are used in connection with the new Institute Clauses. (See Appendix III, pp 166–276, post.)

SCHEDULE

POLICY NUMBER

___

NAME OF ASSURED

___

VESSEL

___

VOYAGE OR PERIOD OF INSURANCE

___

SUBJECT-MATTER INSURED

___

AGREED VALUE
(if any)

___

AMOUNT INSURED HEREUNDER

___

PREMIUM

___

CLAUSES, ENDORSEMENTS, SPECIAL CONDITIONS AND WARRANTIES

162 *Appendix II*

Definitive numbers of the Syndicates and proportions

The List of Underwriting Members of Lloyd's mentioned in the above Table shows their respective Syndicates and Shares therein and is deemed to be incorporated in and to form part of this Policy: It is available for inspection at Lloyd's Policy Signing Office by the Assured or his or their representatives and a true copy of the material parts of it certified by the General Manager of Lloyd's Policy Signing Office will be furnished to the Assured on application.

(2) Insurance Companies' Form

The Institute of London Underwriters
Companies Marine Policy

We, The Companies, hereby agree, in consideration of the payment to us by or on behalf of the Assured of the premium specified in the Schedule, to insure against loss damage liability or expense in the proportions and manner hereinafter provided. Each Company shall be liable only for its own respective proportion.

In Witness whereof the General Manager and Secretary of The Institute of London Underwriters has subscribed his name on behalf of each Company.

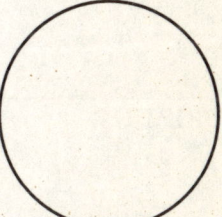

....
General Manager and Secretary
The Institute of London
Underwriters

This Policy is not valid unless it bears the embossment of the Policy Department of The Institute of London Underwriters.

This insurance is subject to English jurisdiction.

SCHEDULE
POLICY NUMBER

NAME OF ASSURED

VESSEL

VOYAGE OR PERIOD OF INSURANCE

SUBJECT-MATTER INSURED

AGREED VALUE
(if any)

AMOUNT INSURED HEREUNDER

PREMIUM

CLAUSES, ENDORSEMENTS, SPECIAL CONDITIONS AND WARRANTIES

THE ATTACHED CLAUSES AND ENDORSEMENTS FORM PART OF THIS POLICY

COMPANIES' PROPORTIONS

For use by the Policy Department
of
The Institute of London Underwriters

APPENDIX III—THE INSTITUTE CLAUSES

The original Lloyd's policy itself was framed as an insurance on ship and goods. To make it apply to other interests and to meet the constantly changing requirements of modern commerce, special clauses or sets of clauses were added to the policy. Many of these sets of clauses have now become standard, eg the clauses issued by the Institute of London Underwriters, and are almost universally introduced into the class of policies to which they apply.[1] These clauses are business stipulations, and must be construed from a business, and not a technical, point of view.[2] The decisions on these special provisions are numerous, but each case turns on the particular language used. If the special clause is inconsistent with the provisions of the printed policy, the special clause must prevail.[3]

In this Appendix are set out some of the more commonly used Institute Clauses.

A new form of Lloyd's policy was introduced in 1982, and in that year and in 1983 new Institute Clauses were introduced.[4]

The principal of these are:

(i)   the Institute Time Clauses (Hulls);[5]
(ii)   the Institute Voyage Clauses (Hulls);[6]
(iii)   the Institute War and Strikes Clauses (Hulls–Time);[7]
(iv)   the Institute War and Strikes Clauses (Hulls–Voyage);[8]
(v)   the Institute Time Clauses (Freight);[9]
(vi)   the Institute Voyage Clauses (Freight);[10]
(vii)   the Institute War and Strikes Clauses (Freight–Time);[11]
(viii) the Institute War and Strikes Clauses (Freight–Voyage);[12]
(ix)   the Institute Cargo Clauses (A);[13]
(x)   the Institute Cargo Clauses (B);[14]
(xi)   the Institute Cargo Clauses (C);[15]
(xii)   the Institute War Clauses (Cargo);[16] and
(xiii) the Institute Strikes Clauses (Cargo).[17]

The date which appears before the heading of each set of clauses is the date when those clauses were introduced.

1 For a complete set of the Institute Clauses, see *Reference Book of Marine Insurance Clauses* compiled by Witherby & Co Ltd and published annually.
2 *Tatham v Burr* [1898] AC at 386. For a general canon of construction, see *Hart v Standard Marine Insurance Co Ltd* (1889) 22 QBD at 501, per Bowen LJ. And as to usage, see s 87 of the Act.
3 *Hydarnes SS Co v Indemnity Mutual Marine Insurance Co* [1895] 1 QB 500, CA; cf *Dudgeon v Pembroke* (1877) 2 App Cas 284. For the effect of the incorporation of the Institute Clauses 'as far as they apply,' see *Otago Farmers' Co-operative Association of New Zealand v Thompson* [1910] 2 KB 145.
4 The new clauses are not without criticism. See e g *Ikerigi Compania Naviera SA v Palmer, The Wondrous* [1992] 2 Lloyd's Rep 566, CA, where Lloyd LJ observed (ibid, at 568): 'The old form of Lloyd's SG policy was subject to a great deal of judicial criticism for 200 years or more. It was to be hoped that the new form of policy introduced in January 1982, and the new Institute Clauses would have made it easier for the parties to define more clearly the intended scope of cover, whether the insurance be on hull, freight or cargo. Unfortunately the present case proves that hope to have been in vain. The two policies are littered with obscurities and infelicities.'
5 See pp 167–195, post.
6 See pp 196–207, post.
7 See pp 208–211, post.
8 See pp 212–215, post.
9 See pp 215–225, post.
10 See pp 225–232, post.
11 See pp 232–235, post.
12 See pp 236–239, post.
13 See pp 239–249, post.
14 See pp 249–256, post.
15 See pp 256–264, post.
16 See pp 264–271, post.
17 See pp 271–276, post.

(1) Hull Clauses

1/10/83 (FOR USE ONLY WITH THE NEW MARINE POLICY FORM)

INSTITUTE TIME CLAUSES

HULLS

(This insurance is subject to English law and practice)

1. Navigation.

1.1   The Vessel is covered subject to the provisions of this insurance at all times and has leave to sail or navigate with or without pilots, to go on trial trips and to assist and tow vessels or craft in distress, but it is warranted that the Vessel shall not be towed, except as is customary or to the first safe port or place when in need of assistance, or undertake towage or salvage services under a contract previously arranged by the Assured and/or Owners and/or Managers and/or Charterers. This Clause 1.1 shall not exclude customary towage in connection with loading and discharging.

1.2   In the event of the Vessel being employed in trading operations which entail cargo loading or discharging at sea from or into another vessel (not being a harbour or inshore craft) no claim shall be recoverable under this insurance for loss of or damage to the Vessel or liability to any other vessel arising from such loading or discharging operations, including whilst approaching, lying alongside and leaving, unless previous notice that the Vessel is to be employed in such operations has been given to the Underwriters and any amended terms of cover and any additional premium required by them have been agreed.

1.3   In the event of the Vessel sailing (with or without cargo) with an intention of being (a) broken up, or (b) sold for breaking up, any claim for loss of or damage to the Vessel occurring subsequent to such sailing shall be limited to the market value of the Vessel as scrap at the time when the loss or damage is sustained, unless previous notice has been given to the Underwriters and any amendments to the terms of cover, insured value and premium required by them have been agreed. Nothing in this Clause 1.3 shall affect claims under Clause 8 and/or 11.

Notes

Warranty as to towage and salvage services. For the meaning of 'warranty,' see 33(1) (p 50, ante). A warranty must be exactly complied with, whether it is material to the risk or not: ibid s 33(3) (p 51, ante). If it is not complied with the insurer is discharged from liability as from the date of the breach of warranty: ibid, s 33(3) (p 51, ante).

Additional premium. Where an insurance is effected on the terms that an additional premium is to be arranged in a given event, and that event happens but no arrangement is made, then a reasonable additional premium is payable: ibid, s 31(2) (p 47, ante).

Measure of indemnity. Normally the measure of indemnity in respect of the insured vessel is that set out in s 68 (total loss) (p 115, ante), and in s 69 (partial loss) (p 116, ante). But the clause set out above limits the measure of indemnity to her scrap value in the circumstances stated.

Clause 8. Claims under Clause 8 which concerns '¾ths Collision Liability' (p 177, post) are not affected.

Clause 11. Claims under Clause 11 which concerns 'General Average and Salvage' (p 181, post) are not affected.

2. Continuation. Should the Vessel at the expiration of this insurance be at sea or in distress or at a port of refuge or of call, she shall, provided previous notice be given to the Underwriters, be held covered at a pro rata monthly premium to her port of destination.

Notes

Purpose of clause. The clause makes certain that insurance cover is available for a further period should the policy normally be due to expire while the vessel is still at sea.

Premium. For the payment of the premium, see s 52 (p 76, ante).

3. Breach of Warranty. Held covered in case of any breach of warranty as to cargo, trade, locality, towage, salvage services or date of sailing, provided notice be given to the Underwriters immediately after receipt of advices and any amended terms of cover and any additional premium required by them be agreed.

Notes

Purpose of clause. The effect of this clause is that if there should be a breach of warranty, as enumerated, underwriters will not avoid the policy, but will hold the assured covered, provided that notice of the breach is given immediately it comes to the knowledge of the assured, and any additional premium is paid.

Additional premium. See p 47, ante.

4. Termination. *This Clause 4 shall prevail notwithstanding any provision whether written typed or printed in this insurance inconsistent therewith.*
Unless the Underwriters agree to the contrary in writing, this insurance shall terminate automatically at the time of

4.1 change of the Classification Society of the Vessel, or change, suspension, discontinuance, withdrawal or expiry of her Class therein, provided that if the Vessel is at sea such automatic termination shall be deferred until arrival at her next port. However where such change, suspension, discontinuance or withdrawal of her Class has resulted from loss or damage covered by Clause 6 of this insurance or which would be covered by an insurance of the Vessel subject to current Institute War and Strikes Clauses (Hulls–Time) such automatic termination shall only operate should the Vessel sail from her next port without the prior approval of the Classification Society,

4.2 any change, voluntary or otherwise, in the ownership or flag, transfer to new management, or charter on a bareboat basis, or requisition for title or use of the Vessel, provided that, if the Vessel has cargo on board and has already sailed from her loading port or is at sea in ballast, such automatic termination shall if required be deferred, whilst the Vessel continues her planned voyage, until arrival at final port of discharge if with cargo or at port of destination if in ballast. However, in the event of requisition for title or use without the prior execution of a written agreement by the Assured, such automatic termination shall occur fifteen days after such requisition whether the Vessel is at sea or in port.

170 Appendix III

A pro rata daily net return of premium shall be made.

Notes

Purpose of clause. The clause indicates that the insurance will terminate in the events specified. It is important to notice that the clause prevails over any provision in the policy inconsistent with it.

Classification Society. A society, eg Lloyd's whose function is to allot a 'class' to a vessel eg '100A1,' which is the highest class.

Clause 6. This clause sets out the perils insured against (p 170, infra).

Institute War and Strikes Clauses (Hulls–Time). These clauses may be added to the policy and are set out at pp 208–211, post.

Charter on bareboat basis. I e a charter-party under which the charterer, and not the shipowner, supplies the officers and crew.

Requisition. A taking over of the vessel by the Government in time of emergency, eg in the Falklands War of 1982.

Return of premium. As to the return by agreement of a proportionate part of the premium, see s 83 (p 137, ante), and as to the enforcement of the return of premium, see s 82 (p 136, ante).

5. Assignment. No assignment of or interest in this insurance or in any moneys which may be or become payable thereunder is to be binding on or recognised by the Underwriters unless a dated notice of such assignment or interest signed by the Assured, and by the assignor in the case of subsequent assignment, is endorsed on the Policy and the Policy with such endorsement is produced before payment of any claim or return of premium thereunder.

Notes

Purpose of clause. The purpose of this clause is to ensure that underwriters are made aware of any assignment of the policy and are provided with conclusive evidence as to who is entitled to receive the amount of any claim or return of premium.

Return of premium. See ss 82–84 (pp 136–140, ante).

6. Perils.
6.1   This insurance covers loss of or damage to the subject-matter insured caused by
6.1.1   perils of the seas rivers lakes or other navigable waters
6.1.2   fire, explosion

6.1.3	violent theft by persons from outside the Vessel
6.1.4	jettison
6.1.5	piracy
6.1.6	breakdown of or accident to nuclear installations or reactors
6.1.7	contact with aircraft or similar objects, or objects falling therefrom, land conveyance, dock or harbour equipment or installation
6.1.8	earthquake volcanic eruption or lightning.
6.2	This insurance covers loss of or damage to the subject-matter insured caused by
6.2.1	accidents in loading discharging or shifting cargo or fuel
6.2.2	bursting of boilers breakage of shafts or any latent defect in the machinery or hull
6.2.3	negligence of Master Officers Crew or Pilots
6.2.4	negligence of repairers or charterers provided such repairers or charterers are not an Assured hereunder
6.2.5	barratry of Master Officers or Crew,
	provided such loss or damage has not resulted from want of due diligence by the Assured, Owners or Managers.
6.3	Master Officers Crew or Pilots not to be considered Owners within the meaning of this Clause 6 should they hold shares in the Vessel.

Notes

This clause sets out the perils insured against. It is to be emphasised that those listed in Clause 6.1 are covered in any event, whereas those listed in Clause 6.2 are covered only where the loss has not resulted from want of due diligence by the assured, owners or managers.

Subject to the provisions of the Marine Insurance Act 1906, and unless the policy otherwise provides, the insurer is liable for any loss proximately caused by a peril insured against: s 55(1) (p 78, ante).

Perils of the sea. The term 'perils of the seas' refers only to fortuitous accidents or casualties of the seas. It does not include the ordinary action of the wind and waves.[1]

It is unsafe to attempt a complete definition of the expression 'perils of the seas,' because in practice the question 'what is a peril of the seas' is inextricably woven up with the further question, 'was the loss proximately caused by the sea peril?'[2] Lord Bramwell tentatively suggested the following definition: 'Every accidental circumstance not the result of ordinary wear and tear, delay, or of the act of the assured, happening in the course of the navigation of the ship, and incidental to the navigation, and causing loss to the subject matter of the insurance.' He then approved an alternative definition given by Lopes LJ, namely, 'In a seaworthy ship damage to goods caused by the action of the sea during transit not attributable to the fault of anybody.'[3]

Buckley LJ (Lord Wrenbury), suggested 'a peril to which the assured would not be exposed if his adventure was not a marine adventure'.[4]

These definitions certainly are open to criticism, but the following points may be noted. First, the term 'peril' denotes something which is accidental and fortuitous. 'The purpose of the policy is to secure an indemnity against accidents which may happen, not against events which must happen.'[5] So scuttling of a vessel by those in charge of her is not a peril of the seas.[6] Secondly, the expression is 'perils *of* the seas,' not 'perils *on* the seas'. For example, the policy enumerates many maritime perils, such as capture, seizure, fire, etc, which are incidental to a marine adventure, but which are not perils of the seas; so, too, risks, not ordinarily covered by the policy, may be expressly covered, eg, the risk of mortality in insurance on cattle, and frozen meat risks. Thirdly, the expression 'perils of the seas' has the same meaning in a marine policy as it has in a bill of lading or charter-party, though its application to the contract is different.[7]

The assured has the burden of proving that there was a loss by perils of the seas, although the degree of proof required is only to show a balance of probabilities in favour of an accidental loss by perils of the seas.[8]

Fire. In order to constitute a loss there must be an actual fire or ignition.[9] Any loss attributable to the fire whether by actual burning or scorching or by smoke will have to be borne by the insurer.[10]

'Fire' in a marine policy is not confined to accidental fire and includes a fire deliberately started by a stranger to the insurance policy.[11]

As to the burden of proof, once it is shown that the loss has been caused by fire, the assured has made out a prima facie case, and the onus is on the insurer to show on a balance of probabilities that the fire was caused or connived at by the assured. Accordingly, if at the end of the day the jury come to the conclusion that the loss is equally consistent with arson as it is with an accidental fire, the onus being on the insurer, the assured would win on that issue.[12]

Explosion. The word 'explosion' in its ordinary meaning includes an eruption without a chemical reaction.[13] But it has also been held to mean an event which was an event which was violent, noisy and one which was caused by a very rapid chemical or nuclear reaction, or the bursting out of gas or vapour under pressure.[14]

Violent theft. The term 'thieves' does not cover clandestine theft, or a theft committed by any one of the ship's company, whether crew or passengers.[15]

In this context the term 'thief' seems only to apply to a person who commits theft by violent means. 'The theft that is insured against in the policy means that which is accompanied by violence (latrocinium), and not simple theft (furtum); it being an old and elementary rule of the law of insurance that *furtum non est casus fortuitus*, is not one of the fortuitous events against which the owner may seek indemnity by insurance, but one which the law presumes the master might have prevented by the exercise of due vigilance, and the loss arising from which he consequently ought to bear.'[16] Some American policies use the words 'pirates and assailing thieves'.

In a case on a bill of lading containing the exceptions 'pirates, robbers, thieves,' it was held that the word 'thieves' applied only to strangers, and not to persons belonging to the vessel; and Archibald J, after pointing out that the words were no doubt copied originally from the ordinary marine policy, expressed the opinion that a similar construction must be put upon both instruments.[17]

To put the matter beyond doubt the present clause states that it covers *violent* theft only.

Jettison. Jettison is the voluntary sacrifice in time of peril of something in or on the ship by throwing it overboard with the intention of preserving the ship and cargo.[18]

The insurance against jettison is independent of any right to general average contribution though the insurer, after payment of the loss would be entitled to such rights as the assured possessed.[19]

Piracy. The term 'pirates' includes passengers who mutiny and rioters who attack the ship from the shore.[20] This definition is not exhaustive, nor is it easy to define the term precisely. In *Republic of Bolivia v Indemnity Mutual Marine Assurance Co Ltd*[21] Kennedy LJ said: 'The authorities show that the word "piracy" is one capable of various shades of meaning, and that, even when used strictly as a legal term, it may be held to cover different subject-matters according as it is considered from the point of view of international or that of municipal lawyers. It seems to me that in the case of a policy like this it ought, if possible, to be construed in the sense which would give it a meaning applicable to the insurance effected by the policy. I do not doubt the general correctness, according to the existing authorities, of the definition given by the late Mr Carver in s 94 of his valuable work on Carriage of Goods by Sea, 4th ed, p 117, where he says: "Piracy is forcible robbery at sea, whether committed by marauders from outside the ship or by mariners or passengers within it. The essential element is that they violently dispossess the master, and afterwards carry away the ship itself, or any of the goods, with a felonious intent."'

More recently, however, the Privy Council has expressed the view that 'actual robbery is not an essential element in the crime of piracy jure gentium, and that a frustrated attempt to commit piratical robbery is equally piracy jure gentium'.[22]

There is no reason to limit piracy to acts outside territorial waters. If a ship is, in the ordinary meaning of the phrase, 'at sea' or if the attack on her can be described as a 'maritime' offence, then for the business purposes of a policy of marine insurance she is in a place where piracy can be committed.[23]

Theft without force or a threat of force is not piracy.[24] The very notion of piracy is inconsistent with clandestine theft.[25]

Accidents in loading etc. This part of Clause 6 was formerly known as the 'Inchmaree' clause taking its name from *The Inchmaree*,[26] where a donkey engine employed in filling the ship's boilers became damaged owing to a valve being closed, which ought to have been open. It was held that the cost of repairing the engine was not covered by the policy in respect of the vessel's hull and machinery, including the donkey engine, since the damage was not caused 'by perils of the seas'. Following on this decision it became customary to include an 'Inchmaree' clause in almost all policies on steamships.

The scope of the present clause is much wider than is necessary to cover merely the circumstances which gave it its origin. It now covers a number of cases where the damage or loss cannot be said to arise from a marine peril, e g (i) breakdown of or accident to nuclear installations or reactors on shipboard or elsewhere; and (ii) contact with aircraft.

The scope of the words 'breakage of shafts or any latent defect in the machinery or hull,' has given rise to a good deal of controversy, but it is now settled that the underwriters are not required to meet the cost of replacing any part of the machinery or hull (including a shaft) which may itself have broken or become unserviceable, owing to the existence of a latent defect, unless the latent defect arose during the currency of the policy.

Underwriters are merely liable to meet the cost of damage caused by a latent defect. Thus, in *Scindia SS (London) Ltd v London Assurance*,[27] the propeller of a ship in dry dock was being removed. This necessitated the withdrawal of the tail shaft, and while this was being done, the tail shaft broke owing to a latent defect, and the propeller fell and was damaged. The insurers admitted liability in respect of the propeller. The shipowners contended that the insurers were liable also for providing and fitting a new shaft. It was held that the claim failed. Referring to the 'Inchmaree' clause included in the policy, Branson J, said:[28] 'It seems to me, therefore, that the proper reading is that the breakage of the shaft itself is not covered, nor can it properly be said that the breakage of the shaft is a loss of or damage to machinery caused by the breakage of the shaft . . . In this case, the only damage, beyond the damage to the propeller, which has been paid for, is the actual damage which happened to the shaft itself, to wit, the breakage of the shaft, and the breakage of the shaft is not caused by the breakage of the shaft.'

The words 'loading, discharging or handling cargo,' were introduced into the clause in 1914 to cover the loss unsuccessfully claimed in *Stott (Baltic) Steamers Ltd v Marten*,[29] where the tackle of a crane lowering a boiler into the hold of a ship broke, causing the boiler to fall and damage the ship's hull, for such loss was there held not to be caused by 'perils of the sea'.

It should be noticed that the clause covers loss, directly caused by negligence of master,[30] officers, crew[31] or pilots provided it has not resulted from want of due diligence by the Assured, Owner or Managers. Whether due diligence has been observed is, of course, a question of fact in each case.[32]

Barratry. The term 'barratry' includes every wrongful act wilfully committed by the master or crew to the prejudice of the owner, or, as the case may be, the charterer.[33]

Thus, if the master scuttles the ship,[34] or fraudulently sells the cargo,[35] or fraudulently deviates,[36] or if the crew wrongfully refuse to discharge cargo,[37] or if the master and crew run off with the ship,[38] these acts amount to barratry.

1 Rules for Construction of Policy, r 7 (p 153, ante).
2 Cf *De Mattos v Saunders* (1872) LR 7 CP 570 at 580, per Willes J; and see s 55, as to proximate cause.
3 *Thames and Mersey Marine Insurance Co v Hamilton* (1887) 12 App Cas at 492 (the *Inchmaree* case); see *Paterson v Harris* (1861) 30 LJQB 354, distinguishing the chemical from the mechanical action of the sea; cf *Blackburn v Liverpool, Brazil and River Plate Steam Navigation Co* [1902] 1 KB 290 (bill of lading case).
4 *Stott (Baltic) Steamers v Marten* (1914) 19 Com Cas 438 at 439; affd [1916] 1 AC 304, HL.
5 Per Lord Herschell in *The Xantho* (1887) 12 App Cas at 509; *The Lapwing* [1940] P 112 (yacht negligently docked so as to be allowed to sit on a dangerous bottom; *held*, that the intervention of those responsible for the docking provided the fortuitous circumstance which entitled the assured to recover for a loss due to a peril ejusdem generis with a peril of the sea, namely, stranding); *N E Neter & Co Ltd v Licenses and General Insurance Co Ltd* [1944] 1 All ER 341, KB (damage to properly stowed cargo caused by rough weather may be fortuitous, even though such weather might be anticipated).
6 *Samuel (P) & Co Ltd v Dumas* [1924] AC 431, 29 Com Cas 239 at 250, HL.

7 *Hamilton v Pandorf* (1887) 12 App Cas 518; *Wilson, Sons & Co v Xantho (Cargo Owners)* (1887) 2 App Cas at 509.
8 *Compania Naviera Santi SA v Indemnity Marine Assurance Co Ltd, The Tropaioforos* [1960] 2 Lloyd's Rep 469 at 473, QB (Commercial Court) (per Pearson J), and the cases cited on that page; *Northwestern Mutual Life Insurance Co v Linard, The Vainqueur* [1974] 2 Lloyd's Rep 398, US Ct of Appeals, Second Circuit (see the judgment of Oakes CtJ, ibid, at 403 where the American cases are reviewed); *N Michalos & Sons Maritima SA v Prudential Assurance Co Ltd, The Zinovia* [1984] 2 Lloyd's Rep 264, QB (Commercial Court); *Rhesa Shipping Co SA v Edmunds, The Popi M* [1985] 2 Lloyd's Rep 1, HL; *R A Houghton and Mancon Ltd v Sunderland Marine Mutual Insurance Co Ltd, The Ny-Eeasteyr* [1988] 1 Lloyd's Rep 60, QB (Commercial Court); *CCR Fishing Ltd v Tomenson Inc, The La Pointe* [1991] 1 Lloyd's Rep 89, Supreme Court of Canada; *Lamb Heading Shipping Co Ltd v Jennings, The Marel* [1992] 1 Lloyd's Rep 402, QB (Commercial Court).
9 *Everett v London Assurance* (1865) 19 CBNS 126 (fire insurance).
10 *Austin v Drewe* (1816) 2 Marsh 130 (fire insurance).
11 *Slattery v Mance* [1962] 1 Lloyd's Rep 60, QB (Commercial Court); *Continental Illinois National Bank and Trust Co of Chicago v Alliance Assurance Co Ltd, The Captain Panagos DP* [1986] 2 Lloyd's Rep 470, QB (Commercial Court) at 510–511 (per Evans J) (affd [1989] 1 Lloyd's Rep 33, CA); *Schiffshypothekenbank Zu Luebeck AG v Compton, The Alexion Hope* [1988] 1 Lloyd's Rep 311 at 317, CA (per Lloyd LJ).
12 *Slattery v Mance* [1962] 1 All ER 525 at 526, [1962] 1 Lloyd's Rep 60 at 62 (per Salmon J). The burden of proof in the case of a loss by fire is, therefore, different from that in a case where a loss by perils of the seas is alleged. See *Compania Naviera Santi SA v Indemnity Marine Assurance Co Ltd, The Tropaioforos* (supra).
13 *Canadian General Electric Co Ltd v Liverpool and London and Globe Insurance Co Ltd* (1980) 106 DLR (3d) 750 (Ont CA) (fire insurance), where a manufacturing plant was insured against damage caused by fire or explosion, and an overheated pressure tank ruptured as a result of water being poured on to it in order to cool it down, and it was held that an 'explosion' had occurred.
14 *Commonwealth Smelting Ltd v Guardian Royal Exchange Assurance Ltd* [1984] 2 Lloyd's Rep 608 (property insurance) at 608 (per Staughton J). In that case the claim for damage to the blower house when a blower disintegrated failed because the predominant cause of the damage was centrifugal disintegration of the impeller and not explosion. (See the judgment of Staughton J, ibid, at 612.) The decision was subsequently affirmed: [1986] 1 Lloyd's Rep 121, CA. (See the judgment of Parker LJ, ibid, 126.)
15 Rules for Construction of Policy, r 9 (p 154, ante).
16 *Shell International Petroleum Co Ltd v Gibbs, The Salem* [1982] 1 All ER 1057 at 1066, CA (per Kerr LJ).
17 *Taylor v Liverpool and Great Western Steam Co* (1874) LR 9 QB 546 at 551.
18 *The Gratitudine* (1801) 3 Ch Rob 240.
19 *Mouse's Case* (1608) 12 Co Rep 63. As to general average contribution, see s 66(3) (p 109, ante).
20 Rules for Construction of Policy, r 8 (p 154, ante); *Kleinwort v Shepard* (1859) 1 E & E 447 (mutiny of Chinese coolies); cf *Johnston v Hogg* (1883) 10 QBD 432 (robbery by Brass River natives); *Republic of Bolivia v Indemnity Mutual Marine Assurance Co* [1909] 1 KB 785, CA (attack by revolutionaries = civil commotion, not piracy).
21 [1909] 1 KB 785 at 802–3.
22 *Re Piracy Jure Gentium* [1934] AC 586 at 600, PC. The opinion was expressed by way of answer to a question referred to the Privy Council under Judicial Committee Act 1833, s 4.
23 *Athens Maritime Enterprises Corpn v Hellenic Mutual War Risks Association (Bermuda) Ltd, The Andreas Lemos* [1982] 2 Lloyd's Rep 483 at 490 (per Staughton J).
24 Ibid, at 491 (per Staughton J).

25 Ibid, at 491 (per Staughton J).
26 *Thames and Mersey Marine Insurance Co v Hamilton* (1887) 12 App Cas 484, HL.
27 [1937] 3 All ER 895, KB. For other cases on this point, see *Oceanic SS Co v Faber* (1906) 11 Com Cas 179, (1907) 13 Com Cas 28, CA; *Wills & Sons v The World Marine Insurance Ltd* (1911) Times, 14 March; *Hutchins Bros Royal Exchange Assurance Corpn* [1911] 2 KB 398, CA; *Jackson v Mumford* (1902) 8 Com Cas 61 (weakness in the design of a connecting rod is not a latent defect); *Irwin v Eagle Star Insurance Co Ltd, The Jomie* [1973] 2 Lloyd's Rep 489, US Ct of Appeals, Fifth Circuit, where it was held that the assured was not entitled to an indemnity in respect of a yacht, which sank due to an air conditioning firm improperly joining together a steel pipe and a brass pipe thus causing electrolysis when the joint was exposed to the presence of air and salt water, for there was no 'latent defect in the hull', but only a mistake by the air conditioning firm in joining steel and brass together (see the judgment of Coleman CtJ, ibid, at 491); *Sipowicz v Wimble, The Green Lion* [1974] 1 Lloyd's Rep 593, District Ct of Southern District of New York, where it was held that the defect was not a 'latent' one because the assured knew of the condition of the metal fastenings and had performed certain work in order to restore them (see the judgment of Cannella DJ, ibid, at 599); *Prudent Tankers Ltd SA v Dominion Insurance Co Ltd, The Caribbean Sea* [1980] 1 Lloyd's Rep 338, where the loss of the vessel had been caused by fatigue cracks in a wedge-shaped nozzle joined to her plate, and the defect was held to be a 'latent' one. (See the judgment of Robert Goff J, ibid, at 347.)
28 [1937] 3 All ER at 898.
29 [1914] 1 KB 442, [1914] 3 KB 1262, [1916] 1 AC 304.
30 See eg *Lind v Mitchell* (1928) 98 LJKB 120, CA (vessel last seen on fire); *Baxendale v Fane, The Lapwing* (1940) 66 Ll L Rep 174 (vessel damaged whilst being cleaned in tidal dock).
31 The American version of the 'Inchmaree' clause refers to 'negligence of master, mariners, engineers or pilots'. See eg *F B Walker & Sons Inc v Valentine* [1970] 2 Lloyd's Rep 429, US Ct of Appeals, Fifth Circuit, and *Rosa v Insurance Co of the State of Pennsylvania, The Belle of Portugal* [1970] 2 Lloyd's Rep 386, US Ct of Appeals, Ninth Circuit, where it was held that even if the crew of another vessel had been negligent in trying to hoist the insured skiff on to their vessel, they were 'mariners' within the meaning of the 'Inchmaree' clause, and the insurers were liable for the loss of the skiff. (See the judgment of Merrill, CtJ, ibid, at 387.)
32 See eg *F B Walker & Sons Inc v Valentine* (supra), where it was held that the failure of the crew to tighten up the main engine stuffing boxes was not due to want of due diligence on the part of the assured (see the judgment of Brown ChJ, ibid, at 430); *Pacific Queen Fisheries v L Symes, The Pacific Queen* [1963] 2 Lloyd's Rep 201, US Ct of Appeals, Ninth Circuit, where the loss of the vessel had resulted from want of due diligence on the part of the assured to prevent the explosion; *Coast Ferries Ltd v Century Insurance Co of Canada, The Brentwood* [1973] 2 Lloyd's Rep 232, Ct of Appeal of British Columbia, where it was held that the loss of the vessel resulted from 'want of due diligence on the part of the assured,' for they had failed to furnish the master with sufficient information about minimum freeboard and trim for the vessel to enable him to exercise sound judgment in loading in the light of his skill and experience. (See the judgment of the Court delivered by Davey J, ibid, at 234.)
33 Rules for Construction of Policy, r 11 (p 154, ante).
34 *Ionides v Pender* (1872) 27 LT 244.
35 *Havelock v Hancill* (1789) 3 Term Rep 277.
36 *Mentz, Decker & Co v Maritime Insurance Co* [1910] 1 KB 132.
37 *Compania Naviera Bachi v Henry Hosegood & Co Ltd* [1938] 2 All ER 189.
38 *Marstrand Fishing Co Ltd v Beer* [1937] 1 All ER 158, KB. See further, *Republic of China, China Merchants' Steam Navigation Co Ltd and United States of America v National Union Fire Insurance Co of Pittsburgh, Pennsylvania, The Hai Hsuan* [1958] 1 Lloyd's Rep 351 (US Court of Appeals), where it was held that the defection of the crews

of vessels, which were owned by the Chinese Nationalist Government, to the Chinese Communist Government, constituted 'barratry'. (See especially the judgment of Soper ChJ, ibit, at 356–357.)

7. Pollution Hazard. This insurance covers loss of or damage to the Vessel caused by any governmental authority acting under the powers vested in it to prevent or mitigate a pollution hazard, or threat thereof, resulting directly from damage to the Vessel for which the Underwriters are liable under this insurance, provided such act of governmental authority has not resulted from want of due diligence by the Assured, the Owners, or Managers of the Vessel or any of them to prevent or mitigate such hazard or threat. Master, Officers, Crew or Pilots not to be considered Owners within the meaning of this Clause 7 should they hold shares in the Vessel.

Notes

Purpose of clause. The clause adds another peril to the 'perils insured against' (see p 170, ante), and perhaps it would have been better to combine it with Clause 6.

Extent of clause. It is to be emphasised that the clause provides cover in respect of pollution damage to the insured vessel and not by her. It is to be noticed that it is subject to the exercise of due diligence to prevent or mitigate the hazard.

8. 3/4ths Collision Liability.

8.1   The Underwriters agree to indemnify the Assured for three-fourths of any sum or sums paid by the Assured to any other person or persons by reason of the Assured becoming legally liable by way of damages for

8.1.1   loss of or damage to any other vessel or property on any other vessel

8.1.2   delay to or loss of use of any such other vessel or property thereon

8.1.3   general average of, salvage of, or salvage under contract of, any such other vessel or property thereon,

where such payment by the Assured is in consequence of the Vessel hereby insured coming into collision with any other vessel.

8.2   The indemnity provided by this Clause 8 shall be in addition to the indemnity provided by the other terms and conditions of this insurance and shall be subject to the following provisions:

8.2.1   Where the insured Vessel is in collision with another vessel and both vessels are to blame then, unless the liability of one or both vessels becomes limited by law, the indemnity under this Clause 8 shall be calculated on the principle of cross-liabilities as if the respective Owners had been compelled to pay to each other such proportion of each other's damages as may have been properly allowed in ascertaining the balance or sum payable by or to the Assured in consequence of the collision.

8.2.2 In no case shall the Underwriters' total liability under Clauses 8.1 and 8.2 exceed their proportionate part of three-fourths of the insured value of the Vessel hereby insured in respect of any one collision.

8.3 The Underwriters will also pay three-fourths of the legal costs incurred by the Assured or which the Assured may be compelled to pay in contesting liability or taking proceedings to limit liability, with the prior written consent of the Underwriters.

EXCLUSIONS

8.4 Provided always that this Clause 8 shall in no case extend to any sum which the Assured shall pay for or in respect of

8.4.1 removal or disposal of obstructions, wrecks, cargoes or any other thing whatsoever

8.4.2 any real or personal property or thing whatsoever except other vessels or property on other vessels

8.4.3 the cargo or other property on, or the engagements of, the insured Vessel

8.4.4 loss of life, personal injury or illness

8.4.5 pollution or contamination of any real or personal property or thing whatsoever (except other vessels with which the insured Vessel is in collision or property on such other vessels).

Note

Purpose of clause. A clause of this nature[1] was first introduced into marine policies as a result of the decision in *De Vaux v Salvador*,[2] where it was held that money payable by the assured to another shipowner in settlement of collision damage was not a loss caused by perils of the sea, and was not accordingly chargeable to the underwriters under the terms of the standard form of marine policy.

At Common Law, the settlement of collision damage, as between shipowners, is made on what is known as the 'single liability principle'.[3] Briefly, this implies that if two vessels collide in such circumstances that both are equally to blame for the collision, the ship sustaining the least damage is liable to pay to the ship sustaining the most damage half the difference between the two amounts of damage. There is only one liability. There are not two liabilities whereby each ship is liable to pay half the cost of the other ship's damage.

As between shipowners, the distinction is not important, unless one shipowner is insolvent, or there is a limitation of liability under the Merchant Shipping Act 1979, s 17. As between shipowner and underwriter, the distinction can, however, be important, especially having regard to the fact that the above clause covers only three-fourths of the assured's collision liability.

Since the decision in *London SS Owners' Insurance Co v Grampian SS Co*[4] which followed the decision in *The Khedive*,[5] the Institute 'Collision' clause has contained the provision that when both vessels are to blame, claims are to be settled on the principle of cross-liabilities (as distinct from the single liability principle) unless the liability of the owners of one or both of the vessels becomes limited by law.

Underwriters have always sought to limit their liability to three-fourths of the amount of collision damage, and it is usual for the remaining one-fourth to be covered with a Protection and Indemnity Association.[6] The risks excluded by the clause are also normally covered with a Protection and Indemnity Association.[7]

The clause is only brought into operation in the event of a collision between the vessel insured and another vessel or vessels, and unless the risks are specifically included, the clause does not cover collision with a wharf of breakwater, or with anything which is not another vessel.[8] Furthermore, the clause covers only collision damages payable in respect of a tort, and does not cover a liability arising in contract.[9]

On the other hand, once there has been a collision with another vessel, underwriters are liable for all damage occasioned thereby, subject to the provisions of Clause 8.4.[10]

---

1 See Ivamy, *Marine Insurance* (4th ed, 1985), pp 170–176.
2 (1836) 4 A & E 420.
3 See *Stoomvaart Maatschappy Nederland v Peninsular and Oriental Steam Navigation Co, The Khedive* (1882) 7 App Cas 795, HL, overruling *Chapman v Royal Netherlands Steam Navigation Co* (1879) 4 PD 157. See also *Young v Merchants' Marine Insurance Co Ltd* [1932] 2 KB 705.
4 (1890) 24 QBD 663, CA.
5 Supra.
6 See p 140, ante.
7 See p 141, ante.
8 *The Niobe* [1891] AC 401, HL (a tug towing *The Niobe* came into collision with, and sunk another vessel, the owners of which recovered damages both from the tug and from *The Niobe*. *The Niobe's* owners were entitled to reimbursement by underwriters under a 'running down' clause); *Margetts and Ocean Accident and Guarantee Corpn Ltd, Re* [1901] 2 KB 792 (a tug coming up river struck an anchor attached by chain to a schooner, and sank. The tug had come into collision with a vessel and underwriters were liable under a 'running down' clause); *Bennett SS Co v Hull Mutual SS Protecting Society Ltd* [1913] 3 KB 372; affd [1914] 3 KB 57, CA (the plaintiffs' vessel damaged the nets attached to a fishing vessel, to the owners of which the plaintiffs had to pay damages. There had been no collision in terms of a 'collision' clause, and the defendants, a P & I Association, were liable to reimburse the plaintiffs, there being no liability on the part of Lloyd's underwriters); *Chandler v Blogg* [1898] 1 QB 32 (the *Newburn* struck a barge which was temporarily sunken, but was capable of being raised and navigated: this was a 'collision'). See also *Merchants' Marine Insurance Co Ltd v North of England Protecting and Indemnity Association* (1926) 32 Com Cas 165, CA (floating crane held not to be 'vessel'); *Richardson v Burrows* (1880) cited Lowndes *Marine Insurance* (2nd ed), p 199, per Lord Coleridge CJ; *Polpen Shipping Co Ltd v Commercial Union Assurance Co Ltd* [1943] KB 161, [1943] 1 All ER 162, KB (collision with a flying-boat not a collision with a 'ship or vessel').
9 See *Furness Withy & Co Ltd v Duder* [1936] 2 All ER 119, KB (vessel being towed collided with its tug, there being a liability towards the tug under the towage contract); *Hall Bros SS Co Ltd v Young, The Trident* [1939] 1 All ER 809, CA (a payment by way of indemnity under French legislation to a French pilot-boat irrespective of negligence is not 'by way of damages').

10 See *France, Fenwick & Co Ltd v Merchants' Marine Insurance Co Ltd* [1915] 3 KB 290, CA; *Burger v Indemnity Mutual Marine Assurance Co Ltd* [1900] 2 QB 348, CA; *The North Britain* [1894] P 77, CA; *Tatham v Burr* [1898] AC 382; *Chapman v James Fisher & Sons* (1904) 20 TLR 319. The provision rendering underwriters liable for a proportion of the legal costs incurred by the assured was introduced as a result of the decision in *Xenos v Fox* (1868) LR 3 CP 630, (1869) LR 4 CP 665.

9. Sistership. Should the Vessel hereby insured come into collision with or receive salvage services from another vessel belonging wholly or in part to the same Owners or under the same management, the Assured shall have the same rights under this insurance as they would have were the other vessel entirely the property of Owners not interested in the Vessel hereby insured; but in such cases the liability for the collision or the amount payable for the services rendered shall be referred to a sole arbitrator to be agreed upon between the Underwriters and the Assured.

Note

Purpose of clause. If it were not for the inclusion of this clause, an assured would be unable to recover collision damage from underwriters, in cases where the collision occurred between two vessels in the ownership of the assured. As the assured cannot sue himself, provision is made for questions of liability or quantum to be referred to a sole arbitrator.

10. Notice of Claim and Tenders.

10.1 In the event of accident whereby loss or damage may result in a claim under this insurance, notice shall be given to the Underwriters prior to survey and also, if the Vessel is abroad, to the nearest Lloyd's Agent so that a surveyor may be appointed to represent the Underwriters should they so desire.

10.2 The Underwriters shall be entitled to decide the port to which the Vessel shall proceed for docking or repair (the actual additional expense of the voyage arising from compliance with the Underwriters' requirements being refunded to the Assured) and shall have a right of veto concerning a place of repair or a repairing firm.

10.3 The Underwriters may also take tenders or may require further tenders to be taken for the repair of the Vessel. Where such a tender has been taken and a tender is accepted with the approval of the Underwriters, an allowance shall be made at the rate of 30 per cent per annum on the insured value for time lost between the despatch of the invitations to tender required by Underwriters and the acceptance of a tender to the extent that such time is lost solely as the result of tenders having been taken and provided that the tender is accepted without delay after receipt of the Underwriters' approval.

Due credit shall be given against the allowance as above for any amounts recovered in respect of fuel and stores and wages and maintenance of the Master Officers and Crew or any member thereof, including amounts allowed in general average, and for any amounts recovered from third parties in respect of damages for detention and/or loss of profit and/or running expenses, for the period covered by the tender allowance or any part thereof. Where a part of the cost of the repair of damage other than a fixed deductible is not recoverable from the Underwriters the allowance shall be reduced by a similar proportion.

10.4 In the event of failure to comply with the conditions of this Clause 10 a deduction of 15 per cent shall be made from the amount of the ascertained claim.

Notes

Purpose of clause. This clause sets out the procedure for ascertaining the amount payable by the underwriters in respect of particular average.

General average. As to general average, see s 66 (p 109, ante).

Fixed deductible. See Clause 12 (p 183, post).

11. General Average and Salvage.

11.1 This insurance covers the Vessel's proportion of salvage, salvage charges and/or general average, reduced in respect of any under-insurance, but in case of general average sacrifice of the Vessel the Assured may recover in respect of the whole loss without enforcing their right of contribution from other parties.

11.2 Adjustment to be according to the law and practice obtaining at the place where the adventure ends, as if the contract of affreightment contained no special terms upon the subject; but where the contract of affreightment so provides the adjustment shall be according to the York–Antwerp Rules.

11.3 When the Vessel sails in ballast, not under charter, the provisions of the York–Antwerp Rules 1974 (excluding Rules XX and XXI) shall be applicable, and the voyage for this purpose shall be deemed to continue from the port or place of departure until the arrival of the Vessel at the first port or place thereafter other than a port or place of refuge or a port or place of call for bunkering only. If at any such intermediate port or place there is an abandonment of the adventure originally contemplated the voyage shall thereupon be deemed to be terminated.

11.4 No claim under this Clause 11 shall in any case be allowed where the loss was not incurred to avoid or in connection with the avoidance of a peril insured against.

Notes

Purpose of the clause. The purpose of the clause is to state the liability of the insurers in respect of salvage, salvage charges and general average.

Salvage charges. These mean the charges recoverable under maritime law by a salvor independently of contract: s 65 (p 107, ante).

General average. See s 66 (p 109, ante). The last part of Clause 11.1 repeats the provisions of s 66(4) as to the enforcement of the right to contribution.

Under-insurance. Ie where the assured is insured for an amount less than the insurable value, or, in the case of a valued policy, for an amount less than the policy valuation: s 81 (p 136, ante).

Foreign adjustment. In English law, the proper place for the adjustment of general average is the place where the adventure ends, and accordingly the law and practice to be applied are the law and practice relating to that place.[1] Such an adjustment is called a foreign adjustment,[2] and it appears that underwriters are also bound so long as the adjustment has been rightly settled in accordance with the law and usages of the foreign place concerned.[3]

The words in the clause, 'as if the contract of affreightment contained no special terms upon the subject,' were included as a result of the decision in *De Hart v Compañia Anonima de Seguros Aurora*.[4]

York–Antwerp Rules 1974. These are set out in Appendix IV (see pp 277–284, post).

Rule XX concerns 'Provision of funds' (see p 284, post). Rule XXI relates to 'Interest on losses made good in general average'. (See p 284, post.)

Exclusion of insurer's liability. Clause 11.4 is in the same terms as s 66(6) (see p 110, ante), which excludes the insurer's liability where the loss was not incurred for the purpose of avoiding, or in connection with the avoidance of, a peril insured against.

---

1 For foreign adjustments, see generally R Lowndes and G R Rudolf, *Law of General Average and the York Antwerp Rules* (11th ed, 1990) paras 50.80–50.87 et seq; *Simonds v White* (1824) 2 B & C 805.
2 *Peters v Warren Insurance Co* (1838) 3 Sumer 389, (1840) 14 Peters 99 (USA); *Simonds v White* (supra); *Dalglish v Davidson* (1824) 5 Dow & Ry KB 6.
3 *Harris v Scaramanga* (1872) LR 7 CP 481; *Newman v Cazalet* (circa 1780) 2 Park's Marine Insurances, 8th ed, p 900; *Walpole v Ewer* (1789) 2 Park's Marine Insurances, 8th ed, p 898; *Hill v Wilson* (1879) 4 CPD 329; *Power v Whitmore* (1815) 4 M & S 141; *Dent v Smith* (1869) LR 4 QB 414; *Hendricks v Australasian Insurance Co* (1874) LR 9 CP 460; *Mavro v Ocean Marine Insurance Co* (1874) LR 9 CP 595, (1875) LR 10 CP 414; *Stewart v West India and Pacific SS Co* (1873) LR 8 QB 88; affd (1873) LR 8 QB 362; *The Mary Thomas* [1894] P 108, CA.
4 *De Hart v Compania Anonoma de Seguros Aurora* [1903] 2 KB 503, CA.

12. Deductible.

12.1 No claim arising from a peril insured against shall be payable under this insurance unless the aggregate of all such claims arising out of each separate accident or occurrence (including claims under Clauses 8, 11 and 13) exceeds .... in which case this sum shall be deducted. Nevertheless the expense of sighting the bottom after stranding, if reasonably incurred specially for that purpose, shall be paid even if no damage be found. This Clause 12.1 shall not apply to a claim for total or constructive total loss of the Vessel or, in the event of such a claim, to any associated claim under Clause 13 arising from the same accident or occurrence.

12.2 Claims for damage by heavy weather occurring during a single sea passage between two successive ports shall be treated as being due to one accident. In the case of such heavy weather extending over a period not wholly covered by this insurance the deductible to be applied to the claim recoverable hereunder shall be the proportion of the above deductible that the number of days of such heavy weather falling within the period of this insurance bears to the number of days of heavy weather during the single sea passage.

The expression 'heavy weather' in this Clause 12.2 shall be deemed to include contact with floating ice.

12.3 Excluding any interest comprised therein, recoveries against any claim which is subject to the above deductible shall be credited to the Underwriters in full to the extent of the sum by which the aggregate of the claim unreduced by any recoveries exceeds the above deductible.

12.4 Interest comprised in recoveries shall be apportioned between the Assured and the Underwriters, taking into account the sums paid by the Underwriters and the dates when such payments were made, notwithstanding that by the addition of interest the Underwriters may receive a larger sum than they have paid.

Notes

Purpose of clause. The clause constitutes an 'excess clause' whereby the assured has to bear the loss up to the amount stated in Clause 12.1, and is similar to an excess clause in a motor policy.

Clause 8. This is the '3/4ths Collision Liability' clause (see p 177, ante).

Clause 11. This is the 'General Average and Salvage' clause (see p 181, ante).

Clause 13. This is the 'Duty of Assured (Sue and Labour)' clause (see p 184, post).

13. Duty of Assured (Sue and Labour).

13.1 In case of any loss or misfortune it is the duty of the Assured and their servants and agents to take such measures as may be reasonable for the purpose of averting or minimising a loss which would be recoverable under this insurance.

13.2 Subject to the provisions below and to Clause 12 the Underwriters will contribute to charges properly and reasonably incurred by the Assured their servants or agents for such measures. General average, salvage charges (except as provided for in Clause 13.5) and collision defence or attack costs are not recoverable under this Clause 13.

13.3 Measures taken by the Assured or the Underwriters with the object of saving, protecting or recovering the subject-matter insured shall not be considered as a waiver or acceptance of abandonment or otherwise prejudice the rights of either party.

13.4 When expenses are incurred pursuant to this Clause 13 the liability under this insurance shall not exceed the proportion of such expenses that the amount insured hereunder bears to the value of the Vessel as stated herein, or to the sound value of the Vessel at the time of the occurrence giving rise to the expenditure if the sound value exceeds that value. Where the Underwriters have admitted a claim for total loss and property insured by this insurance is saved, the foregoing provisions shall not apply unless the expenses of suing and labouring exceed the value of such property saved and then shall apply only to the amount of the expenses which is in excess of such value.

13.5 When a claim for total loss of the Vessel is admitted under this insurance and expenses have been reasonably incurred in saving or attempting to save the Vessel and other property and there are no proceeds, or the expenses exceed the proceeds, then this insurance shall bear its pro rata share of such proportion of the expenses, or of the expenses in excess of the proceeds, as the case may be, as may reasonably be regarded as having been incurred in respect of the Vessel; but if the Vessel be insured for less than its sound value at the time of the occurrence giving rise to the expenditure, the amount recoverable under this clause shall be reduced in proportion to the under-insurance.

13.6 The sum recoverable under this Clause 13 shall be in addition to the loss otherwise recoverable under this insurance but shall in no circumstances exceed the amount insured under this insurance in respect of the Vessel.

Notes

Purpose of clause. The purpose of the clause is to put sue and labour charges on the same basis as salvage and general average.

Institute Time Clauses (Hulls) 185

Taking of reasonable measures. Clause 13.1 is similar to s 78(4) (p 127, ante), and stresses that it applies only where the loss is a peril insured against, as stated in s 78(3) (p 127, ante).

Recovery of reasonable charges. Clause 13.2 is similar to s 78(1) (p 127, ante).

Exclusion of liability for general average and salvage charges. In this respect Clause 13.2 is similar to s 78(2) (p 127, ante). As to 'general average,' see s 66 (p 109, ante), and as to 'salvage charges,' see s 65 (p 107, ante).

Clause 12. This clause is the 'Deductible' clause (see p 183, ante), and the assured will be entitled to claim sue and labour expenses in excess of the amount stated as 'deductible'.

Waiver or acceptance of abandonment. As to acceptance of notice of abandonment, see s 62(5), (6), (p 99, ante), and as to waiver of notice of abandonment, see s 62(8) (p 100, ante).

Sums recoverable additional to loss, otherwise recoverable. Clause 13.6 is similar to s 78(1) (p 127, ante), by which the 'sue and labour' clause is deemed to be supplementary to the contract of insurance.

14. New for Old. Claims payable without deduction new for old.

Note
Purpose of clause. This clause modifies the effect of s 69(1), (2) (p 116, ante), which sets out the measure of indemnity in the case of a partial loss of a ship, and states that it is the reasonable cost of the repairs 'less the customary deductions'.

15. Bottom Treatment. In no case shall a claim be allowed in respect of scraping gritblasting and/or other surface preparation or painting of the Vessel's bottom except that

15.1   gritblasting and/or other surface preparation of new bottom plates ashore and supplying and applying any 'shop' primer thereto,

15.2   gritblasting and/or other surface preparation of:
the butts or area of plating immediately adjacent to any renewed or refitted plating damaged during the course of welding and/or repairs,
areas of plating damaged during the course of fairing, either in place or ashore,

15.3   supplying and applying the first coat of primer/anti-corrosive to those particular areas mentioned in 15.1 and 15.2 above,

shall be allowed as part of the reasonable cost of repairs in respect of bottom plating damaged by an insured peril.

Note

Purpose of clause. The clause modifies the effect of s 69(1), (2) (p 116, ante) in respect of the measure of indemnity in relation to the repair of a ship.

16. Wages and Maintenance. No claim shall be allowed, other than in general average, for wages and maintenance of the Master, Officers and Crew, or any member thereof, except when incurred solely for the necessary removal of the Vessel from one port to another for the repair of damage covered by the Underwriters, or for trial trips for such repairs, and then only for such wages and maintenance as are incurred whilst the Vessel is under way.

Notes

Purpose of clause. This clause limits the amount of wages and maintenance in respect of the master, officers and crew except in the circumstances specified in it.

General average. See s 66 (p 109, ante).

17. Agency Commission. In no case shall any sum be allowed under this insurance either by way of remuneration of the Assured for time and trouble taken to obtain and supply information or documents or in respect of the commission or charges of any manager, agent, managing or agency company or the like, appointed by or on behalf of the Assured to perform such services.

Note

Purpose of clause. The clause emphasises that the assured is not entitled to any indemnity in respect of any expenses which he may have incurred in preparing a claim. The position is the same in other branches of insurance, even though there may be no clause in the policy expressly referring to the matter.

18. Unrepaired Damage.

18.1   The measure of indemnity in respect of claims for unrepaired damage shall be the reasonable depreciation in the market value of the Vessel at the time this insurance terminates arising from such unrepaired damage, but not exceeding the reasonable cost of repairs.

18.2   In no case shall the Underwriters be liable for unrepaired damage in the event of a subsequent total loss (whether or not covered under this insurance) sustained during the period covered by this insurance or any extension thereof.

18.3   The Underwriters shall not be liable in respect of unrepaired damage for more than the insured value at the time this insurance terminates.

Note

Purpose of clause. This clause is similar to s 69(3) (p 116, ante) in respect of the measure of indemnity in the case of a partial loss of a ship.

It also emphasises that the underwriters are not liable if the vessel has not been repaired and is subsequently a total loss. The position is also set out in s 77(2) (p 126, ante).

19. Constructive Total Loss.

19.1 In ascertaining whether the Vessel is a constructive total loss, the insured value shall be taken as the repaired value and nothing in respect of the damaged or break-up value of the Vessel or wreck shall be taken into account.

19.2 No claim for constructive total loss based upon the cost of recovery and/or repair of the Vessel shall be recoverable hereunder unless such cost would exceed the insured value. In making this determination, only the cost relating to a single accident or sequence of damages arising from the same accident shall be taken into account.

Notes

Effect of clause. The effect of this clause is that where a constructive total loss is claimed on the ground that the cost of repairing the ship would be greater than its value when repaired, the insured value is deemed to be the repaired value; and in ascertaining the cost of repairs, the value of the wreck is not to be included.

The former provision is included because of the difficulty of estimating the repaired value of a vessel, and because it is now enacted that, in the absence of any provision to the contrary, it is the actual repaired value which provides the criterion.[1] The latter provision is included *ex abundante cautela*: as the authorities stand at the moment, the value of the wreck is not to be included.

Constructive total loss. See s 60 (p 90, ante).

1 See s 27(4) of the Act following *Irving v Manning* (1847) 1 HL Cas 287. For examples of cases where the policy has contained a contrary provision, see *Marten v SS Owners' Underwriting Association Ltd* (1902) 7 Com Cas 195 (a contrary provision in the policy, but not in the reinsurance policy); *Angel v Merchants' Marine Insurance Co* [1903] 1 KB 811, CA: *North Atlantic SS Co v Burr* (1904) 9 Com Cas 164; *Hall v Hayman* [1912] 2 KB 5; *Helmville Ltd v Yorkshire Insurance Co Ltd, The Medina Princess* [1965] 1 Lloyd's Rep 361 QB (Commercial Court), where the assured failed to prove that the vessel was a constructive total loss, and was held to be entitled to claim for a partial loss only.

20. Freight Waiver.

In the event of total or constructive total loss no claim to be made by the Underwriters for freight whether notice of abandonment has been given or not.

Notes

Purpose of clause. The purpose of the clause is to negative the effect of s 63(2) (p 104, ante), which states that 'on the abandonment of a ship the insurer of her is entitled to any freight in course of being earned, and which is earned by her subsequent to the casualty causing the loss'.

Total loss. See s 68 (p 115, ante).

Constructive total loss. See s 60 (p 90, ante).

Notice of abandonment. See s 62 (p 99, ante).

21. Disbursements Warranty.

21.1　Additional insurances as follows are permitted:

21.1.1　*Disbursements, Managers' Commissions, Profits or Excess or Increased Value of Hull and Machinery.* A sum not exceeding 25 per cent of the value stated herein.

21.1.2　*Freight, Chartered Freight or Anticipated Freight, insured for time.* A sum not exceeding 25 per cent of the value as stated herein less any sum insured, however described, under 21.1.1.

21.1.3　*Freight or Hire, under contracts for voyage.* A sum not exceeding the gross freight or hire for the current cargo passage and next succeeding cargo passage (such insurance to include, if required, a preliminary and an intermediate ballast passage) plus the charges of insurance. In the case of a voyage charter where payment is made on a time basis, the sum permitted for insurance shall be calculated on the estimated duration of the voyage, subject to the limitation of two cargo passages as laid down herein. Any sum insured under 21.1.2 to be taken into account and only the excess thereof may be insured, which excess shall be reduced as the freight or hire is advanced or earned by the gross amount so advanced or earned.

21.1.4　*Anticipated Freight if the Vessel sails in ballast and not under Charter.* A sum not exceeding the anticipated gross freight on next cargo passage, such sum to be reasonably estimated on the basis of the current rate of freight at time of insurance plus the charges of insurance. Any sum insured under 21.1.2 to be taken into account and only the excess thereof may be insured.

21.1.5　*Time Charter Hire or Charter Hire for Series of Voyages.* A sum not exceeding 50 per cent of the gross hire which is to be earned under the charter in a period not exceeding 18 months. Any sum insured under 21.1.2 to be taken into account and only the excess thereof may be insured, which excess shall be reduced as the hire is advanced or earned under the charter by 50 per cent of the gross amount so advanced or earned but the sum insured need not be reduced while the total of the sums insured under 21.1.2 and 21.1.5 does not exceed 50 per cent of the gross hire still to be earned under the charter. An insurance under this Section may begin on the signing of the charter.

21.1.6 *Premiums.* A sum not exceeding the actual premiums of all interests insured for a period not exceeding 12 months (excluding premiums insured under the foregoing sections but including, if required, the premium or estimated calls on any Club or War etc Risk insurance) reducing pro rata monthly.

21.1.7 *Returns of Premium.* A sum not exceeding the actual returns which are allowable under any insurance but which would not be recoverable thereunder in the event of a total loss of the Vessel whether by insured perils or otherwise.

21.1.8 *Insurance irrespective of amount against:*
Any risks excluded by Clauses 23, 24, 25 and 26 below.

21.2 Warranted that no insurance on any interests enumerated in the foregoing 21.1.1 to 21.1.7 in excess of the amounts permitted therein and no other insurance which includes total loss of the Vessel P.P.I., F.I.A., or subject to any other like term, is or shall be effected to operate during the currency of this insurance by or for account of the Assured, Owners, Managers or Mortgagees. Provided always that a breach of this warranty shall not afford the Underwriters any defence to a claim by a Mortgagee who has accepted this insurance without knowledge of such breach.

Notes

Purpose of clause. The purpose of this clause is to prevent shipowners from insuring a ship against all risks for a comparatively low figure, and then making up the total loss value (or over-insuring), at a lower rate of premium by a series of insurances or interests ancillary to the hull insurance.[1] The clause accordingly limits the amount of such ancillary insurances to the percentages specified.

Warranty. For the meaning of 'warranty,' see s 33(1) (p 50, ante).

Effect of breach of warranty. See s 33(3) (p 51, ante).

Acceptance of policy by mortgagee. The word 'accept' in the proviso to Clause 21.2 means 'to take or receive what is offered; to take or receive with consenting mind'.[2]

1 See e g *Outhwaite v Commercial Bank of Greece SA, The Sea Breeze* [1987] 1 Lloyd's Rep 372, QB (Commercial Court), where a managing owners' interest insurance had also been affected.
2 Ibid, at 377–378 (per Staughton J). In this case it was held that two letters written by the mortgagees three months after the vessel was lost did not constitute an 'acceptance' of the policy: ibid, at 378.

22. Returns for Lay-Up and Cancellation.

22.1 To return as follows:

22.1.1 Pro rata monthly net for each uncommenced month if this insurance be cancelled by agreement.

22.1.2 For each period of 30 consecutive days the Vessel may be laid up in a port or in a lay-up area provided such port or lay-up area is approved by the Underwriters (with special liberties as hereinafter allowed)
    (a) .... per cent net not under repair
    (b) .... per cent net under repair.
If the Vessel is under repair during part only of a period for which a return is claimable, the return shall be calculated pro rata to the number of days under (a) and (b) respectively.

22.2 PROVIDED ALWAYS THAT

22.2.1 a total loss of the Vessel, whether by insured perils or otherwise, has not occurred during the period covered by this insurance or any extension thereof

22.2.2 in no case shall a return be allowed when the Vessel is lying in exposed or unprotected waters, or in a port or lay-up area not approved by the Underwriters but, provided the Underwriters agree that such non-approved lay-up area is deemed to be within the vicinity of the approved port or lay-up area, days during which the Vessel is laid up in such non-approved lay-up area may be added to days in the approved port or lay-up area to calculate a period of 30 consecutive days and a return shall be allowed for the proportion of such period during which the Vessel is actually laid up in the approved port or lay-up area

22.2.3 loading or discharging operations or the presence of cargo on board shall not debar returns but no return shall be allowed for any period during which the Vessel is being used for the storage of cargo or for lightering purposes

22.2.4 in the event of any amendment of the annual rate, the above rates of return shall be adjusted accordingly

22.2.5 in the event of any return recoverable under this Clause 22 being based on 30 consecutive days which fall on successive insurances effected for the same Assured, this insurance shall only be liable for an amount calculated at pro rata of the period rates 22.1.2(a) and/or (b) above for the number of days which come within the period of this insurance and to which a return is actually applicable. Such overlapping period shall run, at the option of the assured, either from the first day on which the Vessel is laid up or the first day of a period of 30 consecutive days as provided under 22.1.2(a) or (b), or 22.2.2 above.

Notes

Purpose of clause. The clause provides for the return of the whole or proportionate part of the premium if the policy is cancelled by agreement or if the vessel is laid up.[1]

Enforcement of return of premium. See s 82 (p 136, ante).

1 *North Shipping Co Ltd v Union Marine Insurance Co Ltd* (1918) 24 Com Cas 83; affd (1919) 24 Com Cas 161, CA, p 137, ante (proportionate part of premium to be returned 'for every thirty consecutive days vessel may be laid up in port'); *Hunter v Wright* (1830) 10 B & C 714 (return if ship 'laid up'); *Gorsedd SS Co v Forbes* (1900) 5 Com Cas 413 (return after loss).

The following clauses shall be paramount and shall override anything contained in this insurance inconsistent therewith.

23. War Exclusion. In no case shall this insurance cover loss damage liability or expense caused by

23.1 war civil war revolution rebellion insurrection, or civil strife arising therefrom, or any hostile act by or against a belligerent power

23.2 capture seizure arrest restraint or detainment (barratry and piracy excepted), and the consequences thereof or any attempt thereat

23.3 derelict mines torpedoes bombs or other derelict weapons of war.

Notes

Civil war. A civil war is a war which has the special characteristic of being civil, ie internal rather than external. The words do not simply denote a violent internal conflict on a large scale. A decision on whether such a war exists will generally involve a consideration of (i) whether it can be said that the conflict was between opposing 'sides'; (ii) what were the objects of the 'sides' and how did they set about pursuing them; and (iii) what was the scale of the conflict, and of its effect on public order and the life of the inhabitants. It must be possible to say of each fighting man that he owes allegiance to one side or another, and to identify each side by reference to a community of objective, leadership and administration. It does not necessarily follow that the objectives of all those on any one side must be identical but there must be some substantial community of aim which the allies have banded together to promote by the use of force. There need not always be only two sides, but if the factions are too numerous, the struggle is no more than a melée without the clear delineation of combatants which is one of the distinguishing features of war. A desire to seize or retain the reins of state is not the only motive which can ever put the contestants into a state of civil war. There would be such a war if the objective was not to seize complete political power but to force changes in the way in which power was exercised without fundamentally changing the existing political structure. There would also be a civil war if the participants were activated by tribal, racial or ethnic animosities. It is possible to build up a list of matters which should be considered when deciding on whether internal strife has reached the level of civil war, eg the number of combatants, the number of military and civilian casualties, the amount and nature of the armaments employed, the relative sizes of the territory occupied by the opposing sides, the degree to which the populace as a whole is involved in the conflict, the extent to which each faction purports to exercise legislative, administrative and judicial powers over the territories which it controls.[1]

Rebellion and insurrection. The word 'insurrection' means a rising of the people in open resistance against established authority with the object of supplanting it.[2] 'As regards "rebellion" I adopt the definition in the Oxford English Dictionary (Murray) ". . . organised resistance to the ruler or government of one's country; insurrection, revolt." To this I would add that the purpose of the resistance must be to supplant the existing rulers or at least to deprive them of authority over part of their territory. The dictionary defines "insurrections" in a similar manner, but also suggests the notion of an incipient or limited rebellion. I believe that this reflects the distinction between two exceptions as they are used in the present clause, subject to the rider that a lesser degree of organisation may also mark off an insurrection from a rebellion. But with each exception there must be action against the government with a view to supplanting it.[3]

"Rebellion" and "insurrection" have somewhat similar meanings to each other. To my mind, each means an organised and violent internal uprising in a country with, as a main purpose, the object of trying to overthrow or supplant the government of that country, though "insurrection" denotes a lesser degree of organisation than "rebellion".'[4]

Capture, seizure, arrest. The term 'arrests, [restraints and detainments] . . . refers to political or executive acts, and does not include a loss caused by riot or by ordinary judicial process': Marine Insurance Act 1906, Sch 1, Rules for Construction of Policy, r 10.

In a case in 1883, where a ship, warranted free from capture and seizure, was forcibly seized and practically destroyed in the Brass River by natives, whose object was to plunder the cargo, Cave J, held that this was a 'seizure' within the warranty. After commenting on the various attempts to define the terms 'capture' and 'seizure,' he said, 'The seeming confusion in some of these passages arises from the desire of the authors in question to give a distinct and different meaning to such words as "capture," "seizure," "arrest," "detention," "restraint," and the impossibility of accomplishing the task is shown by their attempts to distinguish between "arrest," "restraint," and "detention." I have no doubt that the word "seizure," like many other words, is sometimes used with more general, and sometimes with more restricted, meaning, and whether it is used in a particular case with the one meaning or the other depends not on any general rule but on the context and the circumstances of the case.'[5]

Illustrations
1. Policy on goods, owned by a Spaniard, from London to Alicante. The ship calls at Corunna, and while there is seized by the Spanish Government for the purposes of transport, there being war between Spain and Morocco. The goods are unloaded and damaged. This is a 'seizure' of goods within the meaning of the policy.[6]
2. Policy on gold from the Transvaal to London, warranted free of capture and seizure. The gold is the property of a company registered in the Transvaal. On 2 October the gold while in transit is seized by the Transvaal Government in anticipation of war, and on 11 October war is declared. This is a 'seizure' within the meaning of the warranty, and the insurer is not liable.[7]

3. Policy on consignment of bulls from England to Buenos Aires. The bulls are prevented from landing under a law prohibiting the importation of live cattle from infected countries. The bulls have to be sent on to another country at great expense. This is a loss through 'restraint of princes'.[8]
4. Voyage policy on a bull to Buenos Aires, the policy being against all risks, including mortality, but stating 'warranted free of capture, seizure, and the consequences of detention'. There having been cattle disease on board, the bull on arrival in Argentina is slaughtered by the local authority. The insurer is protected by the warranty.[9]
5. Time policy on ship. Vessel was alleged to be carrying unmanifested goods and was ordered to be confiscated by an extraordinary military tribunal outside the ordinary judicial system of Vietnam. *Held*, this constituted a loss caused by 'restraint of princes' as it was a 'political or executive act,' and not 'ordinary judicial process'.[10]

1 *Spinney's (1948) Ltd v Royal Insurance Co Ltd* [1980] 1 Lloyd's Rep 406 (fire insurance) at 430 (per Mustill J).
2 *Lindsay and Pirie v General Accident, Fire and Life Assurance Corpn Ltd* [1914] App D 574.
3 *Spinney's (1948) Ltd v Royal Insurance Co Ltd*, supra, at 436 (per Mustill J).
4 *National Oil Co v Zimbabwe (Pte) Ltd v Sturge* [1991] 2 Lloyd's Rep 281, QB (Commercial Court), (marine insurance) at 282 (per Saville J). In this case damage to a pipeline and oil tank farm was held to have been caused by an 'insurrection' by Renamo, an organisation whose aim was to overthrow the Mozambique Frelimo government. (See the judgment of Saville J, ibid, at 284–285.)
5 *Johnston v Hogg* (1883) 10 QBD 432 at 435.
6 *Aubert v Gray* (1862) 32 LJQB 50, Ex Ch.
7 *Robinson Gold Mining Co v Alliance Insurance Co* [1902] 2 KB 489, CA; affd [1904] AC 359, HL.
8 *Miller v Law Accident Insurance Co* [1903] 1 KB 712, CA, rvsg on this point, ibid, [1902] 2 KB 694. But the loss is within the F C and S clause.
9 *St Paul Fire and Marine Insurance Co v Morice* (1906) 11 Com Cas 153.
10 *Panamanian Oriental SS Corpn v Wright* [1970] 2 Lloyd's Rep 365, QB (Commercial Court). (See the judgment of Mocatta J, ibid, at p 377.) The learned judge also said (ibid, at 378) that the interposition of the decision of a Court between the act of Customs officials in initially restraining a ship and the subsequent retention of the ship pursuant to that decision could not prevent the acts of the officials from being executive acts. This case was subsequently reversed on another ground: [1971] 1 Lloyd's Rep 487, CA.

24. Strikes Exclusion. In no case shall this insurance cover loss damage liability or expense caused by

24.1 strikers, locked-out workmen, or persons taking part in labour disturbances, riots or civil commotions

24.2 any terrorist or any person acting from a political motive.

Notes

This clause, although headed 'Strikes Exclusion,' contains other exceptions.

Strike. This has been defined as 'a general concerted refusal by workmen to work in consequence of an alleged grievance,'[1] and includes a 'sympathetic' strike.[2]

Appendix III

Lock-out. This does not include a case where an employer dismisses the workmen because he has no work for them.[3]

Riot. A riot occurs where 12 or more persons who are present together use or threaten unlawful violence for a common purpose and the conduct of them (taken together) is such as would cause a person of reasonable firmness present at the scene to fear for his personal safety.[4] It is immaterial whether or not the 12 or more use or threaten unlawful violence simultaneously.[5] The common purpose may be inferred from conduct.[6] No person of reasonable firmness need actually be, or be likely to be, present at the scene.[7] Riot may be committed in private as well as in public places.[8]

Civil commotion. The term 'civil commotion' is used to indicate a stage between a riot and a civil war.[9] It has been defined to mean an insurrection of the people for general purposes though not amounting to a rebellion.[10] But it is probably not capable of any very precise definition.[11] The element of turbulence or tumult is essential.[12] An organised conspiracy to commit criminal acts, where there is no tumult or disturbance after the acts, does not amount to civil commotion.[13] It is not, however, necessary to show the existence of any outside organisation at whose instigation the acts were done.[14]

Terrorism. The term 'terrorism' is not defined in Clause 24. But the Reinsurance (Acts of Terrorism) Act 1993, s 2(2) gives a useful definition of 'acts of terrorism' when it states: '"Acts of terrorism" means acts of persons acting on behalf of, or in connection with, any organisation which carries out activities directed towards the overthrowing or influencing, by force or violence, of Her Majesty's government in the United Kingdom or any other government de jure or de facto.' 'Organisation' includes any association or combination of persons: Reinsurance (Acts of Terrorism) Act 1993, s 2(3).

1 *Williams Bros (Hull) Ltd v W H Naamlooze Vennootschap Berghuys Kolenhandel* (1915) 21 Com Cas 253 (per Sankey J).
2 *J Vermans' Scheepvaarthedriff NV v Association Technique de l'Importation Charbonnière, The Laga* [1966] 1 Lloyd's Rep 582 at 590 (per McNair J).
3 *Re Richardsons and M Samuel & Co* [1898] 1 QB 261, CA.
4 Public Order Act 1986, s 1(1).
5 Ibid, s 1(2).
6 Ibid, s 1(3).
7 Ibid, s 1(4).
8 Ibid, s 1(5).
9 *Bolivia Republic v Indemnity Mutual Marine Assurance Co Ltd* [1909] 1 KB 785, CA (marine insurance), per Farwell LJ at 801; *Lindsay and Pirie v General Accident Fire and Life Assurance Corpn Ltd* [1914] App D 574; *Levy v Assicurazioni Generali* [1940] 3 All ER 427, PC (fire insurance).
10 *Langdale v Mason* (1780) 2 Park's Marine Insurances 8th Edn 965 (marine insurance), per Lord Mansfield CJ at 967, 968; *Spinney's (1948) Ltd v Royal Insurance Co Ltd* [1980] 1 Lloyd's Rep 406 (fire insurance), per Mustill J at 438.

11 A particular case may be one both of riot and civil commotion: *Motor Union Insurance Co v Boggan* (1923) 130 LT 588, HL (accident insurance), per Lord Birkenhead LC at 591.
12 *London and Manchester Plate Glass Co v Heath* [1913] 3 KB 411, CA (plate glass insurance) per Buckley LJ, at 417; *Pan American World Airways Inc v Aetna Casualty and Surety Co* [1974] 1 Lloyd's Rep 207, District Ct for Southern Dist of New York (aviation insurance) per Frankel DJ at 234.
13 *London and Manchester Plate Glass Co v Heath* (supra).
14 *Lindsay and Pirie v General Accident Fire and Life Assurance Corpn Ltd* (supra).

25. Malicious Acts Exclusion. In no case shall this insurance cover loss damage liability or expense arising from
25.1   the detonation of an explosive
25.2   any weapon of war
and caused by any person acting maliciously or from a political motive.

Note

Explosive. In the Explosives Act 1875 'explosive' means gunpowder, nitroglycerine, dynamite, gun-cotton, blasting powders, fulminate of mercury or of other metals, coloured fires, and every other substance, whether similar to those above mentioned or not, used or manufactured with a view to producing a practical effect by explosion or a pyrotechnic effect; and includes fog-signals, fireworks, fuzes, rockets, percussion caps, detonators, cartridges, ammunition of all descriptions, and every adaptation of preparation of an explosive as above defined: Explosives Act 1875, s 3.

Presumably the word has the same meaning in Clause 25.1.

26. Nuclear Exclusion. In no case shall this insurance cover loss damage liability or expense arising from any weapon of war employing atomic or nuclear fission and/or fusion or other like reaction or radioactive force or matter.

Note

Atomic or nuclear fission and/or fusion. In the Atomic Energy Act 1946 'atomic energy' means the energy released from atomic nuclei as a result of any process, including the fission process, but does not include energy released in any process of natural transmutation or radio-active decay which is not accelerated or influenced by external means: Atomic Energy Act 1946, s 18(1).

Further, in the Nuclear Installations Act 1965: 'nuclear matter' means, subject to any exceptions which may be prescribed—
   (a) any fissile material in the form of uranium metal, alloy or chemical compound (including natural uranium), or of plutonium metal, alloy or chemical compound, and any other fissile material which may be prescribed; and
   (b) any radioactive material produced in, or made radioactive by exposure to the radiation incidental to, the process of producing or utilising any such fissile material as aforesaid: Nuclear Installations Act 1965, s 26.

Presumably the similar words in Clause 26 bear a similar meaning.

1/10/83 (FOR USE ONLY WITH THE NEW MARINE POLICY FORM)
INSTITUTE VOYAGE CLAUSES

HULLS

(This insurance is subject to English law and practice)

1. Navigation.

1.1 The Vessel is covered subject to the provisions of this insurance at all times and has leave to sail or navigate with or without pilots, to go on trial trips and to assist and tow vessels or craft in distress, but it is warranted that the Vessel shall not be towed, except as is customary or to the first safe port or place when in need of assistance, or undertake towage or salvage services under a contract previously arranged by the Assured and/or Owners and/or Managers and/or Charterers. This Clause 1.1 shall not exclude customary towage in connection with loading and discharging.

1.2 In the event of the Vessel being employed in trading operations which entail cargo loading or discharging at sea from or into another vessel (not being a harbour or inshore craft) no claim shall be recoverable under this insurance for loss of or damage to the Vessel or liability to any other vessel arising from such loading or discharging operations, including whilst approaching, lying alongside and leaving, unless previous notice that the Vessel is to be employed in such operations has been given to the Underwriters and any amended terms of cover and any additional premium required by them have been agreed.

Note

This clause is in the same terms as the Institute Time Clauses (Hulls), Clause 1.1 and 1.2.

As to that clause and the notes thereto, see pp 167–168, ante.

2. Change of Voyage. Held covered in case of deviation or change of voyage or any breach of warranty as to towage or salvage services, provided notice be given to the Underwriters immediately after receipt of advices and any amended terms of cover and any additional premium required by them be agreed.

Notes

Purpose of clause. The purpose of the clause is to continue the insurance where there is a deviation, change of voyage or a breach of warranty as to towage or salvage services. (The clause is much wider than its heading suggests.)

Deviation. See s 46 (p 68, ante).

Change of voyage. See s 45 (p 67, ante).

Warranty. As to the meaning of warranty, see s 33(1) (p 50, ante).

Effect of breach of warranty. See s 33(3) (p 51, ante).

Additional premium. See s 31(2) (p 47, ante).

3. Assignment. No assignment of or interest in this insurance or in any moneys which may be or become payable thereunder is to be binding on or recognised by the Underwriters unless a dated notice of such assignment or interest signed by the Assured, and by the assignor in the case of subsequent assignment, is endorsed on the Policy and the Policy with such endorsement is produced before payment of any claim or return of premium thereunder.

Note

This clause is in the same terms as the Institute Time Clauses (Hulls), Clause 5. As to that clause and the notes thereto, see p 170, ante.

4. Perils.

4.1	This insurance covers loss of or damage to the subject-matter insured caused by
4.1.1	perils of the seas rivers lakes or other navigable waters
4.1.2	fire, explosion
4.1.3	violent theft by persons from outside the Vessel
4.1.4	jettison
4.1.5	piracy
4.1.6	breakdown of or accident to nuclear installations or reactors
4.1.7	contact with aircraft or similar objects, or objects falling therefrom, land conveyance, dock or harbour equipment or installation
4.1.8	earthquake volcanic eruption or lightning.
4.2	This insurance covers loss of or damage to the subject-matter insured caused by
4.2.1	accidents in loading discharging or shifting cargo or fuel
4.2.2	bursting of boilers breakage of shafts or any latent defect in the machinery or hull
4.2.3	negligence of Master Officers Crew or Pilots
4.2.4	negligence of repairers or charterers provided such repairers or charterers are not an Assured hereunder
4.2.5	barratry of Master Officers or Crew,
	provided such loss or damage has not resulted from want of due diligence by the Assured, Owners or Managers.
4.3	Master Officers Crew or Pilots not to be considered Owners within the meaning of this Clause 4 should they hold shares in the Vessel.

Note

This clause is in the same terms as the Institute Time Clauses (Hulls), Clause 6. As to that clause and the notes thereto, see pp 170–177, ante.

5. Pollution Hazard. This insurance covers loss of or damage to the Vessel caused by any governmental authority acting under the powers vested in it to prevent or mitigate a pollution hazard, or threat thereof, resulting directly from damage to the Vessel for which the Underwriters are liable under this insurance, provided such act of governmental authority has not resulted from want of due diligence by the Assured, the Owners, or Managers of the Vessel or any of them to prevent or mitigate such hazard or threat. Master, Officers, Crew or Pilots not to be considered Owners within the meaning of this Clause 5 should they hold shares in the Vessel.

Note

This clause is in the same terms as the Institute Time Clauses (Hulls), Clause 7. As to that clause and the notes thereto, see p 177, ante.

6. 3/4ths Collision Liability.

6.1 The Underwriters agree to indemnify the Assured for three-fourths of any sum or sums paid by the Assured to any other person or persons by reason of the Assured becoming legally liable by way of damages for

6.1.1 loss of or damage to any other vessel or property on any other vessel

6.1.2 delay to or loss of use of any such other vessel or property thereon

6.1.3 general average of, salvage of, or salvage under contract of, any such other vessel or property thereon,

where such payment by the Assured is in consequence of the Vessel hereby insured coming into collision with any other vessel.

6.2 The indemnity provided by this Clause 6 shall be in addition to the indemnity provided by the other terms and conditions of this insurance and shall be subject to the following provisions:

6.2.1 Where the insured Vessel is in collision with another vessel and both vessels are to blame then, unless the liability of one or both vessels becomes limited by law, the indemnity under this Clause 6 shall be calculated on the principle of cross-liabilities as if the respective Owners had been compelled to pay to each other such proportion of each other's damages as may have been properly allowed in ascertaining the balance or sum payable by or to the Assured in consequence of the collision.

6.2.2   In no case shall the Underwriters' total liability under Clauses 6.1 and 6.2 exceed their proportionate part of three-fourths of the insured value of the Vessel hereby insured in respect of any one collision.

6.3   The Underwriters will also pay three-fourths of the legal costs incurred by the Assured or which the Assured may be compelled to pay in contesting liability or taking proceedings to limit liability, with the prior written consent of the Underwriters.

EXCLUSIONS

6.4   Provided always that this Clause 6 shall in no case extend to any sum which the Assured shall pay for or in respect of

6.4.1   removal or disposal of obstructions, wrecks, cargoes or any other thing whatsoever

6.4.2   any real or personal property or thing whatsoever except other vessels or property on other vessels

6.4.3   the cargo or other property on, or the engagements of, the insured Vessel

6.4.4   loss of life, personal injury or illness

6.4.5   pollution or contamination of any real or personal property or thing whatsoever (except other vessels with which the insured Vessel is in collision or property on such other vessels).

Note

This clause is in the same terms as the Institute Time Clauses (Hulls), Clause 8. As to that clause and the note thereto, see pp 177–180, ante.

7. Sistership. Should the Vessel hereby insured come into collision with or receive salvage services from another vessel belonging wholly or in part to the same Owners or under the same management, the Assured shall have the same rights under this insurance as they would have were the other vessel entirely the property of Owners not interested in the Vessel hereby insured; but in such cases the liability for the collision or the amount payable for the services rendered shall be referred to a sole arbitrator to be agreed upon between the Underwriters and the Assured.

Note

This clause is in the same terms as the Institute Time Clauses (Hulls), Clause 9. As to that clause and the note thereto, see p 180, ante.

8. Notice of Claim and Tenders.

8.1 In the event of accident whereby loss or damage may result in a claim under this insurance, notice shall be given to the Underwriters prior to survey and also, if the Vessel is abroad, to the nearest Lloyd's Agent so that a surveyor may be appointed to represent the Underwriters should they so desire.

8.2 The Underwriters shall be entitled to decide the port to which the Vessel shall proceed for docking or repair (the actual additional expense of the voyage arising from compliance with the Underwriters' requirements being refunded to the Assured) and shall have a right of veto concerning a place of repair or a repairing firm.

8.3 The Underwriters may also take tenders or may require further tenders to be taken for the repair of the Vessel. Where such a tender has been taken and a tender is accepted with the approval of the Underwriters, an allowance shall be made at the rate of 30 per cent per annum on the insured value for time lost between the despatch of the invitations to tender required by Underwriters and the acceptance of a tender to the extent that such time is lost solely as the result of tenders having been taken and provided that the tender is accepted without delay after receipt of the Underwriters' approval.

Due credit shall be given against the allowance as above for any amounts recovered in respect of fuel and stores and wages and maintenance of the Master Officers and Crew or any member thereof, including amounts allowed in general average, and for any amounts recovered from third parties in respect of damages for detention and/or loss of profit and/or running expenses, for the period covered by the tender allowance or any part thereof. Where a part of the cost of the repair of damage other than a fixed deductible is not recoverable from the Underwriters the allowance shall be reduced by a similar proportion.

8.4 In the event of failure to comply with the conditions of this Clause 8 a deduction of 15 per cent shall be made from the amount of the ascertained claim.

Note

This clause is in the same terms as the Institute Time Clauses (Hulls), Clause 10. As to that clause and the notes thereto, see pp 180–181, ante.

9. General Average and Salvage.

9.1 This insurance covers the Vessel's proportion of salvage, salvage charges and/or general average, reduced in respect of any under-insurance, but in case of general average sacrifice of the Vessel the Assured may recover in respect of the whole loss without first enforcing their right of contribution from other parties.

9.2 Adjustment to be according to the law and practice obtaining at the place where the adventure ends, as if the contract of affreightment contained no special terms upon the subject; but where the contract of affreightment so provides the adjustment shall be according to the York–Antwerp Rules.

9.3 When the Vessel sails in ballast, not under charter, the provisions of the York–Antwerp Rules 1974 (excluding Rules XX and XXI) shall be applicable, and the voyage for this purpose shall be deemed to continue from the port or place of departure until the arrival of the Vessel at the first port or place thereafter other than a port or place of refuge or a port or place of call for bunkering only. If at any such intermediate port or place there is an abandonment of the adventure originally contemplated the voyage shall thereupon be deemed to be terminated.

9.4 No claim under this Clause 9 shall in any case be allowed where the loss was not incurred to avoid or in connection with the avoidance of a peril insured against.

Note

This clause is in the same terms as the Institute Time Clauses (Hulls), Clause 11. As to that clause and the notes thereto, see pp 181–182, ante.

10. Deductible.

10.1 No claim arising from a peril insured against shall be payable under this insurance unless the aggregate of all such claims arising out of each separate accident or occurrence (including claims under Clauses 6, 9 and 11) exceeds .... in which case this sum shall be deducted. Nevertheless the expense of sighting the bottom after stranding, if reasonably incurred specially for that purpose, shall be paid even if no damage be found. This Clause 10.1 shall not apply to a claim for total or constructive total loss of the Vessel, or in the event of such a claim, to any associated claim under Clause 11 arising from the same accident or occurrence.

10.2 Claims for damage by heavy weather occurring during a single sea passage between two successive ports shall be treated as being due to one accident. In the case of such heavy weather extending over a period not wholly covered by this insurance the deductible to be applied to the claim recoverable hereunder shall be the proportion of the above deductible that the number of days of such heavy weather falling within the period of this insurance bears to the number of days of heavy weather during the single sea passage. The expression 'heavy weather' in this Clause 10.2 shall be deemed to include contact with floating ice.

10.3 Excluding any interest comprised therein, recoveries against any claim which is subject to the above deductible shall be credited to the Underwriters in full to the extent of the sum by which the aggregate of the claim unreduced by any recoveries exceeds the above deductible.

10.4 Interest comprised in recoveries shall be apportioned between the Assured and the Underwriters, taking into account the sums paid by the Underwriters and the dates when such payments were made, notwithstanding that by the addition of interest the Underwriters may receive a larger sum than they have paid.

Note

This clause is in the same terms as the Institute Time Clauses (Hulls), Clause 12. As to that clause and the notes thereto, see p 183, ante.

11. Duty of Assured (Sue and Labour).

11.1 In case of any loss or misfortune it is the duty of the Assured and their servants and agents to take such measures as may be reasonable for the purpose of averting or minimising a loss which would be recoverable under this insurance.

11.2 Subject to the provisions below and to Clause 10 the Underwriters will contribute to charges properly and reasonably incurred by the Assured their servants or agents for such measures. General average, salvage charges (except as provided for in Clause 11.5) and collision defence or attack costs are not recoverable under this Clause 11.

11.3 Measures taken by the Assured or the Underwriters with the object of saving, protecting or recovering the subject-matter insured shall not be considered as a waiver or acceptance of abandonment or otherwise prejudice the rights of either party.

11.4 When expenses are incurred pursuant to this Clause 11 the liability under this insurance shall not exceed the proportion of such expenses that the amount insured hereunder bears to the value of the Vessel as stated herein, or to the sound value of the Vessel at the time of the occurrence giving rise to the expenditure if the sound value exceeds that value. Where the Underwriters have admitted a claim for total loss and property insured by this insurance is saved, the foregoing provisions shall not apply unless the expenses of suing and labouring exceed the value of such property saved and then shall apply only to the amount of the expenses which is in excess of such value.

11.5 When a claim for total loss of the Vessel is admitted under this insurance and expenses have been reasonably incurred in saving or attempting to save the Vessel and other property and there are no proceeds, or the expenses exceed the proceeds, then this insurance shall bear its pro rata share of such proportion of the expenses, or of the expenses in excess of the proceeds, as the case may be, as may reasonably be regarded as having been incurred in respect of the Vessel; but if the Vessel be insured for less than its sound value at the time of the occurrence giving rise to the expenditure, the amount recoverable under this clause shall be reduced in proportion to the under-insurance.

11.6 The sum recoverable under this Clause 11 shall be in addition to the loss otherwise recoverable under this insurance but shall in no circumstances exceed the amount insured under this insurance in respect of the Vessel.

Note

This clause is in the same terms as the Institute Time Clauses (Hulls), Clause 13. As to that clause and the notes thereto, see pp 184–185, ante.

12. New for Old. Claims payable without deduction new for old.

Note

This clause is in the same terms as the Institute Time Clauses (Hulls), Clause 14. As to that clause and the note thereto, see p 185, ante.

13. Bottom Treatment. In no case shall a claim be allowed in respect of scraping gritblasting and/or other surface preparation or painting of the Vessel's bottom except that

13.1 gritblasting and/or other surface preparation of new bottom plates ashore and supplying and applying any 'shop' primer thereto,

13.2 gritblasting and/or other surface preparation of:
the butts or area of plating immediately adjacent to any renewed or refitted plating damaged during the course of welding and/or repairs,
areas of plating damaged during the course of fairing, either in place or ashore,

13.3 supplying and applying the first coat of primer/anti-corrosive to those particular areas mentioned in 13.1 and 13.2 above,

shall be allowed as part of the reasonable cost of repairs in respect of bottom plating damaged by an insured peril.

Note

This clause is in the same terms as the Institute Time Clauses (Hulls), Clause 15.
   As to that clause and the note thereto, see pp 185–186, ante.

14. Wages and Maintenance. No claim shall be allowed, other than in general average, for wages and maintenance of the Master, Officers and Crew, or any member thereof, except when incurred solely for the necessary removal of the Vessel from one port to another for the repair of damage covered by the Underwriters, or for trial trips for such repairs, and then only for such wages and maintenance as are incurred whilst the Vessel is under way.

Note

This clause is in the same terms as the Institute Time Clauses (Hulls), Clause 16.
   As to that clause and the notes thereto, see p 186, ante.

15. Agency Commission. In no case shall any sum be allowed under this insurance either by way of remuneration of the Assured for time and trouble taken to obtain and supply information or documents or in respect of the commission or charges of any manager, agent, managing or agency company or the like, appointed by or on behalf of the Assured to perform such services.

Note

This clause is in the same terms as the Institute Time Clauses (Hulls), Clause 17.
   As to that clause and the note thereto, see p 186, ante.

16. Unrepaired Damage.

16.1   The measure of indemnity in respect of claims for unrepaired damage shall be the reasonable depreciation in the market value of the Vessel at the time this insurance terminates arising from such unrepaired damage, but not exceeding the reasonable cost of repairs.

16.2   In no case shall the Underwriters be liable for unrepaired damage in the event of a subsequent total loss (whether or not covered under this insurance) sustained during the period covered by this insurance or any extension thereof.

16.3   The Underwriters shall not be liable in respect of unrepaired damage for more than the insured value at the time this insurance terminates.

Note

This clause is in the same terms as the Institute Time Clauses (Hulls), Clause 18.
   As to that clause and the note thereto, see pp 186–187, ante.

17. Constructive Total Loss.
17.1   In ascertaining whether the Vessel is a constructive total loss, the insured value shall be taken as the repaired value and nothing in respect of the damaged or break-up value of the Vessel or wreck shall be taken into account.

17.2   No claim for constructive total loss based upon the cost of recovery and/or repair of the Vessel shall be recoverable hereunder unless such cost would exceed the insured value. In making this determination, only the cost relating to a single accident or sequence of damages arising from the same accident shall be taken into account.

Note

This clause is in the same terms as the Institute Time Clauses (Hulls), Clause 19. As to that clause and the notes thereto, see p 187, ante.

18. Freight Waiver. In the event of total or constructive total loss no claim to be made by the Underwriters for freight whether notice of abandonment has been given or not.

Note

This clause is in the same terms as the Institute Time Clauses (Hulls), Clause 20. As to that clause and the notes thereto, see pp 187–188, ante.

19. Disbursements Warranty.
19.1   Additional insurances as follows are permitted:

19.1.1   *Disbursements, Managers' Commissions, Profits or Excess or Increased Value of Hull and Machinery.* A sum not exceeding 25 per cent of the value stated herein.

19.1.2   *Freight, Chartered Freight or Anticipated Freight, insured for time.* A sum not exceeding 25 per cent of the value as stated herein less any sum insured, however described, under 19.1.1.

19.1.3   *Freight or Hire, under contracts for voyage.* A sum not exceeding the gross freight or hire for the current cargo passage and next succeeding cargo passage (such insurance to include, if required, a preliminary and an intermediate ballast passage) plus the charges of insurance. In the case of a voyage charter where payment is made on a time basis, the sum permitted for insurance shall be calculated on the estimated duration of the voyage, subject to the limitation of two cargo passages as laid down herein. Any sum insured under 19.1.2 to be taken into account and only the excess thereof may be insured, which excess shall be reduced as the freight or hire is advanced or earned by the gross amount so advanced or earned.

19.1.4   *Anticipated Freight if the Vessel sails in ballast and not under Charter.* A sum not exceeding the anticipated gross freight on next cargo passage, such sum to be reasonably estimated on the basis of the current rate of freight at time of insurance plus the charges of insurance. Any sum insured under 19.1.2 to be taken into account and only the excess thereof may be insured.

19.1.5   *Time Charter Hire or Charter Hire for Series of Voyages.* A sum not exceeding 50 per cent of the gross hire which is to be earned under the charter in a period not exceeding 18 months. Any sum insured under 19.1.2 to be taken into account and only the excess thereof may be insured, which excess shall be reduced as the hire is advanced or earned under the charter by 50 per cent of the gross amount so advanced or earned but the sum insured need not be reduced while the total of the sums insured under 19.1.2 and 19.1.5 does not exceed 50 per cent of the gross hire still to be earned under the charter. An insurance under this Section may begin on the signing of the charter.

19.1.6   *Premiums.* A sum not exceeding the actual premiums of all interests insured for a period not exceeding 12 months (excluding premiums insured under the foregoing sections but including, if required, the premium or estimated calls on any Club or War etc. Risk insurance) reducing pro rata monthly.

19.1.7   *Returns of Premium.* A sum not exceeding the actual returns which are allowable under insurance but which would not be recoverable thereunder in the event of a total loss of the Vessel whether by insured perils or otherwise.

19.1.8   *Insurance irrespective of amount against:*
Any risks excluded by Clauses 20, 21, 22 and 23 below.

19.2   Warranted that no insurance on any interests enumerated in the foregoing 19.1.1 to 19.1.7 in excess of the amounts permitted therein and no other insurance which includes total loss of the Vessel P.P.I., F.I.A., or subject to any other like term, is or shall be effected to operate during the currency of this insurance by or for account of the Assured, Owners, Managers or Mortgagees. Provided always that a breach of this warranty shall not afford the Underwriters any defence to a claim by a Mortgagee who has accepted this insurance without knowledge of such breach.

Note

This clause is in the same terms as the Institute Time Clauses (Hulls), Clause 21. As to that clause and the notes thereto, see pp 188–189, ante.

Institute Voyage Clauses (Hulls)

The following clauses shall be paramount and shall override anything contained in this insurance inconsistent therewith.

20. War Exclusion. In no case shall this insurance cover loss damage liability or expense caused by
- 20.1 war civil war revolution rebellion insurrection, or civil strife arising therefrom, or any hostile act by or against a belligerent power
- 20.2 capture seizure arrest restraint or detainment (barratry and piracy excepted), and the consequences thereof or any attempt thereat
- 20.3 derelict mines torpedoes bombs or other derelict weapons of war.

Note

This clause is in the same terms as the Institute Time Clauses (Hulls), Clause 23. As to that clause and the notes thereto, see pp 191–193, ante.

21. Strikes Exclusion. In no case shall this insurance cover loss damage liability or expense caused by
- 21.1 strikers, locked-out workmen, or persons taking part in labour disturbances, riots or civil commotions
- 21.2 any terrorist or any person acting from a political motive.

Note

This clause is in the same terms as the Institute Time Clauses (Hulls), Clause 24. As to that clause and the notes thereto, see pp 193–194, ante.

22. Malicious Acts Exclusion. In no case shall this insurance cover loss damage liability or expense arising from
- 22.1 the detonation of an explosive
- 22.2 any weapon of war

and caused by any person acting maliciously or from a political motive.

Note

This clause is in the same terms as the Institute Time Clauses (Hulls), Clause 25. As to that clause and the notes thereto, see p 195, ante.

23. Nuclear Exclusion. In no case shall this insurance cover loss damage liability or expense arising from any weapon of war employing atomic or nuclear fission and/or fusion or other like reaction or radioactive force or matter.

Note

This clause is in the same terms as the Institute Time Clauses (Hulls), Clause 26. As to that clause and the note thereto, see p 195, ante.

1/10/83 (FOR USE ONLY WITH THE NEW MARINE POLICY FORM)

INSTITUTE WAR AND STRIKES CLAUSES

HULLS–TIME

(This insurance is subject to English law and practice)

1. Perils. Subject always to the exclusions hereinafter referred to, this insurance covers loss of or damage to the Vessel caused by

1.1 war civil war revolution rebellion insurrection, or civil strife arising therefrom, or any hostile act by or against a belligerent power

1.2 capture seizure arrest restraint or detainment, and the consequences thereof or any attempt thereat

1.3 derelict mines torpedoes bombs or other derelict weapons of war

1.4 strikers, locked-out workmen, or persons taking part in labour disturbances, riots or civil commotions

1.5 any terrorist or any person acting maliciously or from a political motive

1.6 confiscation or expropriation.

Notes

This clause provides cover in respect of the perils excepted by the Institute Time Clauses (Hulls), Clause 23 (war exclusion) and Clause 24 (strikes exclusion), and also provides cover in respect of 'confiscation' and 'expropriation'.

As to the Institute Time Clauses (Hulls) Clause 23 and Clause 24 and the notes thereto, see respectively pp 191 and 193, ante.

Detainment. Where a vessel is detained by reason of the shipowner's failure to pay port dues or an exporter's failure to furnish a foreign currency guarantee, such a detainment is not within Clause 1.2.[1]

'Detainment' includes 'conditional' detainment.[2]

1 *Ikerigi Compania Naviera SA v Palmer, The Wondrous* [1992] 2 Lloyd's Rep 566 at 572, CA (per Lloyd LJ).
2 Ibid, at 571 (per Lloyd LJ).

2. Incorporation. The Institute Time Clauses Hulls 1/10/83 (including 4/4ths Collision Clause) except Clauses 1.2, 2, 3, 4, 6, 12, 21.1.8, 22, 23, 24, 25 and 26 are deemed to be incorporated in this insurance in so far as they do not conflict with the provisions of these clauses.

Held covered in case of breach of warranty as to towage or salvage services provided notice be given to the Underwriters immediately after receipt of advices and any additional premium required by them be agreed.

Notes

This clause shows which of the Institute Time Clauses (Hulls) (see pp 167–195, ante) are incorporated. It is important to notice that they are so incorporated only in so far as they do not conflict with the provisions of the War and Strikes Clauses (Hulls–Time).

Clause 1.2. This is part of the 'Navigation' clause (see p 167, ante).
Clause 2. This is the 'Continuation' clause (see p 168, ante).
Clause 3. This is the 'Breach of warranty' clause (see p 169, ante).
Clause 4. This is the 'Termination' clause (see p 169, ante).
Clause 6. This is the 'Perils' clause (see p 170, ante).
Clause 12. This is the 'Deductible' clause (see p 183, ante).
Clause 21.1.8. This is part of the 'Disbursements warranty' clause (see p 189, ante).
Clause 22. This is the 'Returns for lay-up and cancellation' clause (see p 189, ante).
Clause 23. This is the 'War exclusion' clause (see p 191, ante).
Clause 24. This is the 'Strikes exclusion' clause (see p 193, ante).
Clause 25. This is the 'Malicous acts exclusion' clause (see p 195, ante).

Warranty. See s 33 (p 50, ante).

Effect of breach of warranty. See s 33 (p 51, ante).

Additional premium. See s 31(2) (p 47, ante).

3. Detainment. In the event that the Vessel shall have been the subject of capture seizure arrest restraint detainment confiscation or expropriation, and the Assured shall thereby have lost the free use and disposal of the Vessel for a continuous period of 12 months then for the purpose of ascertaining whether the Vessel is a constructive total loss the Assured shall be deemed to have been deprived of the possession of the Vessel without any likelihood of recovery.

Note

This clause explains that after the time specified the assured is deemed to have been 'deprived of the possession of the vessel without any likelihood of recovery,' and she is, therefore, a constructive total loss within the meaning of s 60(2)(i).
As to constructive total loss, see s 60 (p 90, ante).

4. Exclusions. This insurance excludes
4.1   loss damage liability or expense arising from
4.1.1   any detonation of any weapon of war employing atomic or nuclear fission and/or fusion or other like reaction or radioactive force or matter, hereinafter called a nuclear weapon of war

4.1.2   the outbreak of war (whether there be a declaration of war or not) between any of the following countries:
    United Kingdom, United States of America, France,
    the Union of Soviet Socialist Republics,
    the People's Republic of China
4.1.3   requisition or pre-emption
4.1.4   capture seizure arrest restraint detainment confiscation or expropriation by or under the order of the government or any public or local authority of the country in which the Vessel is owned or registered
4.1.5   arrest restraint detainment confiscation or expropriation under quarantine regulations or by reason of infringement of any customs or trading regulations
4.1.6   the operation of ordinary judicial process, failure to provide security or to pay any fine or penalty or any financial cause
4.1.7   piracy (but this exclusion shall not affect cover under Clause 1.4),
4.2   loss damage liability or expense covered by the Institute Time Clauses—Hulls 1/10/83 (including 4/4ths Collision Clause) or which would be recoverable thereunder but for Clause 12 thereof,
4.3   any claim for any sum recoverable under any other insurance on the Vessel or which would be recoverable under such insurance but for the existence of this insurance,
4.4   any claim for expenses arising from delay except such expenses as would be recoverable in principle in English law and practice under the York–Antwerp Rules 1974.

Note

Clause 4.1.1. This clause repeats the exceptions set out in the Institute Time Clauses (Hulls), Clause 26 (nuclear exclusion). (See p 195, ante.)

Clause 4.1.2. Although loss by war is covered by the War and Strikes Clauses (Hulls–Time), Clause 1.1 (perils) (p 208, ante), the insurers are not liable in the case of a loss by what could be classed as a 'major war', ie one between the world powers set out in the present clause.

Clause 4.1.4. Although loss by 'capture seizure arrest etc' is covered by Clause 1.2 (perils) (p 208, ante), the present clause stresses that where such a loss is brought about by the government etc of the country in which the vessel is owned or registered, the insurers are not liable.

Clause 4.1.5. The word 'infringement' means 'threatened' as well as 'actual' infringement.[1]

Clause 4.1.6. The words 'financial cause' are to be given their ordinary meaning. There is no reason to confine the causes to causes for which the shipowners are responsible. But the financial cause must affect the ship. Otherwise there would be no detainment. Assuming that the ship is detained by a failure to pay money on the part of the cargo interests, it comes within the ordinary meaning of the words 'financial cause'.[2]

York–Antwerp Rules 1974. See Appendix IV, pp 277–284, post.

1 *Ikerigi Compania Naviera SA v Palmer, The Wondrous* [1992] 2 Lloyd's Rep 566 at 571, CA (per Lloyd LJ).
2 Ibid, at 572 (per Lloyd LJ).

5. Termination.

5.1 This insurance may be cancelled by either the Underwriters or the Assured giving 7 days notice (such cancellation becoming effective on the expiry of 7 days from midnight of the day on which notice of cancellation is issued by or to the Underwriters). The Underwriters agree however to reinstate this insurance subject to agreement between the Underwriters and the Assured prior to the expiry of such notice of cancellation as to new rate of premium and/or conditions and/or warranties.

5.2 Whether or not such notice of cancellation has been given this insurance shall TERMINATE AUTOMATICALLY

5.2.1 upon the occurrence of any hostile detonation of any nuclear weapon of war as defined in Clause 4.1.1 wheresoever or whensoever such detonation may occur and whether or not the Vessel may be involved

5.2.2 upon the outbreak of war (whether there be a declaration of war or not) between any of the following countries:
   United Kingdom, United States of America, France,
   the Union of Soviet Socialist Republics,
   the People's Republic of China

5.2.4 in the event of the Vessel being requisitioned, either for title or use.

5.3 In the event either of cancellation by notice of automatic termination of this insurance by reason of the operation of this Clause 5, or of the sale of the Vessel, pro rata net return of premium shall be payable to the Assured.

This insurance shall not become effective if, subsequent to its acceptance by the Underwriters and prior to the intended time of its attachment, there has occurred any event which would have automatically terminated this insurance under the provisions of Clause 5 above.

Notes

Purpose of clause. This clause concerns the right to cancel the policy and also the circumstances in which the policy is automatically cancelled.

Return of premium. See s 83 (p 137, ante).

1/10/83 (FOR USE ONLY WITH THE NEW MARINE POLICY FORM)

INSTITUTE WAR AND STRIKES CLAUSES

HULLS–VOYAGE

(This insurance is subject to English law and practice)

1. Perils. Subject always to the exclusions hereinafter referred to, this insurance covers loss of or damage to the Vessel caused by

1.1 war civil war revolution rebellion insurrection, or civil strife arising therefrom, or any hostile act by or against a belligerent power
1.2 capture seizure arrest restraint or detainment, and the consequences thereof or any attempt thereat
1.3 derelict mines torpedoes bombs or other derelict weapons of war
1.4 strikers, locked-out workmen, or persons taking part in labour disturbances, riots or civil commotions
1.5 any terrorist or any person acting maliciously or from a political motive
1.6 confiscation or expropriation.

Note

This clause provides cover in respect of the perils excepted by the Institute Voyage Clauses (Hulls), Clause 20 (war exclusion) and Clause 21 (strikes exclusion), and also provides cover in respect of 'confiscation' and 'expropriation'.

As to the Institute Voyage Clauses (Hulls) Clauses 20 and 21 and the notes thereto, see respectively, p 207, ante.

2. Incorporation. The Institute Voyage Clauses—Hulls 1/10/83 (including 4/4ths Collision Clause) except Clauses 1.2, 10, 19.1.8, 20, 21, 22 and 23 are deemed to be incorporated in this insurance in so far as they do not conflict with the provisions of these clauses.

Held covered in case of breach of warranty as to towage or salvage services provided notice be given to the Underwriters immediately after receipt of advices and any additional premium required by them be agreed.

Notes

This clause shows which of the Institute Voyage Clauses (Hulls) (see pp 196–207, ante) are incorporated. It is important to notice that they are so incorporated only in so far as they do not conflict with the provisions of the War and Strike Clauses.

Clause 1.2. This is part of the 'Navigation Clause' (see p 196, ante).
Clause 10. This is the 'Deductible Clause' (see p 201, ante).
Clause 19.1.8. This is part of the 'Disbursements Warranty' clause (see p 206, ante).
Clause 20. This is the 'War Exclusion' clause (see p 207, ante).

Clause 21. This is the 'Strikes Exclusion' clause (see p 207, ante).
Clause 22. This is the 'Malicious Acts Exclusion' clause (see p 207, ante).
Clause 23. This is the 'Nuclear Exclusion' clause (see p 207, ante).
Breach of warranty. See s 33(3) (p 51, ante).
Additional premium. See s 31(2) (p 47, ante).

3. Detainment. In the event that the Vessel shall have been the subject of capture seizure arrest restraint detainment confiscation or expropriation, and the Assured shall thereby have lost the free use and disposal of the Vessel for a continuous period of 12 months then for the purpose of ascertaining whether the Vessel is a constructive total loss the Assured shall be deemed to have been deprived of the possession of the Vessel without any likelihood of recovery.

Note

This clause explains that after the time specified the assured is deemed to have been 'deprived of the possession of the vessel without any likelihood of recovery,' and she is, therefore, a constructive total loss within the meaning of s 60(2)(i).

As to constructive total loss, see s 60 (p 90, ante).

4. Exclusions. This insurance excludes
4.1   loss damage liability or expense arising from
4.1.1   any detonation of any weapon of war employing atomic or nuclear fission and/or fusion or other like reaction or radioactive force or matter, hereinafter called a nuclear weapon of war
4.1.2   the outbreak of war (whether there be a declaration of war or not) between any of the following countries:
United Kingdom, United States of America, France,
the Union of Soviet Socialist Republics,
the People's Republic of China
4.1.3   requisition or pre-emption
4.1.4   capture seizure arrest restraint detainment confiscation or expropriation by or under the order of the government or any public or local authority of the country in which the Vessel is owned or registered
4.1.5   arrest restraint detainment confiscation or expropriation under quarantine regulations or by reason of infringement of any customs or trading regulations
4.1.6   the operation of ordinary judicial process, failure to provide security or to pay any fine or penalty or any financial cause
4.1.7   piracy (but this exclusion shall not affect cover under Clause 1.4),
4.2   loss damage liability or expense covered by the Institute Voyage Clauses—Hulls 1/10/83 (including 4/4ths Collision Clause) or which would be recoverable thereunder but for Clause 10 thereof

4.3 any claim for any sum recoverable under any other insurance on the Vessel or which would be recoverable under such insurance but for the existence of this insurance

4.4 any claim for expenses arising from delay except such expenses as would be recoverable in principle in English law and practice under the York–Antwerp Rules 1974.

Notes

Clause 4.1.1. This clause repeats the exceptions set out in the Institute Voyage Clauses (Hulls), Clause 23 (nuclear exclusion) (see p 207, ante).

Clause 4.1.2. Although loss by war is covered under Clause 1 of the Institute War and Strikes Clauses (Hulls—Voyage), Clause 1.1 (perils) (p 212, ante), the insurers are not liable in the case of a loss by what could be classed as a 'major war,' ie one between the world powers set out in the present clause.

Clause 4.1.4. Although loss by 'capture seizure arrest etc' is covered by Clause 1.2 (perils) (p 212, ante), the present clause stresses that where such a loss is brought about by the government etc of the country in which the vessel is owned or registered, the insurers are not liable.

5. Termination.

5.1 This insurance may be cancelled by either the Underwriters or the Assured giving 7 days notice (such cancellation becoming effective on the expiry of 7 days from midnight of the day on which notice of cancellation is issued by or to the Underwriters). The Underwriters agree however to reinstate this insurance subject to agreement between the Underwriters and the Assured prior to the expiry of such notice of cancellation as to new rate of premium and/or conditions and/or warranties

5.2 Whether or not such notice of cancellation has been given this insurance shall TERMINATE AUTOMATICALLY

5.2.1 upon the occurrence of any hostile detonation of any nuclear weapon of war as defined in Clause 4.1.1 wheresoever or whensoever such detonation may occur and whether or not the Vessel may be involved

5.2.2 upon the outbreak of war (whether there be a declaration of war or not) between any of the following countries:
United Kingdom, United States of America, France,
the People's Republic of China,
the Union of Soviet Socialist Republics

5.2.3 in the event of the Vessel being requisitioned, either for title or use

5.3 In the event either of cancellation by notice or of automatic termination of this insurance by reason of the operation of this Clause 5, or of the sale of the Vessel, a return of premium shall be payable to the Assured.

This insurance shall not become effective if, subsequent to its acceptance by the Underwriters and prior to the intended time of its attachment, there has occurred any event which would have automatically terminated this insurance under the provisions of Clause 5 above.

Notes

Purpose of clause. This clause concerns the right to cancel the policy and also the circumstances in which the policy is automatically cancelled.

Return of premium. See s 83 (p 137, ante).

(2) Freight Clauses

1/10/83 (FOR USE ONLY WITH THE NEW MARINE POLICY FORM)

INSTITUTE TIME CLAUSES

FREIGHT

(This insurance is subject to English law and practice)

1. Navigation. The Vessel has leave to dock and undock, to go into graving dock, to sail or navigate with or without pilots, to go on trial trips and to assist and tow vessels or craft in distress, but it is warranted that the Vessel shall not be towed, except as is customary or when in need of assistance, or undertake towage or salvage services under a contract previously arranged by the Assured and/or Owners and/or Managers and/or Charterers. This Clause 1 shall not exclude customary towage in connection with loading and discharging.

Notes

Purpose of clause. The purpose of the clause is to explain the limits of the use to which the vessel may be put.

Warranty as to towage and salvage services. For the meaning of 'warranty,' see s 33(1) (p 50, ante). A warranty must be exactly complied with, whether it is material to the risk or not: s 33(3) (p 51, ante). If it is not complied with, the insurer is discharged from liability as from the date of the breach of warranty: s 33(3) (ante).

2. Craft Risk. Including risk of craft and/or lighter to and from the Vessel.

Note

This clause provides an extension to the cover.

3. Continuation. Should the Vessel at the expiration of this insurance be at sea or in distress or at a port of refuge or of call, the subject-matter insured shall, provided previous notice be given to the Underwriters, be held covered at a pro rata monthly premium to her port of destination.

Note

This clause is in the same words as the Institute Time Clauses (Hulls), Clause 2. As to that clause and the notes thereto, see p 168, ante.

4. Breach of Warranty. Held covered in case of any breach of warranty as to cargo, trade, locality, towage, salvage services or date of sailing, provided notice be given to the Underwriters immediately after receipt of advices and any amended terms of cover and any additional premium required by them be agreed.

Note

This clause is in the same words as the Institute Time Clauses (Hulls), Clause 3. As to that clause and the notes thereto, see p 169, ante.

5. Termination. This Clause 5 shall prevail notwithstanding any provision whether written typed or printed in this insurance inconsistent therewith. Unless the Underwriters agree to the contrary in writing, this insurance shall terminate automatically at the time of

5.1   change of the Classification Society of the Vessel, or change, suspension, discontinuance, withdrawal or expiry of her Class therein, provided that if the Vessel is at sea such automatic termination shall be deferred until arrival at her next port. However where such change, suspension, discontinuance or withdrawal of her Class has resulted from loss or damage covered by Clause 7 of this insurance or which would be covered by an insurance of the Vessel subject to current Institute War and Strikes Clauses Hulls–Time such automatic termination shall only operate should the Vessel sail from her next port without the prior approval of the Classification Society,

5.2   any change voluntary or otherwise, in the ownership or flag, transfer to new management, or charter on a bareboat basis, or requisition for title or use of the Vessel, provided that, if the Vessel has cargo on board and has already sailed from her loading port or is at sea in ballast, such automatic termination shall if required be deferred, whilst the Vessel continues her planned voyage, until arrival at final port of discharge if with cargo or at port of destination if in ballast. However, in the event of requisition for title or use without the prior execution of a written agreement by the Assured, such automatic termination shall occur fifteen days after such requisition whether the Vessel is at sea or in port.

A pro rata daily net return of premium shall be made.

Note

This clause is in the same terms as the Institute Time Clauses (Hulls), Clause 4. As to that clause and the notes thereto, see p 169, ante.

6. Assignment. No assignment of or interest in this insurance or in any moneys which may be or become payable thereunder is to be binding on or recognised by the Underwriters unless a dated notice of such assignment or interest signed by the Assured, and by the assignor in the case of subsequent assignment, is endorsed on the Policy and the Policy with such endorsement is produced before payment of any claim or return of premium thereunder.

Note

This clause is in the same terms as the Institute Time Clauses (Hulls), Clause 5. As to that clause and the notes thereto, see p 170, ante.

7. Perils.
7.1   This insurance covers loss of the subject-matter insured caused by
7.1.1   perils of the seas rivers lakes or other navigable waters
7.1.2   fire, explosion
7.1.3   violent theft by persons from outside the Vessel
7.1.4   jettison
7.1.5   piracy
7.1.6   breakdown of or accident to nuclear installations or reactors
7.1.7   contact with aircraft or similar objects, or objects falling therefrom, land conveyance, dock or harbour equipment or installation
7.1.8   earthquake volcanic eruption or lightning.
7.2   This insurance covers loss of the subject-matter insured caused by
7.2.1   accidents in loading discharging or shifting cargo or fuel
7.2.2   bursting of boilers breakage of shafts or any latent defect in the machinery or hull
7.2.3   negligence of Master Officers Crew or Pilots
7.2.4   negligence of repairers or charterers provided such repairers or charterers are not an Assured hereunder

7.2.5   barratry of Master Officers or Crew,
provided such loss has not resulted from want of due diligence by the Assured, Owners or Managers.

7.3   Master Officers Crew or Pilots not to be considered Owners within the meaning of this Clause 7 should they hold shares in the Vessel.

Note

This clause is in the same terms as the Institute Time Clauses (Hulls), Clause 6. As to that clause and the notes thereto, see p 170, ante.

8. Pollution Hazard. This insurance covers loss of the subject-matter insured caused by any governmental authority acting under the powers vested in it to prevent or mitigate a pollution hazard, or threat thereof, resulting directly from a peril covered by this insurance, provided such act of governmental authority has not resulted from want of due diligence by the Assured, the Owners, or Managers of the Vessel or any of them to prevent or mitigate such hazard or threat. Master, Officers, Crew or Pilots not to be considered Owners within the meaning of this Clause 8 should they hold shares in the Vessel.

Note

This clause is in the same words as the Institute Time Clauses (Hulls), Clause 7. As to that clause and the notes thereto, see p 177, ante.

9. Freight Collision.

9.1   It is further agreed that if the Vessel shall come into collision with any other vessel and the Assured shall in consequence thereof become liable to pay and shall pay by way of damages to any other person or persons any sum or sums in respect of the amount of freight taken into account in calculating the measure of the liability of the Assured for

9.1.1   loss of or damage to any other vessel or property on any other vessel

9.1.2   delay to or loss of use of any such other vessel or property thereon

9.1.3   general average of, salvage of or salvage under contract of, any such other vessel or property thereon,
the Underwriters will pay the Assured such proportion of three-fourths of such sum or sums so paid applying to freight as their respective subscriptions hereto bear to the total amount insured on freight or, if greater, to the gross freight at risk at the time of the collision.

9.2   Provided always that:

9.2.1 liability of the Underwriters in respect of any one such collision shall not exceed their proportionate part of three-fourths of the total amount insured hereon on freight, and in cases in which, with the prior consent in writing of the Underwriters, the liability of the Vessel has been contested or proceedings have been taken to limit liability, they will also pay a like proportion of three-fourths of the costs, appertaining proportionately to the freight portion of damages, which the Assured shall thereby incur or be compelled to pay;

9.2.2 no claim shall attach to this insurance:

9.2.2.1 which attaches to any other insurances covering collision liabilities

9.2.2.2 which is, or would be, recoverable in the terms of the Institute 3/4ths Collision Liability Clause if the Vessel were insured in the terms of such Institute 3/4ths Collision Liability Clause for a value per ton of her gross registered tonnage not less than the equivalent in pounds sterling, at the time of commencement of this insurance, of 66.67 Special Drawing Rights as defined by the International Monetary Fund;

9.2.3 this Clause 9 shall in no case extend or be deemed to extend to any sum which the Assured may become liable to pay or shall pay for or in respect of:

9.2.3.1 removal or disposal, under statutory powers or otherwise, of obstructions, wrecks, cargoes or any other thing whatsoever

9.2.3.2 any real or personal property or thing whatsoever except other vessels or property on other vessels

9.2.3.3 pollution or contamination of any real or personal property or thing whatsoever (except other vessels with which the insured Vessel is in collision or property on such other vessels)

9.2.3.4 the cargo or other property on or the engagements of the Vessel

9.2.3.5 loss of life, personal injury or illness.

Notes

This clause is in similar terms to the Institute Time Clauses (Hulls), Clause 8, and fulfils the same purpose as that clause.

As to that clause and the notes thereto, see p 177, ante.

Special Drawing Rights. For the main provisions of the articles of Agreement of the International Monetary Fund relating to special drawing rights, see Cmnd 7331, arts XV et seq.

10. Sistership. Should the Vessel named herein come into collision with or receive salvage services from another vessel belonging wholly or in part to the same Owners, or under the same management, the Assured shall have the same rights under this insurance as they would have were the other vessel entirely the property of Owners not interested in the Vessel named herein; but in such cases the liability for the collision or the amount payable for the services rendered shall be referred to a sole arbitrator to be agreed upon between the Underwriters and the Assured.

Note

This clause is in the same words as the Institute Time Clauses (Hulls), Clause 9. As to that clause and the note thereto, see p 180, ante.

11. General Average and Salvage.
11.1   This insurance covers the proportion of general average salvage and/or salvage charges attaching to freight at risk of the Assured, reduced in respect of any under-insurance.
11.2   Adjustment to be according to the law and practice obtaining at the place where the adventure ends, as if the contract of affreightment contained no special terms upon the subject; but where the contract of affreightment so provides the adjustment shall be according to the York–Antwerp Rules.
11.3   No claim under this Clause 11 shall in any case be allowed where the loss was not incurred to avoid or in connection with the avoidance of a peril insured against.

Notes

Purpose of clause. The purpose of the clause is to state the liability of the insurers in respect of general average, salvage and salvage charges.

General average. See s 66 (p 109, ante).

Salvage charges. This means the charges recoverable under maritime law by a salvor independently of contract: s 65 (p 107, ante).

Under-insurance. Ie where the assured is insured for an amount less than the insurable value, or, in the case of a valued policy, for an amount less than the policy valuation: s 81 (p 136, ante).

York–Antwerp Rules 1974. These are set out in Appendix IV, pp 277–284, post.

Exclusion of insurer's liability. Clause 11.3 is in the same terms as s 66(6) (p 110, ante), which excludes the insurer's liability where the loss was not incurred for the purpose of avoiding, or in connection with the avoidance of, a peril insured against.

12. Franchise. This insurance does not cover partial loss, other than general average loss, under 3 per cent unless caused by fire, sinking, stranding or collision with another vessel. Each craft and/or lighter to be deemed a separate insurance if required by the Assured.

Notes
This clause excludes a claim for partial loss of freight[1] under 3 per cent of the total freight insured, unless the vessel be stranded, sunk or on fire, but the insurers are nevertheless liable to pay any loss actually caused by fire or collision with another vessel. For the purposes of franchise valuation, the assured can elect to have each craft or lighter treated as a separate insurance.

Partial loss of freight. See s 70 (p 118, ante).

Stranded. It is unsafe to attempt a complete legal definition of 'stranding'. The question is mainly one of fact.

Lord Tenterden said, 'Where a vessel takes the ground in the ordinary and usual course of navigation and management in a tide river or harbour, upon the ebbing of the tide, or from natural deficiency of water, so that she may float again upon the flow of tide or increase of water, such an event shall not be considered a stranding . . . But where the ground is taken under any extraordinary circumstances of time or place, by reason of some unusual or accidental occurrence, such an event shall be considered a stranding.'

Meaning of 'franchise'. If the loss is under 3 per cent of the total freight insured, the insurers are not liable at all.

But if the loss is 3 per cent or over eg 15 per cent, the insurers are liable for the *whole of the loss*. In other words the 'franchise' is not an 'excess clause'.[2]

1 *Wells v Hopwood* (1832) 3 B & Ad 20 at 34; see this passage approved in *Letchford v Oldham* (1880) 5 QBD 538, 545, CA, where the cases are reviewed. Cf *De Mattos v Saunders* (1872) LR 7 CP 570 (ship beached for three days by salvors); *Baker-Whiteley Coal Co v Marten* (1910) 26 TLR 314 (sinking in deep water, not stranding).
2 As eg in the Institute Time Clauses (Hulls), Clause 12 (the 'deductible' clause), by which the assured has to bear a specified amount of the loss concerned. (See p 183, ante.)

13. Measure of Indemnity.
13.1 The amount recoverable under this insurance for any claim for loss of freight shall not exceed the gross freight actually lost.
13.2 Where insurances on freight other than this insurance are current at the time of the loss, all such insurances shall be taken into consideration in calculating the liability under this insurance and the amount recoverable hereunder shall not exceed the rateable proportion of the gross freight lost, notwithstanding any valuation in this or any other insurance.
13.3 In calculating the liability under Clause 11 all insurances on freight shall likewise be taken into consideration.

222 Appendix III

13.4   Nothing in this Clause 13 shall apply to any claim arising under Clause 15.

Notes

This clause relates to the measure of indemnity in the case of a claim for loss of freight, and modifies the effect of s 68 (total loss) (see p 115, ante).

Clause 11. This clause relates to general average and salvage (see p 220, ante).

Clause 15. This clause relates to total loss (see infra).

14. Loss of Time. This insurance does not cover any claim consequent on loss of time whether arising from a peril of the sea or otherwise.

Note

This clause is sometimes known as 'time-charter clause,' and makes it clear that no claim arises in respect of loss of freight arising directly from loss of time.[1]

[1] See *Arnould*, paras 856, 888 and Ivamy, *Marine Insurance* (4th ed, 1985), pp 262–264; *Bensaude v Thames and Mersey Marine Insurance Co Ltd* [1897] AC 609, HL, where a steamer's main shaft broke through a peril of the sea, and the consequent delay resulted in the proper termination of the charter-party by the charterers. This clause prevented the owners from recovering the freight so lost from the freight insurers. See also *Turnbull, Martin & Co v Hull Underwriters' Association Ltd* [1900] 2 QB 402; *Russian Bank for Foreign Trade v Excess Insurance Co Ltd* [1918] 2 KB 123 ('excluding all claims due to delay'); *Roura and Forgas v Townend* [1919] 1 KB 189; *Carras v London and Scottish Assurance Corpn Ltd* [1936] 1 KB 291, CA; *Kulukundis v Norwich Union Fire Insurance Society* [1936] 2 All ER 242, 1488n, CA; *Roberston v Petros M Nomikos Ltd* [1939] 2 All ER 723, HL; *Atlantic Maritime Co Inc v Gibbon* [1953] 2 All ER 1086 at 1101, CA; *Naviera de Canarias SA v Nacional Hispanica Aseguradora SA, The Playa de Las Nieves* [1977] 1 Lloyd's Rep 457, HL, where the insured vessel was off-shore from the time of stranding until the conclusion of repairs. (See the judgment of Lord Diplock, ibid at 459.) This clause does not prevent the assured from claiming under some other clause; see, eg, *Robertson v Petros M Nomikos Ltd* (supra).

15. Total Loss.

15.1   In the event of the total loss (actual or constructive) of the Vessel named herein the amount insured shall be paid in full, whether the Vessel be fully or partly loaded or in ballast, chartered or unchartered.

15.2   In ascertaining whether the Vessel is a constructive total loss, the insured value in the insurances on hull and machinery shall be taken as the repaired value and nothing in respect of the damaged or break-up value of the Vessel or wreck shall be taken into account.

15.3   Should the Vessel be a constructive total loss but the claim on the insurances on hull and machinery be settled as a claim for partial loss, no payment shall be due under this Clause 15.

Notes

Purpose of clause. The purpose of the clause is to explain that freight will be payable in full where there is an actual total loss (s 57) (see p 87, ante) or a constructive total loss of the vessel.

Clause 15.2. This Clause is in the same words as the Institute Time Clauses (Hulls), Clause 19.
As to that clause and the notes thereto, see p 187, ante.

Partial loss. For the meaning of 'partial loss', see s 56(1) (see p 86, ante).

Constructive total loss of freight. As to constructive total loss of freight, see p 91, ante; *Arnould*, paras 1233–1234, and Ivamy, *Marine Insurance* (4th ed, 1985), pp 350–351. There is no mention of constructive total loss of freight in the Act. There can be a total loss of the freight without there being an actual or constructive total loss of the vessel. Greene LJ, said in *Kulukundis v Norwich Union Fire Insurance Society* [1936] 2 All ER at 256, 'Under the principle recently reaffirmed by this Court in the *Carras* case (supra), a shipowner . . . is entitled to claim against his freight underwriter as for a total loss of freight if the vessel suffers such sea damage as will free the shipowner from his obligation under the contract of affreightment to carry the cargo to its destination; provided, of course, that the cargo is not, in fact, carried either by the shipowner himself or by abandonees of ship so as to earn the freight. There may be, perhaps, a further exception where transhipment, though optional to the shipowner, is a reasonable and practicable course. . . . Where the damage can be repaired and no question as to the cost of repairs arises, no difficulty is presented. . . . The difficulty arises where the cost of repairs would be so unreasonable as to justify the shipowner in refusing to incur it, in which case the vessel is said to be lost in a commercial sense.'

16. Returns for Lay-Up and Cancellation.

16.1 To return as follows:
16.1.1 Pro rata monthly net for each uncommenced month if this insurance be cancelled by agreement.
16.1.2 For each period of 30 consecutive days the Vessel may be laid up in a port or in a lay-up area provided such port or lay-up area is approved by the Underwriters (with special liberties as hereinafter allowed)
(a) . . . . per cent net not under repair
(b) . . . . per cent net under repair.
If the Vessel is under repair during part only of a period of which a return is claimable, the return shall be calculated pro rata to the number of days under (a) and (b) respectively.
16.2 PROVIDED ALWAYS THAT
16.2.1 a total loss of the Vessel, whether by insured perils or otherwise, has not occurred during the period covered by this insurance or any extension thereof

16.2.2   in no case shall a return be allowed when the Vessel is lying in exposed or unprotected waters, or in a port or lay-up area not approved by the Underwriters but, provided the Underwriters agree that such non-approved lay-up area is deemed to be within the vicinity of the approved port or lay-up area, days during which the Vessel is laid up in such non-approved lay-up area may be added to days in the approved port or lay-up area to calculate a period of 30 consecutive days and a return shall be allowed for the proportion of such period during which the Vessel is actually laid up in the approved port or lay-up area

16.2.3   loading or discharging operations or the presence of cargo on board shall not debar returns but no return shall be allowed for any period during which the Vessel is being used for the storage of cargo or for lightering purposes

16.2.4   in the event of any amendment of the annual rate, the above rates of return shall be adjusted accordingly

16.2.5   in the event of any return recoverable under this Clause 16 being based on 30 consecutive days which fall on successive insurances effected for the same Assured, this insurance shall only be liable for an amount calculated at pro rata of the period rates 16.1.2(a) and/or (b) above for the number of days which come within the period of this insurance and to which a return is actually applicable. Such overlapping period shall run, at the option of the Assured, either from the first day on which the Vessel is laid up or the first day of a period of 30 consecutive days as provided under 16.1.2(a) or (b), or 16.2.2 above.

Note

This clause is in the same words as the Institute Time Clauses (Hulls), Clause 22. As to that clause and the notes thereto, see p 189, ante.

The following clauses shall be paramount and shall override anything contained in this insurance inconsistent therewith.

17. War Exclusion. In no case shall this insurance cover loss damage liability or expense caused by

17.1   war civil war revolution rebellion insurrection, or civil strife arising therefrom, or any hostile act by or against a belligerent power

17.2   capture seizure arrest restraint or detainment (barratry and piracy excepted), and the consequences thereof or any attempt thereat

17.3   derelict mines torpedoes bombs or other derelict weapons of war.

Institute Time Clauses (Freight) 225

Note

This clause is in the same words as the Institute Time Clauses (Hulls), Clause 23. As to that clause and the notes thereto, see p 191, ante.

18. Strikes Exclusion. In no case shall this insurance cover loss damage liability or expense caused by
18.1 strikers, locked-out workmen, or persons taking part in labour disturbances, riots or civil commotions
18.2 any terrorist or any person acting from a political motive.

Note

This clause is in the same words as the Institute Time Clauses (Hulls), Clause 24. As to that clause and the notes thereto, see p 193, ante.

19. Malicious Acts Exclusion. In no case shall this insurance cover loss damage liability or expense arising from
19.1 the detonation of an explosive
19.2 any weapon of war
and caused by any person acting maliciously or from a political motive.

Note

This clause is in the same words as the Institute Time Clauses (Hulls), Clause 25. As to that clause and the note thereto, see p 195, ante.

20. Nuclear Exclusion. In no case shall this insurance cover loss damage liability or expense arising from any weapon of war employing atomic or nuclear fission and/or fusion or other like reaction or radioactive force or matter.

Note

This clause is in the same words as the Institute Time Clauses (Hulls), Clause 26. As to that clause and the note thereto, see p 195, ante.

1/10/83   (FOR USE ONLY WITH THE NEW MARINE POLICY FORM)

INSTITUTE VOYAGE CLAUSES

FREIGHT

(This insurance is subject to English law and practice)

1. Navigation. The Vessel has leave to dock and undock, to go into graving dock, to sail or navigate with or without pilots, to go on trial trips and to assist and tow vessels or craft in distress, but it is warranted that the Vessel shall not be towed, except as is customary or when in need of assistance, or undertake towage or salvage services under a contract previously arranged by the Assured and/or Owners and/or Managers and/or Charterers. This Clause 1 shall not exclude customary towage in connection with loading and discharging.

Notes

This clause is in the same words as the Institute Time Clauses (Freight), Clause 1. As to that clause and the note thereto, see p 215, ante.

2. Craft Risk. Including risk of craft and/or lighter to and from the Vessel.

Note

This clause is in the same words as the Institute Time Clauses (Freight), Clause 2. As to that clause and the note thereto, see p 215, ante.

3. Change of Voyage. Held covered in case of deviation or change of voyage or any breach of warranty as to towage or salvage services, provided notice be given to the Underwriters immediately after receipt of advices and any amended terms of cover and any additional premium required by them be agreed.

Note

This clause is in the same words as the Institute Voyage Clauses (Hulls), Clause 2. As to that clause and the notes thereto, see p 196, ante.

4. Assignment. No assignment of or interest in this insurance or in any moneys which may be or become payable thereunder is to be binding on or recognised by the Underwriters unless a dated notice of such assignment or interest signed by the Assured, and by the assignor in the case of subsequent assignment, is endorsed on the Policy and the Policy with such endorsement is produced before payment of any claim or return of premium thereunder.

Note

This clause is in the same words as the Institute Time Clauses (Freight), Clause 6. As to that clause and the notes thereto, see p 217, ante.

5. Perils.
5.1   This insurance covers loss of the subject-matter insured caused by
5.1.1   perils of the seas rivers lakes or other navigable waters

5.1.2	fire, explosion
5.1.3	violent theft by persons from outside the Vessel
5.1.4	jettison
5.1.5	piracy
5.1.6	breakdown of or accident to nuclear installations or reactors
5.1.7	contact with aircraft or similar objects, or objects falling therefrom, land conveyance, dock or harbour equipment or installation
5.1.8	earthquake volcanic eruption or lightning.
5.2	This insurance covers loss of the subject-matter insured caused by
5.2.1	accidents in loading discharging or shifting cargo or fuel
5.2.2	bursting of boilers breakage of shafts or any latent defect in the machinery or hull
5.2.3	negligence of Master Officers Crew or Pilots
5.2.4	negligence of repairers or charterers provided such repairers or charterers are not an Assured hereunder
5.2.5	barratry of Master Officers or Crew, provided such loss has not resulted from want of due diligence by the Assured, Owners or Managers.
5.3	Master Officers Crew or Pilots not to be considered Owners within the meaning of this Clause 7 should they hold shares in the Vessel.

Note

This clause is in the same words as the Institute Time Clauses (Freight), Clause 7. As to that clause and the notes thereto, see p 217, ante.

6. Pollution Hazard. This insurance covers loss of the subject-matter insured caused by any governmental authority acting under the powers vested in it to prevent or mitigate a pollution hazard, or threat thereof, resulting directly from a peril covered by this insurance, provided such act of governmental authority has not resulted from want of due diligence by the Assured, the Owners, or Managers of the Vessel or any of them to prevent or mitigate such hazard or threat. Master, Officers, Crew or Pilots not to be considered Owners within the meaning of this Clause 6 should they hold shares in the Vessel.

Note

This clause is in the same words as the Institute Time Clauses (Freight), Clause 8. As to that clause and the notes thereto, see p 218, ante.

7. Freight Collision.

7.1	It is further agreed that if the Vessel shall come into collision with any other vessel and the Assured shall in consequence thereof become liable to pay and shall pay by way of damages to

any other person or persons any sum or sums in respect of the amount of freight taken into account in calculating the measure of the liability of the Assured for

7.1.1 loss of or damage to any other vessel or property on any other vessel

7.1.2 delay to or loss of use of any such other vessel or property thereon

7.1.3 general average of, salvage of or salvage under contract of, any such other vessel or property thereon,

the Underwriters will pay the Assured such proportion of three-fourths of such sum or sums so paid applying to freight as their respective subscriptions hereto bear to the total amount insured on freight or, if greater, to the gross freight at risk at the time of the collision.

7.2 Provided always that:

7.2.1 liability of the Underwriters in respect of any one such collision shall not exceed their proportionate part of three-fourths of the total amount insured hereon on freight, and in cases in which, with the prior consent in writing of the Underwriters, the liability of the Vessel has been contested or proceedings have been taken to limit liability, they will also pay a like proportion of three-fourths of the costs, appertaining proportionately to the freight portion of damages, which the Assured shall thereby incur or be compelled to pay;

7.2.2 no claim shall attach to this insurance:

7.2.2.1 which attaches to any other insurances covering collision liabilities

7.2.2.2 which is, or would be, recoverable in the terms of the Institute 3/4ths Collision Liability Clause if the Vessel were insured in the terms of such Institute 3/4ths Collision Liability Clause for a value per ton of her gross registered tonnage not less than the equivalent in pounds sterling, at the time of commencement of this insurance, of 66.67 Special Drawing Rights as defined by the International Monetary Fund;

7.2.3 this Clause 7 shall in no case extend or be deemed to extend to any sum which the Assured may become liable to pay or shall pay for or in respect of:

7.2.3.1 removal or disposal, under statutory powers or otherwise, of obstructions, wrecks, cargoes or any other thing whatsoever

7.2.3.2 any real or personal property or thing whatsoever except other vessels or property on other vessels

7.2.3.3 pollution or contamination of any real or personal property or thing whatsoever (except other vessels with which the

	insured Vessel is in collision or property on such other vessels)
7.2.3.4	the cargo or other property on or the engagements of the Vessel
7.2.3.5	loss of life, personal injury or illness.

Note

This clause is in the same words as the Institute Time Clauses (Freight), Clause 9. As to that clause and the notes thereto, see p 218, ante.

8. Sistership. Should the Vessel named herein come into collision with or receive salvage services from another vessel belonging wholly or in part to the same Owners, or under the same management, the Assured shall have the same rights under this insurance as they would have were the other vessel entirely the property of Owners not interested in the Vessel named herein; but in such cases the liability for the collision or the amount payable for the services rendered shall be referred to a sole arbitrator to be agreed upon between the Underwriters and the Assured.

Note

This clause is in the same words as the Institute Time Clauses (Freight), Clause 10. As to that clause and the note thereto, see p 220, ante.

9. General Average and Salvage.
9.1	This insurance covers the proportion of general average salvage and/or salvage charges attaching to freight at risk of the Assured, reduced in respect of any under-insurance.
9.2	Adjustment to be according to the law and practice obtaining at the place where the adventure ends, as if the contract of affreightment contained no special terms upon the subject; but where the contract of affreightment so provides the adjustment shall be according to the York–Antwerp Rules.
9.3	No claim under this Clause 11 shall in any case be allowed where the loss was not incurred to avoid or in connection with the avoidance of a peril insured against.

Note

This clause is in the same words as the Institute Time Clauses (Freight), Clause 11. As to that clause and the notes thereto, see p 220, ante.

10. Franchise. This insurance does not cover partial loss, other than general average loss, under 3 per cent unless caused by fire, sinking, stranding or collision with another vessel. Each craft and/or lighter to be deemed a separate insurance if required by the Assured.

Note

This clause is in the same words as the Institute Time Clauses (Freight), Clause 12. As to that clause and the notes thereto, see p 221, ante.

11. Measure of Indemnity.

11.1 The amount recoverable under this insurance for any claim for loss of freight shall not exceed the gross freight actually lost.

11.2 Where insurances on freight other than this insurance are current at the time of the loss, all such insurances shall be taken into consideration in calculating the liability under this insurance and the amount recoverable hereunder shall not exceed the rateable proportion of the gross freight lost, notwithstanding any valuation in this or any other insurance.

11.3 In calculating the liability under Clause 9 all insurances on freight shall likewise be taken into consideration.

11.4 Nothing in this Clause 11 shall apply to any claim arising under Clause 13.

Notes

This clause is in the same words as the Institute Time Clauses (Freight), Clause 13. As to that clause and the notes thereto, see p 221, ante.

Clause 9. This clause relates to general average and salvage (see p 229, ante).

Clause 13. This clause relates to total loss (see infra).

12. Loss of Time. This insurance does not cover any claim consequent on loss of time whether arising from a peril of the sea or otherwise.

Note

This clause is in the same words as the Institute Time Clauses (Freight), Clause 14. As to that clause and the note thereto, see p 222, ante.

13. Total Loss.

13.1 In the event of the total loss (actual or constructive) of the Vessel named herein the amount insured shall be paid in full, whether the Vessel be fully or partly loaded or in ballast, chartered or unchartered.

13.2 In ascertaining whether the Vessel is a constructive total loss, the insured value in the insurances on hull and machinery shall be taken as the repaired value and nothing in respect of the damaged or break-up value of the Vessel or wreck shall be taken into account.

13.3 Should the Vessel be a constructive total loss but the claim on the insurances on hull and machinery be settled as a claim for partial loss, no payment shall be due under this Clause 13.

Institute Voyage Clauses (Freight)

Note

This clause is in the same words as the Institute Time Clauses (Freight), Clause 15. As to that clause and the notes thereto, see p 222, ante.

The following clauses shall be paramount and shall override anything contained in this insurance inconsistent therewith.

14. War Exclusion. In no case shall this insurance cover loss damage liability or expense caused by

- 14.1 war civil war revolution rebellion insurrection, or civil strife arising therefrom, or any hostile act by or against a belligerent power
- 14.2 capture seizure arrest restraint or detainment (barratry and piracy excepted), and the consequences thereof or any attempt thereat
- 14.3 derelict mines torpedoes bombs or other derelict weapons of war.

Note

This clause is in the same words as the Institute Time Clauses (Hulls), Clause 23. As to that clause and the notes thereto, see p 191, ante.

15. Strikes Exclusion. In no case shall this insurance cover loss damage liability or expense caused by

- 15.1 strikers, locked-out workmen, or persons taking part in labour disturbances, riots or civil commotions
- 15.2 any terrorist or any person acting from a political motive.

Note

This clause is in the same words as the Institute Time Clauses (Freight), Clause 18. As to that clause and the note thereto, see p 225, ante.

16. Malicious Acts Exclusion. In no case shall this insurance cover loss damage liability or expense arising from

- 16.1 the detonation of an explosive
- 16.2 any weapon of war

and caused by any person acting maliciously or from a political motive.

Note

This clause is in the same words as the Institute Time Clauses (Freight), Clause 19. As to that clause and the note thereto, see p 225, ante.

17. Nuclear Exclusion. In no case shall this insurance cover loss damage liability or expense arising from any weapon of war employing atomic or nuclear fission and/or fusion or other like reaction or radioactive force or matter.

Note

This clause is in the same words as the Institute Time Clauses (Freight), Clause 19. As to that clause and the note thereto, see p 225, ante.

1/10/83 (FOR USE ONLY WITH THE NEW MARINE POLICY FORM)

INSTITUTE WAR AND STRIKES CLAUSES

FREIGHT–TIME

(This insurance is subject to English law and practice)

1. Perils. Subject always to the exclusions hereinafter referred to, this insurance covers

- 1.1   loss (total or partial) of the subject-matter insured caused by
- 1.1.1   war civil war revolution rebellion insurrection, or civil strife arising therefrom, or any hostile act by or against a belligerent power
- 1.1.2   capture seizure arrest restraint or detainment, and the consequences thereof or any attempt thereat
- 1.1.3   derelict mines torpedoes bombs or other derelict weapons of war
- 1.2   loss (total or partial) of the subject-matter insured arising from loss of or damage to the Vessel caused by
- 1.2.1   strikers, locked-out workmen, or persons taking part in labour disturbances, riots or civil commotions
- 1.2.2   any terrorist or any person acting maliciously or from a political motive
- 1.2.3   confiscation or expropriation.

Note

This clause provides cover in respect of the perils excepted by the Institute Time Clauses (Freight), Clause 17 (war exclusion) and Clause 18 (strikes exclusion), and also provides cover in respect of 'confiscation' and 'expropriation'.

As to the Institute Time Clauses (Freight) Clause 17 and Clause 18 and the notes thereto, see respectively pp 224 and 225, ante.

2. Incorporation. The Institute Time Clauses—Freight 1/10/83 except Clauses 2, 3, 4, 5, 12, 16, 17, 18, 19 and 20 are deemed to be incorporated in this insurance in so far as they do not conflict with the provisions of these clauses.

Held covered in case of breach of warranty as to towage or salvage services provided notice be given to the Underwriters immediately after receipt of advices and any additional premium required by them be agreed.

Notes

This clause shows which of the Institute Time Clauses (Freight) (see pp 215–225, ante) are incorporated. It is important to notice that they are so incorporated only in so far as they do not conflict with the Institute War and Strikes Clauses (Freight–Time).

Clause 2. This is the 'Craft risk' clause (see p 215, ante).
Clause 3. This is the 'Continuation' clause (see p 216, ante).
Clause 4. This is the 'Breach of warranty' clause (see p 216, ante).
Clause 5. This is the 'Termination' clause (see p 216, ante).
Clause 12. This is the 'Franchise' clause (see p 221, ante).
Clause 16. This is the 'Returns for lay-up and cancellation' clause (see p 223, ante).
Clause 17. This is the 'War exclusion' clause (see p 224, ante).
Clause 18. This is the 'Strikes exclusion' clause (see p 225, ante).
Clause 19. This is the 'Malicious acts exclusion' clause (see p 225, ante).
Clause 20. This is the 'Nuclear exclusion' clause (see p 225, ante).

Breach of warranty. See s 33(3) (p 51, ante).

Additional premium. See s 31(2) (p 47, ante).

3. Detainment. In the event that a claim for a constructive total loss of the Vessel is paid on the war risks insurance of the Vessel under Clause 3 (Detainment) of the Institute War and Strikes Clauses—Hulls—Time 1/10/83 or the Institute War and Strikes Clauses—Hulls—Voyage 1/10/83 as a result of the loss of the free use and disposal of the Vessel for a continuous period of 12 months due to capture, seizure, arrest, restraint, detainment, confiscation or expropriation whilst this insurance is in force, the amount insured hereunder shall be paid in full less any claims otherwise arising during the said period of 12 months which have been paid or are recoverable hereunder or under insurances subject to the Institute Time Clauses—Freight 1/10/83 and/or the Institute Voyage Clauses—Freight 1/10/83 and any recoveries made in respect of the said period.

Notes

Institute Time Clauses (Freight). As to these clauses, see pp 215–225, ante.

Institute Voyage Clauses (Freight). As to these clauses, see pp 225–232, ante.

Institute War and Strikes Clauses (Hulls—Time). As to these clauses, see pp 208–211, ante.

Institute War and Strikes Clauses (Hulls—Voyage). As to these clauses, see pp 212–215, ante.

Constructive total loss. See s 60 (p 90, ante)

4. Exclusions. This insurance excludes
4.1 loss (total or partial) or expense arising from
4.1.1 any detonation of any weapon of war employing atomic or nuclear fission and/or fusion or other like reaction or radioactive force or matter, hereinafter called a nuclear weapon of war
4.1.2 the outbreak of war (whether there be a declaration of war or not) between any of the following countries:
United Kingdom, United States of America, France, the Union of Soviet Socialist Republics, the People's Republic of China
4.1.3 requisition or pre-emption
4.1.4 capture seizure arrest restraint detainment confiscation or expropriation by or under the order of the government or any public or local authority of the country in which the Vessel is owned or registered
4.1.5 arrest restraint detainment confiscation or expropriation under quarantine regulations or by reason of infringement of any customs or trading regulations
4.1.6 the operation of ordinary judicial process, failure to provide security or to pay any fine or penalty or any financial cause
4.1.7 piracy (but this exclusion shall not affect cover under Clause 1.2.1),
4.2 loss (total or partial) or expense covered by the Institute Time Clauses—Freight 1/10/83 or which would be recoverable thereunder but for Clause 12 thereof,
4.3 any claim (not being a claim recoverable under the Institute War and Strikes Clauses Freight—Voyage 1/10/83) for any sum recoverable under any other insurance on the subject-matter insured or which would be recoverable under such insurance but for the existence of this insurance,
4.4 loss proximately caused by delay or any claim for expenses arising from delay except such expenses as would be recoverable in principle in English law and practice under the York–Antwerp Rules 1974,
4.5 any claim based upon loss of or frustration of any voyage or adventure.

Notes

Clause 4.1.1. This clause repeats the exceptions set out in the Institute Time Clauses (Freight), Clause 20 (nuclear exclusion) (see p 225, ante).
Clause 4.1.2. Although loss by war is covered under Clause 1 of the Institute War and Strikes Clauses (Freight—Time), Clause 1.1.1 (perils) (p 232, ante), the insurers are not liable in the case of a loss by what could be classed as a 'major war,' ie one between the world powers set out in the present clause.

Institute War and Strikes Clauses (Freight–Time) 235

Clause 4.1.4. Although loss by 'capture seizure arrest etc' is covered by Clause 1.1.2 (perils) (p 232, ante), the present clause stresses that where such a loss is brought about by the government etc of the country in which the vessel is owned or registered, the insurers are not liable.

York–Antwerp Rules 1974. See Appendix IV, pp 277–284, post.

5. Termination.

5.1   This insurance may be cancelled by either the Underwriters or the Assured giving 7 days notice (such cancellation becoming effective on the expiry of 7 days from midnight of the day on which notice of cancellation is issued by or to the Underwriters). The Underwriters agree however to reinstate this insurance subject to agreement between the Underwriters and the Assured prior to the expiry of such notice of cancellation as to new rate of premium and/or conditions and/or warranties.

5.2   Whether or not such notice of cancellation has been given this insurance shall TERMINATE AUTOMATICALLY

5.2.1   upon the occurrence of any hostile detonation of any nuclear weapon of war as defined in Clause 4.1.1 wheresoever or whensoever such detonation may occur and whether or not the Vessel may be involved

5.2.2   upon the outbreak of war (whether there be a declaration of war or not) between any of the following countries:
        United Kingdom, United States of America, France,
        the Union of Soviet Socialist Republics,
        the People's Republic of China

5.2.3   in the event of the Vessel being requisitioned, either for title or use.

5.3   In the event either of cancellation by notice or of automatic termination of this insurance by reason of the operation of this Clause 5, or of the sale of the Vessel, pro rata net return of premium shall be payable to the Assured.

This insurance shall not become effective if, subsequent to its acceptance by the Underwriters and prior to the intended time of its attachment, there has occurred any event which would have automatically terminated this insurance under the provisions of Clause 5 above.

Notes

Purpose of clause. This clause concerns the right to cancel the policy and also the circumstances in which the policy is automatically cancelled.

Return of premium. See s 83 (p 137, ante).

1/10/83 (FOR USE ONLY WITH THE NEW MARINE POLICY FORM)

INSTITUTE WAR AND STRIKES CLAUSES

FREIGHT–VOYAGE

(This insurance is subject to English law and practice)

1. Perils. Subject always to the exclusions hereinafter referred to, this insurance covers
1.1   loss (total or partial) of the subject-matter insured caused by
1.1.1   war civil war revolution rebellion insurrection, or civil strife arising therefrom, or any hostile act by or against a belligerent power
1.1.2   capture seizure arrest restraint or detainment, and the consequences thereof or any attempt threat
1.1.3   derelict mines torpedoes bombs or other derelict weapons of war
1.2   loss (total or partial) of the subject-matter insured arising from loss of or damage to the Vessel caused by
1.2.1   strikers, locked-out workmen, or persons taking part in labour disturbances, riots or civil commotions
1.2.2   any terrorist or any person acting maliciously or from a political motive
1.2.3   confiscation or expropriation.

Note

This clause provides cover in respect of the perils excepted by the Institute Voyage Clauses (Freight), Clause 14 (war exclusion) and Clause 15 (strikes exclusion), and also provides cover in respect of 'confiscation' and 'expropriation'.

As to the Institute Voyage Clauses (Freight) Clauses 14 and 15 and the notes thereto, see p 231, ante.

2. Incorporation. The Institute Voyage Clauses—Freight 1/10/83 except Clauses 2, 10, 14, 15, 16 and 17 are deemed to be incorporated in this insurance in so far as they do not conflict with the provisions of these clauses.

Held covered in case of breach of warranty as to towage or salvage services provided notice be given to the Underwriters immediately after receipt of advices and any additional premium required by them be agreed.

Notes

This clause shows which of the Institute Voyage Clauses (Freight) are incorporated. It is important to notice that they are so incorporated only in so far as they do not conflict with the Institute War and Strikes Clauses (Freight–Voyage).

Clause 2. This is the 'Craft risk' clause (see p 226, ante).
Clause 10. This is the 'Franchise' clause (see p 229, ante).
Clause 14. This is the 'War exclusion' clause (see p 231, ante).
Clause 15. This is the 'Strikes exclusion' clause (see p 231, ante).
Clause 16. This is the 'Malicious acts exclusion' clause (see p 231, ante).
Clause 17. This is the 'Nuclear exclusion' clause (see p 231, ante).

3. Detainment. In the event that a claim for a constructive total loss of the Vessel is paid on the war risks insurance of the Vessel under Clause 3 (Detainment) of the Institute War and Strikes Clauses—Hulls—Time 1/10/83 or the Institute War and Strikes Clauses—Hulls—Voyage 1/10/83 as a result of the loss of the free use and disposal of the Vessel for a continuous period of 12 months due to capture, seizure, arrest, restraint, detainment, confiscation or expropriation whilst this insurance is in force, the amount insured hereunder shall be paid in full less any claims otherwise arising during the said period of 12 months which have been paid or are recoverable hereunder or under insurances subject to the Institute Time Clauses—Freight 1/10/83 and/or the Institute Voyage Clauses—Freight 1/10/83 and any recoveries made in respect of the said period.

Notes

Institute War and Strikes Clauses (Hulls—Time). As to these clauses, see pp 208–211, ante.

Institute War and Strikes Clauses (Hulls—Voyage). As to these clauses, see pp 212–215, ante.

Institute Time Clauses (Freight). As to these clauses, see pp 215–225, ante.

Institute Voyage Clauses (Freight). As to these clauses, see pp 225–232, ante.

4. Exclusions. This insurance excludes
4.1 loss (total or partial) or expense arising from
4.1.1 any detonation of any weapon of war employing atomic or nuclear fission and/or fusion or other like reaction or radioactive force or matter, hereinafter called a nuclear weapon of war
4.1.2 the outbreak of war (whether there be a declaration of war or not) between any of the following countries:
United Kingdom, United States of America, France, the Union of Soviet Socialist Republics, the People's Republic of China
4.1.3 requisition or pre-emption
4.1.4 capture seizure arrest restraint detainment confiscation or expropriation by or under the order of the government or any public or local authority of the country in which the Vessel is owned or registered

238 Appendix III

- 4.1.5   arrest restraint detainment confiscation or expropriation under quarantine regulations or by reason of infringement of any customs or trading regulations
- 4.1.6   the operation of ordinary judicial process, failure to provide security or to pay any fine or penalty or any financial cause
- 4.1.7   piracy (but this exclusion shall not affect cover under Clause 1.2.1),
- 4.2   loss (total or partial) or expense covered by the Institute Voyage Clauses—Freight 1/10/83 or which would be recoverable thereunder but for Clause 10 thereof,
- 4.3   any claim (not being a claim recoverable under the Institute War and Strikes Clauses Freight—Time 1/10/83) for any sum recoverable under any other insurance on the Vessel or which would be recoverable under such insurance but for the existence of this insurance,
- 4.4   loss proximately caused by delay or any claim for expenses arising from delay except such expenses as would be recoverable in principle in English law and practice under the York–Antwerp Rules 1974,
- 4.5   any claim based upon loss of or frustration of any voyage or adventure.

Notes

Clause 4.1.1. This clause repeats the exceptions set out in the Institute Voyage Clauses (Freight), Clause 17 (nuclear exclusion) (see p 231, ante).

Clause 4.1.2. Although loss by war is covered under Clause 1 of the Institute War and Strikes Clauses (Freight—Voyage), Clause 1.1.1 (perils) (see p 236, ante), the insurers are not liable in the case of a loss by what could be classed as a 'major war,' ie one between the world powers set out in the present clause.

Clause 4.1.4. Although loss by 'capture seizure arrest etc' is covered by Clause 1.1.2 (perils) (see p 236, ante), the present clause stresses that where such a loss is brought about by the government etc of the country in which the vessel is owned or registered, the insurers are not liable.

York–Antwerp Rules 1974. See Appendix IV, pp 277–284, post.

5. Termination.

- 5.1   This insurance may be cancelled by either the Underwriters or the Assured giving 7 days notice (such cancellation becoming effective on the expiry of 7 days from midnight of the day on which notice of cancellation is issued by or to the Underwriters). The Underwriters agree however to reinstate this insurance subject to agreement between the Underwriters and the Assured prior to the expiry of such notice of cancellation as to new rate of premium and/or conditions and/or warranties.
- 5.2   Whether or not such notice of cancellation has been given this insurance shall TERMINATE AUTOMATICALLY

5.2.1 upon the occurrence of any hostile detonation of any nuclear weapon of war as defined in Clause 4.1.1 wheresoever or whensoever such detonation may occur and whether or not the Vessel may be involved

5.2.2 upon the outbreak of war (whether there be a declaration of war or not) between any of the following countries:
United Kingdom, United States of America, France, the Union of Soviet Socialist Republics, the People's Republic of China

5.2.3 in the event of the Vessel being requisitioned, either for title or use.

5.3 In the event either of cancellation by notice or of automatic termination of this insurance by reason of the operation of this Clause 5, or of the sale of the Vessel, a return of premium shall be payable to the Assured.

This Insurance shall not become effective if, subsequent to its acceptance by the Underwriters and prior to the intended time of its attachment, there has occurred any event which would have automatically terminated this insurance under the provisions of Clause 5 above.

Notes

Purpose of clause. This clause concerns the right to cancel the policy and also the circumstances in which the policy is automatically cancelled.

Return of premium. See s 83 (p 137, ante).

(3) Cargo Clauses

1/1/82 (FOR USE ONLY WITH THE NEW MARINE POLICY FORM)

INSTITUTE CARGO CLAUSES (A)

RISKS COVERED

1. Risks Clause. This insurance covers all risks of loss of or damage to the subject-matter insured except as provided in Clauses 4, 5, 6 and 7 below.

Notes

This clause emphasises that the cover is against all risks (with specified exceptions set out below). The premium for such cover will be more than that required in the case of the Institute Cargo Clauses (B) (see p 249, post) and the Institute Cargo Clauses (C) (see p 256, post).

Clause 4. This is the 'General Exclusions' clause (see p 241, post).

Clause 5. This is the 'Unseaworthiness and Unfitness Exclusion' clause (see p 242, post).

Clause 6. This is the 'War Exclusion' clause (see p 243, post).

Clause 7. This is the 'Strikes Exclusion' clause (see p 244, post).

2. General Average Clause. This insurance covers general average and salvage charges, adjusted or determined according to the contract of affreightment and/or the governing law and practice, incurred to avoid or in connection with the avoidance of loss from any cause except those excluded in Clauses 4, 5, 6 and 7 or elsewhere in this insurance.

Notes
This clause binds the insurers to accept whatever general average or salvage adjustment may be required by the contract of affreightment, eg the York–Antwerp Rules 1974, or the rules of any foreign law.

General average. See s 66 (p 109, ante).

Salvage charges. See s 65 (p 107, ante).

3. 'Both to Blame Collision' Clause. This insurance is extended to indemnify the Assured against such proportion of liability under the contract of affreightment 'Both to Blame Collision' Clause as is in respect of a loss recoverable hereunder. In the event of any claim by shipowners under the said Clause the Assured agree to notify the Underwriters who shall have the right, at their own cost and expense, to defend the Assured against such claim.

Note
Intention of clause. This clause is intended to deal with the situation which can arise where liability for collision damages falls to be ascertained in accordance with the law of the USA. Under that law, where cargo is lost or damaged in a collision for which both ships are to blame, the cargo-owner may recover in full against the non-carrying ship.[1] Then the non-carrying ship may claim one-half of this sum from the carrying ship.[2] This is an anomalous result because a shipowner is not directly responsible to cargo-owners for damage arising out of negligent

navigation, provided that due diligence has been exercised to make the ship seaworthy.[3] Thus, if a shipowner is solely to blame for a collision, he is usually under no liability to cargo-owners. But if he is partly to blame, he will become indirectly liable to them, as explained above. Shipowners felt aggrieved at this result, and in an endeavour to overcome the difficulty, they normally include a 'both to blame collision' clause[4] in bills of lading, requiring cargo to indemnify them, to the extent that their liability to the non-carrying vessel represents loss or damage to that cargo. The present Institute clause is intended to cover cargo in respect of this indemnity.

1 *The Beaconsfield* 158 US 303 (1894); *The Atlas* 93 US 302 (1876).
2 *The Chattahoochee* 173 US 540 (1899).
3 The Harter Act 1893, s 3; the (United States) Carriage of Goods by Sea Act 1936, s 4(2).
4 In 1952 the legality of the clause was tested in the USA in a case where a bill of lading, *not issued under a charter-party*, contained the clause. The Supreme Court decided that the clause was invalid as being a violation of the rule which in general forbids carriers from stipulating against the negligence of themselves or their employees: *United States of America v Atlantic Mutual Insurance Co* [1952] 1 TLR 1237. But it may be that the decision would be different in the case of a charter-party with bills of lading thereunder, and for this reason the clause is still being used.

EXCLUSIONS

4. General Exclusions Clause. In no case shall this insurance cover
4.1   loss damage or expense attributable to wilful misconduct of the Assured
4.2   ordinary leakage, ordinary loss in weight or volume, or ordinary wear and tear of the subject-matter insured
4.3   loss damage or expense caused by insufficiency or unsuitability of packing or preparation of the subject-matter insured (for the purpose of this Clause 4.3 'packing' shall be deemed to include stowage in a container or liftvan but only when such stowage is carried out prior to attachment of this insurance or by the Assured or their servants)
4.4   loss damage or expense caused by inherent vice or nature of the subject-matter insured
4.5   loss damage or expense proximately caused by delay, even though the delay be caused by a risk insured against (except expenses payable under Clause 2 above)
4.6   loss damage or expense arising from insolvency or financial default of the owners managers charterers or operators of the vessel
4.7   loss damage or expense arising from the use of any weapon of war employing atomic or nuclear fission and/or fusion or other like reaction or radioactive force or matter.

Notes

This clause sets out a number of exceptions to the insurers' liability. It will be noticed that some of these are similar to those in s 55(2) (see p 78, ante).

Wilful misconduct. See 55(2)(a) and the notes thereto (p 78, ante).

Ordinary leakage. See s 55(2)(c) and the notes thereto (p 78, ante).

Ordinary wear and tear. See s 55(2)(c) and the notes thereto (p 78, ante).

Inherent vice or nature. See s 55(2)(c) and the notes thereto (p 78, ante).

Delay. See s 55(2)(b) and the notes thereto (see p 78, ante).

Insufficiency of packing. This has been held to be 'inherent vice'.[1]

Atomic or nuclear fission etc. This part of Clause 4.7 is in words similar to those in the Institute Time Clauses (Hulls), Clause 26 (nuclear exclusion) (see p 195, ante).

1 *F W Berk & Co Ltd v Style* [1955] 3 All ER 625, QB (Commercial Court) (kieselguhr shipped in paper bags); *Gee and Garnham Ltd v Whittall* [1955] 2 Lloyd's Rep 562, QB (Commercial Court).

5. Unseaworthiness and Unfitness Exclusion Clause.

5.1   In no case shall this insurance cover loss damage or expense arising from
> unseaworthiness of vessel or craft,
> unfitness of vessel craft conveyance container or liftvan for the safe carriage of the subject-matter insured,

where the Assured or their servants are privy to such unseaworthiness or unfitness, at the time the subject-matter insured is loaded therein.

5.2   The Underwriters waive any breach of the implied warranties of seaworthiness of the ship and fitness of the ship to carry the subject-matter insured to destination, unless the Assured or their servants are privy to such unseaworthiness or unfitness.

Notes

Seaworthiness. In a voyage policy there is an implied warranty that at the commencement of the voyage the ship shall be seaworthy for the purpose of the particular adventure insured: s 39(1) (see p 58, ante).

Fitness to carry cargo. In a voyage policy on goods there is an implied warranty that at the commencement of the voyage the ship is not only seaworthy as a ship but also that she is reasonably fit to carry the goods to the destination contemplated by the policy: s 40(2) (see p 62, ante).

Waiver of breach of warranty. A breach of warranty may be waived by the insurer: s 34(3) (see p 53, ante).

The effect of the present clause is that any breach of the above implied warranties is waived unless the assured or their servants are privy to such unseaworthiness or unfitness.

6. War Exclusion Clause.
In no case shall this insurance cover loss damage or expense caused by

6.1   war civil war revolution rebellion insurrection, or civil strife arising therefrom, or any hostile act by or against a belligerent power

6.2   capture seizure arrest restraint or detainment (piracy excepted), and the consequences thereof or any attempt thereat

6.3   derelict mines torpedoes bombs or other derelict weapons of war.

Note

This clause is in the same words as the Institute Time Clauses (Hulls), Clause 23. As to that clause and the notes thereto see p 191, ante.

7. Strikes Exclusion Clause.
In no case shall this insurance cover loss damage or expense

7.1   caused by strikers, locked-out workmen, or persons taking part in labour disturbances, riots or civil commotions

7.2   resulting from strikes, lock-outs, labour disturbances, riots or civil commotions

7.3   caused by any terrorist or any person acting from a political motive.

Note

This clause is in words similar to the Institute Time Clauses (Hulls), Clause 24.1 and Clause 24.2 but also excludes liability for loss etc resulting from strikes etc.
    As to Clause 24 and the notes thereto, see p 193, ante.

DURATION

8. Transit Clause.

8.1   This insurance attaches from the time the goods leave the warehouse or place of storage at the place named herein for the commencement of the transit, continues during the ordinary course of transit and terminates either

8.1.1   on delivery to the Consignees' or other final warehouse or place of storage at the destination named herein,

8.1.2   on delivery to any other warehouse or place of storage, whether prior to or at the destination named herein, which the Assured elect to use either

8.1.2.1   for storage other than in the ordinary course of transit or

8.1.2.2 for allocation or distribution,
or
8.1.3 on the expiry of 60 days after completion of discharge overside of the goods hereby insured from the oversea vessel at the final port of discharge,
whichever shall first occur.

8.2 If, after discharge overside from the oversea vessel at the final port of discharge, but prior to termination of this insurance, the goods are to be forwarded to a destination other than that to which they are insured hereunder, this insurance, whilst remaining subject to termination as provided for above, shall not extend beyond the commencement of transit to such other destination.

8.3 This insurance shall remain in force (subject to termination as provided for above and to the provisions of Clause 9 below) during delay beyond the control of the Assured, any deviation, forced discharge, reshipment or transhipment and during any variation of the adventure arising from the exercise of a liberty granted to shipowners or charterers under the contract of affreightment.

Notes

This clause (which was formerly known as the 'warehouse to warehouse' clause) explains when the risk on goods begins and when it ends.[1]

Deviation. If it were not for this clause, deviation would discharge the insurer from liability. See s 46 (p 68, ante).

Delay. If it were not for this clause, delay in the voyage would discharge the insurer from liability. See s 48 (p 70, ante).

Transhipment. See also s 59 (p 90, ante).

'Liberty granted to shipowners.' The 'liberty granted to shipowners' referred to in the clause provides for the contingency of goods being discharged at a place other than the place of destination named in the contract of affreightment, by reason of e g a strike at the port of destination.

1 *Arnould*, paras 521–523, 528, and Ivamy, *Marine Insurance* (4th ed, 1985), pp 122–126. For the construction of the corresponding clause in the Cargo Clauses adopted in July 1924, see *Safadi v Western Assurance Co* (1933) 46 Ll L Rep 140. For other such clauses, see *Westminster Fire Office v Reliance Marine Insurance Co* (1903) 19 TLR 668 (goods held covered 'being temporarily places upon the quay'); *Deutsch-Australische Dampfschiffsgesellschaft v Sturge* (1913) 30 TLR 137 (goods covered 'from the time of leaving the warehouse at point of departure until safely delivered into warehouse or other place for which the goods have been entered'); *Re Traders and General Insurance Association, ex p Continental and Overseas Trading Co Ltd* [1924] 2 Ch 187 (goods covered 'from the time of leaving the shippers' or manufacturers' warehouse'); *Symington & Co v Union Insurance*

Society of Canton Ltd (1928) 34 Com Cas 23, 233, CA (goods covered 'from the time of leaving the shippers' or manufacturers' warehouse during the ordinary course of transit'); *Renton (G H) & Co v Black Sea and Baltic General Insurance Co* [1941] 1 All ER 149, KB (goods covered 'until discharged at port of destination'); *Ide and Christie v Chalmers and White* (1900) 5 Com Cas 212 (the stipulation in a jute contract, 'Insurance . . . to be effected under an FPA policy on usual Lloyd's conditions,' implies a policy containing a 'warehouse to warehouse' clause); *Marten v Nippon Sea and Land Insurance Co Ltd* (1898) 3 Com Cas 164 (a 'warehouse to warehouse' clause, being a usual and common clause, was incorporated into a policy of reinsurance in the usual form); *Overseas Commodities Ltd v Style* [1958] 1 Lloyd's Rep 546, QB (Commercial Court) ('final warehouse'); *John Martin of London Ltd v Russell* [1960] 1 Lloyd's Rep 554, QB (Commercial Court) ('final warehouse'); *Reinhart Co v Joshua Hoyle & Sons Ltd* [1961] 1 Lloyd's Rep 346 ('country damage'). See further the American cases of *Plata American Trading Inc and Nord-Handel Gesellschaft Ruecker-Giehr & Co v Lancashire* [1957] 2 Lloyd's Rep 347 (New York Supreme Court) (tallow pumped from tank to ship), and *Industrial Waxes Inc v Brown* [1958] 2 Lloyd's Rep 626, US Court of Appeals, Second Circuit (assured not entitled to unlimited storage at port of discharge).

9. Termination of Contract of Carriage Clause.

If owing to circumstances beyond the control of the Assured either the contract of carriage is terminated at a port or place other than the destination named therein or the transit is otherwise terminated before delivery of the goods as provided for in Clause 8 above, then this insurance shall also terminate *unless prompt notice is given to the Underwriters and continuation of cover is requested when the insurance shall remain in force, subject to an additional premium if required by the Underwriters*, either

9.1   until the goods are sold and delivered at such port or place, or, unless otherwise specially agreed, until the expiry of 60 days after arrival of the goods hereby insured at such port or place, whichever shall first occur,

or

9.2   if the goods are forwarded within the said period of 60 days (or any agreed extension thereof) to the destination named herein or to any other destination, until terminated in accordance with the provisions of Clause 8 above.

Note

When the contract of affreightment is terminated or the adventure is otherwise terminated before delivery of the goods, the assured must give prompt notice, and if required to do so, will have to pay an additional premium. Where no arrangement as to the payment of the additional premium is made, a reasonable additional premium is payable: s 31(2) (see p 47, ante).

10. Change of Voyage Clause.

Where, after attachment of this insurance, the destination is changed by the Assured, *held covered at a premium and on conditions to be arranged subject to prompt notice being given to the Underwriters.*

Notes

A change of voyage discharges the insurer from liability: s 45(2) (see p 67, ante). This clause avoids this result provided that the assured is willing to pay an additional premium.

Meaning of 'change of voyage'. See s 45(1) (p 67, ante).

Additional premium. See s 31(2) (p 47, ante).

CLAIMS

11. Insurable Interest Clause.

11.1   In order to recover under this insurance the Assured must have an insurable interest in the subject-matter insured at the time of the loss.

11.2   Subject to 11.1 above, the Assured shall be entitled to recover for insured loss occurring during the period covered by this insurance, notwithstanding that the loss occurred before the contract of insurance was concluded, unless the Assured were aware of the loss and the Underwriters were not.

Note

This clause has the same effect as s 6(1) (see p 13, ante).

12. Forwarding Charges Clause. Where, as a result of the operation of a risk covered by this insurance, the insured transit is terminated at a port or place other than that to which the subject-matter is covered under this insurance, the Underwriters will reimburse the Assured for any extra charges properly and reasonably incurred in unloading storing and forwarding the subject-matter to the destination to which it is insured hereunder.

This Clause 12, which does not apply to general average or salvage charges, shall be subject to the exclusions contained in Clauses 4, 5, 6 and 7 above, and shall not include charges arising from the fault negligence insolvency or financial default of the Assured or their servants.

Notes

This clause explains that in the circumstances specified in it the insurers will pay the costs of unloading, storing and forwarding the cargo to its destination.

General average. See s 66 (p 109, ante).

Salvage charges. See s 65 (p 107, ante).

13. Constructive Total Loss Clause. No claim for Constructive Total Loss shall be recoverable hereunder unless the subject-matter insured is reasonably abandoned either on account of its actual total loss appearing to be unavoidable or because the cost of recovering, reconditioning and forwarding the subject-matter to the destination to which it is insured would exceed its value on arrival.

Note

This clause repeats the effect of s 60(1) (p 90, ante) and s 60(2)(iii) (p 91, ante).[1]

1 For a case where the assured failed to prove that there was a constructive total loss of some steel pipes which were insured under a policy containing this clause, see *Boon and Cheah Steel Pipes Sdn Bhd v Asia Insurance Co Ltd* [1975] 1 Lloyd's Rep 452, Malaysia High Court. (See the judgment of Raja Azlan Shah J, ibid, at p 454.)

14. Increased Value Clause.
14.1   If any Increased Value insurance is effected by the Assured on the cargo insured herein the agreed value of the cargo shall be deemed to be increased to the total amount insured under this insurance and all Increased Value insurances covering the loss, and liability under this insurance shall be in such proportion as the sum insured herein bears to such total amount insured.
In the event of claim the Assured shall provide the Underwriters with evidence of the amounts insured under all other insurances.
14.2   **Where this insurance is on Increased Value the following clause shall apply:**
The agreed value of the cargo shall be deemed to be equal to the total amount insured under the primary insurance and all Increased Value insurances covering the loss and effected on the cargo by the Assured, and liability under this insurance shall be in such proportion as the sum insured herein bears to such total amount insured.
In the event of claim the Assured shall provide the Underwriters with evidence of the amounts insured under all other insurances.

Notes

This clause sets out the effect of increasing the 'agreed value' of the cargo.

Agreed value. See s 27 (p 42, ante).

BENEFIT OF INSURANCE

15. Not to Inure Clause. This insurance shall not inure to the benefit of the carrier or other bailee.

Note

Intention of clause. The intention of this clause is to prevent the benefit of the insurance policy from accruing to the carrier or other bailee. Some carriers and bailees, prohibited by statute from contracting out of all liability, include a clause in the contract of carriage or bailment that the benefit of any insurance on the goods shall inure for the benefit of the carrier or bailee.

MINIMISING LOSSES

16. Duty of Assured Clause. It is the duty of the Assured and their servants and agents in respect of loss recoverable hereunder

16.1 to take such measures as may be reasonable for the purpose of averting or minimising such loss, and

16.2 to ensure that all rights against carriers, bailees or other third parties are properly preserved and exercised

and the Underwriters will, in addition to any loss recoverable hereunder, reimburse the Assured for any charges properly and reasonably incurred in pursuance of these duties.

Note

This clause is in similar words to the Institute Time Clauses (Hulls), Clause 13.1 and Clause 13.2 (Duty of Assured (Sue and Labour)), and explains that it is the assured's duty to ensure that all rights against carriers etc are preserved and exercised.

As to the Institute TimeClauses (Hulls), Clause 13 and the notes thereto, see p 184, ante.

17. Waiver Clause. Measures taken by the Assured or the Underwriters with the object of saving, protecting or recovering the subject-matter insured shall not be considered as a waiver or acceptance of abandonment or otherwise prejudice the rights of either party.

Note

This clause is in the same words as the Institute Time Clauses (Hulls), Clause 13.3 (Duty of Assured (Sue and Labour)).

As to that clause and the notes thereto, see p 184, ante.

AVOIDANCE OF DELAY

18. Reasonable Despatch Clause. It is a condition of this insurance that the Assured shall act with reasonable despatch in all circumstances within their control.

Note

In each case it is a question of fact whether or not the assured has acted with reasonable despatch.

LAW AND PRACTICE

19. English Law and Practice Clause. The insurance is subject to English law and Practice.

NOTE: It is necessary for the Assured when they become aware of an event which is 'held covered' under this insurance to give prompt notice to the Underwriters and the right to such cover is dependent upon compliance with this obligation.

1/1/82   (FOR USE ONLY WITH THE NEW MARINE POLICY FORM)

INSTITUTE CARGO CLAUSES (B)

RISKS COVERED

1. Risks Clause. This insurance covers, except as provided in Clauses 4, 5, 6 and 7 below,

1.1	loss of or damage to the subject-matter insured reasonably attributable to
1.1.1	fire or explosion
1.1.2	vessel or craft being stranded grounded sunk or capsized
1.1.3	overturning or derailment of land conveyance
1.1.4	collision or contact of vessel craft or conveyance with any external object other than water
1.1.5	discharge of cargo at a port of distress
1.1.6	earthquake volcanic eruption or lightning,
1.2	loss of or damage to the subject-matter insured caused by
1.2.1	general average sacrifice
1.2.2	jettison or washing overboard
1.2.3	entry of sea lake or river water into vessel craft hold conveyance container liftvan or place of storage,
1.3	total loss of any package lost overboard or dropped whilst loading on to, or unloading from, vessel or craft.

Notes

This clause sets out the perils insured against (subject to specified exceptions).

The cover provided is less than that under the Institute Cargo Clauses (A) (see pp 239–249, ante), and, accordingly, the premium payable is smaller. But it is, of course, larger than under the Institute Cargo Clauses (C) (see pp 256–263, post).

Clause 4. This is the 'General Exclusions' Clause (see p 250, post).

Clause 5. This is the 'Unseaworthiness and Unfitness' clause (see p 251, post).

Clause 6. This is the 'War Exclusion' clause (see p 252, post).

Clause 7. This is the 'Strikes Exclusion' clause (see p 252, post).

Fire. See p 172, ante.

Explosion. See p 172, ante.

General average sacrifice. See s 66 (p 109, ante).

Jettison. See p 173, ante.

Entry of seawater. See under 'perils of the sea' (p 171, ante).

2. General Average Clause. This insurance covers general average and salvage charges, adjusted or determined according to the contract of affreightment and/or the governing law and practice, incurred to avoid or in connection with the avoidance of loss from any cause except those excluded in Clauses 4, 5, 6 and 7 or elsewhere in this insurance.

Note

This clause in the same words as the Institute Cargo Clauses (A), Clause 2 (see p 240, ante).

3. 'Both to Blame Collision' Clause. This insurance is extended to indemnify the Assured against such proportion of liability under the contract of affreightment 'Both to Blame Collision' Clause as is in respect of a loss recoverable hereunder.
In the event of any claim by shipowners under the said Clause the Assured agree to notify the Underwriters who shall have the right, at their own cost and expense, to defend the Assured against such claim.

Note

This clause is in the same words as the Institute Cargo Clauses (A), Clause 3 (see p 240, ante).

EXCLUSIONS

4. General Exclusions Clause. In no case shall this insurance cover
4.1   loss damage or expense attributable to wilful misconduct of the Assured

Institute Cargo Clauses (B) 251

4.2 ordinary leakage, ordinary loss in weight or volume, or ordinary wear and tear of the subject-matter insured

4.3 loss damage or expense caused by insufficiency or unsuitability of packing or preparation of the subject-matter insured (for the purpose of this Clause 4.3 'packing' shall be deemed to include stowage in a container or liftvan but only when such stowage is carried out prior to attachment of this insurance or by the Assured or their servants)

4.4 loss damage or expense caused by inherent vice or nature of the subject-matter insured

4.5 loss damage or expense proximately caused by delay, even though the delay be caused by a risk insured against (except expenses payable under Clause 2 above)

4.6 loss damage or expense arising from insolvency or financial default of the owners managers charterers or operators of the vessel

4.7 deliberate damage to or deliberate destruction of the subject-matter insured or any part thereof by the wrongful act of any person or persons

4.8 loss damage or expense arising from the use of any weapon of war employing atomic or nuclear fission and/or fusion or other like reaction or radioactive force or matter.

Note

This clause is in the same words as the Institute Cargo Clauses (A), Clause 4 except that it also excludes 'deliberate damage to or deliberate destruction of the subject-matter insured or any part thereof, by the wrongful act of any person or persons'.

As to the Institute Cargo Clauses (A), Clause 4, see p 241, ante.

5. Unseaworthiness and Unfitness Exclusion Clause.

5.1 In no case shall this insurance cover loss damage or expense arising from

> unseaworthiness of vessel or craft
> unfitness of vessel craft conveyance container or liftvan for the safe carriage of the subject-matter insured,

where the Assured or their servants are privy to such unseaworthiness or unfitness, at the time the subject-matter insured is loaded therein.

5.2 The Underwriters waive any breach of the implied warranties of seaworthiness of the ship and fitness of the ship to carry the subject-matter insured to destination, unless the Assured or their servants are privy to such unseaworthiness or unfitness.

Note

This clause is in the same words as the Institute Cargo Clauses (A), Clause 5 (see p 242, ante).

6. War Exclusion Clause. In no case shall this insurance cover loss damage or expense caused by
- 6.1 war civil war revolution rebellion insurrection, or civil strife arising therefrom, or any hostile act by or against a belligerent power
- 6.2 capture seizure arrest restraint or detainment, and the consequences thereof or any attempt thereat
- 6.3 derelict mines torpedoes bombs or other derelict weapons of war.

Note

This clause is in the same words as the Institute Cargo Clauses (A), Clause 6 (see p 243, ante).

7. Strikes Exclusion Clause. In no case shall this insurance cover loss damage or expense
- 7.1 caused by strikers, locked-out workmen, or persons taking part in labour disturbances, riots or civil commotions
- 7.2 resulting from strikes, lock-outs, labour disturbances, riots or civil commotions
- 7.3 caused by any terrorist or any person acting from a political motive.

Note

This clause is in the same words as the Institute Cargo Clauses (A), Clause 7 (see p 243, ante).

DURATION

8. Transit Clause.
- 8.1 This insurance attaches from the time the goods leave the warehouse or place of storage at the place named herein for the commencement of the transit, continues during the ordinary course of transit and terminates either
- 8.1.1 on delivery to the Consignees' or other final warehouse or place of storage at the destination named herein,
- 8.1.2 on delivery to any other warehouse or place of storage, whether prior to or at the destination named herein, which the Assured elect to use either
- 8.1.2.1 for storage other than in the ordinary course of transit or
- 8.1.2.2 for allocation or distribution,
  or
- 8.1.3 on the expiry of 60 days after completion of discharge overside of the goods hereby insured from the oversea vessel at the final port of discharge,

whichever shall first occur.

8.2 If, after discharge overside from the oversea vessel at the final port of discharge, but prior to termination of this insurance, the goods are to be forwarded to a destination other than that to which they are insured hereunder, this insurance, whilst remaining subject to termination as provided for above, shall not extend beyond the commencement of transit to such other destination.

8.3 This insurance shall remain in force (subject to termination as provided for above and to the provisions of Clause 9 below) during delay beyond the control of the Assured, any deviation, forced discharge, reshipment or transhipment and during any variation of the adventure arising from the exercise of a liberty granted to shipowners or charterers under the contract of affreightment.

Note

This clause is in the same words as the Institute Cargo Clauses (A), Clause 8 (see p 243, ante).

9. Termination of Contract of Carriage Clause. If owing to circumstances beyond the control of the Assured either the contract of carriage is terminated at a port or place other than the destination named therein or the transit is otherwise terminated before delivery of the goods as provided for in Clause 8 above, then this insurance shall also terminate *unless prompt notice is given to the Underwriters and continuation of cover is requested when the insurance shall remain in force, subject to an additional premium if required by the Underwriters,* either

9.1 until the goods are sold and delivered at such port or place, or, unless otherwise specially agreed, until the expiry of 60 days after arrival of the goods hereby insured at such port or place, whichever shall first occur,

or

9.2 if the goods are forwarded within the said period of 60 days (or any agreed extension thereof) to the destination named herein or to any other destination, until terminated in accordance with the provisions of Clause 8 above.

Note

This clause is in the same words as the Institute Cargo Clauses (A), Clause 9 (see p 245, ante).

10. Change of Voyage Clause. Where, after attachment of this insurance, the destination is changed by the Assured, *held covered at a premium and on conditions to be arranged subject to prompt notice being given to the Underwriters.*

Note

This clause is in the same words as the Institute Cargo Clauses (A), Clause 10 (see p 245, ante).

CLAIMS

11. Insurable Interest Clause.

11.1 In order to recover under this insurance the Assured must have an insurable interest in the subject-matter insured at the time of the loss.

11.2 Subject to 11.1 above, the Assured shall be entitled to recover for insured loss occurring during the period covered by this insurance, notwithstanding that the loss occurred before the contract of insurance was concluded, unless the Assured were aware of the loss and the Underwriters were not.

Note

This clause is in the same words as the Institute Cargo Clauses (A), Clause 11 (see p 246, ante).

12. Forwarding Charges Clause. Where, as a result of the operation of a risk covered by this insurance, the insured transit is terminated at a port or place other than that to which the subject-matter is covered under this insurance, the Underwriters will reimburse the Assured for any extra charges properly and reasonably incurred in unloading storing and forwarding the subject-matter to the destination to which it is insured hereunder.

This Clause 12, which does not apply to general average or salvage charges, shall be subject to the exclusions contained in Clauses 4, 5, 6 and 7 above, and shall not include charges arising from the fault negligence insolvency or financial default of the Assured or their servants.

Note

This clause is in the same words as the Institute Cargo Clauses (A), Clause 12 (see p 246, ante).

13. Constructive Total Loss Clause. No claim for Constructive Total Loss shall be recoverable hereunder unless the subject-matter insured is reasonably abandoned either on account of its actual total loss appearing to be unavoidable or because the cost of recovering, reconditioning and forwarding the subject-matter to the destination to which it is insured would exceed its value on arrival.

Note

This clause is in the same words as the Institute Cargo Clauses (A), Clause 13 (see p 246, ante).

14. Increased Value Clause.

14.1 If any Increased Value insurance is effected by the Assured on the cargo insured herein the agreed value of the cargo shall be deemed to be increased to the total amount insured under this insurance and all Increased Value insurances covering the loss, and liability under this insurance shall be in such proportion as the sum insured herein bears to such total amount insured.
In the event of claim the Assured shall provide the Underwriters with evidence of the amounts insured under all other insurances.

14.2 **Where this insurance is on Increased Value the following clause shall apply:**
The agreed value of the cargo shall be deemed to be equal to the total amount insured under the primary insurance and all Increased Value insurances covering the loss and effected on the cargo by the Assured, and liability under this insurance shall be in such proportion as the sum insured herein bears to such total amount insured.
In the event of claim the Assured shall provide the Underwriters with evidence of the amounts insured under all other insurances.

Note

This clause is in the same words as the Institute Cargo Clauses (A), Clause 14 (see p 247, ante).

BENEFIT OF INSURANCE

15. Not to Inure Clause. This insurance shall not inure to the benefit of the carrier or other bailee.

Note

This clause is in the same words as the Institute Cargo Clauses (A), Clause 15 (see p 247, ante).

MINIMISING LOSSES

16. Duty of Assured Clause. It is the duty of the Assured and their servants and agents in respect of loss recoverable hereunder

16.1 to take such measures as may be reasonable for the purpose of averting or minimising such loss,
and

16.2 to ensure that all rights against carriers, bailees or other third parties are properly preserved and exercised

and the Underwriters will, in addition to any loss recoverable hereunder, reimburse the Assured for any charges properly and reasonably incurred in pursuance of these duties.

Note

This clause is in the same words as the Institute Cargo Clauses (A), Clause 16 (see p 248, ante).

17. Waiver Clause. Measures taken by the Assured or the Underwriters with the object of saving, protecting or recovering the subject-matter insured shall not be considered as a waiver or acceptance of abandonment or otherwise prejudice the rights of either party.

Note

This clause is in the same words as the Institute Cargo Clauses (A), Clause 17 (see p 248, ante).

AVOIDANCE OF DELAY

18. Reasonable Despatch Clause. It is a condition of this insurance that the Assured shall act with reasonable despatch in all circumstances within their control.

Note

This clause is in the same words as the Institute Cargo Clauses (A), Clause 18 (see p 248, ante).

LAW AND PRACTICE

19. English Law and Practice Clause. This insurance is subject to English law and practice.

NOTE: It is necessary for the Assured when they become aware of an event which is 'held covered' under this insurance to give prompt notice to the Underwriters and the right to such cover is dependent upon compliance with this obligation.

1/1/82 (FOR USE ONLY WITH THE NEW MARINE POLICY FORM)

INSTITUTE CARGO CLAUSES (C)

RISKS COVERED

1. Risks Clause. This insurance covers, except as provided in Clauses 4, 5, 6 and 7 below,
1.1   loss of or damage to the subject-matter insured reasonably attributable to

1.1.1 fire or explosion
1.1.2 vessel or craft being stranded grounded sunk or capsized
1.1.3 overturning or derailment of land conveyance
1.1.4 collision or contact of vessel craft or conveyance with any external object other than water
1.1.5 discharge of cargo at a port of distress,
1.2 loss of or damage to the subject-matter insured caused by
1.2.1 general average sacrifice
1.2.2 jettison.

Notes

This clause is in similar words to the Institute Cargo Clauses (B), Clause 1, but it does not cover loss or damage caused by (i) earthquake, volcanic eruption or lightning; or (ii) washing overboard; or (iii) entry of seawater into the vessel; or (iv) total loss of any package lost overboard or dropped whilst loading on to, or unloading from, vessel or craft.

Of course, the premium payable under the Institute Cargo Clauses (C) is less than that under the Institute Cargo Clauses (B).

As to the Institute Cargo Clauses (B), Clause 1, see p 249, ante.

Clause 4. This is the 'General Exclusions' clause (see p 258, post).

Clause 5. This is the 'Unseaworthiness and Unfitness' clause (see p 258, post).

Clause 6. This is the 'War Exclusion' clause (see p 259, post).

Clause 7. This is the 'Strikes Exclusion' clause (see p 259, post).

2. General Average Clause. This insurance covers general average and salvage charges, adjusted or determined according to the contract of affreightment and/or the governing law and practice, incurred to avoid or in connection with the avoidance of loss from any cause except those excluded in Clauses 4, 5, 6 and 7 or elsewhere in this insurance.

Note

This clause is in the same words as the Institute Cargo Clauses (A), Clause 2 (see p 240, ante).

3. 'Both to Blame Collision' Clause. This insurance is extended to indemnify the Assured against such proportion of liability under the contract of affreightment 'Both to Blame Collision' Clause as is in respect of a loss recoverable hereunder.

In the event of any claim by shipowners under the said Clause the Assured agree to notify the Underwriters who shall have the right, at their own cost and expense, to defend the Assured against such claim.

Note

This clause is in the same words as the Institute Cargo Clauses (A), Clause 3 (see p 240, ante).

EXCLUSIONS

4. General Exclusions Clause. In no case shall this insurance cover

4.1   loss damage or expense attributable to wilful misconduct of the Assured

4.2   ordinary leakage, ordinary loss in weight or volume, or ordinary wear and tear of the subject-matter insured

4.3   loss damage or expense caused by insufficiency or unsuitability of packing or preparation of the subject-matter insured (for the purpose of this Clause 4.3 'packing' shall be deemed to include stowage in a container or liftvan but only when such stowage is carried out prior to attachment of this insurance or by the Assured or their servants)

4.4   loss damage or expense caused by inherent vice or nature of the subject-matter insured

4.5   loss damage or expense proximately caused by delay, even though the delay be caused by a risk insured against (except expenses payable under Clause 2 above)

4.6   loss damage or expense arising from insolvency or financial default of the owners managers charterers or operators of the vessel

4.7   deliberate damage to or deliberate destruction of the subject-matter insured or any part thereof by the wrongful act of any person or persons

4.8   loss damage or expense arising from the use of any weapon of war employing atomic or nuclear fission and/or fusion or other like reaction or radioactive force or matter.

Note

This clause is in the same words as the Institute Cargo Clauses (B), Clause 4 (see p 250, ante).

5. Unseaworthiness and Unfitness Exclusion Clause.

5.1   In no case shall this insurance cover loss damage or expense arising from

unseaworthiness of vessel or craft,

unfitness of vessel craft conveyance container or liftvan for the safe carriage of the subject-matter insured,

where the Assured or their servants are privy to such unseaworthiness or unfitness, at the time the subject-matter insured is loaded therein.

5.2 The Underwriters waive any breach of the implied warranties of seaworthiness of the ship and fitness of the ship to carry the subject-matter insured to destination, unless the Assured or their servants are privy to such unseaworthiness or unfitness.

Note

This clause is in the same words as the Institute Cargo Clauses (A), Clause 5 (see p 242, ante).

6. War Exclusion Clause. In no case shall this insurance cover loss damage or expense caused by
6.1 war civil war revolution rebellion insurrection, or civil strife arising therefrom, or any hostile act by or against a belligerent power
6.2 capture seizure arrest restraint or detainment, and the consequences thereof or any attempt thereat
6.3 derelict mines torpedoes bombs or other derelict weapons of war.

Note

This clause is in the same words as the Institute Cargo Clauses (A), Clause 6 (see p 243, ante).

7. Strikes Exclusion Clause. In no case shall this insurance cover loss damage or expense
7.1 caused by strikers, locked-out workmen, or persons taking part in labour disturbances, riots or civil commotions
7.2 resulting from strikes, lock-outs, labour disturbances, riots or civil commotions
7.3 caused by any terrorist or any person acting from a political motive.

Note

This clause is in the same words as the Institute Cargo Clauses (A), Clause 7 (see p 243, ante).

DURATION

8. Transit Clause.
8.1 This insurance attaches from the time the goods leave the warehouse or place of storage at the place named herein for the commencement of the transit, continues during the ordinary course of transit and terminates either
8.1.1 on delivery to the Consignees' or other final warehouse or place of storage at the destination named herein,

8.1.2   on delivery to any other warehouse or place of storage, whether prior to or at the destination named herein, which the Assured elect to use either
8.1.2.1   for storage other than in the ordinary course of transit or
8.1.2.2   for allocation or distribution,
or
8.1.3   on the expiry of 60 days after completion of discharge overside of the goods hereby insured from the oversea vessel at the final port of discharge,
whichever shall first occur.
8.2   If, after discharge overside from the oversea vessel at the final port of discharge, but prior to termination of this insurance, the goods are to be forwarded to a destination other than that to which they are insured hereunder, this insurance, whilst remaining subject to termination as provided for above, shall not extend beyond the commencement of transit to such other destination.
8.3   This insurance shall remain in force (subject to termination as provided for above and to the provisions of Clause 9 below) during delay beyond the control of the Assured, any deviation, forced discharge, reshipment or transhipment and during any variation of the adventure arising from the exercise of a liberty granted to shipowners or charterers under the contract of affreightment.

Note

This clause is in the same words as the Institute Cargo Clauses (A), Clause 8 (see p 243, ante).

9. Termination of Contract of Carriage Clause. If owing to circumstances beyond the control of the Assured either the contract of carriage is terminated at a port or place other than the destination named therein or the transit is otherwise terminated before delivery of the goods as provided for in Clause 8 above, then this insurance shall also terminate *unless prompt notice is given to the Underwriters and continuation of cover is requested when the insurance shall remain in force, subject to an additional premium if required by the Underwriters*, either

9.1   until the goods are sold and delivered at such port or place, or, unless otherwise specially agreed, until the expiry of 60 days after arrival of the goods hereby insured at such port or place, whichever shall first occur,
or
9.2   if the goods are forwarded within the said period of 60 days (or any agreed extension thereof) to the destination named herein or to any other destination, until terminated in accordance with the provisions of Clause 8 above.

Note

This clause is in the same words as the Institute Cargo Clauses (A), Clause 9 (see p 245, ante).

10. Change of Voyage Clause. Where, after attachment of this insurance, the destination is changed by the Assured, *held covered at a premium and on conditions to be arranged subject to prompt notice being given to the Underwriters.*

Note

This clause is in the same words as the Institute Cargo Clauses (A), Clause 10 (see p 245, ante).

CLAIMS

11. Insurable Interest Clause.

11.1   In order to recover under this insurance the Assured must have an insurable interest in the subject-matter insured at the time of the loss.

11.2   Subject to 11.1 above, the Assured shall be entitled to recover for insured loss occurring during the period covered by this insurance, notwithstanding that the loss occurred before the contract of insurance was concluded, unless the Assured were aware of the loss and the Underwriters were not.

Note

This clause is in the same words as the Institute Cargo Clauses (A), Clause 11 (see p 246, ante).

12. Forwarding Charges Clause. Where, as a result of the operation of a risk covered by this insurance, the insured transit is terminated at a port or place other than that to which the subject-matter is covered under this insurance, the Underwriters will reimburse the Assured for any extra charges properly and reasonably incurred in unloading storing and forwarding the subject-matter to the destination to which it is insured hereunder.

This Clause 12, which does not apply to general average or salvage charges, shall be subject to the exclusions contained in Clauses 4, 5, 6 and 7 above, and shall not include charges arising from the fault negligence insolvency or financial default of the Assured or their servants.

Note

This clause is in the same words as the Institute Cargo Clauses (A), Clause 12 (see p 246, ante).

13. Constructive Total Loss Clause. No claim for Constructive Total Loss shall be recoverable hereunder unless the subject-matter insured is reasonably abandoned either on account of its actual total loss appearing to be unavoidable or because the cost of recovering, reconditioning and forwarding the subject-matter to the destination to which it is insured would exceed its value on arrival.

Note

This clause is in the same words as the Institute Cargo Clauses (A), Clause 13 (see p 246, ante).

14. Increased Value Clause.

14.1   If any Increased Value insurance is effected by the Assured on the cargo insured herein the agreed value of the cargo shall be deemed to be increased to the total amount insured under this insurance and all Increased Value insurances covering the loss, and liability under this insurance shall be in such proportion as the sum insured herein bears to such total amount insured.

In the event of claim the Assured shall provide the Underwriters with evidence of the amounts insured under all other insurances.

14.2   **Where this insurance is on Increased Value the following clause shall apply:**

The agreed value of the cargo shall be deemed to be equal to the total amount insured under the primary insurance and all Increased Value insurances covering the loss and effected on the cargo by the Assured, and liability under this insurance shall be in such proportion as the sum insured herein bears to such total amount insured.

In the event of claim the Assured shall provide the Underwriters with evidence of the amounts insured under all other insurances.

Note

This clause is in the same words as the Institute Cargo Clauses (A), Clause 14 (see p 247, ante).

BENEFIT OF INSURANCE

15. Not to Inure Clause. This insurance shall not inure to the benefit of the carrier or other bailee.

Note

This clause is in the same words as the Institute Cargo Clauses (A), Clause 15 (see p 247, ante).

MINIMISING LOSSES

16. Duty of Assured Clause. It is the duty of the Assured and their servants and agents in respect of loss recoverable hereunder

16.1   to take such measures as may be reasonable for the purpose of averting or minimising such loss, and

16.2   to ensure that all rights against carriers, bailees or other third parties are properly preserved and exercised

and the Underwriters will, in addition to any loss recoverable hereunder, reimburse the Assured for any charges properly and reasonably incurred in pursuance of these duties.

Note

This clause is in the same words as the Institute Cargo Clauses (A), Clause 16 (see p 248, ante).

17. Waiver Clause. Measures taken by the Assured or the Underwriters with the object of saving, protecting or recovering the subject-matter insured shall not be considered as a waiver or acceptance of abandonment or otherwise prejudice the rights of either party.

Note

This clause is in the same words as the Institute Cargo Clauses (A), Clause 17 (see p 248, ante).

AVOIDANCE OF DELAY

18. Reasonable Despatch Clause. It is a condition of this insurance that the Assured shall act with reasonable despatch in all circumstances within their control.

Note

This clause is in the same words as the Institute Cargo Clauses (A), Clause 18 (see p 248, ante).

LAW AND PRACTICE

19. English Law and Practice Clause. This insurance is subject to English law and practice.

NOTE: It is necessary for the Assured when they become aware of an event which is 'held covered' under this insurance to give prompt notice to the Underwriters and the right to such cover is dependent upon compliance with this obligation.

1/1/82   (FOR USE ONLY WITH THE NEW MARINE POLICY FORM)

INSTITUTE WAR CLAUSES (CARGO)

RISKS COVERED

1. Risks Clause. This insurance covers, except as provided in Clauses 3 and 4 below, loss of or damage to the subject-matter insured caused by

1.1 war civil war revolution rebellion insurrection, or civil strife arising therefrom, or any hostile act by or against a belligerent power

1.2 capture seizure arrest restraint or detainment, arising from risks covered under 1.1 above, and the consequences thereof or any attempt thereat

1.3 derelict mines torpedoes bombs or other derelict weapons of war.

Note

This clause provides cover in respect of the perils excepted by the Institute Cargo Clauses (A), Clause 6 (war exclusion) (see p 243, ante).

Frustration clause. Three test cases involving the interpretation of this clause were brought before the House of Lords during the Second World War: see *Rickards v Forestal Land, Timber and Rlys Co Ltd et al.*[1]

The following summary of the facts was given by Viscount Simon LC: 'In each of the three cases the claim is by British owners of cargo against Lloyd's underwriters on voyage policies on goods which were shipped in German steamers to places in the British Empire. . . . In each case, the German ship had entered upon the performance of her contract of carriage with the British cargo-owners before the outbreak of war and had not completely performed her contract before the war broke out. Each of these German vessels . . . was subject to German war policy . . . to the effect that, if war threatened between Great Britain and Germany, or if war actually broke out, the ship must take refuge in a neutral port and, if possible, return to Germany with her cargo, or, as a last resort, must scuttle herself rather than be captured. On and after 3 September 1939, there was risk of capture of each of these vessels when outside the territorial waters of any neutral state. The vessels, in each of the three selected cases, deviated from the accustomed and natural course in order to take refuge in other ports in accordance with the general directions which they had received from the German Government. Ultimately they abandoned the contract voyage altogether and made an effort to get back to Germany. Two of them were in danger of being captured in the Allied blockade and accordingly scuttled themselves. The third succeeded in getting through to Hamburg.'[2]

It was decided that there was a constructive total loss when the German captain obeyed the instructions of his government and held the goods as the subject and servant of that government instead of holding them as the bailee of the assured. There had been a 'restraint of princes or peoples'.

But the crucial issue was whether the 'frustration clause' took away from the assured his right to claim for a constructive total loss. On this Viscount Simon said: 'I agree with the Court of Appeal in thinking that the proper interpretation of the frustration clause is not "free of any claim which on the facts might be based on loss of the insured voyage" and that its proper meaning must be "free of any claim which is, in fact, based, because it can only be based, upon loss of the insured voyage".'[3] The result was, therefore, that the underwriters were liable.[4]

1 [1941] 3 All ER 62, HL.
2 Ibid, at pp 64–5.
3 Ibid, at p 66.
4 For a case where underwriters successfully pleaded the 'frustration clause,' see *Atlantic Maritime Co Inc v Gibbon* [1953] 2 All ER 1086, CA.

2. General Average Clause. This insurance covers general average and salvage charges, adjusted or determined according to the contract of affreightment and/or the governing law and practice, incurred to avoid or in connection with the avoidance of loss from a risk covered under these clauses.

Note

This clause is in substantially the same words as the Institute Cargo Clauses (A), Clause 2 (see p 240, ante).

EXCLUSIONS

3. General Exclusions Clause. In no case shall this insurance cover

3.1 loss damage or expense attributable to wilful misconduct of the Assured

3.2 ordinary leakage, ordinary loss in weight or volume, or ordinary wear and tear of the subject-matter insured

3.3 loss damage or expense caused by insufficiency or unsuitability of packing or preparation of the subject-matter insured (for the purpose of this Clause 3.3 'packing' shall be deemed to include stowage in a container or liftvan but only when such stowage is carried out prior to attachment of this insurance or by the Assured or their servants)

3.4 loss damage or expense caused by inherent vice or nature of the subject-matter insured

3.5 loss damage or expense proximately caused by delay, even though the delay be caused by a risk insured against (except expenses payable under Clause 2 above)

3.6 loss damage or expense arising from insolvency or financial default of the owners managers charterers or operators of the vessel

3.7 any claim based upon loss of or frustration of the voyage or adventure

3.8　　　loss damage or expense arising from any hostile use of any weapon of war employing atomic or nuclear fission and/or fusion or other like reaction or radioactive force or matter.

Note

This clause is substantially in the same words as the Institute Cargo Clauses (A), Clause 4 (see p 241, ante), and also states that it does not cover 'any claim based upon loss of or frustration of the voyage or adventure'.

4. Unseaworthiness and Unfitness Exclusion Clause.

4.1　　　In no case shall this insurance cover loss damage or expense arising from

　　　　　unseaworthiness of vessel or craft,
　　　　　unfitness of vessel craft conveyance container or liftvan for the safe carriage of the subject-matter insured,

where the Assured or their servants are privy to such unseaworthiness or unfitness, at the time the subject-matter insured is loaded therein.

4.2　　　The Underwriters waive any breach of the implied warranties of seaworthiness of the ship and fitness of the ship to carry the subject-matter insured to destination, unless the Assured or their servants are privy to such unseaworthiness or unfitness.

Note

This clause is in the same words as the Institute Cargo Clauses (A), Clause 5 (see p 242, ante).

DURATION

5. Transit Clause.

5.1　　　This insurance

5.1.1　　attaches only as the subject-matter insured and as to any part as that part is loaded on an oversea vessel
　　　　　and

5.1.2　　terminates, subject to 5.2 and 5.3 below, either as the subject-matter insured and as to any part as that part is discharged from an oversea vessel at the final port or place of discharge,
　　　　　or
　　　　　on expiry of 15 days counting from midnight of the day of arrival of the vessel at the final port or place of discharge, whichever shall first occur;
　　　　　nevertheless,
　　　　　subject to prompt notice to the Underwriters and to an additional premium,
　　　　　such insurance

5.1.3	reattaches when, without having discharged the subject-matter insured at the final port or place of discharge, the vessel sails therefrom, and
5.1.4	terminates, subject to 5.2 and 5.3 below, either as the subject-matter insured and as to any part as that part is thereafter discharged from the vessel at the final (or substituted) port or place of discharge,

or

on expiry of 15 days counting from midnight of the day of re-arrival of the vessel at the final port or place of discharge or arrival of the vessel at a substituted port or place of discharge, whichever shall first occur.

5.2	If during the insured voyage the oversea vessel arrives at an intermediate port or place to discharge the subject-matter insured for on-carriage by oversea vessel or by aircraft, or the goods are discharged from the vessel at a port or place of refuge, then, subject to 5.3 below and to an additional premium if required, this insurance continues until the expiry of 15 days counting from midnight of the day of arrival of the vessel at such port or place, but thereafter reattaches as the subject-matter insured and as to any part as that part is loaded on an on-carrying oversea vessel or aircraft. During the period of 15 days the insurance remains in force after discharge only whilst the subject-matter is insured and as to any part as that part is at such port or place. If the goods are on-carried within the said period of 15 days or if the insurance reattaches as provided in this Clause 5.2
5.2.1	where the on-carriage is by oversea vessel this insurance continues subject to the terms of these clauses, or
5.2.2	where the on-carriage is by aircraft, the current Institute War Clauses (Air Cargo) (excluding sendings by Post) shall be deemed to form part of this insurance and shall apply to the on-carriage by air.
5.3	If the voyage in the contract of carriage is terminated at a port or place other than the destination agreed therein, such port or place shall be deemed the final port of discharge and such insurance terminates in accordance with 5.1.2. If the subject-matter insured is subsequently reshipped to the original or any other destination, then *provided notice is given to the Underwriters before the commencement of such further transit and subject to an additional premium*, such insurance reattaches
5.3.1	in the case of the subject-matter insured having been discharged, as the subject-matter insured and as to any part as that part is loaded on the on-carrying vessel for the voyage;

5.3.2   in the case of the subject-matter not having been discharged, when the vessel sails from such deemed final port of discharge;

thereafter such insurance terminates in accordance with 5.1.4.

5.4   The insurance against the risks of mines and derelict torpedoes, floating or submerged, is extended whilst the subject-matter insured or any part thereof is on craft whilst in transit to or from the oversea vessel, but in no case beyond the expiry of 60 days after discharge from the oversea vessel unless otherwise specially agreed by the Underwriters.

5.5   *Subject to prompt notice to Underwriters, and to an additional premium if required*, this insurance shall remain in force within the provisions of these Clauses during any deviation, or any variation of the adventure arising from the exercise of a liberty granted to shipowners or charterers under the contract of affreightment.

(for the purpose of Clause 5

'arrival' shall be deemed to mean that the vessel is anchored, moored or otherwise secured at a berth or place within the Harbour Authority area. If such a berth or place is not available, arrival is deemed to have occurred when the vessel first anchors, moors or otherwise secures either at or off the intended port or place of discharge

'oversea vessel' shall be deemed to mean a vessel carrying the subject-matter from one port or place to another where such voyage involves a sea passage by that vessel).

Note

This clause shows when the risk on the cargo begins and ends.

It fulfils the same purpose as the Institute Cargo Clauses (A), Clause 8 (transit clause), the principal differences in the wording being that (i) the risk commences when the cargo or any part of it is loaded on an *oversea vessel*; (ii) in some cases an additional premium is required (see s 31(2), p 47, ante); (iii) there is a provision for on-carriage by aircraft; and (iv) there is an extension of the risk in respect of mines and derelict torpedoes.

6. Change of Voyage Clause. Where, after attachment of this insurance, the destination is changed by the Assured, *held covered at a premium and on conditions to be arranged subject to prompt notice being given to the Underwriters.*

Note

This clause is in the same terms as the Institute Cargo Clauses (A), Clause 10 (see p 245, ante).

7. Anything contained in this contract which is inconsistent with Clauses 3.7, 3.8 or 5 shall, to the extent of such inconsistency, be null and void.

Note

This clause emphasises the paramount importance of the other clauses mentioned in it.

Clause 3.7. This states that there is no cover for 'any claim based upon loss of or frustration of the voyage or adventure' (see p 265, ante).

Clause 3.8. This excludes 'loss damage or expense arising from any hostile use of any weapon of war employing atomic or nuclear fission and/or fusion or other like reaction or radioactive force or matter' (see p 266, ante).

Clause 5. This is the 'Transit' clause (see p 266, ante).

CLAIMS

8. Insurable Interest Clause.

8.1   In order to recover under this insurance the Assured must have an insurable interest in the subject-matter insured at the time of the loss.

8.2   Subject to 8.1 above, the Assured shall be entitled to recover for insured loss occurring during the period covered by this insurance, notwithstanding that the loss occurred before the contract of insurance was concluded, unless the Assured were aware of the loss and the Underwriters were not.

Note

This clause is in the same words as the Institute Cargo Clauses (A), Clause 11 (see p 246, ante).

9. Increased Value Clause.

9.1   If any Increased Value insurance is effected by the Assured on the cargo insured herein the agreed value of the cargo shall be deemed to be increased to the total amount insured under this insurance and all Increased Value insurances covering the loss, and liability under this insurance shall be in such proportion as the sum insured herein bears to such total amount insured.

In the event of claim the Assured shall provide the Underwriters with evidence of the amounts insured under all other insurances.

9.2   **Where this insurance is on Increased Value the following clause shall apply:**
The agreed value of the cargo shall be deemed to be equal to the total amount insured under the primary insurance and all Increased Value insurances covering the loss and effected on the cargo by the Assured, and liability under this insurance

shall be in such proportion as the sum insured herein bears to such total amount insured.

In the event of claim the Assured shall provide the Underwriters with evidence of the amounts insured under all other insurances.

Note

This clause is in the same words as the Institute Cargo Clauses (A), Clause 14 (see p 247, ante).

BENEFIT OF INSURANCE

10. Not to Inure Clause. This insurance shall not inure to the benefit of the carrier or other bailee.

Note

This clause is in the same words as the Institute Cargo Clauses (A), Clause 15 (see p 247, ante).

MINIMISING LOSSES

11. Duty of Assured Clause. It is the duty of the Assured and their servants and agents in respect of loss recoverable hereunder
11.1   to take such measures as may be reasonable for the purpose of averting or minimising such loss, and
11.2   to ensure that all rights against carriers, bailees or other third parties are properly preserved and exercised

and the Underwriters will, in addition to any loss recoverable hereunder, reimburse the Assured for any charges properly and reasonably incurred in pursuance of these duties.

Note

This clause is in the same words as the Institute Cargo Clauses (A), Clause 16 (see p 248, ante).

12. Waiver Clause. Measures taken by the Assured or the Underwriters with the object of saving, protecting or recovering the subject-matter insured shall not be considered as a waiver or acceptance of abandonment or otherwise prejudice the rights of either party.

Note

This clause is in the same words as the Institute Cargo Clauses (A), Clause 17 (see p 248, ante).

AVOIDANCE OF DELAY

13. Reasonable Despatch Clause. It is a condition of this insurance that the Assured shall act with reasonable despatch in all circumstances within their control.

Note

This clause is in the same words as the Institute Cargo Clauses (A), Clause 18 (see p 248, ante).

LAW AND PRACTICE

14. English Law and Practice Clause. This insurance is subject to English law and practice.

NOTE: It is necessary for the Assured when they become aware of an event which is 'held covered' under this insurance to give prompt notice to the Underwriters and the right to such cover is dependent upon compliance with this obligation.

1/1/82   (FOR USE ONLY WITH THE NEW MARINE POLICY FORM)

INSTITUTE STRIKES CLAUSES (CARGO)

RISK COVERED

1. Risks Clause. This insurance covers, except as provided in Clauses 3 and 4 below, loss of or damage to the subject-matter insured caused by
1.1   strikers, locked-out workmen, or persons taking part in labour disturbances, riots or civil commotions
1.2   any terrorist or any person acting from a political motive.

Note

This clause provides cover in respect of some of the perils excepted by the Institute Cargo Clauses (A), Clause 7 (strikes exclusion) (see p 243, ante).

2. General Average Clause. This insurance covers general average and salvage charges, adjusted or determined according to the contract of affreightment and/or the governing law and practice, incurred to avoid or in connection with the avoidance of loss from a risk covered under these clauses.

Note

This clause is in the same words as the Institute Cargo Clauses (A), Clause 2 (see p 240, ante).

EXCLUSIONS

3. General Exclusions Clause. In no case shall this insurance cover

3.1 loss damage or expense attributable to wilful misconduct of the Assured

3.2 ordinary leakage, ordinary loss in weight or volume, or ordinary wear and tear of the subject-matter insured

3.3 loss damage or expense caused by insufficiency or unsuitability of packing or preparation of the subject-matter insured (for the purpose of this Clause 3.3 'packing' shall be deemed to include stowage in a container or liftvan but only when such stowage is carried out prior to attachment of this insurance or by the Assured or their servants)

3.4 loss damage or expense caused by inherent vice or nature of the subject-matter insured

3.5 loss damage or expense proximately caused by delay, even though the delay be caused by a risk insured against (except expenses payable under Clause 2 above)

3.6 loss damage or expense arising from insolvency or financial default of the owners managers charterers or operators of the vessel

3.7 loss damage or expense arising from the absence shortage or withholding of labour of any description whatsoever resulting from any strike, lockout, labour disturbance, riot or civil commotion

3.8 any claim based upon loss of or frustration of the voyage or adventure

3.9 loss damage or expense arising from the use of any weapon of war employing atomic or nuclear fission and/or fusion or other like reaction or radioactive force or matter

3.10 loss damage or expense caused by war civil war revolution rebellion insurrection, or civil strife arising therefrom, or any hostile act by or against a belligerent power.

Note

This clause contains similar exclusions to the Institute Cargo Clauses (A), Clause 4 (general exclusions) (see p 241, ante), Clause 6 (war exclusion clause) (see p 243, ante) and Clause 7 (strikes exclusion clause) (see p 243, ante).

Frustration clause. See the Institute War Clauses (Cargo), Clause 3 (see p 265, ante).

Institute Strikes Clauses (Cargo) 273

4. Unseaworthiness and Unfitness Exclusion Clause.

4.1 In no case shall this insurance cover loss damage or expense arising from
> unseaworthiness of vessel or craft,
> unfitness of vessel craft conveyance container or liftvan for the safe carriage of the subject-matter insured,

where the Assured or their servants are privy to such unseaworthiness or unfitness, at the time the subject-matter insured is loaded therein.

4.2 The Underwriters waive any breach of the implied warranties of seaworthiness of the ship and fitness of the ship to carry the subject-matter insured to destination, unless the Assured or their servants are privy to such unseaworthiness or unfitness.

Note

This clause is in the same words as the Institute Cargo Clauses (A), Clause 5 (see p 242, ante).

DURATION

5. Transit Clause.

5.1 This insurance attaches from the time the goods leave the warehouse or place of storage at the place named herein for the commencement of the transit, continues during the ordinary course of transit and terminates either

5.1.1 on delivery to the Consignees' or other final warehouse or place of storage at the destination named herein,

5.1.2 on delivery to any other warehouse or place of storage, whether prior to or at the destination named herein, which the Assured elect to use either

5.1.2.1 for storage other than in the ordinary course of transit or
5.1.2.2 for allocation or distribution,
or

5.1.3 on the expiry of 60 days after completion of discharge overside of the goods hereby insured from the oversea vessel at the final port of discharge,

whichever shall first occur.

5.2 If, after discharge overside from the oversea vessel at the final port of discharge, but prior to termination of this insurance, the goods are to be forwarded to a destination other than that to which they are insured hereunder, this insurance, whilst remaining subject to termination as provided for above, shall not extend beyond the commencement of transit to such other destination.

5.3   This insurance shall remain in force (subject to termination as provided for above and to the provisions of Clause 6 below) during delay beyond the control of the Assured, any deviation, forced discharge, reshipment or transhipment and during any variation of the adventure arising from the exercise of a liberty granted to shipowners or charterers under the contract of affreightment.

Note

This clause is in the same words as the Institute Cargo Clauses (A), Clause 8 (see p 243, ante).

6. Termination of Contract of Carriage Clause. If owing to circumstances beyond the control of the Assured either the contract of carriage is terminated at a port or place other than the destination named therein or the transit is otherwise terminated before delivery of the goods as provided for in Clause 5 above, then this insurance shall also terminate *unless prompt notice is given to the Underwriters and continuation of cover is requested when the insurance shall remain in force, subject to an additional premium if required by the Underwriters,* either

6.1   until the goods are sold and delivered at such port or place, or, unless otherwise specially agreed, until the expiry of 60 days after arrival of the goods hereby insured at such port or place, whichever shall first occur,
        or
6.2   if the goods are forwarded within the said period of 60 days (or any agreed extension thereof) to the destination named herein or to any other destination, until terminated in accordance with the provisions of Clause 5 above.

Note

This clause is in the same words as the Institute Cargo Clauses (A), Clause 9 (see p 245, ante).

7. Change of Voyage Clause. Where, after attachment of this insurance, the destination is changed by the Assured, *held covered at a premium and on conditions to be arranged subject to prompt notice being given to the Underwriters.*

Note

This clause is in the same words as the Institute Cargo Clauses (A), Clause 10 (see p 245, ante).

CLAIMS

8. Insurable Interest Clause.
8.1   In order to recover under this insurance the Assured must have an insurable interest in the subject-matter insured at the time of the loss.

8.2   Subject to 8.1 above, the Assured shall be entitled to recover for insured loss occurring during the period covered by this insurance, notwithstanding that the loss occurred before the contract of insurance was concluded, unless the Assured were aware of the loss and the Underwriters were not.

Note

This clause is in the same words as the Institute Cargo Clauses (A), Clause 11 (see p 246, ante).

9. Increased Value Clause.
9.1   If any Increased Value insurance is effected by the Assured on the cargo insured herein the agreed value of the cargo shall be deemed to be increased to the total amount insured under this insurance and all Increased Value insurances covering the loss, and liability under this insurance shall be in such proportion as the sum insured herein bears to such total amount insured.

In the event of claim the Assured shall provide the Underwriters with evidence of the amounts insured under all other insurances.

9.2   **Where this insurance is on Increased Value the following clause shall apply:**

The agreed value of the cargo shall be deemed to be equal to the total amount insured under the primary insurance and all Increased Value insurances covering the loss and effected on the cargo by the Assured, and liability under this insurance shall be in such proportion as the sum insured herein bears to such total amount insured.

In the event of claim the Assured shall provide the Underwriters with evidence of the amounts insured under all other insurances.

Note

This clause is in the same words as the Institute Cargo Clauses (A), Clause 14 (see p 247, ante).

BENEFIT OF INSURANCE

10. Not to Inure Clause. This insurance shall not inure to the benefit of the carrier or other bailee.

Note

This clause is in the same words as the Institute Cargo Clauses (A), Clause 15 (see p 247, ante).

MINIMISING LOSSES

11. Duty of Assured Clause. It is the duty of the Assured and their servants and agents in respect of loss recoverable hereunder

11.1   to take such measures as may be reasonable for the purpose of averting or minimising such loss, and

11.2   to ensure that all rights against carriers, bailees or other third parties are properly preserved and exercised

and the Underwriters will, in addition to any loss recoverable hereunder, reimburse the Assured for any charges properly and reasonably incurred in pursuance of these duties.

Note

This clause is in the same words as the Institute Cargo Clauses (A), Clause 16 (see p 248, ante).

12. Waiver Clause. Measures taken by the Assured or the Underwriters with the object of saving, protecting or recovering the subject-matter insured shall not be considered as a waiver or acceptance of abandonment or otherwise prejudice the rights of either party.

Note

This clause is in the same words as the Institute Cargo Clauses (A), Clause 17 (see p 248, ante).

AVOIDANCE OF DELAY

13. Reasonable Despatch Clause. It is a condition of this insurance that the Assured shall act with reasonable despatch in all circumstances within their control.

Note

This clause is in the same words as the Institute Cargo Clauses (A), Clause 18 (see p 248, ante).

LAW AND PRACTICE

14. English Law and Practice Clause. The insurance is subject to English law and practice.

NOTE: It is necessary for the Assured when they become aware of an event which is 'held covered' under this insurance to give prompt notice to the Underwriters and the right to such cover is dependent upon compliance with this obligation.

APPENDIX IV
THE YORK-ANTWERP RULES 1974

Rule of Interpretation. In the adjustment of general average the following lettered and numbered Rules shall apply to the exclusion of any Law and Practice inconsistent therewith.

Except as provided by the numbered Rules, general average shall be adjusted according to the lettered Rules.

Rule A. There is a general average act, when, and only when, any extraordinary sacrifice or expenditure is intentionally and reasonably made or incurred for the common safety for the purpose of preserving from peril the property involved in a common maritime adventure.

Rule B. General average sacrifices and expenses shall be borne by the different contributing interests on the basis hereinafter provided.

Rule C. Only such losses, damages or expenses which are the direct consequence of the general average act shall be allowed as general average.

Loss or damage sustained by the ship or cargo through delay, whether on the voyage or subsequently, such as demurrage, and any indirect loss whatsoever, such as loss of market, shall not be admitted as general average.

Rule D. Rights to contribution in general average shall not be affected, though the event which gave rise to the sacrifice or expenditure may have been due to the fault of one of the parties to the adventure, but this shall not prejudice any remedies or defences which may be open against or to that party in respect of such fault.

Rule E. The onus of proof is upon the party claiming in general average to show that the loss or expense claimed is properly allowable as general average.

Rule F. Any extra expense incurred in place of another expense which would have been allowable as general average shall be deemed to be general average and so allowed without regard to the saving, if any, to other interests, but only up to the amount of the general average expense avoided.

Rule G. General average shall be adjusted as regards both loss and contribution upon the basis of values at the time and place when and where the adventure ends.

This Rule shall not affect the determination of the place at which the average statement is to be made up.

Rule I. Jettison of Cargo. No jettison of cargo shall be made good as general average unless such cargo is carried in accordance with the recognised custom of the trade.

Rule II. Damage by Jettison and Sacrifice for the Common Safety. Damage done to a ship and cargo, or either of them, by or in consequence of a sacrifice made for the common safety, and by water which goes down a ship's hatches opened or other opening made for the purpose of making a jettison for the common safety, shall be made good as general average.

Rule III. Extinguishing Fire on Shipboard. Damage done to a ship and cargo, or either of them, by water or otherwise, including damage by beaching or scuttling a burning ship, in extinguishing a fire on board the ship, shall be made good as general average; except that no compensation shall be made for damage by smoke or heat however caused.

Rule IV. Cutting away Wreck. Loss or damage sustained by cutting away wreck or parts of the ship which have been previously carried away or are effectively lost by accident shall not be made good as general average.

Rule V. Voluntary Stranding. When a ship is intentionally run on shore for the common safety, whether or not she might have been driven on shore, the consequent loss or damage shall be allowed in general average.

Rule VI. Salvage. (*a*) Expenditure by the parties to the adventure in the nature of salvage, whether under contract or otherwise, shall be allowed in general average provided that the salvage operations were carried out for the purpose of preserving from peril the property involved in the common maritime adventure.

Expenditure allowed in general average shall include any salvage remuneration in which the skill and efforts of the salvors in preventing or minimising damage to the environment such as is referred to in Art 13 paragraph 1(*b*) of the International Convention on Salvage 1989 have been taken into account.

(b) Special compensation payable to a salvor by the shipowner under Art 14 of the said Convention to the extent specified in paragraph 4 of that Article or under any other provision similar in substance shall not be allowed in general average.

Rule VII. Damage to Machinery and Boilers. Damage caused to any machinery and boilers of a ship which is ashore and in a position of peril, in endeavouring to refloat, shall be allowed in general average when shown to have arisen from an actual intention to float the ship for the common safety at the risk of such damage; but where a ship is afloat no loss or damage caused by working the propelling machinery and boilers shall in any circumstances be made good as general average.

Rule VIII. Expenses Lightening a Ship when Ashore, and Consequent Damage. When a ship is ashore and cargo and ship's fuel and stores or any of them are discharged as a general average act, the extra cost of lightening, lighter hire and reshipping if incurred and the loss or damage sustained thereby, shall be admitted as general average.

Rule IX. Ship's Materials and Stores Burnt for Fuel. Ship's materials and stores, or any of them, necessarily burnt for fuel for the common safety at a time of peril, shall be admitted as general average, when and only when an ample supply of fuel had been provided; but the estimated quantity of fuel that would have been consumed, calculated at the price current at the ship's last port of departure at the date of her leaving, shall be credited to the general average.

Rule X. Expenses at Port of Refuge etc. (a) When a ship shall have entered a port or place of refuge or shall have returned to her port or place of loading in consequence of accident, sacrifice or other extraordinary circumstances, which render that necessary for the common safety, the expenses of entering such port or place shall be admitted as general average; and when she shall have sailed thence with her original cargo, or part of it, the corresponding expenses of leaving such port or place consequent upon such entry or return shall likewise be admitted as general average.

When a ship is at any port or place of refuge and is necessarily removed to another port or place because repairs cannot be carried out in the first port or place, the provisions of this Rule shall be applied to the second port or place as if it were a port or place of refuge and the cost of such removal including temporary repairs and towage shall be admitted as general average. The provisions of Rule XI shall be applied to the prolongation of the voyage occasioned by such removal.

(b) The cost of handling on board or discharging cargo, fuel or stores whether at a port or place of loading, call or refuge, shall be admitted as general average, when the handling or discharge was necessary for the common safety or to enable damage to the ship caused by sacrifice or accident to be repaired if the repairs were necessary for the safe prosecution of the voyage, except in cases where the damage to the ship is discovered at a port or place of loading or call without any accident or other extraordinary circumstance connected with such damage having taken place during the voyage.

The cost of handling on board or discharging cargo, fuel or stores shall not be admissible as general average when incurred solely for the purpose of restowage due to shifting during the voyage unless such restowage is necessary for the common safety.

(c) Whenever the cost of handling or discharging cargo, fuel or stores is admissible as general average, the costs of storage, including insurance if reasonably incurred, reloading and stowing of such cargo, fuel or stores shall likewise be admitted as general average.

But when the ship is condemned or does not proceed on her original voyage storage expenses shall be admitted as general average only up to the date of the ship's condemnation or of the abandonment of the voyage or up to the date of completion of discharge of cargo if the condemnation or abandonment takes place before that date.

Rule XI. Wages and Maintenance of Crew and other expenses Bearing up for and in a port of Refuge etc. (a) Wages and maintenance of master, officers and crew reasonably incurred and fuel and stores consumed during the prolongation of the voyage occasioned by a ship entering a port or place of refuge or returning to her port or place of loading shall be admitted as general average when the expenses of entering such port or place are allowable in general average in accordance with Rule X(a).

(b) When a ship shall have entered or been detained in any port or place in consequence of accident, sacrifice or other extraordinary circumstances which render that necessary for the common safety, or to enable damage to the ship caused by sacrifice or accident to be repaired, if the repairs were necessary for the safe prosecution of the voyage, the wages and maintenance of the master, officers, and crew reasonably incurred during the extra period of detention in such port or place until the ship shall or should have been made ready to proceed upon her voyage, shall be admitted in general average.

Provided that when damage to the ship is discovered at a port or place of loading or call without any accident or other extraordinary circumstance connected with such damage having taken place during the voyage, then the wages and maintenance of master, officers and crew and fuel and stores consumed during the extra detention for repairs to damage so discovered shall not be admissible as general average, even if the repairs are necessary for the safe prosecution of the voyage.

When the ship is condemned or does not proceed on her original voyage, wages and maintenance of the master, officers and crew and fuel and stores consumed shall be admitted as general average only up to the date of the ship's condemnation or of the abandonment of the voyage or up to the date of completion of discharge of cargo if the condemnation or abandonment takes place before that date.

Fuel and stores consumed during the extra period of detention shall be admitted as general average, except such fuel and stores as are consumed in effecting repairs not allowable in general average.

Port charges incurred during the extra period of detention shall likewise be admitted as general average except such charges as are incurred solely by reason of repairs not allowable in general average.

(c) For the purpose of this and the other Rules wages shall include all payments made to or for the benefit of the master, officers and crew, whether such payments be imposed by law upon the shipowners or be made under the terms or articles of employment.

(d) When overtime is paid to the master, officers or crew for maintenance of the ship or repairs, the cost of which is not allowable in general average, such overtime shall be allowed in general average only up to the saving in expense which would have been incurred and admitted as general average, had such overtime not been incurred.

Rule XII. Damage to Cargo in discharging etc. Damage to or loss of cargo, fuel or stores caused in the act of handling, discharging, storing, reloading and stowing shall be made good as general average, when and only when the cost of those measures respectively is admitted as general average.

Rule XIII. Deductions from Cost of Repairs. Repairs to be allowed in general average shall not be subject to deductions in respect of 'new for old' where old material or parts are replaced by new unless the ship is over fifteen years old in which case there shall be a deduction of one-third. The deductions shall be regulated by the age of the ship from 31 December of the year of completion of construction to the date of the general average act, except for insulation, life and similar boats, communications and navigational apparatus and equipment, machinery and boilers for which the deductions shall be regulated by the age of the particular parts to which they apply.

The deductions shall be made only from the cost of the new material or parts when finished and ready to be installed in the ship.

No deduction shall be made in respect of provisions, stores, anchors and chain cables.

Drydock and slipway dues and costs of shifting the ship shall be allowed in full.

The costs of cleaning, painting or coating of bottom shall not be allowed in general average unless the bottom has been painted or coated within the twelve months preceding the date of the general average act in which case one-half of such costs shall be allowed.

Rule XIV. Temporary Repairs. Where temporary repairs are effected to a ship at a port of loading, call or refuge, for the common safety, or of damage caused by general average sacrifice, the cost of such repairs shall be admitted as general average.

Where temporary repairs of accidental damage are effected in order to enable the adventure to be completed, the cost of such repairs shall be admitted as general average without regard to the saving, if any, to other interest, but only up to the saving in expense which would have been incurred and allowed in general average if such repairs had not been effected there.

No deductions 'new for old' shall be made from the cost of temporary repairs allowable as general average.

Rule XV. Loss of Freight. Loss of freight arising from damage to or loss of cargo shall be made good as general average, either when caused by a general average act, or when the damage to or loss of cargo is so made good.

Deduction shall be made from the amount of gross freight lost, of the charges which the owner thereof would have incurred to earn such freight, but has, in consequence of the sacrifice, not incurred.

Rule XVI. Amount to be made good for Cargo lost or Damaged by Sacrifice. The amount to be made good as general average for damage to or loss of cargo sacrificed shall be the loss which has been sustained thereby based on the value at the time of discharge, ascertained from the commercial invoice rendered to the receiver or if there is no such invoice from the shipped value. The value at the time of discharge shall include the cost of insurance and freight except insofar as such freight is at the risk of interests other than the cargo.

When cargo so damaged is sold and the amount of the damage has not been otherwise agreed, the loss to be made good in general average shall be the difference between the net proceeds of sale and the net sound value as computed in the first paragraph of this Rule.

Rule XVII. Contributory Values. The contribution to a general average shall be made upon the actual net value of the property at the termination of the adventure except that the value of cargo shall be the value at the time of discharge, ascertained from the commercial invoice rendered to the receiver or if there is no such invoice from the shipped value. The value of the cargo shall include the cost of insurance and freight unless and insofar as such freight is at the risk of interests other than the cargo, deducting therefrom any loss or damage suffered by the cargo prior to or at the time of discharge. The value of the ship shall be assessed without taking into account the beneficial or detrimental effect of any demise or time charter-party to which the ship may be committed.

To these values shall be added the amount made good as general average for property sacrificed, if not already included, deduction being made from the freight and passage money at risk of such charges and crew's wages as would not have been incurred in earning the freight had the ship and cargo been totally lost at the date of the general average act and have not been allowed as general average; deduction being also made from the value of the property of all extra charges incurred in respect thereof subsequently to the general average act, except such charges as are allowed in general average.

Where cargo is sold short of destination, however, it shall contribute upon the actual net proceeds of sale, with the addition of any amount made good as general average.

Passenger's luggage and personal effects not shipped under Bill of Lading shall not contribute in general average.

Rule XVIII. Damage to Ship. The amount to be allowed as general average for damage or loss to the ship, her machinery and/or gear caused by a general average act shall be as follows:

(*a*) When repaired or replaced,

the actual reasonable cost of repairing or replacing such damage or loss subject to deduction in accordance with Rule XIII;

(*b*) When not repaired or replaced,

the reasonable depreciation arising from such damage or loss, but not exceeding the estimated cost of repairs. But where the ship is an actual total loss or when the cost of repairs of the damage would exceed the value of the ship when repaired, the amount to be allowed as general average shall be the difference between the estimated sound value of the ship after deducting therefrom the estimated cost of repairing damage which is not general average and the value of the ship in her damaged state which may be measured by the net proceeds of sale, if any.

Rule XIX. Undeclared or Wrongfully declared Cargo. Damage or loss caused to goods loaded without the knowledge of the shipowner or his agent or to goods wilfully misdescribed at time of shipment shall not be allowed as general average but such goods shall remain liable to contribute, if saved.

Damage or loss caused to goods which have been wrongfully declared on shipment at a value which is lower than their real value shall be contributed for at the declared value, but such goods shall contribute upon their actual value.

Rule XX. Provision of Funds. A commission of two per cent of general average disbursements, other than the wages and maintenance of master, officers and crew and fuel and stores not replaced during the voyage, shall be allowed in general average, but when the funds are not provided by any of the contributing interests the necessary cost of obtaining the funds required by means of a bottomry bond or otherwise, or the loss sustained by owners of goods sold for the purpose, shall be allowed in general average.

The cost of insuring money advanced to pay for general average disbursements shall also be allowed in general average.

Rule XXI. Interest on Losses made good in general average. Interest shall be allowed on expenditure, sacrifices and allowances charged to general average at the rate of seven per cent per annum, until the date of the general average statement, due allowance being made for any interim reimbursement from the contributory interests or from the general average deposit fund.

Rule XXII. Treatment of Cash Deposits. Where cash deposits have been collected in respect of cargo's liability for general average, salvage or special charges such deposits shall be paid without any delay into a special account in the joint names of a representative nominated on behalf of the shipowner and a representative nominated on behalf of the depositors in a bank to be approved by both. The sum so deposited together with accrued interest, if any, shall be held as security for payment to the parties entitled thereto of the general average, salvage or special charges payable by cargo in respect to which the deposits have been collected. Payments on account of refund of deposits may be made if certified to in writing by the average adjuster. Such deposits and payments or refunds shall be without prejudice to the ultimate liability of the parties.

APPENDIX V—RULES OF PRACTICE OF THE ASSOCIATION OF AVERAGE ADJUSTERS 1986 (amended 1992)

RULES OF PRACTICE

SECTION A—GENERAL RULES

A1. Adjustments for the consideration of underwriters

That any claim prepared for the consideration of underwriters shall include a statement of the reasons of the average adjuster for stating such a claim, and when submitted in conjunction with a claim for which underwriters are liable, shall be shown in such a manner as clearly to distinguish the claim for consideration from other claims embodied in the same adjustment.

A2. Interest and commission for advancing funds

That, in practice, interest and commission for advancing funds are only allowable in average when, proper and necessary steps having been taken to make a collection on account, an out-of-pocket expense for interest and/or commission for advancing funds is reasonably incurred.

A3. Agency commission and agency

That, in practice, neither commission (excepting bank commission) nor any charge by way of agency or remuneration for trouble is allowed to the shipowner in average, except in respect of services rendered on behalf of cargo when such services are not involved in the contract of affreightment.

A4. Duty of adjusters in respect of cost of repairs

That in adjusting particular average on ship or general average which includes repairs, it is the duty of the adjuster to satisfy himself that such reasonable and usual precautions have been taken to keep down the cost of repairs as a prudent shipowner would have taken if uninsured.

A5. Claims on ship's machinery

That in all claims on ship's machinery for repairs, no claim for a new propeller or new shaft shall be admitted into an adjustment, unless the adjuster shall obtain and insert into his statement evidence showing what has become of the old propeller or shaft.

A6. Water casks

Water casks or tanks carried on a ship's deck are not paid for by underwriters as general or particular average; nor are warps or other articles when improperly carried on deck.

A7. Adjustment; policies of insurance and names of underwriters

That no adjustment shall be drawn up showing the amount of payments by or to the underwriters, unless the policies or copies of the policies of insurance or certificates of insurance, for which the statement is required, be produced to the average adjusters. Such statement shall set out sufficient details of the underwriters interested and the amounts due on the respective policies produced.

A8. Apportionment of costs in collision cases

That when a vessel sustains and does damage by collision, and litigation consequently results for the purpose of testing liability, the technicality of the vessel having been plaintiff or defendant in the litigation shall not necessarily govern the apportionment of the costs of such litigation, which shall be apportioned between claim and counter-claim in proportion to the amount, excluding interest, which has been or would have been allowed in respect of each in the event of the claim or counter-claim being established; provided that when a claim or counter-claim is made solely for the purpose of defence, and is not allowed, the costs apportioned thereto shall be treated as costs of defence.

A9. Franchise charges

The expenses of protest, survey, and other proofs of loss, including the commission or other expenses of a sale by auction, are not admitted to make up the percentage of a claim; and are only paid by the underwriters in case the loss amounts to a claim without them.

SECTION B—GENERAL AVERAGE

Rules of general application

B1. Basis of adjustment

That in any adjustment of general average not made in accordance with British law it shall be prefaced on what principle or according to what law the adjustment has been made, and the reason for so adjusting the claim shall be set forth.

In all cases the adjuster shall give particulars in a prominent position in the average statement of the clause or clauses contained in the charter-party and/or bills of lading with reference to the adjustment of general average.

B9. Claims arising out of deficiency of fuel

That in adjusting general average arising out of deficiency of fuel, the facts on which the general average is based shall be set forth in the adjustment, including the material dates and distances, and particulars of fuel supplies and consumption.

B24. Contributory value of ship

That in any adjustment of general average there shall be set forth the certificate on which the contributory value of the ship is based or, if there be no such certificate, the information adopted in lieu thereof, and any amount made good shall be specified.

B25. Contributory value of freight

That in any adjustment of general average there shall be set forth the amount of the gross freight and the freight advanced, if any; also the charges and wages deducted and any amount made good.

B26. Vessel in ballast and under charter: contributing interests

For the purpose of ascertaining the liability of underwriters on British policies of insurance, the following provisions shall apply:

When a vessel is proceeding in ballast to load under a voyage charter entered into by the shipowner before the general average act, the interests contributing to the general average shall be the vessel, such items of stores and equipment as belong to parties other than the owners of the vessel (eg bunkers, wireless installation and navigational instruments) and the freight earned under the voyage charter computed in the usual way after deduction of contingent expenses subsequent to the general average act. Failing a prior termination of the adventure, the place where the adventure shall be deemed to end and at which the values for contribution to general average shall be calculated is the final port of discharge of the cargo carried under the charter but in the event of the prior loss of the vessel and freight, or either of them, the general average shall attach to any surviving interest or interests including freight advanced at the loading port deducting therefrom contingent expenses subsequent to the general average act.

When a vessel is proceeding in ballast under a time charter alone or a time charter and a voyage charter entered into by the time charterer, the general average shall attach to the vessel and such items of stores and equipment as are indicated above. Failing a prior termination of the adventure, the adventure shall be deemed to end and the values for contribution to general average calculated at the first loading port upon the commencement of loading cargo.

When the charter to which the shipowner is a party provides for York-Antwerp Rules, the general average shall be adjusted in accordance with those Rules and British law and practice and without regard to the law and practice of any foreign port at which the adventure may terminate; and in the interpretation of Rule XI it shall be immaterial whether the extra period of detention takes place at a port of loading, call or refuge, provided that the detention is in consequence of accident, sacrifice or other extraordinary circumstance occurring whilst the vessel is in ballast.

In practice neither time charter hire, as such, nor time charterer's voyage freight shall contribute to general average.

B27. Ulterior chartered freight: contribution to general average

That when at the time of a general average act the vessel has on board cargo shipped under charter-party or bills of lading, and is also under a separate charter to load another cargo after the cargo then in course of carriage has been discharged, the ulterior chartered freight shall not contribute to the general average.

B28. Deductions from freight at charterer's risk

That freight at the risk of the charterer shall be subject to no deduction for wages and charges, except in the case of charters in which the wages or charges are payable by the charterer, in which case such freight shall be governed by the same rule as freight at the risk of the shipowner.

B29. Forwarding charges on advanced freight

That in case of wreck, the cargo being forwarded to its destination, the charterer, who has paid a lump sum on account of freight, which is not to be returned in the event of the vessel being lost, shall not be liable for any portion of the forwarding freight and charges, when the same are less than the balance of freight payable to the shipowner at the port of destination under the original charter-party.

B30. Sacrifice for the common safety: direct liability of underwriters

That in case of general average sacrifice there is, under ordinary policies of insurance, a direct liability of an underwriter on ship for loss of or damage to ship's materials, and of an underwriter on goods or freight, for loss of or damage to goods or loss of freight so sacrificed as a general average loss; that such loss not being particular average is not taken into account in computing the memorandum percentages, and that the direct liability of an underwriter for such loss is consequently unaffected by the memorandum or any other warranty respecting particular average.

B31. Sacrifice of ship's stores: direct liability of underwriters

That underwriters insuring ship's stores, bunker coal or fuel, destroyed or used as part of a general average operation, shall only be liable for those articles as a direct claim on the policy when they formed part of the property at risk at the time of the peril giving rise to the general average act.

B32. Enforcement of general average lien by shipowners

That in all cases where general average damage to ship is claimed direct from the underwriters on that interest, the average adjusters shall ascertain whether the shipowners have taken the necessary steps to enforce their lien for general average on the cargo, and shall insert in the average statement a note giving the result of their enquiries.

B33. Underwriter's liability

If the ship or cargo be insured for more than its contributory value, the underwriter pays what is assessed on the contributory value. But where insured for less than the contributory value, the underwriter pays on the insured value; and when there has been a particular average for damage which forms a deduction from the contributory value of the ship that must be deducted from the insured value to find upon what the underwriter contributes.

This rule does not apply to foreign adjustments, when the basis of contribution is something other than the net value of the thing insured.

That in practice, in applying the above rule for the purpose of ascertaining the liability of underwriters for contribution to general average and salvage charges, deduction shall be made from the insured value of all losses and charges for which underwriters are liable and which have been deducted in arriving at the contributory value.

In adjusting the liability of underwriters on freight for general average contribution and salvage charges, effect shall be given to section 73 of the Marine Insurance Act 1906, by comparing the gross and not the net amount of freight at risk with the insured value in the case of a valued policy or the insurable value in the case of an unvalued policy.

B34. The duty of adjusters in cases involving refunds of general average deposits or apportionment of salvage, collision recoveries, or other funds

That in cases of general average where deposits have been collected and it is likely that repayments will have to be made, measures be taken by the adjuster to ascertain the names of underwriters who have reimbursed their assured in respect of such deposits; that the names of any such underwriters be set forth in the adjustment as claimants of refund, if any, to which they are apparently entitled; and that on completion of the adjustment, notice be sent to all underwriters whose names are so set forth as to any refund of which they appear as claimants and as to the steps to be taken in order to obtain payment of the same.

That in cases where the names of any underwriters are not to be ascertained on completion of the adjustment, notice be sent to the Secretary of Lloyd's, to the Institute of London Underwriters, to the Liverpool Underwriters' Association, and to the Association of Underwriters of Glasgow, notifying such interests as have not been appropriated to underwriters.

And that in cases of apportionment of salvage or other funds for distribution, similar measures be taken by the adjuster to safeguard the interests of any underwriters who may be entitled to benefit under the apportionment.

B35. Memorandum to statements showing refunds in respect of general average deposits

That the following memorandum shall appear at the end of statements which show refunds to be due in respect of General Average Deposits, viz:

Memorandum—Refunds of general average deposits shown in this statement should only be paid on production of the original deposit receipts.

B36. Interest on deposits

That, unless otherwise expressly provided, the interest accrued on deposits on account of salvage and/or general average and/or particular and/or other charges, or on the balance of such deposits after payments on account, if any, have been made, shall be credited to the depositor or those to whom his rights in respect of the deposits have been transferred.

B37. Apportionment of interest on amounts made good

That in practice (in the absence of express agreement between the parties concerned) interest allowed on amounts made good shall be apportioned between assured and underwriters, taking into account the sums paid by underwriters and the dates when such payments were made, notwithstanding that by the addition of interest the underwriter may receive a larger sum than he has paid.

SECTION C—YORK-ANTWERP RULES

C1. Salvage services rendered under an agreement

Expenses for salvage services rendered by or accepted under agreement shall in practice be treated as general average provided that such expenses were incurred for the common safety within the meaning of Rule 'A' of the York-Antwerp Rules 1924 or York-Antwerp Rules 1950.

C2. Commission allowed under York-Antwerp Rules

That the commission of 2 per cent allowed on general average disbursements under Rule XXI of York-Antwerp Rules 1924 and Rule XX of York-Antwerp Rules 1950 or 1974, shall be credited in full to the party who has authorised the expenditure and is liable for payment, except that where the funds for payment are provided in the first instance in whole or in part from the deposit funds, or by other parties to the adventure, or by underwriters, the commission on such advances shall be credited to the deposit fund or to the parties or underwriters providing the funds for payment.

C3. York-Antwerp Rules 1924. Rules X(a) and XX.

That, in practice, where a vessel is at any port or place in circumstances in which the wages and maintenance of crew during detention there for the purpose of repairs necessary for the safe prosecution of the voyage would be admissible in general average under Rule XI of the York-Antwerp Rules 1924, and the vessel is necessarily removed thence to another port or place because such repairs cannot be effected at the first port or place, the provisions of Rule X(a) shall be applied to the second port or place as if it were a port or place of refuge within that Rule and the provisions of Rule XX shall be applied to the prolongation of the voyage occasioned by such removal.

C4. York-Antwerp Rules 1950 and 1974   Rule X(a)

That in practice, in applying the second paragraph of Rule X(a), a vessel shall be deemed to be at a port or place of refuge when she is at any port or place in circumstances in which the wages and maintenance of the Master, Officers and crew incurred during any extra period of detention there would be admissible in General Average under the provisions of Rule XI.

SECTION D—DAMAGE AND REPAIRS TO SHIP

D1. Expenses of removing a vessel for repair

1. For the purpose of ascertaining the reasonable cost of repairs, and subject to any express provisions in the policy, where a vessel is at any port place or location (hereinafter referred to as 'port') and is necessarily or reasonably removed to some other port for the purpose of repairs, either because the repairs cannot be effected at the first port, or cannot be effected prudently, the additional expenses reasonably incurred by the shipowner in removing the vessel (other than any expenses allowable in general average) shall be treated as part of the reasonable cost of repairs.
2. (a) Where the vessel after repairing forthwith returns to the port from which she was removed, the expenses incurred both in removing the vessel to the port of repair and in returning shall be treated as part of the expenses of removal.
    (b) Where the vessel loads a new cargo at the port of repair or proceeds thence to some other port for the same purpose, the expenses shall be calculated as though, but for the repairs, the vessel had previously been engaged to proceed direct from the port from which she was removed to the loading port.

(c) Where, immediately following a casualty, or upon completion of the voyage on which the casualty occurred, the vessel is removed solely to enable repairs to be effected which are essential for continued trading, the expenses may, at the owners' option, be calculated only for the single passage to the repair port.

3. (a) The expenses of removal shall include, inter alia, the cost of any necessary temporary repairs, wages and provisions of crew and/or runners, pilotage, towage, extra marine insurance, port charges, bunkers and stores.

(b) Where by moving the vessel to or from the port of repair any new freight or hire is earned, such net earnings shall be deducted from the expenses of removal.

4. The expenses of removing the vessel for repair shall be charged as follows:

(a) Where the vessel is removed to the port of repair as an immediate consequence of damage for the repair of which underwriters are liable, or the vessel is necessarily taken out of service especially to effect repairs arising from that damage, the whole cost of removal shall be treated as part of the cost of repairing that damage, notwithstanding that the shipowner may have taken advantage of the removal to carry out survey for classification purposes or to effect other average repairs or repairs on his own account.

However, where the vessel is removed for owners' purposes, other than a routine overhaul as in 4(b) below, or as an immediate consequence of damage for which underwriters are not liable, no part of the cost of removal shall be charged to underwriters, notwithstanding that repairs for which they are liable may be carried out at the port of repair.

(b) Where the vessel is removed to the port of repair for routine overhaul at which repairs on both owners' and underwriters' accounts are effected, the expenses of removal shall be apportioned pro rata to the cost (including drydock dues and general services) of all work effected at the port, other than to any damage sustained after the commencement of the removal passage and the cost of any major parts shipped to the repair port from elsewhere.

D2. Fuel and stores used in repair of damage to the vessel

That the cost of replacing fuel and stores consumed either in the repair of damage to a vessel, in working the engines or winches to assist in the repairs of damage, or in moving her to a place or repair within the limits of the port where she is lying, shall be treated as part of the cost of repairs.

D3. Rigging chafed

Rigging injured by straining or chafing is not charged to underwriters, unless such injury is caused by blows of the sea, grounding, or contact; or by displacement, through sea peril, of the spars, channels, bulwarks, or rails.

D4. Sails split or blown away

Sails split by the wind, or blown away while set, unless occasioned by the ship's grounding or coming into collision, or in consequence of damage to the spars to which the sails are bent, are not charged to underwriters.

D5. Dry dock expenses

1. That, in practice, where repairs, for the cost of which underwriters are liable, are necessarily effected in dry dock as an immediate consequence of the casualty, or the vessel is taken out of service especially to effect such repairs in dry dock, the cost of entering and leaving the dry dock, in addition to so much of the dock dues as is necessary for the repair of the damage, shall be chargeable in full to the underwriters, notwithstanding that the shipowner may have taken advantage of the vessel being in dry dock to carry out survey for classification purposes or to effect repairs on his account which are not immediately necessary to make the vessel seaworthy.
2. (a) Where repairs on Owners' account which are immediately necessary to make the vessel seaworthy and which can only be effected in dry dock are executed concurrently with other repairs, for the cost of which underwriters are liable, and which also can only be effected in dry dock,
   (b) Where the repairs, for the cost of which underwriters are liable, are deferred until a routine dry-docking and are then executed concurrently with repairs on Owners' account which require the use of the dry dock, whether or not such Owners' repairs affect the seaworthiness of the vessel,

the cost of entering and leaving the dry dock, in addition to so much of the dock dues as is common to both repairs, shall be divided equally between the shipowner and the underwriters, irrespective of the fact that the repairs for which underwriters are liable may relate to more than one voyage or accident or may be payable by more than one set of underwriters.

3. Sub-division between underwriters of the proportion of dry-docking expenses chargeable to them shall be made on the basis of voyages, and/or such other franchise units as are specified in the policies.

4. In determining whether the franchise is reached the whole cost of dry-docking necessary for the repair of the damage, less the proportion (if any) chargeable to Owners when section (*a*) of paragraph 2 applies, shall be taken into consideration, notwithstanding that there are other damages to which a portion of the cost of dry-docking has to be apportioned in ascertaining the amount actually recoverable.

D6. Tankers—treatment of the cost of tank cleaning and/or gas-freeing

1. That, in practice, where repairs, for the cost of which underwriters are liable, require the tanks to be rough cleaned and/or gas-freed as an immediate consequence of the casualty, or the vessel is taken out of service especially to effect such repairs, the cost of such rough cleaning and/or gas-freeing shall be chargeable in full to the underwriters, notwithstanding that the shipowner may have taken advantage of the vessel being rough cleaned and/or gas-freed to carry out survey for classification purposes or to effect repairs on his account which are not immediately necessary to make the vessel seaworthy.
2. (*a*) Where repairs on Owners' account which are immediately necessary to make the vessel seaworthy and which require the tanks being rough cleaned and/or gas-freed are executed concurrently with other repairs, for the cost of which underwriters are liable, and which also require the tanks being rough cleaned and/or gas-freed,
   (*b*) Where the repairs, for the cost of which underwriters are liable, are deferred until a routine dry-docking or repair period, at which time repairs on Owners' account which also require the tanks being rough cleaned and/or gas-freed are effected, whether or not such Owners' repairs affect the seaworthiness of the vessel,
the cost of such rough cleaning and/or gas-freeing as is common to both repairs shall be divided equally between the shipowners and the underwriters, irrespective of the fact that the repairs for which underwriters are liable may relate to more than one voyage or accident or may be payable by more than one set of underwriters.
3. The cost of fine cleaning specifically for a particular repair or particular repairs shall be divided in accordance with the principles set forth above.
4. Sub-division between underwriters of the proportion of rough tank cleaning and/or gas-freeing and/or fine cleaning chargeable to them shall be made on the basis of voyages, and/or such other franchise units as are specified in the policies.
5. In determining whether the franchise is reached the whole cost of rough cleaning and/or gas-freeing and/or fine cleaning necessary for the

repair of the damage, less the proportion (if any) chargeable to Owners when section (*a*) of paragraph 2 applies, shall be taken into consideration, notwithstanding that there are other damages to which a portion of the cost of rough tank cleaning and/or gas-freeing and/or fine cleaning has to be apportioned in ascertaining the amount actually recoverable.

D7. Particular average on ship: deduction of one-third

The deduction for new work in place of old is fixed by custom at one-third, with the following exceptions:

Anchors are allowed in full. Chain cables are subject to one-sixth only.

Metal sheathing is dealt with, by allowing in full the cost of a weight equal to the gross weight of metal sheathing stripped off minus the proceeds of the old metal. Nails, felt, and labour metalling are subject to one-third.

The rule applies to iron as well as to wooden ships, and to labour as well as material. It does not apply to the expense of straightening bent ironwork, and to the labour of taking out and replacing it.

It does not apply to graving dock expenses and removals, cartages, use of shears, stages, and graving dock materials.

It does not apply to a ship's first voyage.

D8. Scraping and painting

Where the Policy includes a Clause to the effect that:

'No claim shall in any case be allowed in respect of scraping or painting the vessel's bottom'.

(*a*) Gritblasting and/or other surface preparation of new bottom plates ashore and supplying and applying any 'shop' primer thereto

(*b*) Gritblasting and/or other surface preparation of:
  (i) the butts or area of plating immediately adjacent to any renewed or refitted plating damaged during the course of welding and/or repairs
  (ii) areas of plating damaged during the course of fairing, either in place or ashore

(*c*) Supplying and applying the first coat of primer/anti-corrosive to those particular areas mentioned in (*a*) and (*b*) above

shall be allowed as part of the reasonable cost of repairs in respect of bottom plating damaged by an insured peril and shall be deemed not to be excluded by the wording of this Clause. The gritblasting and/or other surface preparation and the painting of all other areas of the bottom is excluded by the Clause.

SECTION E—PARTICULAR AVERAGE ON GOODS

E1. Adjustment on bonded prices

In the following cases it is customary to adjust particular average on a comparison of bonded, instead of duty-paid prices:

In claims for damage to tea, tobacco, coffee, wine, and spirits imported into this country.

E2. Adjustment of average on goods sold in bond

That in consequence of the facilities generally offered to bond goods at their destination, at which terms they are often sold, the term 'Gross Proceeds' shall, for the purpose of adjustment, be taken to mean the price at which the goods are sold to the consumer, after payment of freight and landing charges, but exclusive of Customs duty, in cases where it is the custom of the port to sell or deal with the goods in bond.

E3. Apportionment of insured value of goods

That where different qualities or descriptions of cargo are valued in the policy at a lump sum, such sum shall, for the purpose of adjusting claims, be apportioned on the invoice values where the invoice distinguishes the separate values of the said different qualities or descriptions; and over the net arrived sound values in all other cases.

E4. Allowance for water and/or impurities in picked cotton

When bales of cotton are picked, and the pickings are sold wet, the allowance for water in the pickings (where there are no means of ascertaining it) is by custom fixed at one-third.

There is a similar custom to deduct one-sixth from the gross weight of pickings of country damaged cotton to take account of dirt, moisture and other impurities.

E5. Allowance for water in cut tobacco

When damaged tobacco is cut off, the allowance for water in the cuttings is one-fourth if the actual increase cannot be ascertained.

E6. Allowance for water in wool

Damaged wool from Australia, New Zealand, and the Cape is subject to a deduction of 3 per cent for wet, if the actual increase cannot be ascertained.

SECTION F—GENERAL AVERAGE ADJUSTMENT UNDER ENGLISH LAW AND PRACTICE

F1. Deckload jettison

The jettison of a deckload carried according to the usage of trade and not in violation of the contracts of affreightment is general average.

There is an exception to this rule in the case of cargoes of cotton, tallow, acids and some other goods.

F2. Damage by water used to extinguish fire

That damage done by water poured down a ship's hold to extinguish a fire be treated as general average.

F3. Extinguishing fire on shipboard

Damage done to a ship and cargo, or either of them, by water or otherwise, including damage by beaching or scuttling a burning ship, in extinguishing a fire on board the ship, shall be made good as general average; except that no compensation shall be made for damage by smoke or heat however caused.

F4. Voluntary stranding

When a ship is intentionally run on shore and the circumstances are such that if that course were not adopted she would inevitably drive on shore or on rocks, no loss or damage caused to the ship, cargo and freight or any of them by such intentional running on shore shall be made good as general average, but loss or damage incurred in refloating such a ship shall be allowed as general average.

In all other cases where a ship is intentionally run on shore for the common safety, the consequent loss or damage shall be allowed as general average.

F5. Expenses lightening a ship when ashore

When a ship is ashore in a position of peril and, in order to float her, cargo is put into lighters, and is then at once re-shipped, the whole cost of lightering, including lighter hire and re-shipping, is general average.

F6. Sails set to force a ship off the ground

Sails damaged by being set, or kept set, to force a ship off the ground or to drive her higher up the ground for the common safety, are general average.

F7. Stranded vessels: damage to engines in getting off

That damage caused to machinery and boilers of a stranded vessel, in endeavouring to refloat for the common safety, when the interests are in peril, be allowed in general average.

F8. Resort to port of refuge for general average repairs: treatment of the charges incurred

That when a ship puts into a port of refuge in consequence of damage which is itself the subject of general average, and sails thence with her original cargo, or a part of it, the outward as well as the inward port charges shall be treated as general average; and when cargo is discharged for the purpose of repairing such damage, the warehouse rent and reloading of the same shall, as well as the discharge, be treated as general average. (See *Attwood v Sellar*.)

F9. Resort to port of refuge on account of particular average repairs: treatment of the charges incurred

That when a ship puts into a port of refuge in consequence of damage which is itself the subject of particular average (or not of general average) and when the cargo has been discharged in consequence of such damage, the inward port charges and the cost of discharging the cargo shall be general average, the warehouse rent of cargo shall be a particular charge on cargo, and the cost of reloading and outward port charges shall be a particular charge on freight. (See *Svendsen v Wallace*.)

F10. Treatment of costs of storage and reloading at port of refuge

That when the cargo is discharged for the purpose of repairing, reconditioning, or diminishing damage to ship or cargo which is itself the subject of general average, the cost of storage on it and of reloading it shall be treated as general average, equally with the cost of discharging it.

F11. Insurance on cargo discharged under average

That in practice, where the cost of insurance has been reasonably incurred by the shipowner, or his agents, on cargo discharged under average, such cost shall be treated as part of the cost of storage.

F12. Expenses at a port of refuge

When a ship puts into a port of refuge on account of accident and not in consequence of damage which is itself the subject of general average, then on the assumption that the ship was seaworthy at the commencement of the voyage, the Custom of Lloyd's is as follows:

(a) All cost of towage, pilotage, harbour dues, and other extraordinary expenses incurred in order to bring the ship and cargo into a place of safety, are general average. Under the term 'extraordinary expenses' are not included wages or victuals of crew, coals, or engine stores, or demurrage.
(b) The cost of discharging the cargo, whether for the common safety, or to repair the ship, together with the cost of conveying it to the warehouse, is general average.
The cost of discharging the cargo on account of damage to it resulting from its own *vice propre*, is chargeable to the owners of the cargo.
(c) The warehouse rent, or other expenses which take the place of warehouse rent, of the cargo when so discharged, is, except as under, a special charge on the cargo.
(d) The cost of reloading the cargo, and the outward port charges incurred through leaving the port of refuge, are, when the discharge of cargo falls in general average, a special charge on freight.
(e) The expenses referred to in clause (d) are charged to the party who runs the risk of freight—that is, wholly to the charterer—if the whole freight has been prepaid; and, if part only, then in the proportion which the part prepaid bears to the whole freight.
(f) When the cargo, instead of being sent ashore, is placed on board hulk or lighters during the ship's stay in port, the hulk-hire is divided between general average, cargo, and freight, in such proportions as may place the several contributing interests in nearly the same relative positions as if the cargo has been landed and stored.

F13. Treatment of costs of extraordinary discharge

That no distinction be drawn in practice between discharging cargo for the common safety of ship and cargo, and discharging it for the purpose of effecting at an intermediate port or ports of refuge repairs necessary for the prosecution of the voyage.

F14. Towage from a port of refuge

That if a ship be in a port of refuge at which it is practicable to repair her, and if, in order to save expense, she be towed thence to some other port, then the extra cost of such towage shall be divided in proportion to the saving of expense thereby occasioned to the several parties to the adventure.

F15. Cargo forwarded from a port of refuge

That if a ship be in a port of refuge at which it is practicable to repair her so as to enable her to carry on the whole cargo, but, in order to save expense, the cargo, or a portion of it, be transhipped by another vessel, or otherwise forwarded, then the cost of such transhipment (up to the amount of expense saved) shall be divided in proportion to the saving of expense thereby occasioned to the several parties to the adventure.

F16. Cargo sold at a port of refuge

That if a ship be in a port of refuge at which it is practicable to repair her so as to enable her to carry on the whole cargo, or such portion of it as is fit to be carried on, but, in order to save expense, the cargo, or a portion of it, be, with the consent of the owners of such cargo, sold at the port of refuge, then the loss by sale including loss of freight on cargo so sold (up to the amount of expense saved) shall be divided in proportion to the saving of expense thereby occasioned to the several parties to the adventure; provided always that the amount so divided shall in no case exceed the cost of transhipment and/or forwarding referred to in the preceding rule of the Association.

F17. Interpretation of the rule respecting substituted expenses

That for the purpose of avoiding any misinterpretation of the resolution relating to the apportionment of substituted expenses, it is declared that the saving of expense therein mentioned is limited to a saving or reduction of the actual outlay, including the crew's wages and provisions, if any, which would have been incurred at the port of refuge, if the vessel has been repaired there, and does not include supposed losses or expenses, such as interest, loss of market, demurrage, or assumed damage by discharging.

F18. Treatment of damage to cargo caused by discharge, storing, and reloading

That damage necessarily done to cargo by discharging, storing, and reloading it, be treated as general average when, and only when the cost of those measures respectively is so treated.

F19. Deductions from cost of repairs in adjusting general average

Repairs to be allowed in general average shall not be subject to deductions in respect of 'new for old' where old materials or parts are replaced by new unless the ship is over fifteen years old in which case there shall be a deduction of one-third. The deductions shall be regulated by the age of the ship from 31 December of the year of completion of construction to the date of the general average act, except for insulation, life and similar boats, communications and navigational apparatus and equipment, machinery and boilers for which the deductions shall be regulated by the age of the particular parts to which they apply.

The deductions shall be made only from the cost of the new material or parts when finished and ready to be installed in the ship.

No deduction shall be made in respect of provisions, stores, anchors and chain cables.

Drydock and slipway dues and costs of shifting the ship shall be allowed in full.

The costs of cleaning, painting or coating of bottom shall not be allowed in general average unless the bottom has been painted or coated within the twelve months preceding the date of the general average act in which case one half of such costs shall be allowed.

F20. Freight sacrificed: amount to be made good in general average

That the loss of freight to be made good in general average shall be ascertained by deducting from the amount of gross freight lost the charges which the owner thereof would have incurred to earn such freight, but has, in consequence of the sacrifice, not incurred.

F21. Basis of contribution to general average

When property saved by a general average act is injured or destroyed by subsequent accident, the contributing value of that property to a general average which is less than the total contributing value, shall, when it does not reach the port of destination, be its actual net proceeds; when it does it shall be its actual net value at the port of destination on its delivery there; and in all cases any values allowed in general average shall be added to and form part of the contributing value as above.

The above rule shall not apply to adjustments made before the adventure has terminated.

F22. Contributory value of freight

That freight at the risk of the shipowner shall contribute to general average upon its gross amount, deducting such charges and crew's wages as would not have been incurred in earning the freight had the ship and cargo been totally lost at the date of the general average act and have not been allowed as general average.

UNIFORMITY RESOLUTION

York-Antwerp Rules 1924: application of Rule XIV

That, in practice, in applying Rule XIV of the York-Antwerp Rules 1924, the cost of the temporary repair of the accidental damage there referred to shall be allowed in general average up to the saving to the general average by effecting such temporary repair, without regard to the saving (if any) to other interests.

APPENDIX VI—SHIP'S PAPERS
RULES OF THE SUPREME COURT

(A) RSC Ord 72, r 10—Production of certain documents in marine insurance actions

10. (1) Where in an action in the commercial list relating to a marine insurance policy an application for an order under Order 24, rule 3, is made by the insurer, then, without prejudice to its powers under that rule, the Court, if satisfied that the circumstances of the case are such that it is necessary or expedient to do so, may make an order, either in Form No 94 in Appendix A or in such other form as it thinks fit, for the production of such documents as are therein specified or described.

(2) An order under this rule may be made on such terms, if any, as to staying proceedings in the action or otherwise, as the Court thinks fit.

(3) In this rule 'the Court' means the judge, the district registrar of Liverpool or the district registrar of Manchester, as the case may be.

(B) RSC Appendix A, Form No 94

Order for production of documents in marine insurance action

(Ord 72, r 10)

[*Heading as in action*]

Upon hearing   [and upon reading the affidavit of filed the   day of   19]:

It is ordered that the plaintiff and all other persons interested in this action, and in the insurance the subject of this action, do produce and show to the defendant, his solicitors or agents on oath [*or* by oath of their proper officer] all insurance slips, policies, letters of instruction or other orders for effecting such slips or policies, or relating to the insurance or the subject-matter of the insurance on the ship   , or the cargo on board thereof, or the freight thereby, and also all documents relating to the sailing or alleged loss of the said ship, cargo or freight, and all correspondence with any person relating in any manner to the effecting of the insurance on the said ship, cargo or freight, or any other insurance whatsoever effected on the said ship, cargo or freight, on the voyage insured by the policy sued on in this action, or any other policy whatsoever effected on the said ship, or the cargo on board thereof, or the freight thereby on the same voyage. Also all correspondence between the captain or agent of the ship and any other person with the owner or any person before the commencement of or during the voyage on which the alleged loss happened. Also all books and documents, whatever their nature and whether originals, duplicates or copies, which in anyway relate or refer to any matter in question in this action and which are now in the custody, possession or power of the plaintiff or any other person on his behalf, his or their, or any of their brokers, solicitors or agents, with liberty for the defendant, his solicitors or agents to inspect and take copies of, or extracts from, any of those books or documents. And that in the like manner the plaintiff and every other person interested as aforesaid do account for all other books and documents relating or referring to any matter in question in this action which were once but are not now in his custody, possession and power.

And that [in the meantime all further proceedings be stayed and that] the costs of and occasioned by this application be costs in the action.

Dated the   day of   19

Index

Abandonment
  acceptance of, by insurer 99
  apportionment of freight after 105
  constructive total loss on 90, 98. *See also* CONSTRUCTIVE TOTAL LOSS
  effect of 104–106
  notice of. *See* NOTICE OF ABANDONMENT
  policy without benefit of 9, 106n
  rights on, distinguished from subrogation 104
Accidents in loading
  Institute time clauses, hulls 171, 173, 174
  Institute voyage clauses, hulls 197
Action
  insurance policy, on, generally 37, 38
  insurer, by
    in name of assured 131. *See also* SUBROGATION
    to enforce contribution 135
  meaning 145
  right of, suspended during war 147
Actual total loss
  appearing to be inevitable 91
  freight, in relation to 222, 223, 230
  goods, of, when damage amounts to 86, 87, 88
  meaning 87
  measure of indemnity in case of 115
  notice of abandonment not necessary 87
  presumed, where ship missing 89
  subrogation on payment, right of 131
  suing and labouring clause, additional payment under 127
Ademption of loss 100–101
Adjustment
  general average of 122. *See also* YORK-ANTWERP RULES
  rules of practice 285–303
Advance freight
  effect of abandonment of ship 104–106
  forwarding charges on, liability for 289
  insurable interest in 18–19
  repayment of 18–19
Adventure
  marine
    legality of, implied warranty as to 63

Adventure—*continued*
  marine—*continued*
    meaning 5
    unlawful, insurance of 5, 6, 63
Agent
  assured, of, duty to minimise loss 127
  commission
    Institute
      time clause 186
      voyage clause 204
    whether allowed in average 285
  contract entered into by, ratification 142
  disclosure of material facts by 32, 33
  policy effected by, right of principal to sue 73, 74
Aircraft
  claim arising out of contact with 171, 197, 217, 227
Alien enemy
  illegality of contract with 146, 147
  meaning 147
  property of, mortgagee of 148n, 149n
All risks
  Institute
    cargo clause 239, 249, 256
    strikes clause 271
    war clause 264
  insurance against 6, 7
  limits 6
  meaning 1, 2, 4, 6
Animals
  insurance of 6, 155
Anticipated freight
  insurance interest in 12n, 188, 205, 206
Apportionment
  contract in policy of 125
  expenses incurred under suing and labouring clause 128
  liability in case of negligent collision of 123
  valuation, of, over subject-matter 121, 122
Arson
  burden of proof 172
Assignment
  assignee, right to sue in own name 73

308 Index

Assignment—*continued*
  Institute
    time clauses
      freight 217
      hulls 74, 170
    voyage clauses
      freight 226
      hulls 197
  policy of 73
    after loss 13, 75
    assured has no interest, where 75
    how effected 71
    notice of
      freight 217, 226
      hulls 170, 197
  salvage charges, assignee, whether set-off against 108
  subject-matter insured, of, effect of 20, 21
Association of Average Adjusters
  rules of practice of 285–303
Assured
  assignment of policy by. *See* ASSIGNMENT
  death of, transmission of interest on 21
  defined 1
  disclosure of material particulars by. *See* DISCLOSURE
  duty of
    avert or minimise loss, to 127
    sue and labour 184, 185, 202, 203
  ratification by 142
  relation back of 37
At and from. *See also* VOYAGE POLICY
  effect of use of phrase 40
  form of policy providing for 151
  insurable value of ship under 23n
  rule for construction of 153
  seaworthiness of vessel 63
Atomic weapon
  loss of subject-matter due to 195, 207, 209, 213, 225, 231, 234, 237, 241, 251, 258, 266, 272
Average. *See also* CONTRIBUTION; GENERAL AVERAGE; PARTICULAR AVERAGE
  free of all, meaning 125
  law of place of adjustment, governed by 146
  unless general, meaning 154
  warranty free from, form of 152

Bailee
  Institute cargo clauses as to 247, 248, 255, 270, 275
  insurable interest of 13n
Bankruptcy
  assured, of, transmission of interest on 21

Barratry
  delay caused by 72
  insurance against 171
  loss due to, liability for 79, 80, 152, 197, 218, 227
  meaning 154, 174
Blockade
  insurance of ship running 6
Boat building
  unlawful 64
Both to blame clause
  Institute
    cargo clauses, under 240, 241, 250, 257
    time clauses, under 177, 178
Bottomry bond
  costs of, as general average 284
  insurable interest arising out of 17
Breach of warranty clause. *See also* WARRANTY
  Institute time clauses
    freight 216, 226, 232, 236
    hulls 48, 51, 169, 196, 208, 212
  Institute war and strikes clauses
    freight 232, 236
    hulls 208, 212
Broker
  lien for amount of premium 76
  penalty for arranging gambling policy 157, 158
  responsibility of, for premium 76

Cancellation
  lay-up and, returns for 189–191, 223, 224
Cargo
  damage to, in discharging 281
  improperly stowed 63
  Institute time clauses as to 239–276
  loading or discharging at sea, damage due to 168, 196, 217
  lost or damaged by sacrifice 277
  port of refuge, sale at 301
Carrier
  damage to goods in care of 159
Causa proxima, non remota, spectatur 78
Change of voyage clause 245, 246
Charges of insurance
  insurable interest in 19
  what are 19
Chattels. *See* GOODS
Civil commotion
  exclusion 193, 207, 225, 231, 236
  meaning 194
Civil war
  exclusion 191, 207, 224, 231, 236
  meaning 191

Index 309

Claim and tender clause 180, 181, 200
Clauses
  accidents in loading 171, 173, 174, 197, 217, 227
  actual total loss 222, 223, 230
  additional insurances 188, 189, 205, 206
  agency commission 186, 204
  all risks 239, 249, 256, 264, 271
  assignment 74, 170, 197, 217, 226
  assured, duty of (sue and labour) 184, 185, 202, 203
  at and from 153. *See also* AT AND FROM
  bailee 247, 248, 255, 270, 275
  both to blame
    cargo clauses 240, 241, 250, 257
    time clauses 177, 178
  bottom treatment 185, 203
  breach of warranty
    freight clauses 216, 232, 236
    hulls clauses 48, 51, 169, 208, 212
  broken up, ship to be 168
  change of voyage 196, 197, 226
  claim and tenders, notice of 180, 181, 200
  collision liability
    cargo clauses, under, both to blame 240, 241, 250, 257
    freight 218, 219, 227–229
    hulls 177–179, 198, 199, 218
  constructive total loss 187, 205, 222, 223, 230, 246, 247, 254, 262
  continuation, time clauses
    freight 216
    hulls 168, 169
  craft risk 215, 226
  deductible, what is 183, 201, 202
  delay, as to
    cargo clauses 241, 248, 251, 256, 258, 263
    strike clauses 272, 276
    voyage clauses 218, 228
    war and strikes clauses 210, 234, 238
    war clauses 265, 271
  detainment 208, 209, 213, 233, 237
  deviation, as to. *See* DEVIATION
  disbursements warranty 188, 189, 205, 206
  docking 215, 225
  exclusions
    malicious acts 195, 207, 225, 231
    nuclear 195, 207, 225, 231
    strikes 193, 194, 207, 225, 231, 234, 237, 238
    war 191–193, 207, 209, 210, 213, 224, 231, 234, 237, 238
  forwarding charges 246, 254, 261

Clauses—*continued*
  franchise 221, 229
  free from
    all average, meaning 125
    particular average. *See* PARTICULAR AVERAGE
  frustration 234, 238, 264, 265, 272
  general
    average, as to. *See* GENERAL AVERAGE
    exclusions, cargo 241, 250, 251, 258, 265, 266, 272
  incorporation of 208, 209, 212, 232, 233, 236
  increased value 247, 255, 269, 270, 275
  Institute
    cargo
      (A) 239–249
      (B) 249–256
      (C) 256–263
      strike 271–276
      war 264–271
    time
      freight 215–225, 232–235
      hulls 167–195
    voyage
      freight 225–232
      hulls 196–207
    war and strikes
      freight
        time 232–235
        voyage 236–239
      hulls
        time 208–211
        voyage 212–215
  insurable interest 246, 254, 261, 269, 274, 275
  interest or no interest, effect of 8, 157, 158
  lay-up and cancellation, returns for 189–191, 223, 224
  liberties 244, 253, 260, 268, 274
  loading or discharging at sea, damage due to 168, 196, 217
  loss of time 222, 230
  lost or not lost 151, 152
  malicious acts, exclusion clause 195, 207, 225, 231
  measure of indemnity 221, 222, 230
  navigation 167–169, 196, 215, 225, 226
  new for old 185, 203
  nuclear reaction, damage due to 195, 207, 209, 213, 225, 231, 234, 237, 241, 251, 258, 266, 272
  off-hire, time-charter in 28
  perils 170–174, 197, 208, 212, 217, 218, 226, 227, 232, 236

Clauses—*continued*
  pilot, leave to sail with or without 167, 196, 215, 225
  policy proof of interest 8
  pollution hazard 177, 198, 218, 227
  risks covered 239, 240, 249, 256, 257, 264
  seaworthiness, implied warranty 242
  sistership 181, 199, 220, 229
  strikes, exclusion clause 193, 194, 207, 225, 231, 243, 252, 259
  suing and labouring. *See* SUING AND LABOURING CLAUSE
  termination 169, 170, 211, 214, 215, 238, 239
  tow and assist 167, 196, 215, 225, 226
  transit 3, 4, 153, 243, 244, 252, 253, 259, 260, 266–268, 273, 274
  unrepaired damage 186, 187, 204
  unseaworthiness and unfitness exclusion 242, 243, 251, 258, 259, 266, 273
  wages and maintenance 186, 204, 280, 281
  waiver 128, 152, 187, 205, 248, 256, 263, 270, 276
  war, exclusion clause 191–193, 207, 210, 213, 224, 231, 237, 238, 243, 252, 259
  warehouse to warehouse 3, 4, 243, 244, 259, 260, 273, 274
Collision
  apportionment of costs 286
  both ships owned by same person 132
  clause 123
  Institute
    cargo clauses, under, both to blame 240, 241, 250, 257
    time clauses, under
      liability
        freight 218, 219
        hulls 177, 178, 218
          exclusions 178
      voyage clauses, under
        liability
          freight 227–229
          hulls 198, 199
            exclusions 199
  liability to third parties 123
  negligence, due to, liability for 123
Commission
  agency
    generally 285
    Institute time clause, hulls, in 186
    Institute voyage clause, hulls, in 204
  funds, for advancing 285

Common law
  application of, to marine insurance 146
Company
  adventure of, insurance by shareholder 15
Concealment. *See* DISCLOSURE
Condition. *See also* WARRANTY
  implied, as to commencement of risk 65
Conflict of laws
  marine insurance, in relation to 146
Consideration
  failure of, return of premium on 137–140
Consignee
  insurable interest of 20
Constructive total loss
  abandonment, meaning 98. *See also* ABANDONMENT
  clause 187, 205, 222, 223, 230, 246, 247, 254, 262
  date of cause of action 98
  defined 90, 91
  dual character of 91
  effect of 98
  examples of 92–95
  freight
    clause abandoning claim 187, 205
    in relation to 94, 95, 222, 223, 230
  goods, of 93, 94
  information of the loss, meaning of 100
  measure of indemnity in case of 115
  notice of abandonment 98. *See also* NOTICE OF ABANDONMENT
  partial recovery of subject-matter, effect of 100
  ship, of 92, 93
  subrogation on payment, right of 131
  suing and labouring clause, additional payment under 127
  test as to whether loss amounts to 91, 92
  total loss includes 91
  valuation for, under Institute time clauses 187, 205, 222, 230, 247, 254, 262
  valued policy, in relation to 42
  war, following outbreak of 264
Contingent interest
  whether insurable 14
Continuation clause
  Institute time clauses
    freight 216
    hulls 168, 169
Contraband of war
  meaning 63
  warranty as to 63

Index 311

Contract
agent, by, ratification by principal 142
alien enemy, with, illegality of 147
insurance, implied terms, variation of 142
must be embodied in policy 37
representation pending negotiation of 34, 35
sale of goods, for. *See* SALE OF GOODS
when deemed to be concluded 36
Contribution
double insurance, in case of 49, 135
freight, contributory value of 287
general average
  loss on 109, 122, 302
  meaning 110, 111
  nature of liability for 109–112
insurer's right to, by subrogation 131
right of, when applies 49
ship, contributory value of 287
suing and labouring clause, not recoverable under 127
values for purpose of 282, 283
York-Antwerp Rules, under, 282, 283. *See also* YORK-ANTWERP RULES
Costs
action by insurer in assured's name 131
Covering note
reference to, in legal proceedings 144
Craft risk 215, 226
Crew
barratry of
  excusing deviation or delay 72
  meaning 154
  policy covering loss due to 152, 197, 218, 227
insurable interest in respect of wages 18
misconduct of, liability for loss due to 78
negligence of, policy to cover 197, 217, 227
wages and maintenance of 186, 204, 280, 281

Damage. *See also* REPAIRS
loading or discharging at sea, due to 168, 196, 217
unrepaired 117, 186, 187, 204
Death
assured, of, transmission of interest on 21
Deck cargo
jettison, general average, as 298
to be insured specifically 155
Defeasible interest
whether insurable 14

Delay
excuses for 65, 70, 72
Institute
  cargo clauses, under 241, 248, 251, 256, 258, 263
  strike clauses, under 272, 276
  voyage clauses, under 218, 228
  war and strikes clauses, under 210, 234, 238
  war clauses, under 265, 271
loss caused by, liability for 6, 78, 79
not admitted in general average 297
notice of abandonment, in giving 99
voyage, in, effect of 65, 70, 71
war, caused by 71
Delivery
policy, of, necessity for 39
Deviation
change of voyage distinguished from 68n
effect 68
excuses for 72
Institute
  cargo clauses, under 244, 253, 260
  strike clauses, under 274
  voyage clauses, under 48, 72, 196
  war clauses, under 268
meaning 68
notice to be given 48
several ports of discharge, order of call at 70
'touch and stay', effect of 153
variation of rule by agreement 142
war, caused by 73
Disbursements warranty 188, 189, 205, 206
Disclosure
agent, by 32
assured, by, generally 26, 27
circumstances not necessary to disclose 26, 27
expectations or belief, matters of 34
good faith, generally 24
innocent non-disclosure, effect of 27
material
  facts of 26–30
    illustrations 28–30
  slip as evidence of 144
  representations 33, 34
non-disclosure, evidence as to 24
over-valuation of goods, of 28, 29
ratification by assured, facts discovered before 36, 37
rumour, of 27
Discovery
ship's papers, of 25

Docking clause
freight 215, 225
Double insurance
assured's right of election 138, 139
contribution in case of 135
meaning 16, 48, 49
parties with different interests, by 49, 50
policies of different dates 138
return of part of premium 138, 139

Elections
double insurance, in case of 138, 139
Evidence
contract of marine insurance, of 37
covering note as 144
foreign law, of 146
onus of proof in general average 277
particular usage, of 142, 143
slip as 36, 144
unseaworthiness, of 62
Ex turpi causa non oritur actio
insurance of unlawful adventure 5
Explosion
exclusion 195, 207, 225, 231
insurance against 170, 197, 217, 227
meaning 172
explosive 195

Fire
arson, burden of proof 172
damage by
generally 172
water 298
insurance against 170, 197, 217, 227
Floating policy
delay in commencement of voyage 65
meaning 45
'to follow and succeed', meaning 46
Foreign adjustment clause
Institute time clauses
freight 220
hulls 181, 182
Foreign law
adjustment of average under 287
evidence of 146, 287
Forgery
marine policy, of, offence of 2, 3
Franchise
clause 221, 229
meaning 221
Freight. *See also* ADVANCE FREIGHT
additional insurance permitted under time clauses 188, 205, 206

Freight—*continued*
anticipated, insurable interest in 12n, 188, 205, 206
apportionment after abandonment 105
bill of lading 145
chartered 145, 153, 188, 205, 206
constructive total loss of 94, 95
contributory value of 287
Institute time clauses 215–225, 232–235
Institute voyage clauses 225–232
Institute war and strikes clauses
time 232–235
voyage 236–239
insurable value of, what included in 21, 22
insurance 'at and from', construction of 153
loss of
due to perils insured against, examples 81
general average 282
meaning 144, 155
paid in advance
effect of abandonment of ship 104
insurable interest in respect of 18
repayment of 19
partial loss of, measure of indemnity 118–121
passage money excluded 41
policy on, effect of unseaworthiness of ship 60
pro rata itineris 145n
sacrificed, general average, making good in 302
termination of insurance on 216, 217, 235, 238, 239
total loss of ship, on 94, 95, 105
time clause as to 115, 222, 223
voyage clause as to 115, 230
waiver clause 187, 205
From
construction of 152, 153
Frustration clause
form of 264, 265
strike clauses, under 272
war and strikes clauses, under 234, 238
war clauses, under 265
restraint of princes
meaning 154
policy covering 151

Gaming or wagering contract
marine insurance
as 8, 9, 106n
penalty for 157, 158

General average
act, meaning 109
  under York-Antwerp Rules 277
Average Adjusters' rules of practice 285–303
contribution. *See* CONTRIBUTION
contributory values for 282, 283
cost of bottomry bond 284
damage to machinery and boilers 279
deposits, interest on 291
expenditure, amount recoverable from insurer 109, 110
expenses at port of refuge 279, 280
fire, damage caused extinguishing 278
foreign law, adjustment under 287
Institute
  cargo clauses 240, 250, 257
  strike clauses 271
  time clauses
    freight 220
    hulls 181, 182
  voyage clauses
    freight 229
    hulls 200, 201
  war clauses 265
jettisoning cargo 111, 278
loss
  meaning 109, 110
  period of limitation 110
  salvage charges as 106
  under suing and labouring clause 127
  when insurer not liable 110
losses to be allowed as 277
maritime law distinguished from common law 108
materials burnt for fuel 279
repairs, deductions from cost of 281, 282
salvage charges, volunteer, recovery of 111
ship, freight and cargo, as between 111
wages and maintenance of crew 186, 204, 280, 281
York-Antwerp Rules 277–284. *See also* YORK-ANTWERP RULES
Good faith 24, 25, 27. *See also* DISCLOSURE
Good safety
meaning 153
Goods. *See also* CARGO; SALE OF GOODS
animals not included 155
atomic weapons, loss due to 195, 207, 209, 213, 225, 231, 234, 237, 241, 251, 258, 266, 272
constructive total loss of. *See* CONSTRUCTIVE TOTAL LOSS

Goods—*continued*
damage to, in care of bailee 247, 248, 255, 270, 275
damaged value of, meaning 121n
deck cargo not included 155
fitness of ship to carry, implied warranty as to 62
floating policy on, declaration of interest 45, 46
form of policy insuring 151
gross value of, meaning 120
inherent vice of, loss due to 78, 81, 241, 251, 258, 265, 272
insurable value of, meaning 21
jettisoned by general average act 111
loss due to
  perils of sea, examples 80
  stranding of ship 154
meaning 155
money, whether included in term 145n
partial loss of, measure of indemnity 119, 120
policy on
  deck cargo and animals 41, 155
  effect of unseaworthiness of ship 60
radio-active force, loss due to 195, 207, 209, 210, 213, 225, 231, 234, 237, 241, 251, 258, 266, 272
safely landed, construction of 153
seaworthiness of, warranty as to 62
total loss, when damage amounts to 86
transhipment of, effect on policy 90, 301
undeclared or wrongfully declared 283
voyage policy on, what included in 22
Greenwich time
liabilities determined according to 146
Guarantee
mutual insurance, in relation to 140

Heavy weather
damage by 183, 201, 202
Honour policy
meaning 9
unlawful adventure, insuring 5, 6

Illegality
adventure, of, effect 5, 6, 63
contract with alien enemy 146, 147
Inchmaree clause 173, 176n
Indemnity
marine insurance as contract of 2, 114
measure of 114–131. *See also* MEASURE OF INDEMNITY
third party, by, effect on insurable interest 20

Inherent vice
  all risks policy, exclusion from 6
  goods, of
    contracting out of Act as to 79
    loss due to 78, 81, 241, 251, 258, 265, 272

Institute cargo clauses
  (A) 239–249
  (B) 249–256
  (C) 256–263
  additional premium 48, 245, 246
  change of voyage 48, 67
  form of 160–165
  strike 271–276
  war 264–271

Institute strike clauses. *See also* INSTITUTE WAR AND STRIKES CLAUSES
  bailee 275
  change of voyage 274
  claims 275
  delay, avoidance of 276
  exclusion clauses
    general 272
    unseaworthiness and unfitness 272
  general average under 271
  minimising losses 276
  risks covered by 271
  transit clause 273
  waiver clause 276

Institute time clauses
  freight, as to 215–225, 232–235
    additional premium 48, 216
    aircraft, claim arising out of contact with 217
    assignment 74, 217
    breach of warranty 48, 216
    collision 218, 219
    continuation clause 216
    craft risk 215
    docking 215
    express warranties 55
    foreign adjustment 220
    franchise 221
    general average, adjustment under 220
    malicious acts exclusion 225
    measure of indemnity 221, 222
    navigation 215
    nuclear exclusion 225
    partial loss 119
    perils 217, 218
    pilot, leave to sail with or without 215
    pollution hazard 218
    return
      lay-up and cancellation, for 223, 224
      part of premium, of 217, 223

Institute time clauses—*continued*
  freight, as to—*continued*
    salvage, adjustment under 220
    sistership 220
    strikes exclusion 225
    termination 216, 217
    total loss 115, 222, 223
    war exclusion 224
  hulls, as to 167–195
    accidents in loading 171, 173, 174
    additional premium 48, 51, 168
    agency commission 186
    aircraft, claim arising out of contact with 171
    assignment 74, 170
    bottom treatment 185, 186
    breach of warranty 48, 51, 169
    broken up, ship to be 168
    cargo, loading or discharging at sea, damage due to 168
    claim and tenders, notice of 180, 181
    collision liability 177–179
    constructive total loss, valuation 187
    continuation clause 168, 169
    deductible, what is 183
    disbursements warranty 188, 189
    duty of assured (sue and labour) 184, 185
    exclusions 191–195
    express warranties 55
    foreign adjustment 181, 182
    freight waiver 187, 188
    general average, adjustment under 181, 182
    malicious acts exclusion 195
    navigation 167, 168
    new for old 185
    nuclear exclusion 195
    partial loss 117
    perils 170–174
    pilot, leave to sail with or without 167
    pollution hazard 177
    return
      agreement, by 137
      lay-up and cancellation, for 189–191
      part of premium, of 170, 189, 190
    salvage, adjustment under 181, 182
    sistership 180
    strikes exclusion 193, 194
    successive losses 126
    sue and labour 184, 185
    termination 169, 170
    total loss 115, 126, 187
    tow and assist clause 167
    unrepaired damage 186, 187

Index 315

Institute time clauses—*continued*
hulls, as to—*continued*
wages and maintenance 186
war exclusion 191–193
Institute voyage clauses
freight, as to
additional premium 48, 51, 226
aircraft, claim arising out of contact with 227
assignment 74, 226
breach of warranty 48, 226
change of voyage 226
collision 227–229
craft risk 226
docking 225
express warranties 55
foreign adjustment 229
franchise 229
general average, adjustment under 229
loss of time 230
malicious acts exclusion 231
measure of indemnity 230
navigation 225, 226
nuclear exclusion 231
partial loss 119
perils 226, 227
pilot, leave to sail with or without 225
pollution hazard 227
salvage, adjustment under 229
sistership 229
strikes exclusion 231
total loss 115, 230
war exclusion 231
hulls, as to
additional premium 48, 67, 72, 196
agency commission 204
aircraft, claim arising out of contact with 197
assignment 197
bottom treatment 203
breach of warranty 48, 196
change of voyage 48, 67, 196
claim and tenders, notice of 200
collision liability 198, 199
constructive total loss, valuation 205
deductible, what is 201, 202
deviation 48, 72, 196
disbursements warranty 205, 206
duty of assured (sue and labour) 202, 203
express warranties 55
foreign adjustment 201
freight waiver 205
general average, adjustment under 200, 201

Institute voyage clauses—*continued*
hulls, as to—*continued*
malicious acts exclusion 207
navigation 196
new for old 203
nuclear exclusion 207
partial loss 117
perils 197
pilot, leave to sail with or without 196
pollution hazard 198
salvage, adjustment under 200, 201
sistership 199
strikes exclusion 207
successive losses 126
sue and labour 202, 203
total loss 115
unrepaired damage 204
wages and maintenance 204
war exclusion 207
Institute war and strikes clauses. *See also* INSTITUTE STRIKE CLAUSES; INSTITUTE WAR CLAUSES
freight
time
breach of warranty 232
detainment 233
exclusions 234, 235
incorporation 232, 233
perils 232
return of part of premium 235
termination 235
voyage
breach of warranty 236
detainment 237
exclusions 237, 238
incorporation 236, 237
perils 236
termination 238, 239
hulls
time
breach of warranty 208
detainment 209
exclusions 209, 210
incorporation 208, 209
perils 208
return of part of premium 211
termination 211
voyage
breach of warranty 212
detainment 213
exclusions 213, 214
incorporation 212
perils 212
termination 214, 215

Institute war clauses. *See also* INSTITUTE WAR AND STRIKES CLAUSES
  bailee 270
  claims 269, 270
  delay, avoidance of 271
  exclusion clauses
    general 265, 266
    unseaworthiness and unfitness 266
  frustration clause 265
  general average under 265
  inherent vice, loss due to 265
  minimising losses 270
  risks covered by 264
  salvage charges under 265
  transit clause 266–268
  waiver clause 270
Insurable interest
  advance freight, in respect of 18
  anticipated freight, in 12n, 188, 205, 206
  assignment of subject-matter, effect of 20
  bottomry bond, arising out of 17
  charges of insurance, in respect of 19
  consignee, of 20
  defeasible and contingent interests 14
  defined 10
  essential elements of 11
  examples of 11, 12
  gaming or wagering contracts, avoidance of 8
  inchoate rights, whether amount to 15
  indemnity by third party, effect of 20
  insurance charges 19
  mortgagor and mortgagee, of 20
  nature and extent of, disclosure 41
  necessity for 13
  partial interest, insurance of 15
  re-insurance of risk 16
  respondentia, arising out of 17
  wages, in respect of 18
  when must attach 13
Insurable property
  defined 5
Insurable value
  freight, of 22
  meaning 21
  measure of 21, 22
Insured. *See* ASSURED
Insured value
  Institute cargo clauses, under 247, 254, 262
  Institute time clauses, under
    freight 222, 230
    hulls 187, 205

Insurer
  abandonment of subject-matter, rights on 104
  acceptance of abandonment by 99
  contribution in case of double insurance 49
  defined 1
  gambling policy, penalty for entering into 157, 158
  general average loss
    liability for 109, 110
    when not liable for 110
  liability for loss, extent of 78, 114. *See also* MEASURE OF INDEMNITY
  notice of accident to be given to 168, 196
  policy signed by more than one 39
  re-insurance by 16
  right of subrogation on payment 131
  signature of, on policy 39
  underwriter, meaning 1
Insurrection
  exclusion 191, 207, 224, 231, 236
  meaning of 192
Interest. *See also* INSURABLE INTEREST
  funds, for advancing 285
  general average deposits, on 290
  insured, defined 1
  losses, on, allowance of 284
  recovery of, in action on policy 38
Interest or no interest
  policy providing for
    effect of 8
    penalty for entering into 157, 158
Ireland
  application of Marine Insurance Act to 9

Jettison
  cargo, of, when general average 111, 278
  deckload, of 298
  insurance against 171, 173, 197, 217, 227
  insurer of goods jettisoned entitled to contribution 132
  meaning 173
Joint tenant
  insurable interest of 15

Law merchant
  application of, to marine insurance 146
  usage, evidence of, in relation to 143
Lay-up
  cancellation and, returns for 189–191, 223, 224
Legality
  adventure, of, implied warranty as to 63

Liberty
shipowners, granted to 244, 253, 260, 268, 274
Lien
broker's, for amount of premium 76
Lighter
risk while on, Institute time clause 215, 226
seaworthiness of, whether implied 59
Lloyd's policy
construction of terms in 47, 152–155
form of 151, 152, 160–165
new form 47
several 39
special clauses, use of 166
Lock-out
exclusion 193, 207, 225, 231, 236
meaning 194
Loss. *See also* ACTUAL TOTAL LOSS; CONSTRUCTIVE TOTAL LOSS; PARTIAL LOSS
ademption of 100, 101
all other perils, meaning 154
apportionment between insurers 114
atomic weapon, due to 195, 207, 209, 213, 225, 231, 234, 237, 241, 251, 258, 266, 272
barratry, due to 80, 152
civil commotion, due to 193, 207, 225, 231, 236
collision, due to 123. *See also* COLLISION
delay, due to 6, 78, 79
duty to avert or minimise 127
fire
due to, what included 172
insurance against 170, 197, 217, 227
general average, nature of 277
information of the, meaning of 100
inherent vice of subject-matter, due to 78, 81, 241, 251, 258, 265, 272
insurer's liability for, extent of 78, 114. *See also* MEASURE OF INDEMNITY
interest acquired after 13
malicious acts, due to, clause covering 195, 207, 225, 231
meaning 1
nuclear fission, due to 195, 207, 209, 213, 225, 231, 234, 237
partial. *See* PARTIAL LOSS
particular average 106. *See also* PARTICULAR AVERAGE
perils of the seas, due to, meaning 153
pirates, due to 151, 154, 171, 197, 217, 227
proximate cause of
contracting out of the Act 79
examples 80–82
liability for 78, 79, 81

Loss—*continued*
radio-active force, due to 195, 207, 209, 210, 213, 225, 231, 234, 237, 241, 251, 258, 266, 272
ratification of contract by principal after 142
restraint of princes, due to 142, 151, 154
riot, due to 193, 194, 207, 225, 231, 236
salvage charges, meaning 107. *See also* SALVAGE
stranding, due to, meaning 154. *See also* STRANDING
strikes, due to 193, 207, 225, 231, 236, 243, 252, 259
successive losses
measure of indemnity 126
time clause 187
terrorism, due to 193, 194, 207, 225, 231
test as to whether amounts to constructive total 92
thieves
due to 151, 154
violent theft, due to 171, 172, 173, 197, 217, 227
time, of 222, 230
total distinguished from partial 86
valued policy, under, amount of 42–44
war, due to 191–193, 207, 210, 213, 224, 231, 237, 238, 243, 252, 259
Lost or not lost
form of policy providing for 151, 152
interest acquired after loss 13
rule for construction of clause 152

Malicious acts
exclusion clause 195, 207, 225, 231
Marine adventure
legality of, implied warranty as to 63
meaning 5
unlawful, insurance 5, 6, 63
Marine damage
meaning 6
Marine insurance
definition 1
purpose and object of 6
Marine policy
animals to be insured specifically 155
calculation of time in relation to 146
common law, application of 146
conflict of laws in relation to 146
construction of Marine Insurance Act 149
continuation clause in 168, 169, 216
contract of indemnity, as 2, 114
date of slip as evidence of 144

Marine policy—*continued*
  defined 1
  forgery of 2
  form of 151, 152, 160–165
  gambling, when deemed to be 8, 106n, 157, 158
  implied terms, variation of 142
  law merchant, application to 146
  mutual 140
  notice of assignment of
    freight 217, 226
    hulls 170, 197
  rectification of 144
  sale of goods, duty of seller as to 158, 159
  stipulation as to law governing 146
  transfer of ship, on termination
    freight clause 216
    hulls clause 169
  usage, effect of 143
  war, effect of outbreak of 53, 63, 68, 73, 146, 147, 170. *See also* WAR
  warranty, meaning, in relation to 50, 51
Maritime perils
  meaning 5
  result of 6
Master
  authority to mortgage ship 18
  barratry of
    excuse for deviation or delay 72
    loss due to 79
    meaning 154
    policy covering loss due to 152, 197, 218, 227
  insurable interest in respect of wages 18
  misconduct of, liability for loss due to 78
  negligence of, policy to cover 197, 217, 227
  sale by, liability for loss due to 80
  wages and maintenance of 186, 204, 280
Material representation. *See also* DISCLOSURE
  what is 24–37
Maxims
  aliud est celare aliud tacere 27
  causa proxima, non remota, spectatur 78
  cuilibet licet renunciare juri pro se introducto 54n
  de minimis non curat lex 88
  dolus circuitu non purgatur 79
  ex turpi causa non oritur actio 5
  expressum facit cessare tacitum 143
  furtum non est casus fortuitus 172
  modus et conventio vincunt legem 143

Measure of indemnity
  agreement as to, standard for reaching 114, 115
  apportionment of valuation 121, 122
  collision, in case of 123
  general
    average contribution, in respect of 122
    provisions as to ascertaining 124
  Institute time clauses, under 221, 222
  Institute voyage clauses, under 230
  meaning 114
  'one third new for old', deduction of 116
  partial loss of
    freight 118, 119
    goods 119, 120
    ship 116
  particular average warranty, under 124, 125
  reduction in case of under-insurance 122
  salvage charges, in relation to 122
  scrap value 168
  successive losses, in case of 126
  suing and labouring clause, under 127
  third party, in respect of liability to 123
  time policy, under 117
  total loss, in case of 115
  wooden ships, as to 116
Merchandise. *See* GOODS
Mistake
  rectification of policy in case of 144
Mixed policy
  warranty of seaworthiness as to 59
Mortgage
  ship, of, insurable interests arising by 17
Moveables
  meaning 145
Mutual insurance
  meaning 140, 141

Nationality
  warranty, none implied as to 57
Navigation
  faulty, loss due to 79
  Institute time clauses
    freight 215
    hulls 167–169
  Institute voyage clauses
    freight 225, 226
    hulls 196
  negligent 123
Neutrality
  warranty of, meaning 57
New for old clause 185, 203
Non-disclosure 24–37
  See also DISCLOSURE

Not to inure clause 247, 248, 255, 262
Notice
 accident, of, to insurer 168, 196
 assignment of policy, of
  freight 217, 226
  hulls 170, 197
Notice of abandonment
 acceptance of, by insurer 99–102
 actual total loss, in case of 87
 by whom can be given 100
 examples of 101, 102
 how to be given 99
 information of the loss 100
 necessity for 99
 not accepted, ownership of subject-matter after 104, 105
 partial recovery of subject-matter after 100
 re-insurer, to, whether necessary 16
 waiver of 100
 when unnecessary 99, 102
 withdrawal of 100
Nuclear installations
 breakdown of 171, 197, 217, 227
Nuclear reaction
 damage due to 241, 251, 258, 266, 272
 exclusion clause 195, 207, 209, 213, 225, 231, 234, 237

Off-hire clause 28
One third new for old
 deduction from cost of repairs 116
Open policy
 meaning 42
Over-insurance
 contribution in case of 135
 double insurance as 49
 non-disclosure of, effect 9
 valued policy, under 44

Partial interest
 insurance of 15
Partial loss
 example 86
 followed by total loss
  amount recoverable 126
  time clauses, under 117, 119, 183, 186, 201, 204
 meaning 86
 measure of indemnity
  freight 118, 119
  goods 119, 120
  ship 116
 particular average warranty, under 124–125

Partial loss—*continued*
 subrogation in case of 131
 under-insurance, in case of 136
Particular average
 Average Adjusters' rules of practice 285–303
 bonded prices, adjustment on 297
 meaning 106
 salvage charges as 107
 ship stranded, where 249
 warranty free from
  effect of 124, 125
  form in policy 152
Payment
 deductible from, what is 183, 201, 202
 subrogation on, right of 131
Penalty
 entering into gambling policy, for 157, 158
Perils
 Institute time clauses
  freight 217, 218
  hulls 170–174
 Institute voyage clauses
  freight 226, 227
  hulls 197
 Institute war and strikes clauses
  freight 232, 236
  hulls 208, 212
 perils of the seas, meaning 153, 171, 172
Pilot
 failure to employ, effect of 58
 leave to sail with or without 167, 196, 215, 225
 negligence of, policy to cover 197, 217, 227
 seaworthiness of ship sailing without 58
Pirates
 Institute cargo clauses, under 243
 insurance against loss due to 151, 171, 197, 217, 227
 meaning 154, 173
 theft, where not piracy 173
Policy of insurance. *See also* FLOATING POLICY; MARINE POLICY; TIME POLICY; UNVALUED POLICY; VALUED POLICY; VOYAGE POLICY
 action on, recovery of interest 38
 assignment of 73. *See also* ASSIGNMENT
 at and from
  form of 151
  meaning 40
  rule for construction of 153
 builders' risk policy 64

Policy of insurance—*continued*
  concealment of material facts 26, 27. *See also* DISCLOSURE
  construction of terms in 47, 152–155
  contract
    to be embodied in 37
    when deemed to be concluded 36
  delivery of, necessity for 39
  designation of subject-matter 41
  execution of, at or after contract 36
  floating 45, 46
  forgery of 2
  form in Schedule to Act, use of 47
  form of, re-insurance 16
  hull and machinery, on, what included in 22
  matters to be specified in 38
  meaning 1, 145
  measure of indemnity under 114. *See also* MEASURE OF INDEMNITY
  mixed policy 59
  non-disclosure in 24–37
  premium, payment of 76. *See also* PREMIUM
  reasonable time, meaning 143
  rectification of 144
  risk not covered by 78–82
  signature of insurer, necessity for 39
  signed by two or more insurers 39
  time policy 40
  transhipment of goods, effect of 90
  usage, effect of 142
  valued or unvalued, may be 42
  variation of obligations implied by law 142
  void, return of premium 138
  voyage policy 40
  warranty under 50, 51
    See also WARRANTY
  whether passes to transferee of subject-matter 20
  without benefit of abandonment 9, 106n, 158
Policy proof of interest
  effect of clause 8
  gambling policy, penalty for entering into 157, 158
Pollution hazard
  Institute time clauses
    freight 218
    hulls 177
  Institute voyage clauses
    freight 227
    hulls 198

Premium
  additional, payable in certain event 47, 48, 51, 67, 72, 168, 196, 216, 226, 245, 246
  broker's
    lien for amount of 76
    responsibility for 76
  change of voyage, on 245, 253, 261, 268, 274
  defined 1
  deviation, in case of
    cargo clauses 244, 253, 260
    strike clauses 274
    war clauses 268
  disbursements warranty 189, 206
  mutual insurance, in relation to 140
  reasonable, what is meant by 143
  receipt clause in policy, effect of 77
  return of
    additional insurance 189
    by agreement 137
    enforcement of 136
    failure of consideration 137, 138
    general principle involved 138
    lay-up and cancellation, for, Institute clauses 189, 190, 223, 224
    over-insurance, in case of 138
    part of, Institute clause
      freight 217, 223, 235
      hulls 170, 189, 190, 211
    subject-matter never imperilled 138
    termination, on 211, 214, 235, 239
    void policy, under 138
  to be arranged, effect of 47
  when payable 76
Profits
  insurable value of 23n
Proximate cause
  examples of 80–82
  liability for loss due to 78, 79, 80
    contracting out of Act 79

Radio-active force
  loss of subject-matter due to 195, 207, 209, 210, 213, 225, 231, 234, 237, 241, 251, 258, 266, 272
Ratification
  assured, by, relation back of 36, 37
  contract entered into by agent, of 142
Rebellion
  exclusion 191, 207, 224, 231, 236
  meaning of 192
Receipt
  premium, of, effect of clause in policy 77

Index

Rectification
  policy, of 144
  valuation, defective, of 44n
Reinsurance
  disclosure that policy is reinsurance, whether necessary 41
  examples of 16n, 17n
  interest sufficient to support 16
  meaning of 16
  no notice of abandonment in case of 100
Repairers
  negligence of
    Institute time clauses
      freight 217
      hulls 171
    Institute voyage clauses
      freight 227
      hulls 197
Repairs
  average adjuster, duty of 286
  bottom treatment 185, 203
  deductions from cost of 116
  indemnity for cost of reasonable 116
  reasonable cost of
    meaning 117
    surveyor's fees included in 118n
  scraping and painting 296
  temporary, general average 282
  tenders for 180, 181, 200
  unrepaired damage 117, 186, 187, 204
Representation. *See also* DISCLOSURE; WARRANTY
  material, what is 34
  pending negotiation of contract 33, 34
Respondentia
  insurable interest arising out of 17
Restraint of princes
  meaning 158
  policy covering loss due to 151
Returns clause
  freight 217, 223, 235
  hulls 170, 189, 190, 211
Riot
  exclusion 193, 207, 225, 231, 236
  meaning of 194
Risk
  commencement of 152, 153
  excluded from policy 78
  freight, on 153
  lawful, limited to 6, 7
  meaning 1
  mixed sea and land 3
  passing of, on sale of goods 14, 158
  termination of, at final port 70
Running down clause. *See* COLLISION

Safely landed 153
Sale of goods
  delivery to carrier 159
  insurance, duty of seller as to 159
  port of refuge, forced sale at 301
  risk, passing of 14, 158
Salvage
  charges
    liability for, under particular average warranty 107
    meaning 107
    measure of indemnity in relation to 122
    right to set-off against assignee of policy 108
    under
      cargo clauses 240, 250, 257
      strike clauses 271
      time clauses
        freight 220
        hulls 181, 182
      voyage clauses
        freight 229
        hulls 200, 201
      war clauses 265
    York-Antwerp Rules 107, 277–284
  volunteer, recovery
    as general average 111
    under suing and labouring clause 107
  defined 107, 108
  life, award reflecting 108
  maritime law distinguished from common law 107
  military 108
  policy without benefit of 9, 158
    premium not returnable 139
    statutory prohibition of 158
  services vessel not to undertake clause 167, 196, 215, 225, 226
Seamen. *See* CREW
Seaworthiness
  admitted 242
  burden of proof as to 59
  freight, in relation to policy on 60
  goods
    in relation to policy on 60
    of, whether warranty implied 62
  insufficient crew, effect of 60
  lighter, of, whether implied 59
  mixed policy 59
  pilot, failure to employ, effect of 58
  unseaworthiness and unfitness exclusion clauses 242, 243, 251, 258, 259, 266, 273
  warranty as to 58

Shareholder
insurance of adventure of company by 15
Ship. See also STRANDING
abandonment of 104. *See also* ABANDONMENT
constructive total loss of 90–95. *See also* CONSTRUCTIVE TOTAL LOSS
contributory value of 287
damage to
  as general average 272
  loading at sea, due to 168, 196, 217
detainment 208, 209, 213, 233, 237
form of policy insuring 151
insurable value of, how determined 21, 22
insurance 'at and from', construction of 153
lay-up, period of, warranty as to 55
loss of, due to perils insured against, examples 80–82
machinery, claims for, adjustment 286
meaning 22, 154
missing, total loss presumed 89
name of, in floating policy 45
partial loss of, measure of indemnity 116
port of refuge, resort to 299, 300
repairs to, deduction from cost of 116. *See also* REPAIRS
seaworthiness of, sailing without pilot 58
seaworthy, when deemed to be 58–60
ship's papers
  disclosure of 25
  implied condition as to 56
transfer of
  freight clause 216
  hulls clause 169
under construction, policy of 3
Signature
insurer, of, on policy 39
Sistership clauses
Institute time clause
  freight 220
  hulls 181
Institute voyage clause
  freight 229
  hulls 199
Slip
admissible as evidence in legal proceedings 36, 37, 38, 144
initialling of, effect of 36
meaning 1
nature of 144
Stamp duty
liability to, saving for 145
unstamped slip admissible as evidence 36, 37, 144

Stranding
exception in case of 152, 249, 257
meaning 154, 221
voluntary 298
York-Antwerp Rules, under 278
Strikes
exclusion clause 193, 207, 225, 231, 236, 243, 252, 259
Institute clauses 271–276. *See also* INSTITUTE WAR AND STRIKES CLAUSES
meaning 193
Subject-matter
abandonment of 90, 91. *See also* CONSTRUCTIVE TOTAL LOSS
  notice of 99–102. *See also* NOTICE OF ABANDONMENT
damage due to inherent vice
  cargo clauses 241, 251, 258
  strikes clauses 272
  war clauses 265
inherent vice of
  contracting out of Act as to 79
  loss due to 78, 81, 241, 251, 258, 265, 272
insurer's right to, on payment 131
ownership of, if notice of abandonment not accepted 104, 105
Subrogation
costs of action in assured's name 131
devaluation of currency, effect of 133
examples 132, 133
nature of 131
right of, generally 131
Successive losses
amount recoverable 126
Institute time clauses, under 187
Suing and labouring clause
amounts recoverable under 127
  apportionment 128
  examples 128, 129
duty of assured 184, 185, 202, 203
form of, under
  policy 152
  time clauses 184, 185, 202, 203
waiver clause as supplement to 128

Take a line
meaning 1
Tenant in common
insurable interst of 15
Termination clause
contract of carriage clause 245
Institute time clauses
  freight 216, 217
  hulls 169, 170

Termination clause—*continued*
  Institute war and strikes clauses
    freight
      time 235
      voyage 238, 239
    hulls
      time 211
      voyage 214, 215
Terrorism
  exclusion 193, 207, 225, 231
  meaning 194
Theft
  violent
    insurance against 171, 197, 217, 227
    meaning 172, 173
Thieves
  meaning 154, 172
  pirates, where not 173
  policy covering loss due to 151
Third party
  liability to, measure of indemnity in case of 123
Time
  calculation of 146
  definite period of, definition of 40
  Institute clauses 167–195, 215–225, 232–235. *See also* INSTITUTE TIME CLAUSES
  loss of 222, 236
  reasonable
    despatch clauses 248, 256, 263, 271, 276
    meaning 143
Time clauses
  freight 215–225
  hulls 116, 137, 167–195
Time policy
  indemnity, measure of, time for determining 117
  meaning 40
  proportionate refund of premium under 136
  seaworthiness of ship
    disclosure as to 33
    warranty as to 58
  ship, on, what included in 22, 23
Total loss. *See also* ACTUAL TOTAL LOSS; CONSTRUCTIVE TOTAL LOSS
  meaning 86
  measure of indemnity 115
  partial loss distinguished 86
Touch and stay
  liberty to 151
  meaning 153
Tow and assist clause 167, 196, 215, 225, 226

Transhipment
  goods, of, effect on policy 90, 301
Transit clause 3, 4, 153, 243, 244, 252, 253, 259, 260, 266–268, 273, 274

Uberrima fides 24. *See also* DISCLOSURE
Under-insurance
  effect of 122, 126, 181, 182, 200, 220
Underwriter. *See* INSURER
Unlawful adventure
  insurance of 5, 6, 63
Unseaworthiness. *See* SEAWORTHINESS
Unvalued policy
  double insurance in relation to 49
  freight, partial loss of 118, 119
  goods, partial loss of 119, 120
  insurable value under 22
  meaning 42
  measure of indemnity under 2, 114
  over-insurance under, return of premium 138
Usage
  construction of policy according to 142, 143

Value
  apportionment of, over subject-matter 121, 122
  goods, of, how ascertained 121, 122
  insurable, measure of 21, 22
  scrap 168
Valued policy
  amount payable under 2
  apportionment of loss under 42–44
  conclusiveness of fixed value 42, 43
  double insurance in relation to 49
  freight, partial loss of 118, 119
  goods, partial loss of 119, 120
  meaning 42
  measure of indemnity, under 114
  valuation, when set aside 22
  wagering contract, whether 43
Vessel. *See* SHIP
Voyage
  change of
    force majeure, due to 67
    Institute voyage clause 196, 197, 226
    involuntary 68
    meaning 67
  delay in 72
  departure, alteration of port of 66
  destination, alteration of 66
  deviation from 68. *See also* DEVIATION
  implied condition as to commencement of risk 65
  several ports of discharge specified 70

Voyage policy
  delay, effect of 70
  final port, meaning 70
  form of 151, 152
  generally 40
  goods, on, what included in 22
  implied
    condition as to commencement of voyage 65
    warranty as to
      fitness to carry goods 62
      seaworthiness 58–60, 62
  meaning 40

Wagering policy
  marine insurance, when amounting to 8
  no return of premium under 138
  'without benefit of abandonment' 9, 106n

Wages
  insurable interest in respect of 18
  maintenance, and 186, 204, 280, 281

Waiver
  clause 128, 152, 187, 205, 248, 256, 263, 270, 276
  notice of abandonment, of 100

War
  breach of warranty 52
  capture, seizure, arrest, meaning 192
  change of destination, causing 68
  civil war, meaning 191
  constructive total loss, causing 264, 265
  contraband of, meaning 63
  convoy, sailing with 53, 56
  delay, causing 71
  deviation, causing 73
  effect of outbreak of 53, 63, 68, 73, 146, 147, 170, 264
  enemy property, mortgagee of 148n, 149n
  exclusion clauses 191–193, 195, 207, 210, 213, 224, 231, 237, 238, 243, 252, 259
  Institute clauses 264–271. *See also* INSTITUTE WAR AND STRIKES CLAUSES; INSTITUTE WAR CLAUSES
  Institute time clauses exclusion
    freight 224, 225
    hulls 191–193
  Institute voyage clauses exclusion
    freight 231
    hulls 207
  Institute war and strikes clauses
    freight 234, 236
    hulls 209, 210, 213, 214

War—*continued*
  insurrection, meaning 192
  notice of abandonment unnecessary 102
  rebellion, meaning 192
  risks
    insurance against 5, 7
    ship running blockade 5, 6
  ship missing during, who bears loss 89
  suspension of right of action during 147

Warehouse to warehouse clause
  effect of 3, 4
  under Institute
    cargo clauses 243, 244, 259, 260
    strike clauses 273, 274

Warranty. *See also* CONDITION
  breach of
    effect 48, 51, 52
    Institute clauses as to
      freight 216, 226, 232, 236
      hulls 48, 51, 169, 196, 208, 212
    onus of proof 51
    when excused 53
  change of circumstances affecting 53
  collateral stipulation, distinguished from 51
  contraband, as to 63
  disbursements 188, 189, 205, 206
  express, meaning and examples 54, 55
  fitness of ship to carry goods, as to 58, 59
  free from average
    effect of 124, 125
    form in policy 152
  good safety, as to 57
  kinds of, distinguished 51
  legality of adventure, as to 63
  marking of tins, as to 52
  nationality, of, not implied 57
  nature of 50, 51
  neutrality, of 56
  seaworthiness of
    goods, as to 62
    ship, as to 58, 242

Wear and tear
  loss caused by
    all risks policy, exclusion from 6
    contracting out of the Act as to 79
    liability for 78

Without benefit of salvage
  clause providing for
    effect of 8, 9, 106n, 157
    penalty for 157
    premium not returnable 139

Wreck
  cutting away, under York-Antwerp Rules 278

Wreck—*continued*
  value of, under Institute clauses
    freight 222, 230
    hulls 187, 205

York-Antwerp Rules 1974
  assessment of contributory values under 113n, 282, 283
  Average Adjuster's rules of practice, application in 291, 292
  cargo lost or damaged by sacrifice 282
  cash deposits, treatment of 284
  cutting away wreck 278
  damage to
    cargo
      by sacrifice 282
      in discharging 281
    machinery and boilers 279
    ship 283
  deductions from cost of repairs 281, 282
  delay, loss due to 277
  expenses at port of refuge 279
  extinguishing fire on shipboard 278
  general average
    act, meaning 277
    contributory values 282, 283
    disbursements, commission allowed 291
    form of clause as to 240
    in relation to 113n
    losses to be allowed as 277

York-Antwerp Rules 1974—*continued*
  Institute time clauses, application to
    freight 220
    hulls 181
  Institute voyage clauses, application to
    freight 229
    hulls 201
  Institute war and strikes clauses, application to
    freight 234, 238
    hulls 210, 214
  interest on losses 284
  interpretation 277
  jettison of cargo 278
  lightening ship when ashore 279
  loss of freight 282
  materials burnt for fuel 279
  onus of proof 277
  provision of funds 284
  sacrifice for common safety 278
  salvage
    charges payable under 107, 291
    remuneration 278
  temporary repairs 282
  undeclared or wrongfully declared cargo 283
  uniformity resolution 303
  values to be used 278
  voluntary stranding 278
  wages and maintenance of crew 280, 281

Printed in Great Britain
by Amazon